THE SHAPE OF APOCALYPSE IN
MODERN RUSSIAN FICTION

# THE SHAPE OF APOCALYPSE IN MODERN RUSSIAN FICTION

DAVID M. BETHEA

PRINCETON UNIVERSITY PRESS

PRINCETON, NEW JERSEY

Copyright © 1989 by Princeton University Press
Published by Princeton University Press,
41 William Street,
Princeton, New Jersey 08540
In the United Kingdom:
Princeton University Press,
Guildford, Surrey

Library of Congress Cataloging-in-Publication Data

Bethea, David M., 1948–
The shape of apocalypse in modern Russian fiction / David M. Bethea.
p.   cm.
Bibliography: p.
Includes index.
ISBN 0–691–06746–5 (alk. paper)
1. Russian fiction—19th century—History and criticism.
2. Russian fiction—20th century—History and criticism.
3. Apocalyptic literature—History and criticism. I. Title.
PG3096.A65B48 1989
891.73'09382—dc19                                      88-12639
                                                       CIP

This book has been composed in Linotron Aldus

Clothbound editions of Princeton University Press books are
printed on acid-free paper, and binding materials are
chosen for strength and durability.
Paperbacks, although satisfactory, for personal collections,
are not usually suitable for library rebinding

Printed in the United States of America by
Princeton University Press,
Princeton, New Jersey

FOR KIM AND EMILY

# Contents

A Note on the Transliteration     xi

Preface     xiii

Introduction: Myth, History, Plot, Steed     3

ONE    *The Idiot*: Historicism Arrives at the Station     62

TWO    *Petersburg*: The Apocalyptic Horseman, the Unicorn, and the Verticality of Narrative     105

THREE    *Chevengur*: On the Road with the Bolshevik Utopia     145

FOUR    *The Master and Margarita*: History as Hippodrome     186

FIVE    *Doctor Zhivago*: The Revolution and the Red Crosse Knight     230

Afterword: The End and Beyond     269

Works Cited     277

Index     297

We hoped; we waited for the day
The state would wither clean away,
Expecting the Millennium
That theory promised us would come,
It didn't.
                    —W. H. Auden, *New Year Letter*

The rider on the white horse! Who is he then? . . . He is the royal one, he is my very self and his horse is the whole *mana* of a man. He is my very me, my sacred ego, called into a new cycle of action by the Lamb and riding forth to conquest, the conquest of the old self for the birth of the new self . . .
                    —D. H. Lawrence, *Apocalypse*

What tense would you choose to live in?

"I want to live in the imperative of the future passive participle—in the 'what ought to be.' "

I like to breathe that way. . . . It suggests a kind of mounted, bandit-like, equestrian honor. That's why I like the glorious Latin "Gerundive"—it's a verb on horseback. . . .

Such was the dialogue I carried on with myself as I rode horseback through the variegated terrain of wild and cultivated uplands, nomadic territories, and vast pasturelands of Alagez.
                    —Osip Mandelshtam, *Journey to Armenia*

# A Note on the Transliteration

The system of transliteration I have used is that recommended by Professor
J. Thomas Shaw in his *The Transliteration of Modern Russian for English-
Language Publications* (Madison, 1967). In the text itself as well as in the
substantive sections of notes, I have used Shaw's "System I," which is a
modified version of the Library of Congress system for the purpose of "nor-
malizing" personal and place names for the generalist Western reader. References to secondary literature in the text and notes are to *abbreviated* titles
(the complete bibliographical information being found in the "Works
Cited"). In the "Works Cited" section and in transliteration of words as
words I have used "System II," which is the unmodified Library of Congress system, with the diacritical marks omitted. It is hoped that any confusion that might arise from the combination of these two systems (e.g.,
"Andrey Bely" in the text but "Andrei Belyi" in the "Works Cited") will
be compensated for by the increased readability afforded the non-specialist
and the greater precision afforded the specialist.

# Preface

"There are," as the philosopher Nikolay Berdyaev once wrote, "two dominant myths which can become dynamic in the life of a people—the myth
about origins and the myth about the end. For Russians it has been the
second myth, the eschatological one, that has dominated." This statement,
which fairly revels in its lack of qualifiers and scant context in the original
(*The Russian Idea*), would undoubtedly strike the historian as excessive, yet
at the same time it expresses an idea, *the Russian idea*, which many writers
have taken to be true and have assumed as a point of departure for their
fictions. The objective and received truths of this statement are not at all
the same, just as the objective and received truths of America's "chosen"
status, its "manifest destiny," are different. This study, which is essentially
about the "End" of history as presented in selected works of modern Russian fiction, has, as is usually the case in such matters, a history of its own.
The original conception developed in response to what I saw to be a distinct
gap in the existing scholarship and criticism: while the Western, or more
precisely Anglo-American tradition has been blessed with a number of
studies about apocalypse as both historical and literary phenomenon, there
has as yet been no sustained attempt to bring what is known about the
Russian view of the *eskhaton* to bear on the form of Russian prose fiction.
The works of those such as M. H. Abrams (*Natural Supernaturalism*), Norman Cohn (*The Pursuit of the Millennium*), and Frank Kermode (*The Sense
of An Ending*) have become classics in their fields for anyone interested
either in the roots of Western apocalyptic or in the impact that social and
cultural models of the End have had on literary form. Yet this tradition and
these models have a decidedly *Western* bias, and Russian historiographers
and philosophers of history have never been comfortable with their country's ability, or inability, to fit western paradigms. For our purposes, therefore, these studies are at best anachronistic (*if* Russian cultural models are
indeed, belatedly, becoming "westernized") and at worst irrelevant (*if* Rus-

sia's Byzantine and Asiatic legacies, together with the Western one, have made these models unique and indigenous). When no less an authority than Abrams can claim that "the nation possessed of the most thoroughly and enduringly millennial ideology . . . is America" ("Apocalypse: Theme and Variations" 357), one has to wonder, as did Lévi-Strauss in his exposure of Sartre's insider's cultural bias, how "savage" at times can be the sophistication of the Western mind.

The tasks I set myself in these pages are several: (1) to provide close analytical readings of five major novels, which, though written in different periods, are each related to the others through their prominent allusions to the Book of Revelation and through their common concern with the narration of history (and historical closure); (2) to take some of the generalizations about the "messianic" and "eschatological" impulse in the Russian historical character and show how, in each context, they provide powerful models for structuring these works of fiction; (3) to indicate where this theme of apocalypse actually enters into the realm of narrative structure, where it takes on dynamic shape and expands into a moving picture of history in crisis; and (4) to outline a possible typology for these "apocalyptic fictions" that would, with its essentially Christian orientation and implication of a God-Author beyond the Finis of history, stand as a kind of countermodel to the Socialist Realist classic, with its essentially Marxist orientation and implication that immanent laws within history guide our steps toward a secular paradise. These tasks, which now seem crucial to the integrity of the project, were not obvious at the outset. Like Ivan Petrovich Belkin, Pushkin's endearing but feckless historiographer in "The History of the Village Goryukhino," I had to order the material in a way that seemed consistent and honest in view of the "facts," which brings me to the question of the shape of my narrative, itself about the fictionalized shape of history.

A good deal of intellectual energy has been expended and ink spilled (or computer diskettes filled) in recent theoretical discussions about the "open" boundary between history and fiction, between facts as such and their inevitable narration. In the Russian context this issue goes back at least as far as Karamzin and Pushkin: Karamzin began as a belletrist and ended his career as Russia's "first historian and last chronicler"; Pushkin, fascinated by the difference between fact and artifact, explored these very boundaries in such later works as *The Tales of Belkin*, the already mentioned "The History of the Village Goryukhino," and *The Captain's Daughter*. As intriguing as all this may be, I must confess that as "historiographer" I have for some time had the distinct impression that it was not I who was "prefiguring" my field of study, enclosing facts within the "meta-" viewpoint of a (hi)story, but the facts themselves that were constantly shaping and changing the rough sketch first dictated by intuition. Thus, if what follows has a bias, as indeed it must, this bias is not naive; it has been checked and re-checked against the information supplied by specific authors, texts, and contexts. The reader has every right to call my arrangement of the facts a "fiction," just one of many possible narratives, but it is my underlying argument, one shared not only by these authors but also by the very structure of their works, that not all such narratives are created equal.

In order to free my narrative from the heavy hand of an a priori theoretical framework, which seemed to me essentially dishonest (it was the works, not the binding idea "from outside," that came first), I began each chapter as a "chronicler" rather than as a "historiographer." My aim was to read and analyze each work *on its own terms*. Hence the first mental draft envisioned five very different studies linked loosely by a common *theme* ("revolution and revelation"). Only later, in the course of analysis, did the theoretical considerations, the narrative interstices out of which a chronicle becomes a history, emerge. This is not to say that my priorities are the only appropriate ones, or that an opposite ordering of the material (theory over close reading or, in structuralist linguistic terms, *langue* over *parole*) would not be possible and even rewarding, but simply that these priorities seemed to me the best way of dealing with the concept of apocalypse as it surfaced in specific texts and contexts, with their own agendas and dialogues perhaps quite different from ours. To borrow Hayden White's terminology in *Metahistory* for the possible paradigms (formist, organicist, mechanistic, contextualist) available to one "explaining" (narrating) history, my approach is fundamentally contextualist.

Nevertheless, it would be equally disingenuous of me to claim that, as work progressed, the idea of apocalypse, and thus the theoretical issues involved when inscribing the biblical End in narrative form, did not loom larger, attracting more of my attention and requiring additional effort to raise my perspective from the synchronic flatland of the individual text to the heady atmosphere of diachrony, the mountain aerie or "overview" from which some of the most important works in Russian literature could be seen as reworkings, in *their* time and place, of the same biblical plot. Although my study does not pretend to be a literary history of "apocalyptic fiction" on Russian soil (the very idea of a series of close readings militates against breadth of coverage), it posits, in skeletal form, the existence of such a history. For each of the novels treated—Dostoevsky's *The Idiot*, Bely's *Petersburg*, Platonov's *Chevengur*, Bulgakov's *The Master and Margarita*, and Pasternak's *Doctor Zhivago*—is an active participant in a formidable web of allusion and intertextuality; this web leads back to Pushkin, Gogol, and *their* views (as refracted through the novel or narrative poetic form) of Russian history in the first half of the nineteenth century, at a time when modern Russian historiography and historical consciousness were being born. (The symbolist poet Innokenty Annensky probably said it best: "Pushkin and Gogol—our two-faced Janus. Two mirrors on the door that separates us from our past.") In other words, these works, dominated as they are by the overwhelming sense that national history and biblical plot are in a state of fatal alignment or parallax, continually look from the "presents" of their contexts *back* to a pre-history, or "epic past," when Russia's future was a still open book. This "Great Time," as the scholar of myth Mircea Eliade would call it, may be the old *Rus'* before the Petrine reforms or some folk ideal such as the underwater kingdom of Kitezh. More importantly, it is the necessary "before" that preceded a "fall" into history and that allowed these writers to explain the shape of what followed, up to, and in some cases *beyond*, the events depicted in their apocalyptic presents. As I demonstrate in the Introduction, the works of Pushkin and Gogol are significant as late "pre-history" because the tensions driving them—the temporal "old"/"new," the spatial "East"/"West"—are, while ominous, far from being resolved and because the dynamic images (Bronze Horseman, troika) embodying historical momentum and radical change are, while not "apocalyptic" in context, capable of becoming so in the eyes of later generations, when social and political ferment in the second half of the nineteenth century made the threat of revolution seem imminent and inevitable.

The Introduction sketches the salient features of the Russian apocalyptic tradition and attempts a brief typology of what will be called "apocalyptic fiction," dwelling in some length on the role played by the images of the horse and train in this tradition and typology. Thereafter, each subsequent chapter has the same basic format: a discussion of the historical and biographical contexts out of which the work in question grew precedes and introduces an in-depth reading of the text itself. The important difference between "apocalypse" and "utopia," between a divinely inspired conclusion to history leading to an atemporal ideal (the New Jerusalem) and a humanly engineered conclusion to history leading to a secular paradise (one model being the classless society), becomes an issue only in the work of Platonov. All the other authors write works whose epistemological point of departure is essentially Christian and apocalypticist; Platonov, whose novel is related to the others structurally and typologically, blurs and confuses the Christian and Marxist approaches to history under the influence of the philosopher Nikolay Fyodorov. Thus *Chevengur* is included in this study as the expression of yet another artistic means, together with those of the "Christian" Bulgakov and Pasternak, of dealing with the fact that the End (and Beginning) promised by the revolution was a failure, was *not* equivalent to the one foretold in Revelation. Dostoevsky, whose *Idiot* was written before the revolutions of 1905 and 1917, and Bely, whose *Petersburg* was written between them, create texts permeated with a nervousness and urgency that

enters into every aspect of their structure and style and shows their perceived position in history to be "after" the fall and "before" (*right* before
in Bely's case) the End. Depending on its time of writing, therefore, each
work possesses a "prospectivist" or "retrospectivist" view of the revolution
that must be integrated not only philosophically but structurally into its
view of biblical apocalypse or (in Platonov's case) utopia. The Afterword
suggests its own retrospective view of the typology as well as a prospective
view of where that typology, faintly and in various subterranean guises,
may still be operating.

   If I had to describe my approach, or what I hope is my approach, it would
be, as a distinguished colleague once said of his ideal marriage of criticism
and scholarship, "structuralism with a human face." The categories and
paradigms adduced to marshal one's material should, ideally, be both ger-
mane and open-minded, be capable of engaging the text as it speaks and
listens to the realities of society, polity, culture, and art. In the language of
Yury Tynyanov, a formalist who did become a structuralist with a human
face, the "auto-function" (that which links similar elements within different systems of discourse) and the "syn-function" (that which links different
elements within the same work) are constantly flexed in a very real, yet
often subtle and invisible equipoise. This is the hidden musculature, as it
were, that operates below the surface of otherwise arbitrary literary signs
to give the text its homeostatic dynamism, its historical personality—what
it meant "then" and what it means "now." What is ironic in the case of
these authors of apocalyptic fictions is that they, in varying degrees of consciousness, used *the very limitations* of the novel form to imply a reality
beyond it. Feeling all the integumentary tugs of their works' hidden musculature and knowing that words were all they had to project what was
finally dumb to human figuration, they nevertheless undertook to incorporate Western civilization's ultimate figure of closure in a form that traces
its generic origins to the concepts of openness, contingency, desacralization,
irreverent laughter, perpetual contact with "profane" time and space.
Therefore, while the thinking of those such as Mikhail Bakhtin, Arthur
Danto, Mircea Eliade, Michel Foucault, Edmund Leach, Claude Lévi-
Strauss, Yury Lotman, and Hayden White has been a constant goad to my
own and a source of many of the ordering principles in this book, I do not
always agree with them.

   Any reader of these Russian apocalypticists should know how, for example, Foucault's now famous prediction of the end of "Man" and the humanistic tradition—"a face drawn in sand at the edge of the sea"—would
fit into their fundamentally Christian systems of thought and their artistic
structures. This statement, after all, is Foucault's adaptation, a century
later, of Nietzsche's most provocative pronouncement. But Dostoevsky was

horrified (though also fascinated, to be sure) by history "as such," without God; forestalling Nietzsche, he answered history's inquisitorial proof that "God is dead" with a non-verbal kiss; and against the diamond hard and sharp postulates of Raskolnikov he offered up the stammering meekness of Sonya, whose voice acquired authority only when another voice, coming from the Book, spoke through hers. Thus it seems fair to assume that, at least for Dostoevsky and the tradition that followed, not all voices, regardless of their logical persuasiveness and flair for *ore profundo* (Foucault's being a prime example), are created equal. For what Dostoevsky and the others were trying to do was logically (but not mythopoetically) impossible—the incorporation of life's openness within the closure of God's plot. And to explain this through the immanent binary rules of discourse posited by structuralism or through the relentless accretions to meaning provided by the ubiquitous "other" of post-structuralism is to deny a priori the essential ingredient in an apocalypticist view of the world—that there is such a thing as "revelation," as a radical and total shift in time-space relations, and that it comes *from beyond*. Hence the thinkers to which I freely resort to counterbalance the ones just listed are usually Russian Orthodox in faith and, in several cases, they actually influenced, as metaphysical god-fathers, the novels being discussed: Nikolay Berdyaev, Sergey Bulgakov, Georgy Fedotov, Pavel Florensky, Georgy Florovsky, Nikolay Fyodorov, Ivan Kireevsky, Alexey Khomyakov, Konstantin Leontiev, Vasily Rozanov, and Vladimir Solovyov.

Any work such as this is not only a formal dialogue, but an almost endless causerie with those friends and colleagues patient enough to listen and respond to my ideas and to read parts or all of the manuscript in its fledgling form. These individuals will forgive me for not saying more about their contributions, the much appreciated "sub-plots" from "outside" and "others" that found their way into the shape of my narrative: Vladimir Alexandrov, Mark Altshuller, Stephen Baehr, Nina Berberova, Thomas Beyer, Edward J. Brown, Sergej Davydov, Caryl Emerson, Herman Ermolaev, Efim Etkind, Joseph Frank, Boris Gasparov, George Gibian, Eugene Klimoff, George Krugovoy, Eric Pervukhin, Ellendea Proffer, Gary Rosenshield, Natalya Sadomskaya, Thomas Shaw, Victor Terras, Anatoly Vishevsky, Slava Yastremski, Alexander Woronzoff. Much-needed time for research on the early stages of the project was provided by a year-long fellowship from the American Council of Learned Societies and a semester grant from the Graduate School at the University of Wisconsin-Madison. Thanks are also due to Mary Heins, Tali Mendelberg, Hana Pichova, Adrienne Shirley (this last of Princeton University Press), and Sonia Yetter-Beelendorf, all of whom spent long hours helping me prepare and edit the manuscript in its various stages. Parts of this study have appeared, in modified form, elsewhere and are here so noted: "On the Shape of Apocalypse in Modern Russian Fiction: Towards a Typology" (in *Issues in Russian Literature Before 1917: Proceedings from the III World Congress of Soviet and East European Studies*, ed. J. Douglas Clayton [Columbus: Slavica, 1988]); "Remarks on the Horse/Train as a Space-Time Image in Russian Literature from 1820 to 1920" (in *Russian Literary Mythologies: From the Golden Age to the Silver Age*, eds. Boris Gasparov and Robert P. Hughes [*California Slavic Studies*, forthcoming]); "The Role of the *eques* in Pushkin's *Bronze Horseman*" (in *Pushkin Today*, eds. David M. Bethea and J. Thomas Shaw [Bloomington: Indiana University Press, forthcoming]); "Historicism Arrives at the Station: The Image of the Train and the Shape of Time in *The Idiot*" (*California Slavic Studies* [forthcoming]); "History as Hippodrome: The Apocalyptic Horse and Rider in *The Master and Margarita*" (*Russian Review*, 41 [October 1982], 373–99). The quotation from W. H. Auden's *New Year Letter*, copyright 1941 and renewed 1969 by W. H. Auden, is reprinted with permission of Random House, Inc., from *W. H. Auden: Collected Poems*, edited by Edward Mendelson. The quotation from Yeats's "The Second Coming" is reprinted with permission of Macmillan Publishing Company from *The Poems of W. B. Yeats: A New Edition*, edited by Richard J. Finneran, copyright 1924, by Macmillan Publishing Company, renewed 1952 by Bertha Georgie Yeats, and with permission of A. P. Watt Ltd. on behalf of Michael B. Yeats and Macmillan London Ltd. I dedicate this book to my favorite listener and reader, an expert on the beauty and fragility of plots and on their extratextual ties, and to a future listener, whose story is just beginning.

Madison, Wisconsin

THE SHAPE OF APOCALYPSE IN

MODERN RUSSIAN FICTION

# Introduction:
# Myth, History, Plot, Steed

As far as I know, this [statue of Lenin in front of the Finland Station]
is the only monument to a man on an armored car that exists in the
world. In this respect alone, it is a symbol of a new society. The old
society used to be represented by men on horseback.
—Joseph Brodsky,
"A Guide to a Renamed City"

## MYTH

Humankind has always lived in time, but it has not always lived in history.
Archaeologists and anthropologists provide countless examples of societies,
"ancient" in time or "primitive" in development, where time was experienced mythically rather than historically, where only those details of life
that fit into and recapitulated the master plot of a sacred tale were worthy
of remembrance.[1] The British social anthropologist Bronislaw Malinowski
defined myth as

> . . . not merely a story but a reality lived. It is not of the nature of
> fiction, such as we read today in a novel, but it is a living reality, be-
> lieved to have once happened in primaeval times, and continuing ever
> since to influence the world and human destinies. . . . Myth is to the
> savage, what, to a fully believing Christian, is the Biblical story of the
> Creation, of the Fall, of the Redemption by Christ's sacrifice on the
> Cross. As our sacred story lives in our ritual, in our morality, as it
> governs our faith and controls our conduct, even so does his myth for
> the savage (*Magic, Science and Religion* 100).

The phrases most operative in this passage are "a reality lived," "believed
to have happened once in primaeval times," and "continuing ever since to
influence the world and human destinies." "History," on the contrary, is

---

[1] Perhaps the best-studied recent example of an older, indigenous culture that has taken on
the structural models of Christian apocalyptic (imported via missionaries) is the Melanesian
Cargo cult. See Lawrence, *Road Belong Cargo*, and Worsley, *The Trumpet Shall Sound*.

3

perceived as the very opposite of myth—the desacralization of the past, the recording of events as they actually happened, without reference to some prefiguring master plot. What characterizes the "archaic" as opposed to the "modern" human being, according to Mircea Eliade, is that the former is able, through ritual, to return periodically "to the mythical time of the beginning of things" and thereby to abolish "concrete, historical time," whereas the latter, having been cut off from this Great Time through the gradual process of desacralization and secularization, must "make himself, within history" (*Myth* ix).[2] To cite just one example of how ritual served (and serves) as a shield against duration and chaos, the Babylonian New Year festival (*akîtu*) is based on the story of an underwater "carnival" king (Tiamat) who destroys the status quo, humiliates the "real" sovereign (Marduk), and casts the participants back into a pre-time of deluge and darkness; virtually at the same time, and at the dawn of the new year, order is restored, chaos is reconfigured through the act of creation, and a sacred union (hierogamy), symbolizing the rebirth of the human being and the world, is celebrated. Here the parallels with the Christian sacrament of baptism (the ritual death of the old man followed by a new birth), which in earlier times took place on Easter and New Year's Day, are obvious (Eliade 55–59).

In the venerable confrontation between history and myth the Judaeo-Christian tradition has often been seen as a turning point. Put simply, the Old Testament prophets explained the vagaries of fate and the periodic debacles of the chosen people, the "remnant of Israel" (Zephaniah 3:13), not by relating these events to a continually recaptured great past but by replacing them within a plot of *things to come*, as trials to be borne in order to make the Israelites worthy of their status and mission. "They [the prophets] insisted," writes Amos Funkenstein, "that God's immense, universal powers were manifested by the very plight of the chosen people: only God could employ the mightiest empires as 'rods of wrath' to purge Israel, while these empires were unaware of their role in the divine plan, of their objective role in history (Isaiah 10:5–7)" ("A Schedule" 46). One can immediately see the difference between this view of time and that, say, expressed implicitly in Hesiod's myth of declining world ages (Golden, Silver, Copper, Age of Heroes, Iron) and explicitly in Plato's doctrine of reciprocating cosmic cycles (the *Politicus*), where panplanetary conjunctions are linked with various terrestrial adversities to make a statement about the human being's continuous rise and fall as a moral being (Reiche, "The Archaic Heritage" 27–29). With the Judaeo-Christian tradition, humanity had "en-

---

[2] Cf. in this regard Engels' remark in a letter to Ernst Bloch that "We *make our history ourselves*" (my emphasis; cited in Williams, *Marxism and Literature* 85).

tered" history (not of course yet history in the modern, secular sense) and that history had a straightforward movement and teleological coloring. The human being had also, as we learn in Genesis, *fallen* from privileged status in the Garden of Eden (the Judaeo-Christian "Great Time") *into* profane time and an imperfect world, and there was *no way back*.

The figure whose interpretation of the biblical plot from a Christian standpoint was most influential for the Western Roman Catholic tradition was St. Augustine (A.D. 354–435). Through his doctrine of the three stages of salvation (the *ante legem* before Moses, the *sub lege* during and after him, and the culminating—for this world—*sub gratia* initiated by Christ) and through his periodization of history into Six World Ages (with the Seventh located *outside* of time), he consolidated the "historiosophy" of the prophets and gave it a christocentric reading that was to dominate for centuries (Reeves, "Medieval Attitudes" 41). Pivotal to this reading was the conviction, expressed in *The City of God*, that the Christ example was unique, unrepeatable, and end-determined. As Funkenstein explains further,

> It is very clear that the apocalyptic tradition does not exclude eternal return, at times even alludes to it under the influence, perhaps, of Iranian tradition. Nor indeed does the Bible exclude eternal return—it simply is outside the horizon of biblical imageries. The *uniqueness* of history, or at least of its central event, became thematic only in the Christian horizon. Against Origen's theory of world succession, Saint Augustine insisted that Christ came only *once* for all times. The difference is rather that while the apocalyptic writer takes his proof from Scripture and history, the Greek philosopher relies on astronomical-cosmological speculations ("A Schedule" 50; see also Pelikan, *Jesus* 21–33).

So with the Judaeo-Christian model the Great Time of the past (the Garden of Eden) was cast into the future (the New Jerusalem), and the steady organ bass of apocalyptic thinking came gradually to drown out the Greek music of the spheres.[3] Ironically, the figure of the circle, distinct from that of the repeating cycle, was not eliminated entirely, since the New Jerusalem not only replaced but was a *return* to the lost garden as a reward for trials suffered in the name of the faith, the shape of history becoming, in Karl Löwith's apt formulation, "one great detour to reach in the end the beginning" (*Meaning in History* 183).

But what is meant precisely by the term "apocalyptic thinking" and how

---

[3] The ancient Greek interest in astrological signs and configurations continued in the Christian tradition well into the Middle Ages and is prominent in such writers as Dante.

does it relate to the "bookish," "scribal" nature of the revealed message? There are so many apocalypses and so many non-biblical myths of the End that this is no easy question to answer. In an effort to locate certain finite transhistorical categories, such scholars of myth as Franz Cumont and Eliade have been apt to cast their narratives all the way back to ancient Iranian legends about an end of the world by fire, which then, presumably, migrated westward—the *ekpyrosis* that occupies a central position in the religious systems of Stoicism, the Sibylline Oracles, and Judaeo-Christian literature (Cumont, "La Fin du monde" 29–96; Eliade, *Myth* 124). Biblical scholars, however, seem to be more restrained in their application of terminology; they draw a sharp line between "eschatology," or knowledge of the end (*eskhaton*), which any culture may announce it possesses, and "apocalypticism," or the "distinctive form of teaching about history and its approaching End" found in the Judaeo-Christian tradition (McGinn, "Early Apocalypticism" 6).[4] It may clarify matters, therefore, to view apocalypticism as "a species of the genus eschatology," with the implication that there is "an important difference between a general consciousness of living in the last age of history and a conviction that the last age itself is about to end, between a belief in the reality of the Antichrist and the certainty of his proximity (or at least of the date of his coming), between viewing the events of one's own time in the light of the End of history and seeing them as the last events themselves" (McGinn, *Visions* 3–4). In this regard, the "whole-sale invasion of Persian religious ideas into post-exilic Judaism as the determining factor in the rise of apocalypticism are now generally discounted," having been supplanted by more plausible "gradualist" theories about the interaction of Canaanite mythology and Near Eastern Wisdom traditions with indigenous Judaism (or Judaisms) as it existed in the Hellenistic world (McGinn, "Early Apocalypticism" 14). Thus the "genre" of the apocalypse, according to those who have examined it most closely, is now believed to have arisen in the third and second centuries B.C. under the impulse of a Jewish nationalism, which was itself a natural outgrowth of, rather than a radical departure from, the "proto-apocalyptic" phases associated with the Canaanite and Wisdom antecedents.

---

[4] "Apocalypticism in its Jewish origins is distinguishable from two related terms common in biblical theology and the history of religions: *eschatology* and *prophecy*. Apocalypticism is a species of the genus eschatology, that it, it is a particular kind of belief about the last things—the End of history and what lies beyond it. Scriptural scholars have used the term *apocalyptic eschatology* to distinguish the special teachings of the prophets. (Apocalyptic eschatology may be seen as equivalent to the frequently used term *Apocalyptic*, formed in imitation of the German *Apocalyptik*.) Valuable as the distinction may be in the realm of biblical studies, the picture will obviously become blurred in later Christian history when elements of both forms of eschatology will frequently be mingled" (McGinn, *Visions* 3–4).

The Revelation of John, or the Apocalypse, as it is known by its Greek name, is only one of a number of extant apocalyptic texts, some from the Intertestamental period and entirely Jewish in origin (I Enoch, Daniel), others from Christianity's first century (the synoptic Gospels, I and II Thessalonians), and others still from the later Patristic tradition (Shepherd of Hermas, Testament of the Lord, Apocalypse of Peter, Vision of Paul). Still, the Apocalypse of John, which is now generally thought to have been written c. 90–95 A.D., has become the most famous (or notorious) of all apocalypses, the one most laymen have in mind when they speak of *the* Apocalypse. And it in turn has become the text that has most palpably influenced our Western views of history as a plot with: (1) a beginning by divine fiat (the creation), (2) a tale of early catastrophe (the fall of Adam and Eve), (3) a later privileged moment of crisis (the incarnation, crucifixion, and resurrection), and (4) a final crescendo with awesome dénouement (the *Parousia*, or Second Coming, of Christ, followed by the replacement of the old world by a "new heaven and new earth") (Abrams, "Theme and Variations" 343–44). Narratologically speaking, the Apocalypse, which both comes *at the end* of the Bible and tells of *the end* of human history, allows that history to have a coherent and meaningful *beginning* and *middle* because it provides a fitting conclusion (Kermode, *Sense* 5–8). Hence, while some scholars still argue that apocalypticism as a balance of myth, method, and way of life existed only for about two hundred years (or until the early Christians grew tired of "standing on tiptoes" [Pelikan, *Jesus* 24] in the shadow of disconfirmation), most will agree with Funkenstein that "the fascination with historical time and its structure was the most important contribution of the apocalyptic mentality to the Western sense of history" (Funkenstein, "A Schedule" 49, 57). Precisely how the Johannine conclusion, with its elaborate figures and haunting codes, dovetails with the real events of contemporary history has been a source of endless debate, and no less endless carnage, from the beginning. It has left its signature on page after page of Christian history, constituting the vast "underthought" of orthodoxy and millenarian heterodoxy (Manichaean, Messalian, Paulician, Bogomilian, Patarian, Albigensian) alike (Manuel, *Utopian Thought* 48).

What do all apocalypses have in common, how are we able to speak of them as a distinct genre? A recent volume of *Semeia* answers the question in the following way:

"Apocalypse" is a genre of revelatory literature with a narrative framework, in which a revelation is mediated by an otherworldly being to a human recipient, disclosing a transcendent reality which is both temporal, insofar as it envisages eschatological salvation, and spatial, insofar as it involves another, supernatural world (Collins, "Towards the Morphology of a Genre" 9).

In the broadest terms, a member of the elect is deeply troubled by the affairs of his church in this world. It may be the pseudonymous Daniel, one of the *maskîlîm* or wise teachers, who must try to make sense of the persecution of the Jews under the Hellenizing program of Antiochus IV Epiphanes (167– 164 B.C.), a kind of "proto-Antichrist" (McGinn, "Early Apocalypticism" 8); or it may be John, sent into exile on the island of Patmos by the Emperor Domitian (A.D. 81–96), who must try to find justification for similar persecution of the early Christians by Rome. The seer is allowed to understand through an apocalypse, a "disclosing" or "uncovering," which translates into a series of visions of the glorious End. Hence the various magnificent figures, such as the four beasts of Daniel 7 or the beast rising out of the sea of Revelation 13, have *ex eventu* referents in history (i.e., the Babylonians, Medes, Persians, Greeks, Romans), but at the same time are colorful, compelling, and abstract enough to provide ready-made source material for subsequent "seers." The Whore of Babylon could be the Roman Empire in one epoch and the Church of Rome in another; the beast could be *Nero redivivus* in one context and a concupiscent pope, later called an "Antichrist,"[5] in another. What is significant is that the tribulations of the profane present, of *human beings in history*, are rendered understandable and therefore bearable by reference to a suprahistorical intelligence (God) who, standing *beyond* the Beginning and the End, sends His messenger (the angel of Revelation 1:1) to one of His faithful (the "servant John") with a divine preview of history's "Finis"—that spatial metaphor for a non-temporal paradise called the New Jerusalem. Just as Christ's life culminated in a triadic pattern of trial-crucifixion-resurrection, so now does the life of humanity, that is, universal history, promise to culminate in a similar pattern (thus the *Second Coming* of Christ) of present crisis-coming judgment-final vindication (McGinn, "Early Apocalypticism" 9).

As the *Semeia* volume shows, the genre of apocalypse has numerous permutations: it may contain a review of universal history up to the present moment of crisis or it may involve a purely personal eschatology; the revelation itself may be presented in the form of a vision or a speech or a dialogue; the seer may go on an otherworldly journey (a Judaeo-Christian version of the utopian *topos*)[6] or may be visited in his or her realm, etc. Yet

---

[5] In the New Testament the name "Antichrist" does *not* appear in Revelation, but only in I and II John.

[6] It is of course moot to argue which impulse came first—the apocalyptic or the utopian. After all, Plato's presentation of his ideal republic, which Thomas More used as an important point of departure in his text, antedates the appearance of Christian apocalyptic. The foremost

whatever the particular variations, certain basic elements, what might be termed the epistemological "deep structure" of apocalypse, hold firm: (1) history is a unity or totality *determined* by God but at the same time so configured as to allow humanity, or more precisely, a member of the elect, to *choose* between Christ and Antichrist, between the truth coming from beyond and the mirage of worldly power, well-being, etc. that passes for truth in the here and now; (2) the moment of decision has arrived and the initial stage in the climactic pattern of crisis-judgment-vindication has begun; and (3) this coming End is viewed as tragic and retributive for those who have chosen not to uphold the faith and as triumphant for those who have (McGinn, "Early Apocalypticism" 4–6, 10–12). Above all, the apocalypticist mentality and its scribal expression in the genre of apocalypse imply the interplay of spatio-temporal *oppositions* and of one's place within them: old/new, here/there, determinism from beyond/free choice from within, the historically mired Whore of Babylon/the ahistorical New Jerusalem, etc. The perceived resolution of all opposition comes, logically enough, at the climax of the Book of Revelation. The Beast, the symbol of benighted power in this world, brings about the destruction of the Whore of Babylon (originally Rome), "the great harlot . . . with whom the kings of the earth have committed fornication" (Revelation 17:1–2). Against this sense of tumultuous discord is presented the marriage of the Lamb and the Bride, Christ and the "holy city . . . coming down out of the heaven from God" (Revelation 21:10). In effect, the final vision of the Christian hierogamy has achieved a kind of narrative optical illusion—a view of the "outside" of history from the "inside," a projection of an all-encompassing and all-resolving "then" from the vantage of a beleaguered "now."

---

American scholars of utopia, Frank and Fritzie Manuel, isolate and historicize the utopian urge in the following way:

> Utopia is a hybrid plant, born of the crossing of a paradisaical, otherworldly belief of Judeo-Christian religion with the Hellenic myth of an ideal city on earth. The naming took place in an enclave of sixteenth-century scholars excited about the prospect of a Hellenized Christianity. While we may loosely refer to ancient and medieval works with some utopian content as utopias, the Western utopia is for us a creation of the world of the Renaissance and the Reformation. . . . But the relation of the utopian to the heavenly always remains problematic. Utopia may be conceived as a prologue or foretaste of the absolute perfection still to be experienced; it then resembles the Days of the Messiah or the Reign of Christ on earth of traditional Judaism and Christianity, with the vital addition of human volition as an ingredient in the attainment of that wished-for state. Or the utopia, though originally implanted in a belief in the reality of a transcendental state, can break away from its source and attempt to survive wholly on its own creative self-assurance. Whether the persistence of the heavenly vision in a secularized world, if only in some disguised shape, is a necessary condition for the duration of utopia is one of the unresolved questions of Western culture (*Utopian Thought* 15–17).

The record of how, time and again, the apocalypticist urge provoked historical confrontation in the West is immense, and can only be touched on in these preliminaries. Suffice it to say that of all the individuals who attempted to transpose the principal figures and codes of the Johannine text to the terms of contemporary reality, two were pivotal to the course of Western apocalypticism—St. Augustine and Joachim of Fiore (1145–1202). In his classic *The Pursuit of the Millennium*, Norman Cohn has written a social history of the volatile fit between the apocalyptic plot and its numerous adaptations among sectarian movements of Northern and Central Europe during the Middle Ages. Whatever the sects (Tafurs, Flagellants, Taborites) and whatever the social basis for their unrest (religious fervor during the Crusades, fear of the Black Death, deteriorating economic conditions in feudal Europe), the pattern was uniform: these were the saving remnant whose role it was to usher in the End and inherit a renovated kingdom. In this context, the Bishop of Hippo's earlier declaration that the millennium, that is, the thousand-year period of Revelation 20:1–6 during which Satan would be temporarily bound and the martyrs would reign with Christ over the world,[7] was coterminous with the reign of the church did little to dissuade what was often a rag-tag band of wanderers, itself socially disenfranchised, that saw that church as a haven of simony, voluptuousness, and the spirit of Antichrist. Officially, then, this move to legitimize the historical church as the only "City of God" on earth had enormous ramifications, not the least of which was to defuse the urgent need to look for a future Golden Age, since apparently it was already here. As we discover in *City of God* (xviii: 52–53), it is not our place to tease out a divine fretwork of apocalyptic signs from the welter of current affairs: these prophecies are, in R.A. Markus' summation of the Augustinian position, "not to be read as referring to any particular historical catastrophe, but to the final winding up of all history; and the time of that no man can know" (*Saeculum* 152–54).

But in the popular, sectarian consciousness, which could not help from

---

[7] "In a strict sense, millenarianism, or chiliasm, was originally limited to a prophetic conviction, derived from a commentary on the fourth verse of the twentieth chapter of the Apocalypse of John, to the effect that Christ would reign for a thousand years on earth. The pivotal events of the transition to the days of the millennium were depicted in well-worn images of catastrophe: During a time of troubles empires crumble, there are titanic struggles of opposing armies, vast areas of the world are devastated, nature is upheaved, rivers flow with blood. On the morrow, good triumphs over evil, God over Satan, Christ over Antichrist. As existential experience the millennium of early Christianity is the counterpart of the Days of the Messiah in much of Jewish apocalyptic. The bout of violence reaches a grand climax, and then and only then is there peace—primitive priapic scenes are the inescapable analogy" (Manuel and Manuel, *Utopian Thought* 46–47).

noticing the disparity between the historical and ideal churches, the millenarian impulse remained strong. This is especially true after Joachim, a
seminal mystic of the Catholic Middle Ages, reversed Augustinian doctrine
and gave the people back their millenarianism with his triadic periodization
of history:

> Joachim's originality lay in his affirmation that the threefold pattern
> of history was as yet incomplete and that the work of the Holy Spirit,
> the Third Person, must shortly be made manifest in a further stage of
> spiritual illumination. Recasting the traditional Pauline pattern he ex-
> panded his famous doctrine of the three *status* in history: the first,
> beginning with Adam and ending with the Incarnation, has been char-
> acterized by the work of the Father; the second, beginning back in the
> Old Testament (to overlap with the first) and continuing until Jo-
> achim's own day, belonged to the Son; the third, with a double origin
> in the Old Dispensation and the New and about to come to fruition in
> the near future, would see the full work of the Holy Spirit completed.
> *Here was a magnificent programme of progress which offered an ad-
> vance still to come within history.* Its novelty is well illustrated by the
> fact that Joachim departs decisively from the Augustinian tradition by
> placing the Sabbath Age of the World and the opening of the Seventh
> Seal of the Church clearly within history and identifying them with
> the third *status* (my emphasis; Reeves, "Medieval Attitudes" 49–50;
> see also Reeves, *The Influence of Prophecy*).

The thirteenth century, as Russia fell under the Mongol Yoke to the East,
was a time of great eschatological fervor and anxiety in Europe. 1260 was,
in the popular imagination, the year in which Joachim's prophecies were to
come true, and the Franciscan Spirituals, whose apocalyptic hopes and fears
are presented in Umberto Eco's recent novel *The Name of the Rose*, were
to be the original inheritors of the third *status*. But as routinely happens in
these matters, disconfirmation makes it possible for later generations to re-
calculate and retranslate the numbers and signs into their own "chosen"
*status*. Thus Joachim's placement of this third age of the Holy Spirit *within*
history was enormously influential for the development of apocalyptic
thought in the West. It surfaces, *mutatis mutandis*, in the programs of
Müntzer, Campanella, Lessing, in the Third State of Auguste Comte, in
Marx's Higher Stage of Communism, in Teilhard's Noösphere, as well as in
countless nationalisms, from Savonarola's Florence to Hitler's Third Reich
(Manuel, *Utopian Thought* 33, 63). Even Columbus' discovery of a new
world in 1492 (the year the old world was scheduled to end in Russia) is
largely a product of this tradition (Reeves, "Medieval Attitudes" 62 ff.).
And in the Russian context it can be seen in modern guise in the tripartite

periodization of history advanced by such thinkers as Vladimir Solovyov and Dmitry Merezhkovsky.

## HISTORY

It is difficult to imagine two students of Russian cultural history more unalike than the émigré philosopher Nikolay Berdyaev and the Soviet structuralist and semiotician Yury Lotman. Yet on one issue they are both in unequivocal agreement—the relentlessly *eschatological* shape of those cultural models (of history, of life, and of the two as presented in literature) that have been the focus of Russia's popular and literary imagination for centuries. Berdyaev—who was powerfully influenced by Dostoevsky and who came to maturity on the eve of the revolution, when the thought systems of various Christian mystics and Marxists were brought to a boil by the expectation of a new millennium—could still claim as late as 1946 that "Russians are either apocalypticists or nihilists. Russia is an apocalyptic revolt against antiquity. . . . This means that the Russian people, according to their metaphysical nature and calling in the world, are a people of the end [*narod kontsa*]" (*Russkaia ideia* 195). Lotman—who came to prominence in the 1960s as the leader of the Tartu School of structural poetics and who has written a series of pioneering works on the thesis that art does not passively "reflect" life but actually provides models and norms that social life then tries to imitate and incorporate—argues that "The historical fate of Western thought . . . developed in such a way that, beginning with the Middle Ages and continuing up to recent times, the idea of progress occupied a dominant position in both scientific and social thinking, coloring the whole of culture for entire historical periods. On the other hand, in the history of Russian social thought there dominated, over the course of entire historical periods, concepts of an eschatological or maximalist type" ("Spory o iazyke" 173). Whether both of these writers, the one more "intuitive" and given to broad, unqualified generalization and the other more "contextualist" and given to a meticulous sifting of evidence, are "objectively" correct is ultimately beside the point, since they are continuing a dialogue about the *received* notions of Russia's past, present, and future that is central to any discussion of their country's historical identity.

The binary oppositions by which Russians have tended to define themselves from their first steps into literacy have had, according to Lotman and Boris Uspensky, a profound impact on the eschatological view of national history passed down through the centuries. In the Roman Catholic West earthly life was from very early on "conceived of as admitting three types of behavior [on the model of heaven-purgatory-hell]: the unconditionally sinful, the unconditionally holy, and the neutral, which permits eternal salvation after some sort of purgative trial. In the real life of the medieval West a wide area of neutral behavior thus became possible, as did neutral societal institutions, which were neither 'holy' nor 'sinful,' neither 'pro-state' nor 'anti-state,' neither good nor bad" ("Binary Models" 32). In Russia, however, "duality and the absence of a neutral axiological sphere led to a conception of the new not as a continuation, but as a *total eschatological change*" (my emphasis; "Binary Models" 32).[8] Of these oppositions, argue Lotman and Uspensky, none are more important than the fundamental temporal distinction between "old" and "new" and the fundamental spatial distinction between "east" and "west." These terms shift valence as times and audiences change. More central to our discussion, the very distinctions between space and time can overlap and interpenetrate, suggesting that in point of fact they are extensions of each other.

This means that to a structuralist like Lotman what is determinative in Russian cultural history is the ongoing clash between "outsiders" and "insiders," between those of a "now" versus those of a "then" temporality. Indeed, a number of historians have analyzed the major turning points of Russian history—the Christianization of *Rus'* in 988, the period of the Mongol Yoke (1240–1480), the origins of the formula "Moscow the Third Rome" and the growth of religious nationalism in the late fifteenth and early sixteenth centuries, the Great Schism led by the Old Believers in the 1660s, and the Petrine reforms in the first quarter of the eighteenth century—in precisely these terms (see, e.g., Obolensky, "Russia's Byzantine Heritage"). The cast of "outsiders" (Byzantium, Turko-Mongol Empire, Western Europe) may change and what is "traditional" or "iconoclastic" may fluctuate depending on the point of view of the speaker/participant, but Lotman and Uspensky's point is well-taken: Russia has tended to define itself by radically breaking, or at least *by seeing itself* as radically breaking, with an earlier period. This break is never, to be sure, as clean and final as the principals might imagine for the very reason that the earlier period which is supposedly overcome is preserved willy-nilly in the cultural memory as a necessary opposition. After 988, paganism was not forgotten but remembered because its gods became the devils of the "Christian" world

---

[8] Again, a Western observer, or "outsider," may wish to question the existence of a now almost mythical past of a "neutral axiological sphere" among medieval Catholics, especially if one considers the widespread appeal of the proto-revolutionary, millenarian heterodoxies—which decidedly did *not* admit any middle ground in questions of judgment and faith—studied by Cohn, but if by this the authors mean that, as a result of the Renaissance, Reformation, and Enlightenment, the notions of "progress" and a human-centered view of the world associated with the rise of a middle class came gradually to dominate—but never to eliminate entirely—the "either/or" mentality of apocalypticism in the West, then their formulation appears more defensible.

(Volos/Veles→*volosatik* or "wood goblin") or because their previous function was preempted by a Christian counterpart (Volos/Veles→St. Blaise [Vlasy], St. Nicholas, St. George) (Uspenskii, "Kul't Nikoly"). Whereas Hilarion, in his celebrated "Sermon on Law and Grace" (c. 1037–1050), likens the "new" faith of the Russians to the enfranchised bride Sarah and thus to *New* Testament grace but the "old" faith of Byzantium to the handmaiden Hagar and thus to *Old* Testament law, the archpriest Avvakum will, in another era, resort to a diametrically opposed system of contrasts. To the leader of the Old Believers, as we shall see shortly, the Nikonian reforms of the 1660s were a betrayal of sacred tradition; what was "unorthodox," including the three-figured sign of the cross, was a fall from a better past into the "now" of the Antichrist.

But to return to our topic, Russian history has been subject not only to the distant thunder of eschatology, which views any present *saeculum* in light of the *eskhaton*, but also to the specific tremors and oscillations of apocalypticism, which, like a kind of divine seismograph, shows history's explosive conclusion to be near and predictable as soon as the shape of current events are keyed to certain texts of Judaeo-Christian tradition. As suggested earlier, "eschatological" can imply any radical break with the past, while "apocalyptic" implies the salient features of Judaeo-Christian historiosophy: history is determined by God the author, the plot is now coming to a close in the rhythm of crisis-judgment-vindication, the figures of the Johannine and other apocalyptic texts have begun to appear to the "seers" of contemporary history, etc. Here the same opposition of old/new applies, but now it is given a narrower interpretation. In general, "eschatologists" may be dour or eupeptic, depending on which side of the break they place themselves and their generation.[9] That is to say, they may be either *apocalypticists*, if they see the present *transitus* as an ultimate judgment "from beyond" on their fallen fellows (as well as a simultaneous vindication of their own faith), or *utopians* (or millenarians *avant le lettre*), if they see contemporary reality simply as a stage to pass through in order to reach that "no place" which passes for a terrestrial New Jerusalem. Thus, al-

---

[9] Cf. Sergey Bulgakov in "Pravoslavnaia èskhatologiia": "Eschatologism may have two images [*dva obraza*], light and dark. The latter has its place when it arises as a result of historical fright and a certain religious panic: it was this sort [of eschatologism that was produced by] the Russian schismatics—the self-immolators who wanted to destroy themselves in order to save themselves from the reigning Antichrist. But characteristic of eschatologism can be (and should be) a bright image with its impulse toward the Coming Christ. As we proceed in history, we come to meet Him [*idem k Nemu navstrechu*], and the rays [of light], emanating from His future coming to the world, can be felt. . . . Thus the Second Coming of Christ is not only terrible for us, since He will come as our Judge, but also glorious, since He will come in His glory, and this Glory is also the glorification of the world and the fullness that has come to pass in all creation" (385).

though there are countless permutations and no hard-and-fast laws in these matters, the apocalypticist tends to interpret the old/new opposition by making the first element positive (the original, pristine faith) and the second element negative (contemporary impiety and desecration), while the utopian tends to do the reverse, making a fetish of what is new, "enlightened," "advanced," such as technology (usually seen in Russia's case as coming from the West), and denigrating what is old, "superstitious," and "ignorant," such as religious tradition (usually seen in Russia's case as indigenous).[10] Ultimately, however, the apocalypticist and utopian cannot be said to translate simply into opposite sides of one eschatological coin; they have radically different conceptions of what constitutes narrative authority in the historiographical process. To the one, this authority comes from God, who is outside human (hi)story; to the other, this authority comes from human beings, who can make themselves and their ideal POLIS within history, *if* only they really try.

While our focus in these pages is primarily the nineteenth century and that "prehistory" of Russian apocalyptic consciousness leading up to Dostoevsky and the modern period, I would like to dwell briefly on several episodes from earlier Russian history. These episodes loom large because over time they became a fertile source for the kind of end-determined, "right-angled" view of national history perpetuated by later writers, social theorists, and public figures. Moreover, they have striking similarities that gradually entered into the Russians' myths about themselves, their nation, and their ruler. The first has to do with the formula "Moscow the Third Rome," and, while generally traceable to the pronouncements of the Pskovian monk Philotheus in the early sixteenth century,[11] encompasses a larger series of

---

[10] Utopians can, to be sure, select as a model a golden agrarian age in the past, but I have in mind those—Alexander Bogdanov and Alexey Gastev would be prime examples in the modern Russian context—who take the streamlined euchronia, the "high tech" urban center, as the destined goal of history. See the Manuels (*Utopian Thought* 20) for the difference between "eutopia" and "euchronia": "In the bosom of a utopia of agrarian calm felicity a utopia of endless, dynamic change in science and technology was born. This switch to euchronia was heralded with the awakened sleeper of Sébastien Mercier's *L'An 2440* and with the utopian projections in the Tenth Epoch of Condorcet's *Esquisse*. The vision of a future society of *progrès indéfini* predominates through the emergence of Marx on the utopian landscape. Paradoxically, un-Christian utopia represented a resurgence of a strong millenarian, paradisaical, and apocalyptic current in secular form. The free rational choices of the Morean Utopian lawgiver or the Renaissance architect were abandoned to history: Utopia became less Hellenized and more Judeo-Christian. Older rhythms of thought from millenarianism and Joachimism were secularized, and translations of Judeo-Christian apocalyptic rhetoric into new forms became the stuff of the transformation." Again, on the parallels between utopia and apocalyptic paradise, see *Utopian Thought* 33–63.

[11] Evidence for the emergence of the myth of Moscow the Third Rome can be found in texts that pre-date Philotheus' formulation, such as "The Tale of the White Cowl" (late fifteenth

dates and events: the Council of Ferrara-Florence (1438–39), the fall of Constantinople in 1453, the projected end of the world in 1492, the writings of Philotheus c. 1510–24, and the crowning of Ivan IV as tsar in 1547. The second involves the Great Schism of the 1660s and the Petrine reforms which followed in the early years of the eighteenth century. These two constellations of events are not only related to each other but are seminal to an understanding of Russia's historical identity *before* its writers of secular history, such as Karamzin, began to try to disentangle the myth from the reality. It was these myths, whose precise historical provenance was often forgotten or ignored, that those coming after either tried to live up to or to live down, but rarely reacted to neutrally.

An essential element of Byzantine ideology inherited by the Russians was the notion of *basileus*, of the emperor who is simultaneously spiritual and secular leader of his Christian realm.[12] Even though the *basileus* is largely a "messianic" concept (McGinn, *Visions* 28), it does have important ties with the Eastern Christian apocalyptic tradition through the *Revelations of the Pseudo-Methodius* (wr. late seventh century). According to the latter, there would appear a Last World Emperor, whose role it was to defeat the Ishmaelites (read Islam) and then journey to Jerusalem to hand over his crown to God, at which moment the time of the Antichrist would commence (McGinn, *Visions* 70–73; Alexander, *Byzantine Apocalyptic Tradition* 13–60). The *basileus* myth itself goes back to Constantine (288?–337), who united Christianity and imperial Rome during his reign and built a new capital in Byzantium, which was renamed Constantinople and which, from the latter part of the fourth century, came to be known as the "New Rome." This second, "Eastern" Rome acquired additional status when the first, "Western" Rome was sacked by Alaric in 410. But by the fifteenth century Constantinople, which up to then had been successful at fending off Eastern marauders, was itself under imminent threat of falling to the Ottoman Turks. Its church delegates were eager to strike a bargain with a now renovated Rome at the Council of Ferrara-Florence. Moscow, on the other hand, which for some time had seen the rival Latinists as "old," "corrupt," "fallen," and "Western" (especially after the excommunication of Michael Cerularius, patriarch of Constantinople, and the resulting schism of 1054), interpreted the union as perfidy. The actual fall of Constantinople in 1453

---

century), but it was Philotheus who first made the case explicitly and concisely ("Both Romes fell, the third endures, and a fourth there will never be" [cited in Zenkovsky, *Medieval Russian Epics* 323]).

[12] The attributes "spiritual"/"secular" were originally not opposed, but merely different profiles of one divinely inspired countenance. See Cherniavsky, "Khan or Basileus"; and Obolensky, "Russia's Byzantine Heritage." For much of this discussion of Philotheus, I am indebted to D. Stremooukhoff's fine study "Moscow the Third Rome."

became proof a fortiori both of God's displeasure and of the Russians' own elect status. Already profoundly under the spell of messianism through the imported concept of the *basileus*, Moscow was soon faced with the prospect of either liberating Constantinople (thereby fulfilling its role as the "fair-skinned tribe" in the prophetic script of the pseudo-Methodius)[13] *or* declaring itself the third and last Rome and its tsar[14] the *basileus*. When the end of the world did not occur in 1492 (the last year of the seventh millennium in the Byzantine calendar), Moscow was free to pursue the second alternative.

Strangely enough, the fall of Constantinople, the passing of the year 1492, *and* the rise of Moscow as the Third Rome were essentially a reading of the Christian plot or *mythos* into contemporary history, but with a different twist. History was not yet secularized, and thus its meaning had still to come from outside. What could be "apocalyptic," or a justification for negative happenings, in the case of Constantinople could also be "messianic," or a justification for "chosen" status, in the case of Moscow.[15] This distinction is borne out with remarkable vividness in the exegesis of Philotheus. Taking his cue from earlier remarks by Zosimius, metropolitan of Moscow, and borrowing his figures from the Apocalypse of Ezra,[16] Philotheus identifies the *third* head of the twelve-winged eagle (IV Ezra 12:23) with Moscow, which had recently coopted the two-headed eagle as its coat of arms. Yet Philotheus is also apparently aware that this image of a three-headed beast could have *negative* connotations, such as the *passing* of worldly empires on the model of Daniel's four beasts. Thus in the epistle "Against the Astrologers and the Latins" (c. 1524) he shifts his emphasis from the third head of the eagle to the Woman Clothed in the Sun (Revelation 12:2), whom he perceives as Russia fleeing into the desert of true faith away from the false capitals of Rome and Constantinople. What is particularly striking about this case being made for Russia's manifest destiny is that Philotheus was arguing, like a Russian Augustine, against his native Pskovians, who saw Moscow as the seat of the Antichrist (Pskov had recently fallen under the rule of Vasily III, who deprived the ancient city of

---

[13] According to the prophetic script of the pseudo-Methodius, Constantinople was to be liberated by the Last World Emperor and his fair-skinned tribe, after which the final confrontation with the Antichrist would take place and the End of the world would follow (Sackur, *Sibyllinische Texte* 89–94; cited McGinn, *Visions* 75–76).

[14] The title began to gain currency under Ivan III (ruled 1462–1505).

[15] On the distinction between "messianism," "millenarianism," and "apocalypticism," see McGinn, *Visions* 28–36.

[16] The Apocalypse of Ezra was itself based in part on the Book of Daniel, an important Old Testament apocalyptic text. See Stremooukhoff, "Moscow" 113.

its rights and dispersed much of the population), and against the Latins, who maintained that the true Christian empire was still located in the West.

When Ivan IV had himself crowned tsar in 1547 amid much pomp,[17] he in effect consolidated the notion of Russia as holy empire and himself as *basileus*, which latter fact was soon recognized by the Eastern church. Indeed, beginning with the early sixteenth century scribal attempts were made to trace the Russian princely dynasties back to Augustus via his brother Prus, ruler of Prussia; this meant that these princes "were heirs of the two Romes not only spiritually or eschatologically, as they were for the monk Philotheus, but historically, virtually dynastically" (Cherniavsky, *Tsar* 42). Moreover, the shift from saintly prince, with his filial, "Christlike" role, to pious tsar, with his paternal, "God-like" one, was not lateral but *vertical*. It was, concludes Cherniavsky, "a raising of his functions to a higher, *apocalyptic* level; his person could not be made more exalted in any case" (Cherniavsky, *Tsar* 40).

With the coming of the Great Schism in the next century, the terms of spatio-temporal opposition remain essentially the same, but their values are reversed. The questions of ritual and doctrine now, as in the cases studied by Cohn in Northern and Central Europe, have an ever stronger *social* undercurrent. It is as if the Pskovians' cries in the wilderness, which in their time were limited to one or two cities (Novgorod also experienced apocalyptic forebodings in the early sixteenth century), had spread to a larger area and begun to rival in resonance the voices of official doctrinal reason. The Old Believers, it should be recalled, made their case to a *significant* portion of the population, with as many as twenty percent of the Russians of the time joining their ranks and embracing the *political theology* of the Schism (Cherniavsky, "Old Believers" 4–5). Above all, Avvakum and his followers were a sectarian movement that saw their golden age of harmony and piety *in the past*. As Berdyaev writes, "The Schism was a departure from history because history was controlled by the prince of this world, the Antichrist, who had penetrated to the upper levels of the church and state. The Orthodox kingdom was going underground. The genuine kingdom was the City of Kitezh [a popular version of paradise], located beneath the lake" (*Russkaia ideia* 14). Hence the seventeenth century in general and the decade of the Schism in particular were times of great social upheaval, including the civil wars of the Time of Troubles, the peasant unrest in the 1630s, the town rebellions in the 1640s and 1650s, the Cossack uprisings in the 1660s and 1670s, and the *streltsy fronde* in the 1680s and 1690s. Indeed, it would be no exaggeration to say that the Schism and the Petrine reforms (which the

---

[17] This was, to be sure, not the first time that a Muscovite grand prince had borne the title, but it was the first time that the crowning had been surrounded by such august celebration.

Old Believers led the reaction against) were *the* moment in Russian history when the oppositions of old/new and east/west entered into a particularly fateful alignment with the Russians' myths about themselves and the governance of their state. The very facts of broad popular appeal and interpenetration of the political, social, and theological realms suggest that this time was perceived as a "turning point" not only for the Avvakumians but for all those coming later who, with the emergence of "historical consciousness" in the early nineteenth century, would wrestle with their country's identity as "Eastern" or "Western," as a renovation of a golden past or a radical thrust into an enlightened future. The replacement of Moscow the Third Rome by St. Petersburg, the secular Western city of the Antichrist, would become a central theme, for example, of *The Idiot* and *Petersburg*, two of the "apocalyptic fictions" to be treated in this study; both pre-1917, these works present imperial Russia fast entering a state of crisis and eclipse. Similarly, the fate of the original capital, renovated to its former status after the revolution, would be the subject of *The Master and Margarita* and *Doctor Zhivago*, novels that show the city as a parodic Whore of Babylon and a fallen (and ultimately risen) Third Rome, respectively.

If the apocalyptic mood in medieval Russia never disappeared entirely, it reasserted itself with a vengeance in 1644, when the government printing office released the so-called *Book of Cyril*, which contained various South Slavic and Ukrainian apocalyptic writings. It was at approximately this same time that the monk Kapiton, founder of a hermitage in the north (Totma), first began to spread his theology—known pejoratively as *kapitonovshchina*—of flight from this world, imminent apocalypse, and self-immolation (Cherniavsky, "Old Believers" 16). Kapiton's activities served as a prelude to those of the Old Believers three decades later; an important shift in political theology was augured by the claim, made by one of his followers, that Tsar Alexis (ruled 1645–76) was "not tsar but a horn of the Antichrist" (Barskov, *Pamiatniki* 333; see also Smirnov, *Vnutrennie voprosy* 31 ff.). In this cryptic comment we already see the beginnings of an assault on the myth of *basileus* that will be carried far and wide by the Old Believers. The apocalyptic expectations of *kapitonovshchina* began to heat up again when the Patriarch Nikon decreed changes in church ritual in 1652–54. These reforms in ritual, which affected the way one made the sign of the cross, the number and manner of prostrations, and the hallelujah glorification, were not the first undertaken at the initiation of a tsar;[18] along with the abovementioned social tensions, however, their endorsement of Greek and South Slavic "purity" held the match to the powder keg of broad reaction. At first, the small group of Moscow preachers led by Avvakum

---

[18] Witness Ivan IV's well-known *Stoglav* Council in 1551.

was kept in check, but they persisted in their ecclesiastical rebellion. Attempts at compromise were rebuffed by the Avvakumians—the Fathers Avvakum, Fyodor, Lazar, and Epiphany—and the Patriarchal Council of 1666–67 passed intact the Nikonian reforms and declared the "old" practices and texts heretical. Those who continued to resist were anathematized, while the Avvakumians themselves were exiled to the far north (Pustozersk), where, in 1682, they were burned at the stake.

This skeletal account gives little sense of how closely apocalyptic theology was intertwined with the Council's work and the subsequent fate of the Avvakumians and their converts.[19] The Schism forced the Old Believers to rethink the essential terms entering into their Russian understanding of the economy of salvation. If Moscow was turning its back on its heritage as the Third Rome, then there was only one conclusion to draw—it was not the holy but the *unholy* city, the seat of the Antichrist. Nikon and Tsar Alexis were precursors of the Antichrist, whose appearance was scheduled for 1666 (the date of the convening of the Council and a convenient cipher for the beast's number, 666 [Revelation 13:18]). Messianism was turned inside out into apocalypticism; Russia's manifest destiny as the *New* Rome and world savior was transformed into its manifest destiny as traducer of sacred (here "old") tradition, as the Antichrist. In the words of the Old Believer monk Avraamy, "There will no longer be any further delay; everywhere is Russia's last [moment], and from hour to hour worse things happen" (Barskov, *Pamiatniki* 162).

By the late seventeenth century the Old Believer movement had spilled over into the impressionable, often uneducated public far beyond anything imagined by the original group of four. Numerous zealots were writing hundreds, if not thousands, of apocalypses of their own, preaching fiery sermons in the northern woods, and, when hemmed in too closely by the authorities (in 1684 it was made a *secular, state* crime, with punishment of death, to practice the schismatic faith), burning themselves alive to protest this world. Equally significant, these same *starovery* provided important ideological impetus for popular rebellion: consider, for example, the now

---

[19] To shift the context a little, the Great Reform movement—the West's version of the Schism—which originated in Luther's Germany a century and a half earlier and soon spread to Calvin's Geneva and Zwingli's Zurich, involved a quite similar apocalyptic theology. Only the terms, not perhaps unexpectedly, were reversed: the Wittenberg preacher (who, like Avvakum, was excommunicated in 1521 for insisting that popes and their councils can err) stood for "newness"—for a translation of the Bible into colorful German vernacular, for congregational singing, for lay reception of the eucharistic bread and wine, etc.; the traditions of the Roman Catholic church, especially those connected with the practice of granting indulgences, were seen as "old"—as belonging to the temporal rather than the universal church, to the Antichrist rather than Christ. Of course Luther, like most late medieval Christians, fully believed that his children would live to see the Second Coming.

generally acknowledged connection between the Old Believers and the revolt of Stenka Razin in 1670–71 and the uprising of the *streltsy* in 1682.
And so, "beginning with the insurrection of 1682, every popular uprising
in Russia—the continued *streltsy* troubles, the Cossack rebellions under Peter I (Azov, Astrakhan, Bulavin's uprising), and the climax of the great uprising of Pugachev under Catherine II—was fought under the banner of the
Old Belief: the restoration of old rituals, icons, and books was inextricably
connected with the program of massacring the aristocracy and abolishing
serfdom" (Cherniavsky, "Old Believers" 20).[20]

In other words, with the coming to power of Peter I (ruled 1682–1725),
the fury of the Old Believers' apocalypticism reached its peak and the true
*raskol* began. Peter, who spelled his name with a foreign alphabet, was seen
as the Antichrist incarnate; his city, with its Western architecture, its predominance of European spires over Orthodox cupolas, as un-Russian and
thereby unholy; his new calendar, which "stole eight years from God," as
a turning away from Biblical time; and his chosen title—*imperator* (emperor)—as the ultimate derogation of his sacred role as tsar. Peter's desacralization of Russia's past went much further than the shearing of boyars'
beards—the number of variations on the Peter as Antichrist myth attests to
this. But the main issue remained one of divine genealogy: as *basileus*,
Peter was supposed to be God's appointed servant on earth; yet rather than
accepting this role, he had made of himself a *zemnoi bog*, a god on earth
(Cherniavsky, "Old Believers" 33). It is indeed ironic that the Old Believers
were so devoted to the "old," including the belief in their ruler as *basileus*,
that they devised stories about Peter's changeling status. After all, to them
this colossal figure of evil could not be both tsar *and* Antichrist.

The seventeenth century was not only a time of great turmoil for the
myth of the tsar as *basileus*, however. It was also the time when the second
great myth, that of "Holy Russia" (*Sviataia Rus'*) and her people (*narod*),
first gained wide currency as something independent of, and indeed in many
ways opposed to, the myth of the tsar.[21] As Alexander Solovyov first estab-

----

[20] To glance ahead for a moment, both Blok and Bely, in the years leading up to 1917, would
become fascinated by the tradition tying together apocalypticism, revolution, and sectarian
heterodoxy. After 1917, writers such as Pilnyak and Platonov would translate the same apoc-
alypticist-sectarian nexus into Bolshevik legend: the former's *okhlomony* (*Mahogany*) and the
latter's Chevengurians are in fact modern Old Believers who are attempting to keep the faith
of the revolution alive in times of compromise and "secularization" (the NEP—New Economic
Policy).

[21] It could conceivably be argued that the notions of "Russian Land" (*russkaia zemlia*), dat-
ing back to Kievan times, and "Holy Russia" are analogous. Here, however, the operative term
is *holy*, which was first joined with *Rus'* in the sixteenth century, in Kurbsky's correspondence. Paszkiewicz links the older term *Rus'* and the Christian religion, but without the specific
use of *sviataia* (*Origins of Russia* 12).

lished, the term "Holy Russia" initially appeared in Prince Andrey Kurbsky's correspondence with Ivan IV as an *indictment* of the tsar's action—the émigré prince lamented that Ivan had "dishonored [himself] and the holyrussian land" (*Russkaia Istoricheskaia Biblioteka* 31: 134; cited in Cherniavsky, *Tsar* 107). But only with the Time of Troubles (*Smutnoe vremia*) in the early seventeenth century, when Russia was without a tsar and had to preserve its Orthodox essence intact against Polish Catholic intervention, did the term gain popular acceptance and begin to appear in numerous folk songs and epics:

> Russia was "Holy Russia" because it was the land of salvation, expressed in its icons, saints, people, and ruler. But the historical origin of the term indicates its concrete limits: "Holy Russia" was *what remained*, during the Time of Troubles, after Tsar and State and church hierarchy were gone; it was the *concentrated essence* of Russia, visible when the form of Russia was destroyed. Hence, both on the transcendental and concrete levels "Holy Russia" was an absolute, immutable, because the land of salvation could not change except catastrophically, nor could the Russian essence change without losing itself (my emphasis; Cherniavsky, *Tsar* 116).

Here was a spatial myth that existed "no-place" but was capable of sustaining those like the Old Believers as they confronted the specter of tsar turned Antichrist and the Third Rome turned Whore of Babylon. Where, one might ask, could this "Holy Russia" be found? It could be found in the *narod*, in the villages and monasteries, lower gentry and simple folk that kept the faith alive when the tsar was absent and the Poles were at the gates of Moscow. So too could it be found in those preachers in the northern woods who burned themselves alive because their tsar had disappeared and because the only way back to the past, to the underwater kingdom of Kitezh, was through fiery death. Thus "Holy Russia," though born of a specific time and place, became something nonhistorical, transcendental. *Rus'*, the name for "old" Russia, could be *Sviataia*, "Holy," but the *Imperiia*, "Empire," could only be *Rossiiskaia*, a secular "Russian" formed from the "new" noun *Rossiia* (Cherniavsky, *Tsar* 119). And it was between these two essentially opposing myths, that of the tsar and that of the people of "Holy Russia," that the intelligentsia, the group of educated Russians who were located *outside* either myth,[22] found themselves when, returning obsessively to the question of Russia's identity, they made cultural history in the nineteenth century.

---

[22] Generally speaking, the intelligentsia saw themselves as belonging neither to the tsar's reactionary government nor to the *narod*'s difficult daily life and customs. See below.

It would be futile to try to define with any precision "Holy Russia" and its ephemeral boundaries within the *narod*. What can be proposed is that the term, as a cultural model, inevitably raises issues of mythical, as opposed to historical, time. Each of its later champions—Khomyakov, Zhukovsky, Vyazemsky, Tyutchev, Dostoevsky, Fyodorov, Berdyaev—was forced to accommodate a contingent, problem-ridden present by casting back to this nonhistorical past or by projecting it into the future. Moreover, the moment in Russian cultural history at which this all-important opposition became actual and operative, entering into the very structure of the Russian language, was again the seventeenth century, the same epoch-making period of the Schism. The Soviet scholar A. M. Panchenko has demonstrated that, beginning with the second half of the seventeenth century, one can add to the already familiar oppositions of old/new and foreign/domestic the new opposition of mythical time/secular history. This may seem, prima facie, simply another variation on the old/new antinomy, but Panchenko thinks otherwise. The grounds for argument between Nikon and Avvakum were not necessarily tradition and innovation in a true *historical* sense (since in matters of ritual and doctrine almost any scriptural source can be adduced to buttress the priority and hence the authority of one's argument); on the other hand, the grounds for argument between the traditionalists and the new teachers of imported baroque culture who came to prominence during the reigns of Tsars Alexis and Peter could, and probably did have, considerable import for the development of Russian historical consciousness. In this case, the polemic between the Old Believers and such "New Enlighteners" as Simeon of Polotsk, Silvester Medvedev, Stephan Yavorsky, and St. Dimitry of Rostovsk was not so much over doctrine— though that was the pretext—as over *historical time*. "It was not a historiographical but a historiosophical argument—an argument about a historical ideal, about historical distance, about the interrelation between man and time, about eternity and the perishable, about the past, present, and future" (Panchenko, "Istoriia i vechnost' " 191).

Using an approach not unlike Lotman's, Panchenko breaks these two conceptions of time into the medieval, that valorized by the Old Believers, and the proto-modern, that valorized by the New Enlighteners. The first sees "human existence, taken *in toto*, as an *echo of the past*—more precisely, of those events from the past which are identified with eternity" (my emphasis; Panchenko, "Istoriia i vechnost' " 191). This "echo" is intimately bound to the Orthodox understanding of weekly and yearly cycles, each of which "renews," in small or large scale, the resurrection of Christ. Within the family circle (or "cycle"), the same echo principle was at work: individual members, as descendants, were often given names from one semantic "family" to underscore the belief that their role was to recapitulate the "clannish fate" (*rodovaia sud'ba*) of their ancestors. Here the renewal is never innovative, never a break with the past, but always a reconfirmation of human contact with eternity. In other words, Panchenko's revealing analysis is in remarkable accord with what Eliade has written about sacred time in archaic or primitive societies. The future does not yet exist (hence the Apocalypse for the Old Believers is *now*) because the profane present is constantly annulled in favor of a periodic return to eternity. According to Orthodox ritual, the "man who fasts, confesses, and takes communion each time 'renews himself.' That is, he purifies himself of sinful [outer] layers, grows closer to the ideal. 'Renewal' is a kind of 'aging' [*odrevlenie*: lit: 'making ancient'] of man, in which the qualities of the ideal show through with greater clarity" (Panchenko, "Istoriia i vechnost' " 192).

For the New Enlighteners, however, many of whom had been through the Kiev Academy and were influenced by Polish (that is, "Western," post-Renaissance) models, historical time was not something to be banned; rather it was something to be learned and understood. These were men of books and libraries, whereas Avvakum was a man of one book in principle and few books in practice. When, for example, the latter was blessed early in his career by a confessor, the formula used included "by *the* [apocalyptic!] Book of Ephrem the Syrian" (cited in Panchenko, "Istoriia i vechnost' " 194). This is not to say that the culture of the Old Believers was one of ignorance and obscurantism, as Simeon and his colleagues would submit, but simply that the book, like the icon, was something sacred, immutably true, in no need of duplication. The book, and the Great Time of which it told, possessed human beings; human beings did not possess the book. With the Enlighteners, on the other hand, the Russian, to use again Eliade's formulation, *entered* history as secular time. To be sure, this was not seen by them as a "fall" into history—quite the opposite, since Russia was being *raised* out of the darkness—but it would seem so to later, more nostalgic, generations. These scholars "proclaimed the idea of a *unified, civilized* time, removing, in effect, the distinction between eternity and perishable existence"; history became " 'interesting' in and of itself, independent of its relation to God, eternity, and the soul"; and history, most importantly, no longer "predetermined the fate of [one's] descendants, their earthly existence. The past was dead" (Panchenko, "Istoriia i vechnost' " 195).

Not fortuitously, the gradual emergence of secular literature, as well as of its disguised forms in the works of those still closely associated with the church, marked this shift in historical consciousness. Simeon's verse plays written in the 1670s provide compelling evidence of the change in process. The first, about Nebuchadnezzar, would appear by its title to be an adaptation of the church ritual then referred to as *chin peshchnogo deistva* (lit.

"rite of the furnace action": see Karlinsky, *Russian Drama* 1–14).[23] It was this ritual, which took place at Christmastime and symbolically recalled the immaculate conception (just as the youths were not burned in the furnace, so was the Virgin not harmed by the fiery Holy Spirit entering her natural body), that the tsar himself had traditionally participated in. Now, however, it was subject to ban, and consequently Simeon's play has none of this symbolic overlay. In fact, the principal focus of the play is the "comedic" (plays at this time were called *komedii*), "verisimilar" historical parallels between the ancient king and the current Tsar Alexis. Hence the *faith* (*vera*) implicit in the Christmas ritual (*chin*) was being eroded by the *culture* of the "comedy" (Panchenko, "Istoriia i vechnost' " 196). The similarities (and differences) between Nebuchadnezzar and Alexis served to indicate how *future* generations would interpret the deeds of the present tsar. History began to stretch out into the future, to appear endless. Even questions of the Last Judgment, which so vexed the Old Believers, became more personal than collective, more "literary" than "literal." The numerous works of the Russian baroque that deal with the Apocalypse—the "Pentateugum" of Andrey Belobotsky and the anonymous "Staircase to Heaven" are two of the best known—do so thematically rather than ritually. Conversely, the actual ritual during Shrovetide—when the patriarch wiped clean the icon of the Last Judgment in the Uspensky Cathedral (the act of "renewal") and blessed and sprinkled water over the tsar—was abolished. Like Augustine defending his church and faith against the apocalypticists, St. Dimitry, one of the New Enlighteners, could claim: "To us the Last Judgment is more personal [*komuzhdo svoi*] than general, and as for the time itself of the terrible judgment day, it is not for us to ask. It is enough to believe that it will come . . . but when it will come, do not inquire . . . about that day and hour no one knows" (*Rozysk o raskol'nicheskoi brynskoi vere* 62; cited in Panchenko, "Istoriia i vechnost' " 198).

Russia's transition from theocratic to secular state was obviously more complex and continuous than our schematic retelling of it allows, yet in the final analysis there is no minimizing the vast significance of the Petrine reforms and the figure of Peter himself. Nineteenth-century social thought and historiography abound with comparisons, optimistic and pessimistic, utopian and apocalyptic, that interpret the present and predict the future by attempting to solve the riddle of the Petrine Sphinx. Even such a respected historian as S. M. Solovyov considered Peter "*the* hero of Russian history, probably the only hero, and the last one. . . . [He] concludes the epic period of Russian history and opens the era of civilization for Russia. . . . The

---

[23] *Of the King Nebuchadnezzar, the Golden Calf, and the Three Youths Not Burned in the Furnace.*

change under him was most radical: from epic to history—from prehistory to history proper. Only since Peter has Russia become an 'historic' nation" (cited in Florovsky, "The Problem" 127). This is a gross oversimplification, as most modern historians would now admit, but again, as a cultural model and narrative *mythos* to be strenuously rejected (the Slavophiles) or equally strenuously embraced (the Westernizers), it maintained its potency into the nineteenth century and, in some cases, beyond.

Thus flanked by an "enlightened" vanguard whose task it was to legitimize the tsar's role, the Petrine myth emerged in its purest form as a tale of long overdue change—not evolutionary, but revolutionary, not ameliorative, but total, instantaneous, seemingly *ex nihilo*, and of course eschatological. Antiokh Kantemir proclaimed that through the "wise commands" of Peter Russia had become, *"in a moment's time,"* "a new people" (my emphasis; *ss* 75).[24] And just as Simeon had earlier compared Alexis to Nebuchadnezzar, so now Feofan Prokopovich compared Peter to Saint Vladimir, the Christianizer and "enlightener" of Russia, in his tragicomedy of the same name (see Lotman and Uspenskii, "Binary Models" 52–56; and Karlinsky, *Russian Drama* 24–29). "New" suddenly had a positive valence, as it had for Hilarion, and what was "old"—including the obstreperous Orthodox priests thinly disguised as "pagan sorcerers" in Prokopovich's play—was ignorant and evil.[25] In effect, the notions of progress and enlightenment championed by the new cultural spokesmen carried with them the spatial image of futurity, the *put'* (path) that was to become the root metaphor for directing and marshalling the "historical present" (ultimately a *contradictio in adjecto*) in the collective imagination of the emerging intelligentsia. What was totally "new" or "reborn" had to *go* somewhere, to *look* for something. Disenfranchised by Peter's meritocracy and table of ranks and raised on a steady diet of "progressive" European principles, the hereditary nobility (*stolbovoe dvorianstvo*) were to become leading members of the intelligentsia and the creators of the new literature. Not only did they see their own power and wealth ebbing away, they were forced to witness the decline of their peasants, the principal victims in this political and economic realignment (see Lotman, "Ideinaia struktura"). "The Russian nobleman of the nineteenth century normally lacked strong roots in any particular area and had no real feeling of attachment to a specific locality

---

[24] Compare, for example, the following lines about Stalin written by the Georgian poet N. Mitsishvili in the mid-thirties and translated by Pasternak: "You have achieved the unachievable: / You have remade [*peresozdal*] people's minds and souls, / Your hand with sickle has covered a continent, / And with hammer has gone to the ends of the earth" (*Poèty Gruzii* 85–86).

[25] It is significant that the opponent of the pagan sorcerers is not a churchman but a Greek philosopher. See Karlinsky, *Russian Drama* 26.

and to a family estate on which his ancestors had lived for generations. . . . There is little evidence of the attachment to and the ties with the ancestral home which characterized the mentality of the western nobleman" (Raeff, "Home, School, and Service" 295–307). Reared by nursemaids and tutors who had no "rights" to him, sent to a school which offered a completely Western education, the young nobleman grew up with a distinctly rationalistic and didactic cast of mind, neither totally Muscovite nor French, but one that obviously anticipated that of the nineteenth century *intelligent* (Roberts, "Russia and the West" 256). In a word, the educated nobleman of the eighteenth century found himself "*doubly cut off*: from his own people's past, which he had learned to scorn and reject, and from Western Europe, which had not yet fully accepted him and of which he still did not feel the equal" (my emphasis; Raeff, "Russia's Perception" 262–63).

The almost hypnotic attraction of the *put'*, with its spatialization of temporal desire, is an essential ingredient in the messianic and apocalyptic roles that the nineteenth-century intelligentsia assigned to the long-suffering *narod*. It was felt that the various roads, paths, and ways invoked to describe Russian historical time should in the end, and *at the end*, have a destination. With remarkable ingenuity, the present was overcome by finding some popular trapdoor to a sacred—usually pre-Petrine—past or by scaling the ladder of Western, post-Enlightenment knowledge to a brighter future. Yet in either case the *temporal* ideal was equally removed, equally *distant* from the *intelligent* "outsider." Berdyaev, whose own work grew out of the late nineteenth-century tradition, resorts to the same matrix of images (spatiality standing in for temporality) when he states with characteristic aplomb that "Russians are *beguny* [a sect whose name means "runners," those running *from* this world] and bandits. And Russians are wanderers [*stranniki*] in search of God's truth" (*Russkaia ideia* 10). It is only a short step from this account of the sectarian genesis of Russian restlessness and "flight" to a *general* spatialization of the urge for temporal reintegration experienced by all great Russian writers:

> Russians always thirst for another life, another world; they always experience displeasure at what is. There belongs to the structure of the Russian soul an eschatological directedness. The urge to wander [*strannichestvo*] is a very characteristic Russian phenomenon, and as such unknown to the West. The wanderer walks the boundless Russian land and never settles down [*osedaet*], never becomes attached to anything. The wanderer searches for the truth, for the Kingdom of Heaven; he is directed into the distance. The wanderer has no abiding earthly city, but is directed toward the City-to-Come [*Grad Griadushchii*]. The people [*narodnyi sloi*] have always singled out from their

midst such wanderers. Yet in spirit the most creative representatives of Russian culture—Gogol, Dostoevsky, L. Tolstoy, Vl. Solovyov, and all the revolutionary intelligentsia—have also been wanderers. There exists not only a physical, but a spiritual urge to wander. This is the inability to be at ease with anything finite, the directedness toward what is infinite. But this is also an eschatological directedness, an expectation that there will be an end to all that is finite, that a final truth will be revealed, that in the future some sort of extraordinary occurrence will take place. I would call this a messianic sensibility, to an equal degree characteristic of those [coming] from the people [*narod*] and of those of higher culture. Russians are, to a greater or lesser extent, consciously or unconsciously, chiliasts. Westerners are much more sedentary [*osedlye*], more attached to the perfected forms of civilization; they value their present and are more concerned with the successful management of the earth (*Russkaia ideia* 199).

As is often the case, Berdyaev's generalizations could be relegated to the musty files of *Geistesgeschichte* were it not for the influence such notions had on leading nineteenth century thinkers, who in turn, with their own mix of *mythos* and political agenda, cast an imposing shadow on the "authors" of the revolution at the turn of the twentieth century. One need only recall how attached Lenin was to his executed brother's copy of *What Is to Be Done?* (1863),[26] itself a kind of utopian fairy tale with an ideal future (cast in the present) and a plucky Cinderella (Vera Pavlovna) who wins both her prince and her happy kingdom (a Russian version of the Fourierian phalanstery) in the bargain. From the late eighteenth to the early twentieth century nearly every major historian, philosopher, and author (as well as countless minor ones) tried to come to terms with the familiar old/new, east/west oppositions, and, as social tensions increased and anarchy and revolution became more probable, they saw the conclusion to the historical plot rise into view either as a utopian triumph devoutly to be wished or as an apocalyptic *ekpyrosis* (great fire) or *kataklysmos* (great flood) anxiously to be awaited.

The most prominent landmarks are now commonplace in the annals of intellectual and cultural history and can be touched on here in telegraphic fashion:

(1) the Masonic "catastrophists" (Semyon Bobrov, Matvey Dmitriev-Mamonov, A. M. Kutuzov, Sergey Shirinsky-Shikhmatov) and other proto-Decembrists who forecast an end to the Russian Empire either by

---

[26] The title was to reappear as one of Lenin's most important reinterpretations of Marxist doctrine.

flood or by fire,[27] and who set down a tradition to be reworked by Pushkin, Vladimir Pecherin, Vladimir Odoevsky, Mikhail Dmitriev, and others;

(2) the preaching of St. Seraphim (1759–1833) about another order of time beyond this world and his prediction that the visit of a tsar to a nunnery would initiate a period of great upheaval and carnage;[28]

(3) the heated debate over the "old" and "new" styles in Russian literature carried on by the Shishkovites and Arzamasians in the early years of the century;

(4) the broad interest in history spurred by many things: the defeat of Napoleon in 1812, the monumental work of Karamzin that followed, the sharp disagreements in print between Pushkin and Polevoy over the authority of the great historiographer in the post-Decembrist Uprising years, the spate of historical studies that appeared in the 1830s and that derived authority either from the idealism of Hegel and Schelling (Polevoy, Ivan Kireevsky, Pogodin) or from the skepticism of Niebuhr and Von Ranke (Kachenovsky), the emergence into prominence of the historical novels of Bulgarin, Lazhechnikov, Zagoskin, and, in general, the dogged search for a legitimate national identity promoted during the reign of Nicholas I (ruled 1825–55);

(5) Chaadaev's famous critique, from the viewpoint of conservative French Catholic philosophy (de Bonald, de Maistre), of Russia's past (or absence thereof: "Isolated from the world, we have given nothing to the world, we have taken nothing from the world; we have not added a single idea to the mass of human ideas; we have contributed nothing to the progress of the human spirit" [*Phil Letters* 41]), his premonition that some great turning point was at hand and that the establishment of the Kingdom of Heaven upon earth was imminent, and his radical *volte-face* in *Apologie d'un fou* (1836), when the lack of an historical past is suddenly transformed into the promise of a future ("the future is ours" [*Phil Letters* 175]);

(6) the search by the Slavophiles (chiefly Ivan Kireevsky, Alexey Khomyakov, and Konstantin Aksakov) for an ideal past in the concepts of *sobornost'* (the spirit of "free unity") and *obshchina* (the peasant commune), their desire to project that past into the future as the *telos* of Russian history, and their radical rejection of the Catholic and Protestant West—the one's "unity without freedom" (i.e., socialism) and the other's "freedom without unity" (i.e., the "egoism" of Max Stirner);

[27] For the poetic treatment of the great flood (*kataklysmos*) and great fire (*ekpyrosis*) see, e.g., Bobrov's "The Fate of the Ancient World" (1789?) and Dmitriev-Mamonov's "Fire" (1811?).

[28] The visit would turn out to be made by Nicholas II in July 1903 and was seen to usher in the two revolutions. See Clark and Holquist, *Mikhail Bakhtin* 133–34, 372.

(7) Belinsky's provocative *mot*, echoing Chaadaev's earlier historical claims, that "we have no literature" (*PSS* I: 22);

(8) Herzen's nagging fear of revolution ("This lava, these barbarians, this new world, these Nazarenes who are coming to put an end to the impotent and the decrepit . . . they are closer than you think" [*SS* VI: 58–59]), his skepticism about apocalypse and historical destiny ("history is all improvisation, all will, all extempore" [*SS* VI: 34–35), his disenchantment with 1848, and yet his hope, during the period of "Russian Socialism," that his country—especially the *Eastern* frontier of Siberia—in its "newness" and "openness," could save the world from the corruption and philistinism of the European bourgeoisie;

(9) Bakunin's translation of Left Hegelianism into the joy of destruction (recall his notorious "Die Lust der Zerstörung ist auch eine schaffende Lust" ["The desire for destruction is also a creative desire"]) and total negation of the past;

(10) Dostoevsky's neurotic hatred of Switzerland, his falling out with Turgenev over the subject of Germany versus Russia, his savage parodies of the "men of the sixties," his anxiety over the rising tide of anarchy, terrorism, and *nechaevshchina*, and his predictions, especially in sections of *Diary of a Writer* written in the 1870s, that the Antichrist was afoot and the End was near ("The Antichrist is coming to us! He is coming! And the end of the world is near—nearer than they think" [Timofeeva, "God raboty" 170]);

(11) Leontiev's conservative scorn for equality, progress and enlightenment, his rejection of drab and tasteless European dress and habits, his eerie sense of living at the edge of an abyss, his legendary desire to "freeze Russia lest she rot," and his conviction that "we suddenly, from the depths of our state bowels [*gosudarstvennye nedra*] . . . will give birth to the Antichrist" and "will end history, destroying humanity in a bloodbath of universal equality" ("Nad mogiloi Pazukhina" VII: 425);

(12) Fyodorov's utopian attempt, in *The Philosophy of the Common Cause* (1906, 1913), to render apocalyptic retribution "from beyond" unnecessary through a program of universal brotherhood, scientific discovery, and literal resurrection—molecule by molecule—of one's ancestors;

(13) Vladimir Solovyov's conviction near the end of his life that the twentieth century would be "an epoch of last great wars, civil disorders, and revolutions," that "Panmongolism" would reign, and that as a result of a universal intermixing of East and West there would emerge a "superman . . . a great thinker, writer, and public figure," whose activities on the stage of history would appear as a kind of photographic negative, or anti-image, of Jesus Christ (*Tri razgovora* 193, 199).

These are just a few of the moments that, taken together, gave our novelists the overwhelming sensation of apocalypse and *Endzeit*. I do not mean to suggest that there is a direct or simple correlation between these ideas themselves and the structure (as opposed to the themes per se) of the novels under discussion, but only that certain assumptions about the meaning of Russian history—it is meaningful because it is ending soon, and any ending, whether punitive or expiative, confers meaning—can also be made about the meaning of Russian history and individual biography as presented in narrative fiction. The time has come, however, to look more closely at what this means.

## PLOT

We have been speaking primarily of Russian history and the views of participants/spectators as to that history's alleged beginning and end. As we move to a discussion of fictional narrative and its presentation of a *Russian* apocalypse, it would be well to state several givens. First, as Arthur Danto has rigorously argued, there is a fundamental difference between historical crisis as viewed (or "lived") by a participant (say, Avvakum) and that same crisis as viewed by the historian (say, Michael Cherniavsky) looking back and narrating it (*Narration and Knowledge* 342–63). The participant *projects* an ending, but the historian *knows* that that is how things turned out; the participant is still "inside" (hi)story, but the historian is by definition "outside" it, located temporally and spatially at that much invoked "meta-" level whence he or she can presumably, objectively and dispassionately, describe and therefore explain how the chronicle of events became history, how, in formalist terms, the "fable" (*fabula*) became a "plot" (*siuzhet*), the "story" (*histoire*) a "discourse" (*discours*) (Chatman, *Story and Discourse* 19).

Thus it is the historian's special role to generate, in Danto's terminology, "narrative predicates"—those statements which, when applied to objects, "do so only on the assumption that a future event occurs," and which are seen as "retrospectively *false* . . . if the future required by the meaning-rules of these predicates fails to materialize" (*Narration and Knowledge* 349–50). Such narrative predicates make a special claim on the future, but it is a future *only* from the viewpoint of the participant. From the viewpoint of the historian it is *already past*: e.g., "Lenin's arrival at the Finland Station *would* [a modal the participant might have hoped for but could not know for certain] unify the revolutionary movement and contribute to the collapse of the Provisional Government." On the other hand, while the historian can narrate the past, he or she *cannot* narrate the future; the very closedness of the past (the historian is located outside it) implies that the future is open and that, in this new context, the historian must trade the role of narrator for that of participant/spectator (he or she is inside and part of that which is still unfolding). *"The very structure of narrative,"* concludes Danto, "entails the openness of the future, for only then can it in any way depend upon the present" (*Narration and Knowledge* 353).

So much has been written about the essential isomorphism of historical and fictional narratives[29] that we tend to overlook the more basic difference between the narrative predicates characteristic of them.[30] The historian, if consistent and not given to narrating what cannot, *historically*, be known, is limited to a description of the past, meaning that his or her "meta"-viewpoint is only privileged vis-à-vis the participants of those already accomplished events and "turning points" at issue. To *know* the End from one's own viewpoint, from *one's present*, is to break the rules of a narrative predicate, and therefore to posit what for the *historical* narrative is an impossibility. "If the knowledge of the narrator [historian] were made available to the characters [participants, spectators], the structure of narration would be destroyed" (*Narration and Knowledge* 356). Danto is assuming, as indeed he must, that there is no higher viewpoint *outside* of and enclosing the historian's future which can be known and narrated as history. Yet this very stricture, essential to the integrity of historical narration, does not necessarily bind the unfolding of fictional narrative. Perhaps the most fundamental, ahistorical argument advanced by the "apocalyptic fictions" we will be examining is that narrators, like historians, do stand in a position of "metacognitive" superiority to their characters, *but* these characters can, if sensitive to the signs/symbols in these stories, know ("intuit") what their

[29] Both historical and fictional narrators select out and "prefigure" their material, both tell "stories," even if one is based primarily on "fact" and the other, with varying degrees of subterfuge, embraces its fictionality, etc. A fine recent distillation of the argument is found in Gearhart, *The Open Boundary* 3–28, but see also Barthes, "Historical Discourse"; Braudy, *Narrative Form in History and Fiction*; Gallie, *Philosophy and the Historical Understanding*; Gossman, "History and Literature"; J. Hillis Miller, "Narrative and History"; and White, *Metahistory*. Gearhart's book is useful for its non-flamboyant discussion of the contributions of many of the chief participants in this dialogue, including Louis Althusser, Roland Barthes, Arthur Danto, Paul de Man, Jacques Derrida, Michel Foucault, W. B. Gallie, Claude Lévi-Struass, and Hayden White.

[30] Cf. Bakhtin's position on the difference between novel and history as explained by Michael Holquist in *The Dialogic Imagination*: "But histories differ from novels in that they insist on a homology between the sequence of their own telling, the form they impose to create a coherent explanation in the form of a narrative on the one hand, and the sequence of *what* they tell on the other. This templating of what is enunciated with the act of enunciation is a narrative consequence of the historian's professional desire to tell 'wie es eigentlich gewesen ist' ["how it really was"]. The novel, by contrast, dramatizes the gaps that always exist between what is told and the telling of it, constantly experimenting with social, discursive and narrative asymmetries (the formal tetralogy that led Henry James to call them 'fluid puddings')" (xxviii).

narrators know. This is not of course *historical* knowledge as Danto would define it, but to the characters (and to their narrators and authors) it *is* knowledge (one would probably have to call it "mystical" or "revelatory") nonetheless.[31]

In other words, the protagonists of these novels, who in several cases write versions of their own stories, may be paradoxically characterized not only as "chroniclers" but, in a sense, as "historians"—they are given, by their narrator or author, a *fore*knowledge of the future *from the present*. Located on the inside, they are vouchsafed *aperçus* that could come only from the outside. And, strange to say, not only does this not destroy narrative, it makes it rich and mystifying. We are constantly presented with Escher-like optical illusions, with narrative hierarchies that, like staircases climbing upward and simultaneously back into themselves, are both circular *and* open. For just as in fiction a character can have knowledge that by rights should only belong to the narrator (the Master "knows" that the stranger at Patriarchs Ponds *is* the Devil), so too can the narrator, circumscribed by the work's beginning and end, have knowledge that should only belong to the author. Such then is the epistemological Phrygian Cap coming between the narrative hierarchies of historiography and fiction writing. The novel can play with, indeed be obsessed by, the meaning of history, but it can also freely undermine the logic of the narrative predicate without which historiography is impossible.

At this point I would like to offer a rough typology of a sub-genre of the modern Russian novel which I call the "apocalyptic fiction." Along the way I will also suggest why certain current assumptions about novelistic form in general and narrative in particular do not always account for the "structure" of these works, which routinely question their own limits as verbal art only to posit a non-verbal (or non-verbalizable) meaning lying *beyond*. This is to say, in the first place, that an apocalyptic fiction is not an apocalypse, but a modern equivalent of one, a kind of sacred text or version of *the Book* through which the character and the narrator and, by implication, the reader—all in their separate, self-enclosed realms—are made privy to a "secret wisdom" from another space-time. For our purposes the following

---

[31] To "narrate the world" in this way is to do something very similar to what Karl Solger and Friedrich Schlegel discussed and Ludwig Tieck, E.T.A. Hoffmann, and Heinrich Heine practiced under the rubric of "Romantic Irony." The romantic ironist, however, sees the character as the author's plaything, just as a human being is a puppet held up by a mocking deity's strings. To put it another way, the boundary-line between story and teller, narrative and narrator, is to be crossed only by "the fully-conscious artist whose art is the ironical presentation of the ironic position of the fully-conscious artist" (Muecke, *Irony* 20). Yet for these Russian writers and the tradition they were creating, the narrative hierarchy does not have to be in the shape of a closed and vicious circularity.

characteristics might be selected out as determinative in apocalyptic fiction: (1) a canonical subtext that plays an important role both thematically and structurally in the parent text (in our case the Apocalypse of John); (2) a living tradition with which the work enters into dialogue and against which it asks to be read (i.e., the work is not an isolated phenomenon); (3) an apocalyptic "set" or predisposition to read current historical crisis through the prism of the Johannine structures and figures (here, the Revolution as eschatological turning point to be either anticipated or retrospectively evaluated: see Kermode, "Apocalypse and the Modern" 86); and (4) an apocalyptic plot whose "deep" or mythological structure in modern novelistic terms is a recapitulation of the essential movement of the Johannine text.

Rather than looking at these novels through the either/or optic of structuralism or poststructuralism—that is, they are *either* self-regulating, self-inscribing linguistic units whose "anatomies" can be classified and dissected with the appropriate narratological *langue* (Tomashevsky, Barthes, Todorov, etc.) *or* they are generic anarchists whose chief raison d'être is to subvert convention and tradition and to exist in what Bakhtin would call a zone of maximum openness with reality—we will see them as verbal forms that are *simultaneously aware of their openness and closedness,* and of the boundary between *Wahrheit* and *Dichtung.* As Frank Kermode has aptly remarked, these are the fragile "fictions of concord," the "plots of, or against, the world and time" that, neither pure reality nor pure myth, fully acknowledge the modern world's skepticism about holistic pattern and yet somehow are able to provide form enough to make sense of our lives (Kermode, *Sense* 59; "Apocalypse and the Modern" 101).

Let us now examine more closely the various elements of an apocalyptic fiction. To begin with, each of the novels in question alludes significantly to the Johannine text. These allusions are not merely thematic overlay, that is, their function is not limited to drawing the reader's attention to the fate of individual Russian heroes and Russian history caught at "biblical" turning-points or crises. Rather, we are invited to view the mythic "zone" of novelistic space (i.e., the themes, figures, and passages taken from Revelation) and the realistic "zone" of novelistic space (i.e., the openness and contingency of contemporary life and history) as being in profound dialogic interaction. It is not simply that the mythic zone subsumes and determines the realistic zone in a straightforward and simplistic allegory or that the realistic zone upstages and undermines the authority of the mythic zone in an irreverent parody, but that genuine meaning—what it really signifies to experience apocalypse and revelation *in our time*—must be sought in a full-scale and honest confrontation between the two.

Myshkin cannot be understood only—if at all—as the triumphant Christ of the Second Coming; nor can the manifest weaknesses of the Master or

Yury Zhivago be explained away by calling them Christ figures; nor can we disentangle *Petersburg*'s plot (in both senses of the word) by acknowledging the very real parallels planted there between the Bronze Horseman and the Antichrist. If the Christian myth does have the last word in these works, *enclosing* the aimless flux of chronos in a higher pattern, it is not an easily won victory. Rogozhin murders Nastasya Filippovna and Myshkin goes mad; Dudkin murders Lippanchenko and Nikolay Apollonovich almost blows up his father; the Master and Margarita die at the hands of the same Pilate who executed Yeshua when they drink the gift of his poison wine; Sasha Dvanov follows his fisherman father into Lake Mutevo and suicide; and Yury Zhivago dies a broken man, having lived the last years of his life in the house of a former servant, while Lara disappears into the camps and their orphan daughter is left to fend for herself. In each case, to read these heroes' and heroines' actions *within* history (or history as represented as narrative) is to read them as failure. Yet to conclude from this that the primary function of the apocalyptic subtext is parodic is, as most readers would readily affirm, to misinterpret something very basic. What Pasternak's title character says in high seriousness could be applied (with certain reservations) to the entire tradition we are investigating: "All great, genuine art resembles and continues the Revelation of St. John: it always meditates on death and thus always creates life" (*Doctor Zhivago* 78).

The question of tradition in these novels is potentially vexed for the simple reason that they can be said to form a conscious and coherent whole only from our position "on the outside," and then presumably only with a good deal of typological tampering. "Conscious" and "coherent" to which historian, which narrator? Julia Kristeva's concept of *intertextualité* ("the transposition of one or more *systems* of signs into another") is useful in this connection only if one is interested in isolating the boundaries of the novel as *textual system* and then demonstrating how, in time, those same boundaries are contaminated and "transposed" (*Desire and Language* 15). As even the casual reader can see, these five novels do not form an "intertext" in the sense of master grid of biographical influence or literary provenance. The lines of influence are more tangled than that and in any case may go back further, often to Pushkin and Gogol, who were perceived in this tradition as mediators between Russia's "epic past" and the modern historical present. For example, Dostoevsky alludes prominently to Pushkin in *The Idiot*; Bely to Pushkin, Gogol, Dostoevsky and others in *Petersburg*; Platonov to Dostoevsky in *Chevengur*; Bulgakov to Pushkin, Gogol, and Dostoevsky in *Master and Margarita*; and Pasternak to Pushkin and the Symbolists in *Doctor Zhivago*. It is probably more accurate to say that these Russian novelists were reacting to the unique injunctions of their moment and to the sense of national crisis that had to be narrated and "domesti-

cated" into meaningful structures for them personally. Their eccentric nov-
elization of history brings to mind such celebrated Western apocalypticists
as Robert Musil and D. H. Lawrence; the latter's view of historical epochs
as a neo-Joachimist triad dominated by "Law," "Love," and the "Com-
forter" is uncannily similar to the ideas of Vladimir Solovyov and Merezhkovsky, just as his urge to translate an apocalyptic fervor into personal
myth is rivaled only by that of Andrey Bely. Any quasi-Proppian analysis
which advances a "master plot" at the expense of the "living" and changing
aspects of the tradition cannot do justice to the existence in history, the
historicity, of these forms.

What can be said without oversimplifying the case about the tradition of
apocalyptic fiction on Russian soil is the following:

(1) the already mentioned eschatological orientation in cultural consciousness, which had its genesis in earlier centuries and which assumed an
ever greater prominence with the rise of historiosophical/historiographical
debate in the nineteenth century, was still experienced as *real* and *vital* by
these writers and was incorporated into the structure of their fictions.[32] All
of these works provide compelling cases of how context, text, and subtext
interact, since in them the authors borrow from given bodies of *Russian*
messianic or eschatological thought and adapt them to their own purposes—
for Dostoevsky, it was the Slavophiles; for Bely, Vladimir Solovyov; for
Bulgakov, Pavel Florensky; for Platonov and Pasternak, Nikolay Fyodorov.

(2) In terms of richness and breadth of apocalyptic literature, there is
nothing to compare in the Russian context with the Symbolist period and
with the theme of "last things" in the many novels, stories, poems, essays
and philosophical causeries of Vladimir Solovyov, Dmitry Merezhkovsky,
Vasily Rozanov, Valery Bryusov, Maximilian Voloshin, Alexey Remizov,
Alexander Blok, Andrey Bely, and others. Indeed, it could be said without
exaggeration that the "new" Soviet literature and the doctrine of Socialist
Realism that it eventually engendered were logical—if often forced—extensions of this culture of "last things," and that the long-awaited *transitus*
from old to new, end to beginning, then to now, was not only historically
determined, as many wished to believe, but also *predetermined* by this essentially Christian myth, ancient, potent, yet ever mutable.[33] And

[32] As an aside one could mention the intelligentsia tradition of defining the perceived boundaries of epochal change with the help of certain root spatial and temporal metaphors: Radishchev's *Journey from St. Petersburg to Moscow*, Herzen's *From the Other Shore* and *Ends
and Beginnings*, Turgenev's *On the Eve*, Chernyshevsky's "The Russian at the Rendezvous,"
Dobrolyubov's "When Shall the Real Day Come?" Bely's *The Beginning of the Century* and
*Between Two Revolutions*, Vyach. Ivanov's *Furrows and Boundaries*, etc.

[33] This connection is especially clear in the various "salvation programs," the plans to
achieve secular, *physical* immortality, that surface either explicitly or implicitly in many So-

(3) taken together, these five works represent various responses of the novel form (from roughly 1860 to 1960) to the central apocalyptic event of modern Russian consciousness, which they either predict or "prophesy," as in the cases of Dostoevsky and Bely, or look back on with the wisdom of disconfirming hindsight, as in the cases of Platonov, Bulgakov, and Pasternak.

It has long been maintained that as the idea of history as divinely inspired human activity with an imminent conclusion from without gave way to the idea of history as secular progress with an immanent conclusion here on earth the historical "plot" was constantly modified to include an ever wider and disparate reality. This plot, asserts Kermode, made its way not only into our histories but into our fictions—secular humanity's answer to *the Book*. In *Natural Supernaturalism* M. H. Abrams has further contributed to the discussion by demonstrating that the vast history of apocalyptic literature in the West reached its highwater mark during the period of the French Revolution: the millenarian enthusiasm and hopes for a new age found in the early works of the English and German romantics (especially Blake, Southey, Wordsworth, Coleridge, Schelling, Hölderlin, and Hegel) were severely tested in the wake of Jacobin terror. The end of history as they knew it—which *should* have come with the revolution but did not—was dealt with not by rejecting apocalypticism out of hand but by turning to an *artistic re-visioning* of reality which was able to accommodate the specter of disconfirmation. Thus, the central distinction between much of the earlier and later works of these poets and historians (from Wordsworth's *Descriptive Sketches* to his *Prelude*, from Coleridge's *Religious Musings* to his *Rejection: An Ode*, from Blake's *Marriage of Heaven and Hell* to his *Jerusalem*, etc.) involved a shift in emphasis from an "apocalypse of revolution," or a universal eschatology achieved through sudden and violent political means, to an "apocalypse of consciousness,"[34] or a personal escha-

---

viet works. Irene Masing-Delic, in her forthcoming study *Death and Immortality in Russian Twentieth Century Literature*, identifies a number of texts, including Khlebnikov's *Ladomir*, Ognyov's "Eurasia," and Zabolotsky's *Columns* and *The Triumph of Agriculture*, where this theme of the literal overcoming of death is prominent.

[34] Cf. Abrams' statement (*Natural Supernaturalism* 332) on the English and German romantics before the French Revolution and the Russian symbolists before the October Revolution: "[Their works] are written in the persona of the visionary poet-prophet, 'the Bard,' who present, past, and future sees; they incorporate the great political events of their age in suitable grandiose literary forms, especially the epic and 'the greater Ode'; they present a panoramic view of history in a cosmic setting, in which the agents are in part historical and in part allegorical or mythological and the overall design is apocalyptic; they envision a dark past, a violent present, and an immediately impending future which will justify the history of suffering man by its culmination in an absolute good; and they represent the French Revolution (or else a coming revolution which will improve on the French model) as the critical event which sig-

tology achieved through the agency of the poetic imagination. For the romantics of the post-revolutionary era the New Jerusalem was to be achieved, in Abrams' words, "not by changing the world but by changing the way we see the world" (*Natural Supernaturalism* 347; "Theme and Variations" 363). And without ignoring important cultural differences, I would also propose that for Russian apocalypticists like Bulgakov and Pasternak, who wrote *after* 1917 and who had to make sense of the revolution's excesses and failings, this same shift to a personal eschatology and to an artistic, as opposed to a political, revisioning of reality is readily apparent.

Finally, as far as tradition is concerned, it can be argued that these works, and others like them, constitute a resilient set of counter-models to the Socialist Realist classic, and this may be one reason why they have become *the* tradition to be studied in the Western academy. Katerina Clark has described how certain elements of the Socialist Realist "master plot" can adapt to historical context and still remain cohesive (e.g., a hero's being historically "spontaneous" [*stikhiinyi*] or "conscious" [*soznatel'nyi*] can be characterized as positive or negative depending on the time and place of writing; *The Soviet Novel* 46–67). What the Socialist Realist classic is able to do with a remarkable economy of means is to "fabulize" a Marxist view of history by manipulating certain powerful and hallowed mythical categories: the Bolshevik hero, such as Gleb Chumalov, has been in touch with an epic past—he participated in 1917, performed legendary feats of heroism at the front, and knows people, like Shibis, who *saw* Lenin. And this contact with a sacred past confers the "right stuff" on Gleb; it allows him to confront and overcome a problem-ridden present (NEP) and make his way toward, but never actually to, the *telos* of communism. Likewise, *Mother* freely borrows the semantics of religious conversion to generate enthusiasm for the indisputable destiny of Gorky's Marxist "elect." Our primarily "Christian" authors, on the other hand, incorporate into their narratives a different view of history. Because meaning is not immanent or historically determined (that is, it does not come "from within"), it must be generated by comparing the *disjunction* between character and narrator, narrator and reader, and ultimately reader and God. What prevents dramatic irony in the Socialist Realist classic (the narrator does not play with character or reader because "enlightenment" is not relative and because "realism" implies a maximum proximity to history and a maximum distance from fiction) is precisely what makes meaning so richly polysemous in these relentlessly unrealistic works about the climax of Christian history. Here too we find characters "from beyond," as shall be suggested in more detail in a moment,

---

nals the emergence of a regenerate man who will inhabit a new world uniting features of a restored paradise and a recovered Golden Age."

but their function, in terms of the purpose or goal of history, is entirely different.

What are the essential elements of the "apocalyptic plot" and how do they relate to the works under discussion? First, each of these novels in a fundamental way is about *the End*. A number of contemporary critics have made studies of the device of closure in the modern novel, with the implication that, regardless of strategies for sealing off, or leaving open, a narrative,[35] the entire structure of a work is inevitably "end-determined," that is, it is emplotted backwards, from, as it were, its "Finis" to its "Once upon a time . . ." Yet it is not enough to say that these works are simply end-determined; both on the level of biography and on the grander level of Russian history, their narratives invoke the shadow of the biblical End. They are a search—and herein the spatial metaphor of the "path" or "road" (*put'*) necessarily enters discussion—for the meaning of the *Russian* apocalypse. Their heroes' and heroines' stories are Russia's stories, and in much the same way as the reader of the Socialist Realist classic is urged to draw analogies between the fate of a member of the elect and the country at large (that is, there is an unmistakable homology between development of a Bolshevik hero and the shape of Marxist historiography), so too is the reader of these works drawn to see a connection between personal death and the end of national, even world history. Not for nothing does each of these novels conclude, and most begin, with a crucial death: Marie and Nastasya Filippovna in *The Idiot*, Lippanchenko and Nikolay's parents in *Petersburg*, Sasha Dvanov's father and Sasha himself in *Chevengur*, Berlioz and the Master and Margarita in *The Master and Margarita*; and Yury's mother and father and Yury himself in *Doctor Zhivago*. As we proceed closer to 1917 (that is, from Dostoevsky to Bely), this parallelism between personal and national ends becomes more and more fraught with anxiety (and more and more formally complex). As suggested, however, those works written after 1917 (*Chevengur*, *Master and Margarita*, and *Doctor Zhivago*), when the connection between revelation and revolution has been disconfirmed and a qualitatively new era has *not* begun, still make comparisons between personal and national history, but use different strategies in order to avoid a literal prediction of the end of Russian history within time (e.g., Menippean satire/"mock apocalypse" in the case of *The Master and Margarita*, the secularization of the apocalyptic through Fyodorovian philosophy in the cases of Platonov and Pasternak).

To speak of the apocalyptic plot in narrative terms is also to make certain

---

[35] E.g., the relation of end to beginning and middle may be "circular" or "parallel" or "incomplete" or "tangential," etc. See Torgovnik, *Closure* 3–19, as well as Friedman (*Turn of the Novel*), D. A. Miller (*Narrative and Its Discontents*), and Richter (*Fable's End*).

assumptions about the shape of Christian *Heilsgeschichte*. Despite their considerable variety, sophistication, and lack of orthodoxy (or Orthodoxy), these authors' views of history share a concern with those of the biblical prophets about the nature, compass, and narrative presentation of the End—what would it look like from "here" or from "there"? how can its projected significance be read backwards to provide meaningful pattern in one's life now? what in this conclusion to history's plot is "fictitious"—the result of an insufficiently informed reading of the signs—and what is "real"—the result of a truly *higher* understanding? If scholars of biblical texts such as Collins can speak of the "genre" of apocalypse in descriptive terms, then perhaps we can speak of a subset of the modern novel which takes the core elements of the biblical genre and adapts them to its own hybrid form. Among the assumptions about the narrative shape of history that enter into the biblical genre and that are relevant to our discussion are the following:

(1) History is *determined* by God's plot, but the individual is *free* to choose between positive and negative fields of action within that plot. In narratological terms, this means that characters are limited both as "actants" once they act and as verbal constructs once their action is described, but that they can free themselves from this epistemological prison and, as it were, *unwrite* their biographies once they know what the narrator/author does.[36]

(2) The latter, tumultuous stage of history which these modern novelists as "prophets" are describing follows the same *triadic pattern* of crisis-judgment-vindication found in Revelation and other canonical apocalypses. However, whereas the initial stages of crisis and judgment are usually self-evident, the final stage of vindication may not be, and depends on whether a higher authorial viewpoint of all-embracing unity and resolution—the novelistic equivalent of the biblical marriage of the Lamb and the Bride—can be posited from "within" the text.

(3) History is a *totality*, and its movement from beginning to end is also a *return*—from a paradise of innocence (the Garden of Eden) to a paradise *earned* through suffering (the New Jerusalem).[37] In each of these novels the period of innocence or grace is "not of this world" and is experienced as a separate, enclosed epic past which took place prior to the principal action and which preceded the hero's and/or heroine's "fall into" history: Myshkin's "fairy tale" romance with Marie in Switzerland and Nastasya Filip-

---

[36] A compelling example of this situation is presented in the mock apocalyptic ending to Nabokov's *Invitation to a Beheading*.

[37] This movement, by the way, which is both a progression and a return, evokes the image of the romantic spiral, an image alluded to either explicitly or implicitly in several of the works under discussion and serving in them as an important structural principle. For more on the romantic spiral, see Abrams, *Natural Supernaturalism* 183–87.

povna's idyllic life at Otradnoe before the seduction by Totsky; Nikolay Apollonovich's dashing presence as an Ivan Tsarevich before his attempted rape of Sophia Petrovna; the Kitezh-like realm that Sasha's father goes to look for in Lake Mutevo and that, as the symbol of what separates parent from child, haunts and simultaneously moves Sasha forward in his search for the Bolshevik City of the Sun; the Master's and Margarita's life with their novel and the lottery money before the work is finished and "crucified" by the literary establishment; Yura's adolescent notions about sex before he sees the frightening galvanism joining Komarovsky and Lara, and Lara's own virginal symmetry and beauty before these are shattered by the lawyer's "Roman" ethic. This paradise lost is then projected into the future, beyond the present crisis (and its boundaries as "text"), as the *telos* of personal and national history; if it is to be recaptured at all, it is only *at the end*, through suffering and death (compare, for example, the final resting place of the Master and Margarita *outside* history and the salvational status of the *late* Yury Zhivago's poetry). And

(4) an understanding of history, which all apocalypses profess to provide, is possible only by looking for signs—in artistic terms, symbols—of God's will in the otherwise baffling "text" of current events. Such "revelations" normally involve a conflation of narrative's mythical and realistic "zones": the buffoon Lebedev reading a central passage from Revelation to a brooding Nastasya Filippovna; the half-literate Styopka regaling the alcoholic Dudkin with popular versions of the Second Coming. Too marked to be dismissed as parody, they might better be seen as those charged moments when another, authoritative voice from beyond intrudes into the text to speak of the End.

Another salient element of the apocalyptic plot is the messenger from a different temporality and spatiality who announces/reveals to the characters of this world that the end is at hand. To recall the basic terms of Collins' definition: " 'Apocalypse' is a genre of revelatory literature with a narrative framework, in which *a revelation is mediated by an otherworldly being* to a human recipient, disclosing a transcendent reality which is both temporal, insofar as it envisages eschatological salvation, and spatial, insofar as it involves another, supernatural world." In the Johannine text itself, this messenger is the angel of God who provides the prophet with his vision and who takes his place "betwixt-and-between" the heavenly and earthly realms. The fact that the angel appears from somewhere outside history to a member of humanity trapped within history (and mortality) is the very essence of the revelation (*apokalypsis*). These novels also provide such a mediating figure, although often thinly disguised in what remains of a "realistic" tradition. Logically enough, his appearance in the lives of other characters usually raises questions of his or their sanity.

In *The Idiot*, this figure is the title character, that passionate advocate of beginnings (his offer of marriage at Nastasya Filippovna's birthday party) and ends (his thoughts on execution) who has come to fallen Petersburg and to life "in the middle" with his epileptic visions of an existence outside time; in *Petersburg*, it is the Bronze Horseman (and the Unicorn), who announces to the lesser characters that their end, and that of Russia, is imminent; in *Chevengur*—Sasha's father, who, having plunged into the lake, already knows the secret of death for which his son spends the entire novel searching; in *Master and Margarita*—Woland, who knows that there is a historical Jesus, a Satan, and an existence beyond death (which he brings Berlioz) and whose appearance sets off the race around the streets of Moscow that lands Ivan (a modern-day St. John?) in Rimsky's asylum; and in *Doctor Zhivago*, this figure is the mysterious Evgraf, the "angel of death," who, "as though falling from the skies," appears to Yury during his bout with typhus, helps to raise him, like Lazarus, from the dead, and at the same time encourages him to write poetry, the most tangible evidence of Zhivago's "talent for life." All these figures, then, come from or have access to a different temporality, and it is their role to enter history ("life in the middest") with messages, often cryptic or difficult to translate into the logic of everyday speech, about eschatological salvation ("life at the end").

What this also means, to subvert for a moment Bakhtin's logic with regard to novelistic discourse, is that this voice is not merely that of any other, whose status is equal and equally contingent, but that of *the Other*, whose status is transcendent and uniquely resonant.[38] It is true that Myshkin's efforts to follow this voice and forego judgment only bring judgment with a vengeance; then again, to think this way is to judge him and the other protagonists *within history, within the text*. The voice that speaks to Myshkin during his epileptic aura, before his falling sickness, or to Homeless each Easter season when the injection, his symbolic crucifixion, releases him from his nightmare and puts him back in touch with a radiant and calm Master and Margarita, or to Yury at the moment of poetic inspiration when he becomes St. George and the wolves closing in on the house at Varykino become the dragons of history, is the voice from *outside time*. And while it does not ignore the reality principle,[39] it does, contrary to Bakhtinian the-

---

[38] Bakhtin, on the other hand, would undoubtedly argue that the notion of human dialogue outside of time is literally inconceivable, a *contradictio in adjecto*. To speak of a Voice from outside time is, according to him, to release the listening hero (and reader) into a kind of "audiencelessness" (impossible) or "*neotvetstvennost'* " (*un*responsiveness in various senses). Be this as it may, it is my contention that these novelists were attempting to project the narrative equivalent of just such an optical (or auditory) illusion. Their model for divine utterance is potentially non-binding with regard to the speaker's time and space (what has been said can be *unsaid*) in precisely the way that *human* dialogue is not.

[39] Again, it cannot be emphasized enough that all these characters are feckless in the eyes of history.

ory, suggest that human dialogue can be inscribed in divine monologue, that diachrony can unfold within a synchronous pattern.

No sketch of the apocalyptic plot would be complete without mention of its chief protagonist and antagonist, Christ and Antichrist. As suggested earlier, none of these novels is a transparent allegory promoting literalist notions of the End. Instead they are hybrid forms that often apply principles of irony and parody to subvert the received wisdom (whether it be Christian or Marxist) of the Orthodox view. In the final analysis, however, they are not simply subversive or ironic but committed to a vision of their own, which is often mystical or quasi-gnostical and, in the cases of Bely, Bulgakov, and Pasternak, tightly linked with the gift of artistic creation.[40] The marked presence of Christ-like figures in nearly all of our novels—Myshkin ("Prince Christ"), the white Domino and Unicorn, the Master, Yury Zhivago—does *not* imply, at least in any obvious way, that these are versions of the triumphant Lord of the *Parousia* come to defeat the forces of the Beast and oversee the climax of human history.

The creators of these characters are too conscious of what history has wrought *since* Christ first made his appearance and supposedly conferred on time a unique meaning "from the end" to rely on the sort of "sudden relief expedition from the sky" (Jones, *Eternal Gospel* 5) that appealed to the religious imagination of first and second century Christians. According to the typology set out by Theodore Ziolkowski in *Fictional Transfigurations of Jesus*, there is a danger in overinterpreting the "Christ-like" character in modern literature. If the features characterizing this hero do not add up to a consistently emplotted portrait, complete with the chief topoi, of the life of Jesus, then we are dealing with atmosphere and scattered allusion, but not with "fictional transfiguration." Thus, for instance, the majestic Pieter Peeperkorn in Mann's *The Magic Mountain* falls into the category of a modern transfiguration because his stay at the International Sanitorium Berghof has its climax in a parodic last supper and betrayal, while the character of Myshkin, for all its Christ-like qualities, does not (*Transfigurations* 3–6, 104–5). Still, even if some of these Russian novels *do* have characters who come closer to a "transfigured" Christ,[41] this may not be what is ultimately significant. Ziolkowski's definition turns out to be too limited for our purposes, particularly when the chief focus in these Russian novels is on death, judgment, and *the end* of history. We are not here dealing with a

[40] Platonov's work offers the clearest example of the collision of utopian and apocalypticist worldviews and, as the product of a proletarian dreamer deeply disenchanted by NEP, can rely on no higher belief in the transcendent value of language; it is thus unique in its pessimism and dark use of parody.

[41] E.g., not only does the Master share many of Yeshua's traits, but his burning of the manuscript is obviously linked with the crucifixion of the historical Jesus.

simple paradigm of *Jesus redivivus* or *imitatio Christi* (examples of which abound in the ecstatic tradition of socialist literature), but with the Christ-like figure who must live *near the end* of his own and (in Dostoevsky and Bely at least) his nation's history. None of these characters is the avenging Lamb of Revelation, the eerie field marshall on white charger come to scatter the forces of the unrighteous. Each must bear the judgment of history, his cross, and each must try to deal with what the end means for his time. Yet by now it should be obvious that if there is a way out, if history is to be transfigured, and if the humiliated Christ is to become victorious, it is through *the Book*.

Conversely, all those figures in these novels whose purpose it is to bring judgment are in essence fictional incarnations of the view that history, after Hegel and Marx, is its own highest court.[42] They are punishers, avenging horsemen, not Christ-like but Antichrist-like figures. Among them we find Rogozhin, who is associated in the dream of Ippolit (the "unleasher of horses") with the beast of Revelation and with the great dumb *mashina*, the "iron horse" and its relentless ride, that crushes the most beautiful being in the world; the Bronze Horseman, who pours his molten essence into Dudkin, the second Evgeny, and bids him kill Lippanchenko; Kopyonkin, the quixotic knight of the revolution, who kills out of comradely feelings and whose Proletarian Strength, the Bolshevik Rosinante, tramples everything underfoot; Pilate, the Rider of the Golden Spear, who executes Yeshua against his wishes and who threatens Cayaphas with a flood of Arab horsemen; and Strelnikov, the executioner, who from his armored train strikes out against the enemies of the revolution.

## STEED

Mention of the avenging horseman brings us to the final element of the apocalyptic plot—the means it has at its disposal for propelling itself for-

[42] "Hegel's program was avowedly theological, was seen by him specifically as a regrounding of Christian revelation within the newly glimpsed limits of an intelligible human history. Thus, for instance, God brooding over the abyss becomes in Hegel Being in that moment of identity before its first self-estrangement through negation, and thus the Biblical creation of the universe becomes the process of self-estrangement through which Being splits off from itself into a realm of brute matter, *and thus Apocalypse becomes the reconciliation of all contradiction and the abolition of all differences in an Absolute Spirit that, in a last negation of negation, resumes all things into itself.* . . . For Hegel, the notion of reality unfolding through contradictions and rising to ever-higher levels until Spirit at last becomes conscious of itself constituted no new Revelation but only (and here was the originality of Hegelian philosophy as he saw it) Revelation in its *immanent* form. *History discovering its own meaning from the inside,* humanity grasping itself not as the arbitrary creation of some absent sky-deity but as the Spirit gradually becoming manifest to itself" (my emphasis; Dowling, *Jameson, Althusser, Marx* 44–45).

ward, for moving, as fictional history, from beginning to middle to end. Since all of these novels, as apocalyptic templates, begin in a time of crisis, their starting points are not the biblical garden, but a time much closer to the Johannine climax. This proximity to catastrophe has important implications for the form their stories take. What will be suggested, following but not necessarily agreeing with Bakhtin, is that these novelists need some concrete way to visualize the rapid and ominous passage of time in space. To make a pun that Bely (if not my reader) would approve of, they need to find a way to translate theodicy, or a justification of God's plot in the face of recalcitrant reality, into "the odyssey," or the journey down history's road. Bakhtin's term for this artistic translation is the *chronotope* (lit: "time-space"), that is, the place(s) in the text where the novelist seeks to "materialize time in space," to work out an equation for the spatialization of human temporal desire within the terms permitted by one's historical context. For Bakhtin the chronotope is much more than a traditional generic rubric; it is, as Caryl Emerson has recently pointed out, a "category of consciousness," an "assumption about the workings of time and space" that every author must make in seeking to "totalize" his or her world. It always contains an element of *evaluation* that tethers it to the author's "here" and "now" and, in this sense, it *cannot be transcended* (*Boris Godunov* 5–6; see also Medvedev, *Formal Method* 129–30). Perhaps the most obvious way— at least to the Western mind—for the novel as personal/national history to show movement is through the time-honored figure of the road, which in modern times of doubt, anxiety, and irony tends to be beset by all manner of thresholds, crossroads, borders, and spatio-temporal choices.

All of our novels are dominated by the haunting presence of a "threshold city," the end of history's road or the place where all paths converge as history prepares for eschatological change. Thus the two prerevolutionary novels are set in the doomed imperial capital of Petersburg and the three postrevolutionary novels are set either in the "fallen" Third Rome of Moscow or in the beclouded *Civitas Solis* of Chevengur. These cities are the precise focal points where, to apply Eliade's terminology, the "profane center" (e.g., the Whore of Babylon) and the "sacred center" (e.g., the New Jerusalem) meet, where the modern seer, straddling two different temporalities, catches glimpses of an otherworldly order in the midst of worldly chaos and revolution. Related to this phenomenon of mythical centering is what the structural anthropologist Edmund Leach, analyzing the binary elements of biblical narrative, defines as "liminality"—that is, the rules governing the *limen*, the place "betwixt-and-between" the sacred and profane where the prophet experiences revelation:

Fined down to its essentials the argument [about thresholds] runs something like this. Uncertainty generates anxiety, so we avoid it if we can. The categories of language cut up the world into unambiguous blocks. The individual is either a man or a beast; either a child or an adult; either married or unmarried; either alive or dead. *In relation to any building I am either inside or outside. But to move from one such clear state to its opposite entails passing through an ambiguous 'threshold,' a state of uncertainty where roles are confused and even reversed.* This marginal position is regularly hedged by taboo.

This finding clearly has an important bearing on my general topic of the relevance of anthropology to biblical studies. *For, after all, mediation between opposites is precisely what religious thinking is all about.*

Thresholds, both physical and social, are a focus of taboo for the same reason that, in the Bible, inspired sacred persons, who converse face to face with God, or who, in themselves, have attributes which are partly those of mortal man and partly those of immortal God, *almost always experience their inspiration in a 'betwixt and between' locality, described as 'in the wilderness,' which is neither fully in This World nor in The Other (Structuralist Interpretations 15–16).*

The means that these Russian novelists find to place their heroes in a sacred-tabooed zone "betwixt-and-between" are rather obvious: Myshkin's idiocy and sexual ambivalence, Nikolay's androgynous status and Dudkin's alcoholic delirium, Sasha Dvanov's role as dreamy *durak* (as opposed to *umnik*), the Master's insanity, Yury's moments of illness and inspiration. More importantly, this state of social or psychological or artistic liminality is also associated with *sites* steeped in the Russian eschatological tradition.[43] It is, for example, at just such a sacred-profane site that Nastasya Filippovna must choose between the opposing versions of time represented by her prospective grooms, Myshkin and Rogozhin; or that Apollon Apollonovich, Nikolay Apollonovich, Dudkin, Lippanchenko, and Sophia Petrovna must learn what it means to be "doomed irrevocably" by the retributive horseman; or that the Chevengurians must labor to build a new life whose result is mass death; or that the Master and Margarita must experience first crucifixion, then resurrection at the hands of their artistic child; or that Yury, on the eve of the revolution, must look for his Christmas star in the same candle in the window that Lara has asked Pasha Antipov to light as she sets out to shoot Komarovsky, the cause of her "fall."

What is equally intriguing, however, is that in these apocalyptic fictions, in these novels that progress by (fore)telling the end, the journey down history's road is accelerated and foreshortened, for we are near the end and about to reach it. Taking their cue from perhaps the best-known of all passages—Revelation 6:1–8, which depicts history's movement through four

[43] The one exception being Chevengur, which follows a popular utopian model.

stages of horse and rider—these novelists develop elaborate symbolic net-
works around the image of the horse and its modern counterpart, the train
("the iron horse"). I would like to propose that the horse is a powerful
visual tool in the hands of these verbal artists precisely because it is capable
of telescoping in one economical image several traditions (the imperial, the
folkloric, the religious) and because its inherent qualities (speed, beauty,
elemental forces, comradeship, martial prowess) make it an ideal symbol for
eschatological transit, for the tumultuous "ride" from one space-time to
another.[44]

Imperially, the steed sets the ruler or the aristocratic knight (*eques*) apart
from the common people. If the ancient Egyptians discerned something un-
dignified about seating their ruler on horseback and thus preferred the chariot, the Greeks had no such scruples and in fact placed great emphasis on
horsemanship. One aspect of Alexander's "greatness" that has come down
to us was his prowess on horseback (it was said that his horse Bucephalus
would accept no other rider), including his discomfiting of Darius from his
chariot as depicted in a famous mosaic. The steed continued to acquire significance, becoming the attribute not simply of the *eques*, but, especially
during the Roman Empire, of the emperor: witness the famous equestrian
monument to Marcus Aurelius first erected on the Capitol as a symbol of
his majesty and authority and later preserved during the Christian era only
because it was rechristened "Constantine" (thus linking the notion of pa-
pacy to empire) and moved to the Lateran. After a hiatus of almost a millennium, the equestrian reemerged in the monuments of Donatello, Verrochio, Bologna, Mochi, and Bernini, and in the sketches of Leonardo.
Particularly noteworthy about the Renaissance treatment is the fact that the
*concetto* (the conceit or "spark" for the entire project) for the *Reiterstand-
bild* underwent gradual change: the horse and rider were slowly separated
as part of an ensemble decorating a ducal tomb (e.g., that of Cangrande
[1330] in Verona); the *eques* now no longer had to be a sovereign, but could
be a mere *condottiere*, or captain of mercenary forces (e.g., Donatello's *Gat-
tamelata* [1448–50] in Padua); and the steed became more animated and
full of latent power to the point that, in Leonardo's sketches and especially
in Bernini's sculpture of Constantine the Great (1654–70), it finally reared
up on its hind legs. Bernini's equestrian monument occupies such a prominent place in this genealogy because it is located on the Scala Regia (the

---

[44] In my treatment of the imperial and folkloric equine traditions I have relied extensively
on the following sources: Anuchin, "Sani, lad'ia i koni"; Janson, "The Equestrian Monument"; Lipets, *Obrazy*; Levitine, "The Problem of Portraits"; and Watson, "Horsemanship."
See also Giamatti, "Headlong Horses"; Viach. Ivanov, "Opyt istolkovaniia"; Jobes, *Dictionary of Mythology* 789–91; Potapov, "Kon' "; B. Rowland, "The Horse"; Sirotina, "Obraz
konia."

main landing of the Vatican), thereby forming the first image of papal authority that a visitor encounters, and because Constantine is presented at that moment of revelation—the "moving stasis" of the rearing horse captures this *concetto* perfectly—when he sees the cross in the sky and prepares himself to conquer in its name.

This first completed statue of the rearing horse became, significantly, the model for the Louis XIV equestrian monument at Versailles, which in turn would influence Falconet as he worked on the Bronze Horseman for Catherine.[45] When Bernini's statue arrived in France, Louis' advisers urged that the rock support on which the statue rested be reconfigured in a representation of flames: at the time it was felt to be politically wiser to play down the imperial connotations and to recast the horseman in the role of a latter-day Marcus Curtius hurling himself into the abyss to save his earthquake-riven capital. Ironically, however, the earthquake was not to be forestalled, and in the wake of 1789 all royal equestrian statues in France save this one (which was conveniently located across the lake from the palace in a far corner of the park) were destroyed. And it is a double if not triple irony that Falconet, who supposedly despised Bernini, returned to the master's *concetto* (the rock rather than the flames) and that his statue of Peter the Great would have such an hypnotic effect on generations of the Russian intelligentsia faced with a similar specter of revolution (Janson, "The Equestrian Monument" 157–89).

Bernini had originally wished to represent Louis on a rocky summit, "in full possession of that Glory which . . . has become synonymous with his name" (Janson 166–67), an idea which Falconet felt was justifiably transposable to the Russian context. Moreover, the snake being trampled underfoot was an allegory for defeated envy. But the Russian time-space in which this bronze "text" was erected quickly changed meaning. The tsar as modern Marcus Aurelius did not arguably mean much to the Russians,[46] but the

---

[45] Bernini had virtually finished the statue of Louis before he (Bernini) died, but since it underwent various changes once it reached French hands (see below), it is the sculptor's terracotta *bozzetto* which most accurately preserves his intentions.

[46] Lednicki (*Pushkin's 'Bronze Horseman'* 33–34) shows that Falconet, in his correspondence with Catherine and Diderot, openly *opposed* a recreation of the original Marcus Aurelius. He much preferred the idea of "Peter-the-pacifist" and "Peter-the-legislator," with outstretched hand in a *protective* gesture (*main protectrice*). Nevertheless, in the court's efforts to legitimize Peter's role by tying the tsar to an older classical model, the connection with the Moscow horseman (St. George) was not avoided, especially in later generations (Blok, for example, was to compare specifically the rival horsemen: see Hackel, *The Poet* 41). Moreover, the fact that Falconet's equestrian was *rearing* (as opposed to the original Marcus Aurelius on the Capitoline) gave the monument an energy and *dynamic* relation to its surrounding space which was of course not lost on Pushkin. Here the main issue is not what Falconet or Catherine intended, but what those coming after read *into* the statue and its present context as cultural myth. For

tsar as Christ-like St. George slaying the serpent (the pagan forces) of history did. Long before this, in the late sixteenth century, foreigners visiting the court of Ivan the Terrible's son Fyodor Ivanovich mentioned the existence of "a golden medal portraying St. George mounted on a horse," which was worn on the sleeve or hat of the recipient as a sign of "the highest honor that can be bestowed for any service whatsoever."[47] In any event, the *apocalyptic* connotation of the horse and rider is very much in evidence on one of the extant flags of Ivan the Terrible, where we find Christ mounted on a white charger, surrounded by twenty-seven angels on horseback, and escorted by the archangel Michael with his winged steed. The official order of St. George, the most popular of all Russian military medals and the only tsarist decoration to survive (in altered form, of course) into Soviet times, was instituted in 1769, that is, some thirteen years before the unveiling of Falconet's statue on Petersburg's Senate Square. So while Peter had done his best to secularize the imperial iconography, it retained a religious referent after his death, even perhaps in Falconet's borrowed *concetto*. To subsequent generations the Moscow horseman could be seen as having moved—against his will—to the city of Peter, St. George as having traded his lance for an arm pointed imperiously into Russia's future, and the serpent impaled by the lance as having become a snake trampled underfoot by the tsar's steed.[48]

Whether its rider was Christ or Antichrist, the majestic steed became *the* symbol of Russia rearing up into the space between the old and the new. If writers like, Pushkin did not, for reasons of artistic temperament or histo-

---

an excellent (though not entirely objective) discussion of Pushkin's understanding of Falconet's work, see Lednicki, *Pushkin's 'Bronze Horseman'* 25–42. Pushkin's view of the dynamic between rider and steed is given a structuralist interpretation in Zholkovsky, *Themes* 69–75.

[47] These words belong to Giles Fletcher, an envoy of England's Queen Elizabeth I who visited Russia during the reign of Fyodor Ivanovich. See Durov, *Russkie i sovetskie nagradnye medali* 4. It is intriguing to note that on some of these medals there was simply a horseman, *without the defeated dragon*, or a *unicorn*. Some scholars attest that the dragon *came later*—that is, after the solitary horseman—during the late fifteenth century, when Moscow was considering the significance of the fall of Constantinople and adopting as state emblem the two-headed eagle. For more on the history of the St. George medal and order on Russian soil, see Lakier, *Russkaia geral'dika* 1: 228–31, 290–91; and Speransov, *Zemel'nye gerby Rossii* 25–26.

[48] As I argue in "The Role of the *eques* in Pushkin's *Bronze Horseman*," the confrontation(s) between Peter and Evgeny in Pushkin's poem in fact revolves around their opposing roles as "pagan" versus "sacred" riders. When in the first confrontation, for example, Evgeny is frozen *astride* a stone lion (the heraldic symbol of Yury Dolgoruky, founder of *Moscow*), which in turn stands guard over one of Petersburg's *new* houses (instead of over the *vetkhii domik*, the "little old house" of Parasha, Evgeny's fiancée), it can be said that the hero's various attributes as "Moscow horseman" have been undercut and parodied by their transference to the seat of the Bronze Horseman, the new city's all-powerful *kumir* (idol) and cruel tutelary spirit.

riosophical conviction, choose to make the connection between the monument and the apocalyptic *end* of Russian history (that connection would be established later), the reason was not, as we have seen, for any lack of eschatological tradition.[49] Peter could be viewed in opposite ways: by enlighteners as a St. George stamping out ignorance and obscurantism so that Russia could leap into a better future; by sectarians as a man-god who had betrayed his role as tsar to become emperor and hence Antichrist. But regardless of one's a priori beliefs about the direction of Russian history, Peter on horseback came to signify a radical and total shift in time-space relations, the visual equivalent of his new calendar. That this tradition was later undermined by other equestrians, notably Paolo Trubetskoy's satiric monument to Alexander III in which Peter's spirited charger comes to resemble a hippopotamus, should not be seen as a serious challenge to, but as confirmation of, the remarkable potency of Falconet's work, which from Pushkin's poem on retained a mythical status, either positive or negative. The statue of a triumphant Lenin arriving at the Finland Station *on his armored car (bronevik)* is of course further evidence that even the Soviets felt compelled to tap into a later, but transparently similar, version of the imperial equestrian.

Underlying our discussion of Falconet's and Pushkin's horsemen is another, larger issue. The Western tradition of equestrian statuary takes its roots from the notion of controlling, of "reining" in, a wild and passionate "body politic." The centaur is half brute beast; Euripides' Hippolytus (like his namesake in Dostoevsky's *The Idiot*) lives up to his etymology as an "unleasher of horses"; and, perhaps most influential, Plato's *Phaedrus* presents the human soul in the allegorical guise of a chariot driven by reason and drawn by noble and ignoble horses—all these images have created a context in which countless writers depict royal heroes as both "reining" and

[49] Pushkin, who was a highly irreverent Voltairian in his youth (the anti-religious element persists in his work only until about 1826) did not have what we would call today an apocalyptic "turn of mind." But he did take for granted that his readers and correspondents would have some knowledge of the last book of the Bible. There are in all five indisputable mentions of the apocalypse in Pushkin's literary works (including drafts) and letters. (See the "large" Academy edition: I: 162–63, III: 860, XII: 174, XIII: 29, XIV: 121.) Most of these references are parodic, that is, Pushkin tended to use them in a comic rather than serious context, referring to himself during the first Boldino autumn (1830), for example, as sending regards from his "Patmos" (letter to M. P. Pogodin of November 1830 in XIV: 121). On another occasion, Pushkin includes an allusion to the Pale Horse of Revelation in a draft of the poem "Verses composed during a night of insomnia," but then removes it, presumably because he did not want the elements of this mythological system to invade his art on a serious level. In an interesting unpublished recent paper ("The Apocalyptic Theme in Pushkin's 'Count Nulin' ") the émigré scholar Boris Gasparov alleges the presence of the apocalyptic subtext in *Count Nulin*, one of Pushkin's humorous long poems, but his findings are still, in my opinion, inconclusive.

"reigning" (Watson, "Horsemanship" 275). Among the ancient and modern authors who have adopted the Platonic metaphor or its correlate myth
of the overproud Phaeton, one might mention Philo Judaeus, Plutarch, Augustine, Prudentius, Dante, Ariosto, Chaucer, Luther, Sidney, Spenser,
Bunyan, Burton, Herbert, Jonson, and especially Shakespeare (Watson,
"Horsemanship" 275–79; see also Giamatti, "Headlong Horses"; and Rowland, "The Horse and Rider Figure").[50] Whether presenting the fatal error
of Macbeth's vaulting ambition in an image of Phaeton, or equating the loss
of Richard II's solar (regal) status to Bolinbroke's mastery of his (Richard's)
roan Barbary, or implying that Hal has come of age when he "uncolts"
Falstaff and defeats his rival horseman of the "hotspur," Shakespeare returns incessantly to what he perceives as a necessary parallelism between
ruling one's own passions and ruling those of the people (Watson, "Horsemanship" 277ff.). This, after all, is the notion of noble horsemanship from
which, etymologically and culturally, the *chivalric* tradition grew. He who
could control his own steed and unhorse his opponent was the ideal knight;
and victory in combat was all the evidence needed to establish nobility and
status. Hence in Western literature as in statuary it was essential *to keep
distinct* the notions of horseman and horse, rider and ridden.

In Russia, however, where a tsar such as Peter was associated by a significant segment of the population with what was *new* and *revolutionary* and
the people with what was *old* and *orthodox*, this Western formula could not
be so easily transplanted. If Catherine and her German "enlighteners"
could insist on viewing Falconet's work as an expression of Peter's proud
design to control the elements (and, by implication, the wild force of the
people), then those of another generation could also see the tsar as that
figure which, by turning Russia westward and upsetting the *status quo*,
*unleashed* rather than reined in the passions of his people. As Pushkin himself remarked in a plan (1830) for a work about the nobility: "Pierre I est
tout à la fois Robespierre et Napoleon (la révolution incarnée)"—"*Peter I is
at one and the same time Robespierre and Napoleon (the revolution incarnate)*" (PSS XII: 205; see also Lednicki, *Pushkin's 'Bronze Horseman'* 30–
31). This very issue of Peter's unreining/unbridling became, among others,
a focus in *The Bronze Horseman* for Pushkin's quiet polemics with his
friend, the great Polish poet Adam Mickiewicz.[51] The latter had recently, in

[50] Even Freud felt "spurred on" by the metaphor when comparing the roles of ego and id:
"One might compare the relation of the ego to the id with that between a rider and his horse.
The horse provides the locomotive energy, and the rider has the prerogative of determining
the goal and of guiding the movements of his powerful mount towards it" (*New Introductory
Lectures* 108; cited in Watson, "Horsemanship" 276).

[51] Depending on context and audience, Pushkin's attitude toward his country could be both

the *Digression* of Part III of *Forefather's Eve*, criticized his "Muscovite friends"—singling out "the bard of the Russian people"—for their chauvinistic response to the Polish uprising of 1830–31. And one of his chief images for describing his (the oppressed Pole's) version of Russian history is that of Peter's steed racing out of control: "His charger's reins Tsar Peter *has released*; / He has been flying down the road, perchance, / And here the precipice checks his advance" (translated and cited in Lednicki, *Pushkin's 'Bronze Horseman'* 29; my emphasis).[52] Pushkin, with his genius for absorbing the most disparate viewpoints and making them his own, implies an answer to Mickiewicz in his introduction (Peter is magisterial and in control) *at the same time* that he makes "a crack . . . in the smooth surface of panegyrism" in the story that follows (Lednicki, *Pushkin's 'Bronze Horseman'* 52). The link between a natural and social unleashing is never stated in the poem, and yet this buried kinship is, to "gallop" ahead of ourselves a moment, one reason—perhaps *the* reason—why a Western formula signifying imperial *order* became in time a Russian formula signifying *apocalyptic chaos*. Thus it will be our argument that Pushkin's *Bronze Horseman*, drawing as it does from sculptural, iconographic, and heraldic traditions which join Marcus Aurelius and St. George, Europe and Russia, not only marks the moment of maximal equipoise in the fictional depiction of Russian history but also is itself, with its unique stand-off of styles and thematics (eighteenth-century "panegyric"/nineteenth-century "realistic")[53] and counterpointing of introduction and narrative sections, a perfect formal expression of that balance (see Lednicki, *Pushkin's 'Bronze Horseman'* 49–50). Peter and his city are both splendid *and* cruel, and therein lies the enigma of Pushkin's masterpiece.[54]

The question of the folkloric roots of the equine image is admittedly more vague and indeterminate, shrouded, as it were, in the mists of the popular memory/collective unconscious. Here its chief expression in the nineteenth-century literary tradition is found not in Pushkin but in Gogol, whose celebrated panegyric on Russia's destiny in the context of a troika

---

condemnatory and patriotic, just as his view of Peter's place in history was a complex mix of fascination and repugnance.

[52] Lednicki (*Pushkin's 'Bronze Horseman'* 28–30) suggests further that Mickiewicz's image of the unreined steed owes a debt to Pushkin's earlier poem "To Licinius" (1815), where the overproud hero (and by implication Russia) is threatened with a fall because he can no longer control his chariot.

[53] For the shift from panegyric (Kantemir, Trediakovsky, Sumarokov, Lomonosov, Derzhavin, etc.) to realistic (Gogol, Dostoevsky, etc.) treatment of Peter and his city, see Antsyferov, *Dusha*.

[54] Later commentators on the meaning of the city's mounted *genius loci*, including Dostoevsky, will ignore the capital's splendor—or see it in decline—and foreground its cruel, tyrannical side.

ride had an immense impact on later generations of writers, including a
strikingly apocalypticist reworking in Blok (see Chapter Two below). Folk-
lorically, the horse has always possessed distinct connotations. There is, to
begin with, the most obvious—the *bogatyrskii kon'* (hero's steed) of epic
poem and folktale, the brave, wise, and prophetic friend of Ilya or Dobrynya
that leaps over mountains with the speed of an arrow and tramples the enemies of sacred Russia (see Lipets, *Obrazy batyra* 124–249). Less well-
known but equally potent source material for the popular imagination is the
practice, widespread and ancient, of killing and burying a horse with its
master. D. Anuchin, the eminent late nineteenth-century Russian anthropologist who examined primitive burial mounds (*kurgany*) in Slavic countries, came to the conclusion (echoed more recently by Eliade) that the horse
is "pre-eminently the funerary animal" ("Sani"; *Myth* 67). The horse is
buried with its master not only to show respect but also to give the deceased
a way of traveling to the other world. This notion of conveyance is reinforced in the tradition of the sledge (*sani*), which carries the individual from
an earthly home to the final resting place and which also is drawn by the
horse.[55] Similarly, the figure of a horse's head or "little horse" (*konek*) was
placed on a Russian peasant's hut to protect the family within from disaster
and their flock from disease or infertility (P. A. Rovinskii, "Zemlia i volia"
438). If the *konek* was smashed by others or fell apart on its own, it meant
that either death or some great misfortune was in store for the head of the
household. Finally, in the peasant consciousness, and in its modern representation in the works of such poets as Esenin and Klyuev, the horse's head
was the symbol of the popular cosmos (*izbianyi kosmos*), of the link between the sun ("there") and the earth ("here"), and of motion upward and
outward into unknown regions.[56] Therefore, the horse not only had important ties with the ritual of sacrifice and burial but also with the mythical
*put'* (path) joining the little world of the peasant's hut to the great world
beyond (Bazanov, *S. Esenin* 70–77).

Beyond this, however, the horse has long had another, darker side in the
popular consciousness—that associated with the "Scythian" marauder. It is
at this point that the Russian tradition comes close to the generally positive
or romanticized images of the Argentinian gaucho and the American cow-
boy, with the important difference that the latter horsemen were seen to
"open up" (but not civilize) parts of their countries, while the Mongols
imposed their "yoke" on a flourishing Kievan state. All of these roving men
on horseback stood for something quite different from the chivalric tradi-

[55] The barque or boat (*lad'ia*) also suggests a "crossing-over"—cf. the river Styx and the
ferryman Charon of Greek mythology—but without the help of a horse.

[56] Cf. Eliade's statement, in *Shamanism: Archaic Techniques of Ecstasy*, that the horse "fa-
cilitates the trance, the ecstatic flight of the soul to forbidden regions" (470).

tion—volatile, unrestrained movement, freedom coupled with lawlessness, a nomadic lack of culture. As we see in the poems of such modern "Scythians" as Voloshin and Blok (in the latter especially the "chivalric" and "Mongol" notions of horse and rider often alternate and compete), the revolution conjured up past ghosts of mounted chaos sweeping into "European" Russia from the East. Ironically, as Blok maintained in the tortured logic of his essays, if its purpose was to bring down the corrupt edifice of European civilization, this "second coming" of Russia's Eastern origins was not without its cathartic truth. The "pagan" as opposed to "chivalric" horseman came to be an important *pre*figuring element in the intelligentsia's quest to understand its "Russianness." Russians, as Berdyaev said so often, needed a *put'* (path) of their own, regardless of where that path led; they were *stranniki*, wandering truth-seekers, and they despised the "sedentary" (*osedlyi*) European. Borges' recent eulogy of the gaucho and of the latter's doomed attempt to conquer time and history by conquering space comes eerily close to certain "Scythian" passages in Zamyatin[57] and others and indicates to what extent this popular myth of wanderlust is not unique or indigenous:

> The figure of the man on the horse is, secretly, poignant. Under Attila, the "Scourge of God," under Genghis Khan, and under Tamerlane, the horseman tempestuously destroys and founds extensive empires, but all he destroys and founds is illusory. His work, like him, is ephemeral. From the farmer comes the word "culture" and from cities the word "civilization," but the horseman is a storm that fades away ("Stories of Horsemen" 8).

To presume from the above that Gogol's Chichikov is a nineteenth-century Genghis Khan come to rape and pillage in a provincial backwater is, prima facie, not a little far-fetched. He is cultured (albeit superficially), his background is urban, he has a passion for order—in short, all the terms in Borges' formula are reversed. Yet everything that Chichikov creates and destroys is *illusory*. And more important, it is when Chichikov disappears

---

[57] "The essence of the spiritual revolutionary was captured by Zamjatin's description of the Scythian: 'Over the green steppe speeds alone a wild horseman with streaming hair—the Scythian. Where is he speeding? Nowhere. Why? For no reason. He speeds simply because he is a Scythian, because he has become one with the steed, because he is a centaur, and because freedom, solitariness, his steed, the wide steppe are most dear to him.' The galloping Scythian symbolized freedom, unending movement, and solitariness—freedom to reject the present in the name of the distant future, unending movement as a guarantee of man's progress in the face of universal philistinism, and solitariness because the spiritual revolutionary and heretic was always an isolated figure who stood apart from the masses" (Shane, *Zamjatin* 18). See also the description of the centaur, of one who "has become one with the steed," in *We* when D-503 looks down at the world beyond the Green Wall from within the spaceship Integral.

into the wide-open spaces at the end of part one that Gogol's narrator abandons himself to lyrical ruminations on the troika and Russia's destiny and we enter a strange and privileged narrative space in the text.[58] Here the horse-drawn troika (the Russian chariot) symbolizes the shift from everyday time (the provincial town) to epic time (the grand *openness* of Russia's future). We are meant to "cross over" with Chichikov (he is indeed a kind of mock-epic Charon) and rise above this world (he is also, at a higher level, a kind of Elijah). At the same time, Gogol's imperatives exhort us to enter into the sheer nervous excitement of the ride, the combination of pleasure *and* fear that the passenger feels as the troika and Russia hurtle into the future. Thus, along with Pushkin's poetic treatment of Falconet's statue, Gogol's folk-inspired apotheosis of the troika becomes another potent image of eschatological change to be adopted and reworked by later writers.

It is, to be sure, a risky enterprise to extrapolate a shape for Russian cultural history from scattered examples of the equine motif. The term "Trojan horse" means something quite different to us than it did to the Greeks, just as the horse that brought death to Prince Oleg in the Primary Chronicle is not—because of the *context* in which it is presented—the horse of Pushkin's adaptation. I would like to propose, however, that many nineteenth-century Russian writers combined myth and realism in their use of the horse and that this intentional modal confusion suggests that the above-mentioned traditions were very much alive. We have already discussed Pushkin and Gogol, and, while space does not permit further treatment of them here, there are other examples in their work that lend credibility to our assumptions.[59] To turn our attention elsewhere, Chatsky, the famous

---

[58] For more on the poetics of space in Gogol, see Lotman, "Problema khudozhestvennogo prostranstva."

[59] In Pushkin one could cite, for example, his poetic reworking of the legend of the prophetic Oleg and his important lyric "The Devils." In the first work it is predicted that the prince will die because of his steed, so Oleg cautiously remains apart from the horse until after the latter is dead. The prophecy comes true, however, and the connotation of equine-inspired doom is realized when Oleg, come to visit the remains of his faithful friend, is fatally bitten by a snake lying in wait in the horse's skull. "The Devils" describes how the speaker's sleigh is caught in a snowstorm and how the horses, frightened by the eerie atmosphere, lose their way. The animals' wild movements and lack of a road/destination *could* symbolize several things at this juncture of Pushkin's career (1830), not the least of which being his own troubled feelings about his forthcoming marriage. Gogol often used some form of horse-drawn conveyance as a *way out* of a difficult situation: Podkolyosin in *Marriage* makes a quick exit in a carriage rather than proceed to the altar, and the tormented Poprishchin in "The Diary of a Madman" imagines his escape from madness and the terrible conditions of the asylum in terms of a heavenly bound troika (another Elijah motif). The equine motif also appears at the end of the story "The Carriage" and the fragment "Rome," but its demonic connotations are perhaps most evident at the end of "Nevsky Prospect": "When the entire city [Petersburg] is transformed into thunder and flash, myriads of carriages careen off bridges, postilions shout and jump off horses, and

hero of Griboedov's *Woe from Wit* (1833), does not merely ask for his carriage at the end of the play; rather, he exclaims that "he is no more a rider" whose destination is Moscow and that he is going into the world to look for a more worthy residence. His departure is thus a direct appeal to the audience, a kind of "crossing-over" into their space-time and into their notion of Russia's historical *put'*. In other words, Griboedov uses, *before Gogol*, the formula of an equine exit from a fallen world.

In Lermontov's poetry and prose a spirited horse is repeatedly associated with a beautiful maiden: both horse and maiden may be destroyed (or "broken" or "run to death") by the speaker's or protagonist's passionate but fickle nature. One obvious example of this appears in *A Hero of Our Time* (1840), where Bela's death is inextricably linked first with Pechorin's cynical horse-trading and then with his efforts to "break" her, and where his loss of Vera finds an objective correlative in the death from exhaustion of his horse. A remarkably similar case can be found in Turgenev's "First Love" (1860), when Vladimir is shattered by the discovery that his father is having an affair with Zinarda, the object of his impossible adolescent infatuation. Indeed, in this instance passion becomes something much more than innocent horseplay; it is a galvanic force that binds "rider" to "mount" (the father is repeatedly referred to as a formidable horseman who *curbs* Zinaida much as he curbs his mare Electric) in a sadomasochistic duel until the moment when a blow delivered by his riding crop shows the unsuspecting boy the depth of their attraction. (It may well be that the sophisticated and well-read Turgenev was playing with a modern version of the Renaissance simile that linked the sex act with a man's domineering position "in the saddle.") And of course the most celebrated example of this cruel male horsemanship belongs to Tolstoy, whose elaborate description of the horse race in *Anna Karenina* (wr. 1873–77) makes an unmistakable connection between Vronsky "in the saddle" on the mare Frou-Frou, breaking her back with his careless riding, and Vronsky in relation to Anna, "crushing" her so much that she hurls herself beneath a train.[60]

In *Crime and Punishment* (1866), Raskolnikov's terrifying dream of the mare beaten to death by a peasant is modeled on a similar description in

---

the devil himself lights the streetlamps for the sole purpose of showing everything in an unreal guise" (*PSS* III: 46). As a folk symbol of Russia on the move, the troika was invoked regularly by members of Pushkin's pleiad: see, e.g., the spirited poem "Again the Troika" by Vyazemsky. Other writers (primarily poets) who developed the equine motif at this time, or earlier, include: Batyushkov ("The Song of Harold the Brave"), Bestuzhev-Marlinsky ("Saatyr"), Derzhavin ("The Chariot"), Kyukhelbeker ("Svyatopolk," "Rogday's Hounds"), Kozlov ("The Nocturnal Ride"), Krylov ("The Rider and the Steed"), Zhukovsky ("The Song of the Arab [Sung] over the Grave of his Horse," "Svetlana," "Lenora," "The Knight Rollon").

[60] For more on the connection between the steeplechase and the train ride in *Anna Karenina*, see the discussion in Chapter One.

Nekrasov's long poem *About the Weather* (wr. 1863–65). Nekrasov and Dostoevsky replace the powerful male steed (*kon'*) of folklore with the bedraggled nag (*kliacha*)—this female horse symbolizes the silent (non-verbal), long-suffering Russia of Lizaveta, Sonya, and the *narod* (see Chapter One). While "aristocratic" writers like Lermontov, Turgenev, and Tolstoy tend to conflate the curbing, breaking, or destroying of a high-strung mare with the "painful pleasure" of romantic love, Dostoevsky and Nekrasov, though in their own ways sadomasochistic, expand the mare image into a more "popular" horse, one not ridden by a privileged rider but compelled to draw a heavy burden in the workaday world. In fact, as is further argued in Chapter One, only with Dostoevsky does the horse (and its modern version the train) begin to assume a definite and indisputable *apocalyptic* resonance; Russian history has now entered a new and ominous stage, and for the first time personal and national *ends* are embodied in variations on the same image cluster. Finally, two notable equine allusions are provided by Leskov and Chekhov in the latter part of the nineteenth century. In Leskov's "Enchanted Pilgrim" (1873) Ivan Flyagin is a *koneser* (or "connoisseur" of the *kon'*—the pun is Leskov's), an expert tamer of horses, an extravagant drinker and male specimen of epic proportions, and a saintly and sinful *strannik* (McLean, *Leskov* 241–55); Chekhov's description of a popular world falling apart in an orgy of drunkenness and ignorance ("The Peasants" [1897]) is again symbolized by a horse, crazed by a fire and running out of control.

Dostoevsky's work suggests itself as a turning point in this tradition and our logical point of entrance because several of his major works, and *The Idiot* in particular, witness a joining of the notions of biblical end and the current direction of Russian history in the image cluster of the horse/train.[61] Personal tragedy expands into imminent national tragedy, and the

---

[61] An excellent introduction to the mythic connotations of the horse and train in nineteenth-century Russian literature is found in Baehr, "The Troika and the Train" (forthcoming). Baehr's study provides numerous examples of how the horse and train were perceived as opposing concepts (old/new, traditional/modern, natural/mechanical, etc.) in both the popular and the educated imagination. Particularly pertinent to our survey are his comments about the various reworkings of the Bronze Horseman myth into railway terms: Vyazemsky's "Pyotr Alekseevich" (1867), a poem in which the tsar's mount becomes an "imperial tender" and his title "crowned engineer" (*ventsenosnyi mashinist*); or Nekrasov's "The Railroad" (1864), another poem about, among other things, the abused and forgotten workers who haunt the Moscow-Petersburg railroad as it is built by Count Pyotr Andreevich Kleinmichel (a surrogate for Nicholas I): the ghosts of these "little men" come to utter their "threatening exclamations" in much the same way that Evgeny, in Pushkin's poem, once uttered his demented challenge to the equestrian statue. For additional discussion on the theme of the railroad in nineteenth century Russian literature, see Gesemann, "Zur Rezeption"; and Al'tman, "Zheleznaia doroga."

metaphorical ride of Nastasya Filippovna, who is, on a mythical level, Russia "the fallen bride," is repeatedly presented as a composite of the third and fourth horses of Revelation (6:5–8) and of the railroad network that is poisoning the "waters of life" (7:17, 8:10, 21:6). Living in a later, more skeptical time, and fearing that the "religion" of rationality that the "men of the sixties" had imported from the West would lead to universal destruction, Dostoevsky reverses the terms of the chivalric epic—the genre in which a poet like Spenser could still equate England's progress toward a New Jerusalem of ideal governance with a knightly quest on horseback.[62] Now the rider does not hold the reins but is driven by a diabolical machine toward the terminus of death. In such apocalyptically oriented writers as Dostoevsky and Leontiev, the train, with its domination over horse-drawn conveyance in the second half of the nineteenth century, gradually becomes the equivalent of the Petrine steed: it is once again the victory of the false "new" over the genuine "old," of godless European enlightenment over orthodox, organic Rus'.[63] The train is so threatening as a symbol of doom (in the popular consciousness it was given not the neutral name *poezd*, but the marked one, *mashina*—the ultimate machine and handiwork of the Antichrist[64]) because it moves, like "atheistic" logic, along iron rails without any higher reason for being and because it reaches its destination, which in these apocalyptic fictions is often associated with death, with only a mechanical explanation of how it got there. Since the train is perceived as a *self-enclosed* ensemble of origin/destination, coach, rails, and telegraph,[65] the passenger feels *cut off* from nature and the outside world and begins to

---

[62] A more appropriate model of course, and one which actually surfaces in the text of *The Idiot*, is *Don Quixote*, a work which parodies and "novelizes" the by then dated model of the chivalric quest. It also plays an important role in Platonov's *Chevengur*, which focuses on the Bolshevik quest for a new and better world. See Chapter Three.

[63] American writers and thinkers experienced some of the same reservations about the incursion of the machine world—especially the train—into pristine America, although, to be sure, there seems to have been more sheer fascination with the idea of progress and less of Russia's apocalyptically-tinged fears. See Leo Marx's classic *The Machine in the Garden* 194–98, 209–16, 227–65. Of all American writers, Hawthorne was probably the one most mesmerized by the mythological aura surrounding the appearance of the iron horse in his country: see, e.g., his chapter "The Flight of Two Owls" in *The House of Seven Gables* as well as his story "The Celestial Railway."

[64] For example, in a "physiological sketch" ("Zheleznaia doroga mezhdu Peterburgom i Moskvoi" [The Railroad between Petersburg and Moscow]) that appeared in volume 54 of the journal *The Contemporary* (*Sovremennik*) for 1855 (43–71), the author ("S") repeatedly refers to the train as a *mashina* and dwells on the fears of his passengers toward the new form of transportation: " 'Oh, tell me, please, isn't it dangerous to ride on the railroad?' asks a stout lady" on the very first page (43). A related, but popular (*narodnyi*) fear of the train is expressed by the character Fyoklushka in A. Ostrovsky's play *The Storm* and by one of Tolstoy's peasants in *War and Peace*. For more on the railroad motif and its "chronotopic" possibilities, see Chapter One.

[65] The telegraph was added at a later point to aid in communication and prevent accidents.

experience the space-time of the journey in *relative terms*.[66] Moreover, the shift from individual, aristocratic rider to collective, *driven* passengers (Dostoevsky was again one of the first to stress this melting-pot atmosphere of "many-voicedness" in his description of a third class coach) makes the train a perfect "vehicle" for the expression of tumultuous social change.[67] The train continues to be a powerful, and often apocalyptically colored symbol for both the popular and literary imagination well into the twentieth century: there is, for example, Esenin's famous race between flesh-and-blood colt and iron horse in "Sorokoust"; Mandelshtam's blending of the notions of music and iron, of a passing age rent by the screeching of train whistles, in his poem "Concert at the Station" (see Ronen, *An Approach* xvii–xx); Artem Vesyoly's duel between bull and train in *Russia Drenched in Blood*; Andrey Platonov's and fellow proletarians' fervent belief that the train, as quintessential machine, would be the liberating force in the new Soviet era; V. Ilenkov's metaphor of Soviet society as train and the party as the "driving axle" in the novel by the same name (see Clark, "Little Heroes" 190–91); and more recently there is Solzhenitsyn's description of the dismantling of "true-timbered" (*kondovaia*) Russia and the demise of its best representative in terms of a railway accident ("Matryona's Homestead"); and Venedikt Erofeev's tragicomic tale, punctuated with allusions to Revelation, of another doomed train-ride into alcoholic oblivion and death (*From Moscow to the End of the Line* [*Moskva-Petushki*]).

Thus, perhaps more than any other single ingredient of the apocalyptic plot it is the "chronotopic" picture of the horse/train that has had the most far-reaching implications for the *shape* of the various authors' thinking as *inscribed* in the movement of the different stories. Following Dostoevsky's lead, Bely, Platonov, Bulgakov, and Pasternak return, *mutatis mutandis*, to this image cluster as a way into the larger issue of how to conceptualize ("emplot") the movement of history—is it, for instance, linear, circular, or spiralic? It is presumably not fortuitous that, together with that of the train, the image of the horse has remained one of the most durable and rich in all Russian literature and culture: witness its prominent place (usually in some form of the chivalric, folkloric/Scythian, or apocalyptic *topos*) in the works of Blok, Bely, Voloshin, and other Symbolists; in Esenin, Klyuev, and the

---

[66] See Schivelbusch, *The Railway*. In general Schivelbusch is a rich source of information on how the nineteenth century European perception of space and time was radically changed by the presence of the train. He also provides numerous examples of the train in popular and elitist literature of the time.

[67] In the "physiological sketch" referred to above there is a good deal made of the different classes (first, second, and third) on the train and their respective attitudes, from boisterous to reserved, toward the journey. Dostoevsky was clearly laying claim to this recent phenomenon in his vivid presentation of the third class coach carrying Myshkin, Rogozhin, and Lebedev in the opening pages of *The Idiot*.

peasant poets; in Shershenevich, Mariengof, Gruzinov, and the Russian Imagists. The list could go on to include Mandelshtam, Tsvetaeva, Babel, Sholokhov, the émigré poet Vladimir Korvin-Piotrovsky—even Vs. Ivanov, Efim Dorosh, I. Gudov, and other converts to high Stalinist Socialist Realism (Clark, *Soviet Novel* 139, 277).[68] And one most remarkable recent example, Joseph Brodsky's poem about the black horse, has been shown by the Soviet scholar O. V. Simchenko to trace its ancestry to Anna Akhmatova and her recollection of 1936, the eve of the great purges: "Life [placed] us at the reins [lit. 'under the bridle'—*pod uzdy*] of a Pegasus that [was] somehow reminiscent of the Pale Horse of Apocalypse or the Black Horse of the verses [i.e., Brodsky's] that [were] yet to be born" (cited in Simchenko, "Tema pamiati" 506). To be sure, not all of these writers employ the equine image within the explicit semantic field of "apocalypse," yet such a meaning may not be far off, especially if the given passage raises the issue of the shape and direction of Russian history and the end-time of the revolution. In this larger sense, one may go so far as to say that the Russian tradition of apocalyptic fiction is a unique metaphorical "unbridling" or "unreining" of those same relentless cultural categories (old/new, East/West, pagan/orthodox) that had pursued the collective consciousness of the intelligentsia for centuries.

In the West, perhaps for the reasons advanced by Berdyaev and Lotman, or perhaps because the potent combination of national myth and fanatic millenarianism driving the human imagination down "history's road" came to be questioned sooner, few modern writers of the "large form" (especially after the Great War) enter into the living tradition of "apocalyptic fiction" as I have tried to define it.[69] Only someone like D. H. Lawrence, whose novels are considered by many to go against the grain of Anglo-American modernism, rivals these Russian novelists in his persistent telescoping of personal, national, and biblical myths of the End (and Beginning). Let us then close our introductory remarks with Lawrence, who apparently had his own "Scythian" streak and who too felt compelled to seat his apocalyptic fervor "in the saddle":[70]

[68] For specific examples of the equine motif in the works of the symbolists, see Chapter Two.

[69] This is not to say that the apocalyptic theme fades from Western literature (and culture) after World War I. On the contrary, it is quite evident in the works of modern drama—witness the plays of Girandoux, Ionesco, Beckett, Genet, and others (see Valency, *The End of the World* 419–37). And it is present in prose works as recent as Pynchon's *Gravity's Rainbow*. Nonetheless, the underlying faith in a *Christian* resolution to the biblical plot has become increasingly untenable, and what is now called "apocalyptic" is more and more the *end as nothingness* (an especially vivid theme in, say, Beckett). It is my argument that Russian writers such as Bulgakov and Pasternak fall more into a Christian tradition of *Apocalyptik* that is perhaps anachronistic by Western standards.

[70] Compare, for example, the following passage from Lawrence's *Apocalypse* and the passionate scene of Ursula and the horses at the conclusion of *The Rainbow*.

Horses, always horses! How the horse dominated the mind of the early races, especially in the Mediterranean! You were a lord if you had a horse. Far back, far back in our dark souls the horse prances. He is a dominant symbol: he gives us lordship: he links us, the first palpable and throbbing link with the ruddy-glowing Almighty of potence: he is the beginning even of our godhead in the flesh. And as a symbol he roams the dark under-world meadows of the soul. He stamps and threshes in the dark fields of your soul and mine. The sons of god who came down and knew the daughters of men and begot the great Titans, they had "the members of horses," says Enoch.

Within the last fifty years man has lost the horse. Now man is lost. Man is lost to life and power—an underling and a wastrel. While horses thrashed the streets of London, London lived. . . .

But the rider on the white horse is crowned. He is the royal one, he is my very self and his horse is the whole *mana* of a man. He is my very me, my sacred ego, called into a new cycle of action by the Lamb and riding forth to conquest, the conquest of the old self for the birth of the new self. . . .

The true action of the myth, or ritual-imagery, has been all cut away. The rider on the white horse appears, then vanishes. But we know why he has appeared. And we know why he is paralleled at the end of the Apocalypse by the last rider on the white horse, who is the heavenly son of Man riding forth after the last and final conquest over the "kings." The son of man, even you or I, rides forth to the small conquest; but the Great Son of Man mounts his white horse after the last universal conquest, and leads on his hosts (*Apocalypse* 125–28).

# ONE

---

## *The Idiot*:
## Historicism Arrives at the Station

> That devilish Iron Horse, whose ear-rending neigh is heard throughout the town, has muddied the Boiling Spring with his foot, and he it is that has browsed off all the woods on Walden shore, that Trojan Horse, with a thousand men in his belly, introduced by mercenary Greeks! Where is the country's champion, the Moore of Moore Hall, to meet him at the Deep Cut and thrust an avenging lance between the ribs of the bloated pest?
>
> —Henry David Thoreau, *Walden*

> What is this that man has done?
> He has set off on the iron road,
> And I feel the threat of our iron century.
> —Fyodor Glinka, "Two Roads"

For good or for ill, Russian literature has long been known for its so-called messianism, and there is no writer who struggled more than Dostoevsky to give legitimacy to the "Russian idea," to the belief that Russian history is uniquely inscribed with a Biblical End. Yet Dostoevsky was no mystic, at least in the sense of one who tries to peer *beyond* the End and tell about it (see, e.g., Rozenblium, "Tvorcheskie dnevniki" 13–15). If he had occasion to resort to the figures and codes of Revelation,[1] he did so allusively, for as a novelist he was keenly aware that his texts must first be grounded firmly in nineteenth-century history and that whatever lies on the other side of personal death is not to be captured *in words*, is not the stuff of a story told over time. As his epoch's most eloquent voice in the dialogue between logic (*rassudok*) and belief (*vera*), he apparently had similar thoughts about the

---

[1] A perceptive discussion of the effect of Dostoevsky's apocalypticism on the narrative structure of his "threshold" works—particularly *Diary of a Writer*—is found in Morson, *Boundaries* 24–26, 33–38. For possible apocalyptic motifs in *The Idiot*, see Cox (*Between Heaven and Earth* 164–91), Leatherbarrow ("Apocalyptic Imagery"), and especially Hollander ("Apocalyptic Framework"). See as well Mochulsky, *Dostoevsky* 353–62; Peace, *Dostoyevsky* 109–24; and Dostoevskii, *PSS* IX: 393, 439, 442, 445–48.

promised interregnum of the Antichrist and the Second Coming of Christ as prophesied by John of Patmos.

Modern criticism often speaks of novels as being "end-determined"[2] or somehow written in reverse, with the shadow of a foreordained conclusion cast backwards over the various elements of narrative structure. Such an approach, one suspects, could certainly be applied to much of Dostoevsky's writing, and to *The Idiot* especially, of whose haunting final scene the author wrote his niece S. A. Ivanova, "almost the whole novel was thought out and written for the sake of the dénouement" (Dolinin II: 138).[3] But it would be a mistake to do so too hastily, if only because the neat and self-regarding "structure" touted by modern criticism is such a vexed issue in the context of Dostoevsky the great vitalist. The implicit danger in reading Dostoevsky through Western eyes is to impose cultural paradigms and critical orthodoxies which have limited meaning when projected back to the Russia of the 1860s and 1870s. In this regard, *The Idiot* has been a powerful magnet for some spectacular misreadings.[4] René Girard's fascinating but remarkably uninformed account of what he calls the "Dostoevskian apocalypse" in *Deceit, Desire, and the Novel* is a prime example of this (see 256–91). Indeed, if we are to judge by what Dostoevsky had to say about the logically closed ideologies swarming in the air of his time, he would have harsh words for the way that language has evolved from a medium of ethical choice to a system of systems. In the end one would have to agree with Edward Wasiolek who, as the Western scholar most familiar with Dostoevsky's notebooks, points out that *The Idiot* is, of Dostoevsky's major fiction, the work most resistant to "elegant" structural analysis: "We cannot go to *The Idiot* with theories of the organic fitness of every part, of the necessity of every positioning, every image, every sound. . . . Structure, I hazard, is never as exquisite as our current theories would have it, at least not in this novel" (*Notebooks* 9).

One issue is not in doubt: as the threat of revolution entered the public consciousness, Dostoevsky and the tradition his work grew out of became

---

[2] The phrase is Frank Kermode's. See his influential *The Sense of An Ending* as well as Friedman (*Turn*), D. A. Miller (*Narrative and Its Discontents*), Richter (*Fable's End*), and Torgovnik (*Closure*).

[3] For the sake of consistency I will be using the *Russian* calendar in all references to Dostoevsky's correspondence. During the period under discussion (1860s) the Russian calendar lagged behind the Western calendar by twelve days.

[4] Such misreadings would include, in my opinion, Krieger's making the smug and ultimately judgmental Radomsky into the author's mouthpiece ("Dostoevsky's 'Idiot' " 49–51); Lord's conclusion that Myshkin is a "princely humbug" and "an open sore, a paranoic introvert" (*Dostoevsky* 84, 88); and Dalton's interpretation of Rogozhin's attempt on Myshkin's life in terms of the hero's sexual fantasies and Freudian "primal scene" logic (*Unconscious Structure* 107–16).

increasingly obsessed by the notion of apocalypse. Whether or not history, in Herzen's metaphor, followed a "libretto," the threat of a communist-inspired "violent tempest—dreadful, bloody, unjust, and swift"—was something that people anticipated, depending on their political orientation and the part they saw themselves playing in the unfolding drama, with either fear or joy (*ss* VI: 104). Moreover, this apocalypticism could not but leave some trace on how Dostoevsky's fiction is composed and narrated.[5] Here *The Idiot* is particularly noteworthy: it is Dostoevsky's first major work in which the apocalypse, as metaphor for "anti-life" (death), "anti-history" (timelessness), and indeed "anti-narrative" (end, silence) is ironically the prime mover of plot. There is good reason why the novel has been called Dostoevsky's most "untidy masterpiece" (Wasiolek, *The Notebooks* 19) and why efforts to invest it with a structure it apparently lacks have so often gone awry. This central paradox—namely, that *The Idiot* is about an end it cannot tell but only *foretell*—is the subject of this chapter. To pose the question in terms of the novel's life in our own times: this end, foretold, held in linguistic limbo by the "différance" of Dostoevsky's telling—is it a true End, a transcendental presence whose "time has come"? or is it simply an end like any other, a provisional presence that resolves nothing and leaves everyone, characters, reader, and author, stuck on the tracks of an ongoing historicism? I will briefly establish a context for Dostoevsky's apocalypticism within his epoch and his own oeuvre, then look more closely at how the novel gathers narrative momentum and proceeds toward its end. Our focus will be on the image of the train, which as metaphor for mechanical force, "iron logic," and unregenerate chronos, is both the chief semantic and compositional source of this momentum and one possible key to Dostoevsky's conceptualization of the role of apocalypse in history.

The most authoritative statement ever made by Dostoevsky on the idea of the End came in a notebook entry of April 16, 1864, as he stood vigil at the bier of his first wife. The occasion provided ample opportunity to contemplate the nature of death, the possibility of resurrection, and the meaning of history. The entry itself is especially interesting both because of its unguarded frankness and because of its timing on the eve of Dostoevsky's major period—the first part of *Notes from Underground* had just appeared that March and *Crime and Punishment* and the other novels were soon to follow. It is also striking that the questions raised by Dostoevsky as he rea-

---

[5] The studies by Cox, Leatherbarrow, and Hollander mention numerous possible apocalyptic motifs, but they stop short of showing how an apocalyptic framework might affect the actual narrative structure of *The Idiot*. For the understanding of apocalyptic time (the difference between *chronos* and *kairos*) as it applies to *The Idiot*, see Holquist (*Dostoevsky* 102–23) and Terras ("Dissonans" 64).

soned passionately with himself are directly implicated in the themes and story-line of *The Idiot*, the novel written after *Crime and Punishment*, in the first years of Dostoevsky's self-imposed exile in Western Europe (September 1867–January 1869).

Masha is lying on the table. Will Masha and I ever see each other again?

It is impossible to love one another *as oneself* according to Christ's commandment. . . . Only Christ could do this, but Christ was eternal [*vekovechnyi*], an eternal ideal [*ot veka ideal*], toward which man strives and must, by the laws of nature, strive. At the same time, after the appearance of Christ as *the ideal of man in the flesh* it became clear as day that . . . the highest use to which man can put his personality is . . . to destroy, as it were, that *I*, to give it back in full to each and every one selflessly and wholeheartedly. And this is the greatest happiness. Thus the law of *I* merges with the law of humanity and in this merging both [the *I* and the *all*] . . . attain the highest goal of their individual development.

It is precisely this that is the paradise of Christ. All history—both that of mankind and of each man separately—is only the development of, struggle with, urge for, and attainment of this goal.

But if this is the ultimate goal of mankind (at whose attainment there will no longer be a need to develop . . . [and], therefore, to live), then it follows that man, having once attained [his goal], also ends his earthly existence. Hence man on earth is a being that is only developing, and therefore not completed, but transitional.

But to attain such an exalted goal is, to my mind, totally senseless, if in the attainment of the goal all is snuffed out and disappears, that is, if there is no more life for man upon the attainment of the goal. It follows then that there is [i.e., there must be] a future life in paradise . . .

NB. The Antichrists are mistaken when they attempt to refute Christianity with the following main point of refutation: (1) "Why doesn't Christianity reign on earth if it is [the] true [religion], why does man suffer to this day and not become a brother to others?"

Well, it's not easily understandable why—because this is the ideal of the future, completed life of man, while earthly man is in a transitional state. This ideal will come, but it will come after the attainment of [life's] goal, when man will have been completely reborn by the laws of nature into another form which neither marries nor is given in marriage;[6] and, secondly, Christ himself taught this lesson only as an ideal,

[6] The phrase "neither marries nor is given in marriage" is an allusion to Matthew 22:30.

prophesying that until the end of the world there would be struggle and development (his teaching about the sword) for such are the laws of nature, because on earth life is developing, while there [i.e. the other world] is an existence which is complete in its synthesis, eternally joyous and full, for which, it would seem, "time" shall be no more. . . .[7]

Hence man strives on earth for an ideal that *opposes* his nature. When man doesn't fulfill the ideal of striving for the ideal, that is, doesn't *in an act of love* make a sacrifice of his *I* to other people or another being (Masha and I), he experiences suffering and calls that suffering sin. Hence man must constantly experience a suffering which is counterbalanced by the heavenly [*raiskii*] delight in fulfilling the law, that is, by sacrifice. Herein lies our [sense of] balance on earth. Otherwise the Earth would be without meaning (*Neizdannyi Dostoevskii* 173–75).

I have quoted this extraordinary passage at length because in it we see the mind of a great story-teller trying, step by step, to compose a plot for life that *encompasses* death. As in the finale of *The Idiot*,[8] where Myshkin and Rogozhin contemplate the corpse of Nastasya Filippovna, Dostoevsky strikes repeatedly at the mystery of this ultimate threshold. The fascination with spatio-temporal brinks and border-crossings that is his hallmark[9] and that so marks the writing of *The Idiot*[10] is here distilled to a radical essence of logic and belief. Dostoevsky works back from the fact of his wife's death to the story of every human life. Death frames life, gives it a conclusion so that what has come before can have a beginning, middle, and end (see Kermode, *Sense* 58–59). Yet only if the conclusion can be set, as it were, in a larger story does this structure have a meaning, and the forward movement ("struggle and development") a goal (the synthesis of "Masha" and "I"). Dostoevsky's Christian logic is trying to posit the ultimate story whose au-

---

[7] The allusion to Revelation 10:6 ("there shall be no more time"; in RVS, "there should be no more delay") will be taken up at significant moments by Myshkin and Ippolit in *The Idiot*. See below.

[8] Cf. the similar situation in "The Meek One" ("Krotkaia"). There too the silence of a dead woman is juxtaposed with the arguments raised by her conscience-stricken husband.

[9] "Everywhere and in everything I go to extremes; all my life I have always overstepped the mark" (letter of August 16, 1867 to A. Maykov in Dolinin II: 29). On the threshold in Dostoevsky see Arban, "Porog"; and Bakhtin, *Problemy* 71–74, 85, 170–74, 204–6.

[10] Dostoevsky's obsessive preoccupation with debts, deadlines, and gambling up to and during the writing of *The Idiot* suggests that at some level he *needed* to feel the danger of a crisis situation in order to bring out untapped resources within himself, to perform at the threshold of nervous (and often epileptic) collapse. He even came to look at *The Idiot* in gambling terms as his last possible wager: "In a word, I am throwing myself into the novel as though into an attack [*na ura!*]—headfirst, everything on one card, what will be, will be!" (letter of October 9, 1867 to A. Maykov in Dolinin II: 47).

thorial viewpoint cannot be known. To resort to the language of narratology, without some larger emplotment of faith, humanity's attempts to serialize the tale of its strivings *beyond* life's conclusion are deprived of any absolute or meaningful placement in time. There is no divine "draft," no "Finis" in paradise, only endless embellishment and retardation.

In short, although Dostoevsky's internal monologue does not express the argument so explicitly, the future author of *The Idiot* is feeling his way toward the head-on collision between Christianity and historicism, between an atemporal ideal and the relentless march of chronos, that lies at the center of his most elusive plot. Indeed, many of the motifs that reappear, artistically shaped, in *The Idiot* are set forth here in unmediated fashion: the silent corpse and what it means; Christ as an ideal that entered history and became flesh; the final tableau and tragic ensemble of competing loves; the sense of harmony and synthesis—Dostoevsky's metaphor for God—that, like a freely rotating eyeball, sees the present (life "in the middest") from the vantage of eternity (life "at the end"). All of these are vital to the plot of *The Idiot*, and we will return to them in due course. For the moment suffice it to say that Dostoevsky was sensitive to the dangers of positivistic thinking that lie in wait for the vacillating believer.[11] His unkind words for the "Antichrists," "atheists," and "materialists" of the 1860s are evidence of this.[12] And, as shall be seen shortly, Dostoevsky felt that the logic of such thinking condemned the (hi)story of a human life and a people to be told in terms of a tragic and unavoidable end.

As an artist, Dostoevsky had to find a way to invest these tensions ("here" / "there," "now" / "then") in story form. He needed some verbal picture of interlocking time-space relations to embody the notions of personal and national history that occurred to him in *his* time. This picture, which Bakhtin has termed the chronotope, is the novelist's (or narrative poet's) way of translating notions of time (open/closed, public/private, changing/static) into ready-made images of narrative space (the public square, the road).[13] One of the most celebrated and visually arresting means of proceeding down the road of life and history is the steed which, as we have seen, entered Russian literature and culture—both reflecting the shape of contemporary history and, indeed, contributing to that shape—as a powerful symbol for contemporary readers. In the Russian context, the horse was employed both

[11] As Dostoevsky said of himself in a now famous letter of late February 1854 to N. D. Fonvizina, "I am a child of the century, a child of faithlessness and doubt until now and (I know this) until the grave" (Dolinin I: 142).

[12] In a letter of August 16, 1867 to A. Maykov, Dostoevsky called the 1860s a period that "in terms of its crisis and reforms is nearly as important as that of Peter" (Dolinin II: 27).

[13] See the discussion of the chronotope in the Introduction.

as local color (a mode of conveyance, a domestic animal) and as mythical image (a symbol of imperial might or manifest destiny), so that in certain works it actually became a focal point where opposing concepts of time (everyday-epic) could intersect and collide. Here the horse's role in folkloric and chivalric tradition elided with its role in the emerging realistic tradition; the site of this collision—the "cliff" over the "abyss" in Petersburg in Pushkin's *The Bronze Horseman*, the "steppe" in Gogol's *Dead Souls*—functioned as an all-important visual field for organizing the reader's response to contemporary history.

Thus, Senate Square served as the "betwixt-and-between" site where different classes of people (Peter-Evgeny) and the different times they represented could have their "duel." And the steppe, with its sprawling expanse and seemingly endless horizon line, became a metaphor for the openness and infinite possibility of Russian historical time, a time whose direction and meaning were as yet unknown: "Whither art thou soaring away to, then, Russia? Give me thy answer! But Russia gives none" (Guerney 304). As he entered on the period of his major fiction, Dostoevsky turned with increasing fervor to the central questions of Russia's history, to the "whither" and "why" raised by his forebears. His later works constantly take into account the time and space that has been traveled *since* these earlier historical poses first captured the attention of contemporary audiences.

Although the horse's role in the chronotope of Pushkin and Gogol was not, properly speaking, "apocalyptic"—that is, no *explicit* connection was made between its movement and the End prophesied in the Book of Revelation—one thing is certain: over time, this role began to acquire an increasingly dark coloration. What was once implicit was now, under the pressure of contemporary history, "revealed" to subsequent generations. If in the first half of the nineteenth century certain thinkers, notably Chaadaev and Herzen, had seen Russia's lack of a significant past as an opportunity to avoid the pitfalls of Western bourgeois civilization (Herzen visualized this as the pristine "openness" of Siberia), then in the second half of the century others such as Leontiev and Solovyov saw their country's historical mission more pessimistically, in terms of closure, not openness. Leontiev, for example, so feared the process of democratization promoted by the left that he claimed that "Russian society . . . is racing faster than any other along the path of universal mixing [*vsesmeshenie*], and, who knows . . . suddenly we may . . . give birth to the Antichrist" ("Nad mogiloi Pazukhina," s vii: 425). In addition, the myth surrounding Petersburg in Pushkin's poem was gradually being re-finished by other "catastrophists": rather than the floodwaters that were often seen in early nineteenth-century poetry (V. Odoevsky, Lermontov, M. Dmitriev, V. Pecherin) as a *natural* form of retribution, by the turn of the century it was the notion of a flaming end (*ekpyrosis*), to be fueled by terrorist bombs and the *man-made* fires of social revolution, that came to dominate the descriptions of this doomed city.[14]

Dostoevsky's later fiction marks a distinct turning point in this tradition: in it the connection between the end of the biblical plot and the direction of Russian history is made explicit. Dostoevsky was the first Russian prose writer[15] to visualize the movement of an individual life and a national history in terms of the apocalyptic horse and rider. That which was left unsaid in the duel between Evgeny and the Bronze Horseman is now fully articulated in the love triangle of Myshkin, Rogozhin, and Nastasya Filippovna as it is emplotted in the Petersburg world of the 1860s. Dostoevsky's allusions to a coming apocalypse can be traced to a visit to the 1862 London Exhibition, which he subsequently described in *Winter Notes on Summer Impressions* (1863). Here he voices his disgust at the Western "worship of Baal" for the first time, but the reference seems, in context, closer to a metaphor for corruption than to a literal prophecy.[16] By the 1870s, however, and particularly in *The Diary of a Writer*, Dostoevsky had apparently begun to insist on an actual and imminent coming of the Antichrist: "The Antichrist is coming to us! He is coming! The end of the world is near—nearer than they think" (Timofeeva, "God raboty" 170).[17] Sometime during the

[14] Examples are provided by Odoevsky's *Russian Nights*, Lermontov's (?) "The Flood" ("Navodnenie"), M. Dmitriev's "The Submerged City," Pecherin's *The Triumph of Death*, and others. See Antsyferov, *Dusha*; and Weidlé, *Zadacha* 203–27. Numerous examples of the apocalyptically-tinged fire motif in turn-of-the-century literature are found in the novels of Valery Bryusov (*The Fiery Angel*), Remizov (*The Pond, Sisters in the Cross*), and Bely (*Petersburg*). In *Sisters* (1910), for example, the Bronze Horseman is portrayed as a fireman—an allusion which Bely seems to have known, since his character Sophia Petrovna ("Holy Wisdom, daughter of Peter") has a vision of the Bronze Horseman which turns into a fire truck speeding to a fire. See as well *Fiery Russia*, Remizov's book about the revolution.

[15] To be sure, there had been a number of Russian "eschatologists" before Dostoevsky. These might include such eighteenth- and nineteenth-century figures (mainly poets) as A. M. Kutuzov, Semyon Bobrov, S. A. Shirinsky-Shikhmatov, M. A. Dmitriev-Mamonov, and V. S. Pecherin. The use of apocalyptic motifs by most of these figures traces to their ties with freemasonry rather than to medieval Russian tradition. In any event, Dostoevsky is the first major Russian prose writer of whom it can be said that both the form and substance of his work bears the influence of the text of Revelation. For more on the early Russian eschatologists, see Lotman and Uspenskii, "Spory o iazyke."

[16] "Something final has taken place here, taken place and come to an end. It is like a Biblical picture, something out of Babylon, a prophecy from the Apocalypse coming to pass before your eyes" (v: 70). Parenthetical references to Dostoevsky are to the *Polnoe sobranie sochinenii*. Roman and Arabic numerals refer to volume and page numbers respectively. The English translation of *The Idiot* used in this study is that of Magarshack and is abbreviated in the text as "Mag." Liberal changes have been made in the Magarshack translation for the sake of semantic clarity and precision.

[17] Compare: "As a matter of fact, what awaits the world not only in the remaining quarter of this century but even (who knows?) perhaps in this very year? There is unrest in Europe—

intervening years between the publication of *Winter Notes* and the serialization of *Diary* Dostoevsky had shifted his focus from individual to national salvation, from death as a personal apocalypse to revolution as a political one. And, indeed, a closer look reveals evidence of this shift in the three long novels written during this period—*Crime and Punishment* (1866), *The Idiot* (1868–69), and *The Devils* (1871–72).

In *Crime and Punishment*, as mentioned earlier, Raskolnikov's dream of the mare draws heavily on a similar description in Nekrasov's long poem *About the Weather* (wr. 1863–65) (*PSS* II: 169–70). Nekrasov and Dostoevsky replace the powerful male steed (*kon'*) of folklore with a bedraggled female nag (*kliacha*), implying that this horse symbolizes the silent (nonverbal), long-suffering Russia of the *narod*.[18] The potential murderer raises his hand against a world of "Christian" time, the world of Lizaveta, Sonya, and Raskolnikov's own child-self. This horse is a far cry from the proud steed of Peter, raised on its haunches and poised, like Russia, to leap into the future,[19] or the spirited troika of Gogol, emerging, like Russia again, from the multiform countryside onto the highroad of history. Here the death of the horse is still not "apocalyptic," since the narrator stops short of linking its end with the larger shape of Russian history. It can be inferred, however, that human beings are capable of bringing on their own end and the end of those around them as soon as they replace *higher* reason (guided by moral "intuition") by *lower* reason (simple verbal logic), thus enabling the conclusion that murder can be an act of the mind alone. That Dostoevsky was now coming closer to an apocalyptic view of Russian history, with Raskolnikov's dilemma expanding into the larger issue of Russia "at the crossroads," is seen in the hero's last dream in Siberia. Raskolnikov is finally made to understand, by the sprung logic of a dream, what his mind has managed to avoid throughout the long and circuitous telling of his story up to this moment: when used to measure morality, reason is a plague (see the locusts that have "human faces" and are arrayed like "horses for battle"

---

of this there can be no doubt. . . . It is obvious that the time has come for something eternal, millenarian, for that which has been preparing itself in the world since the very beginning of its civilization" (January 1877; xxv: 6); "Everyone senses that something final has begun, that an end is coming to former things. . . . [and] a step is being taken toward something already completely new . . . and this step is being taken by Russia" (April 1877; xxv: 94). See the illuminating discussion in Morson, *Boundaries* 33–38.

[18] This dream has important links to an episode in Dostoevsky's youth when he witnessed the beating of a peasant by a government courier. See Frank, *Seeds* 70–73.

[19] We will have occasion to speak again of the equine image of "turning," "*re*-turning" (*re*-volution), and "crossing-over" in the next chapter. In the meantime, cf. the famous "purple passage" (Chapter Two) in Bely's *Petersburg* where Russia is compared to Peter's apocalyptic steed standing poised on its haunches.

of Revelation 9:1–11), presumably emanating from the West,[20] that will bring on the wholesale destruction of humanity. Immediately following this revelation Raskolnikov has his silent conversion ("They [Sonya and Raskolnikov] wanted to speak, but couldn't find the words") and his story crosses a narrative threshold that words cannot describe ("But here begins another story . . .") (VI: 421–22).

In *The Idiot*, which will be examined more closely in a moment, Dostoevsky makes broad use of the Johannine Apocalypse, including pointed reference to the third and fourth horses of Revelation 6:1–8. By this time the nagging premonition that *mundi termino appropinquante* was entering the author's consciousness through a variety of channels: (1) the patriotic feelings he felt moved to express in frank correspondence with his friend the poet Apollon Maykov, who during this same period (February–July 1868) was working on a new verse translation of the Apocalypse (Dolinin II: 102); (2) his growing anxiety as he followed the latest news from Russia, including details of the Zhemarin murders (to be reproduced in *The Idiot*) in the March 10th issue of *The Voice*; (3) his close-hand view of Mikhail Bakunin and the Russian revolutionary movement in exile at a conference in Geneva the previous fall (September 1867); and (4) his gathering animus against Europe (especially Switzerland), which was beginning to reach a fever pitch.[21] Dostoevsky embodies these concerns in his art not only thematically but *structurally*; he visualizes the shape of contemporary history, including what he felt to be the critical 1860s, by reincarnating the flesh-and-blood horse of biblical and folkloric tradition in the horse of modern times—the train (see Bazanov, *S. Esenin* 153–58). Similarly, the open road that once lured Chichikov and his vegetative Russia into a future of epic proportions becomes the rails of historicist logic that lead to a radically different terminus, one in which Russia's sleeping beauty can never be awakened.

By the writing of *The Devils*, the apocalyptic movement that began in *Crime and Punishment* and gathered momentum in *The Idiot* reaches national and international proportions. The narrative opens with a description of Stepan Trofimovich Verkhovensky, the "free thinker" of the 1840s, who is modeled on the famous Professor Timofey Granovsky and represented as "father" to the coming minions of the Antichrist, as progenitor of the "Time of Troubles" that begins two decades later. As a way into the mentality of those early years, when Dostoevsky himself fell under the sway of the liberal Belinsky and then the more radical Petrashevsky Circle (see Frank, *Seeds* 159–291), the narrator hilariously recounts a poem written by Stepan Trofimovich in his youth, a parody of the minor poet and one-time

---

[20] In the actual text from the "depths of Asia."

[21] See, e.g., letters of August 16, 1867–March 20, 1868 to A. Maykov in Dolinin II: 24–103.

liberal V. S. Pecherin.[22] But the humorous veil of parody is torn by a thrust of high seriousness when the reader suddenly realizes that the silly decorative image of a "youth of indescribable beauty [entering] on a black horse" (x: 10)[23] is in fact the Stavrogin of the 1860s. Like Stepan Trofimovich, the handsome and daring Stavrogin was modeled on a real-life figure of the 1840s, Nikolay Speshnev, a revolutionary of almost mesmerizing charm.[24] Significantly, the youth "depicts death, which all peoples are thirsting for" (x: 10).[25] In the characterization and field of action accorded to Stavrogin then, whose name, suggestive of the Antichrist, is a combination of *stavros* ("cross") and *rog* ("horn"), Dostoevsky takes the final step begun in the earlier works: he joins the image of the apocalyptic horseman with that of the coming revolution, and thereby makes explicit what had hitherto been largely implied. When later in the novel Pyotr Verkhovensky ecstatically identifies Stavrogin with "the leader of the flagellants, Ivan Filippovich, [who] had been seen ascending into heaven on a chariot before a multitude of people" (x: 326), we are confronted not only with a cherished folk image—the prophet Elijah (Ilya)—but, more importantly, with a Gogolian vision of horse-drawn deliverance, of movement up and out of this world and time. Dostoevsky's irony of course is that what for the benighted people appears to be a savior is in fact a parody, a mask, a straw man, and that what seems like an ascent into a better place and time is on the contrary a descent into revolution, chaos, death.

Dostoevsky's last significant use of the horse-and-rider motif comes in *The Adolescent* (1875), his penultimate novel. Arkady Dolgoruky, the title character, has a vision of Petersburg, the new Babylon, as it disappears into an abyss. All that remains of the city's original splendor is the striking outline of the bronze statue on the "hotly breathing, *driven* [*zagnannyi*] steed"

[22] Pecherin is the same "eschatologist" mentioned above in an earlier note (14). His polemic with the liberal Herzen over the significance of trains figures prominently in Lebedev's long digression on the Apocalypse in *The Idiot* (VIII: 305–16). See discussion below.

[23] In Pecherin's original the rider is, significantly, on a *white horse*. See his *Torzhestvo smerti*, in Ginzburg, *Poety 1820–1830-kh godov* II: 483.

[24] A number of commentators have also mentioned the name of the notorious anarchist Mikhail Bakunin in connection with Stavrogin.

[25] Dostoevsky seems to be playing off both Pecherin and the apocalyptic equine motif when he has Pyotr Verkhovensky link his idol Stavrogin with "the leader of the flagellants, Ivan Filippovich, [who] had been seen ascending into heaven on a chariot before a multitude of people" (x: 326). Pecherin also has waves of doom appear in "triumphant chariots" (*Torzhestvo* II: 483). Here the assumed patronymic "Filippovich" (son of Filip—"lover of horses") may be noteworthy when seen against the names of the two characters in *The Idiot* most influenced by the apocalyptic subtext—Nastasya *Filippovna* and *Ippolit* ("unleasher of horses"). To what extent Dostoevsky and his readers were aware of such Greek etymologies is, however, open to doubt. See below.

(XIII: 113)²⁶: Pushkin's steed, once a prime mover of Russia's imperial ambitions and a symbol of its national will, is being driven from the stage of Russian history (see Dolgopolov, "Roman A. Belogo" II: 219). To Dostoevsky at least, its time has come and gone. In the years to follow, as the "realistic" novel yields its position of privilege to shorter forms with their fin-de-siècle aesthetic and metaphysical concerns, the Symbolists will be responsible for an explosive proliferation of this same equine motif (see Chapter Two). But, closer to the coming revolution and consumed by an ever greater and more self-destructive urgency, they will reverse the formula and equate the soon-to-be-unleashed fury of the *narod* with the force of an avenging Bronze Horseman. Still employing the mythological imagery of Dostoevsky and his predecessors, they will stand his essentially conservative political worldview on its head. In Bely's *Petersburg* in particular, the ambiguous historical role of Peter—is he an authoritarian father-figure or a rebellious son?—will be seen as a chief source of apocalyptic tension, and the Bronze Horseman and the new Evgeny (Dudkin), as paternal and filial extensions of the same chaos, will join hands in a pact with universal death.²⁷

*The Idiot* is the first of Dostoevsky's novels, and indeed one of the first Russian novels,²⁸ in which the railroad assumes a significant role. The first railroad in Russia, a short line, had been opened between Petersburg and Tsarskoe Selo as early as 1837,²⁹ and Moscow was joined to Petersburg by

²⁶ On Dostoevsky's changing attitudes toward the mythical character of Petersburg, see Weidlé, *Zadacha* 203–27.

²⁷ On this tradition of a split role for the tsar, see Lotman and Uspenskii, "Spory o iazyke" 268–79.

²⁸ The only immediate impact of the first (St. Petersburg—Pavlovsk and Tsarskoe Selo) railway line on Russian "literature" was in the area of vaudeville: P. S. Fyodorov's "A Trip to Tsarskoe Selo by Railway" (performed seventeen times in Petersburg between 1838 and 1841). By the early 1840s, the theme of the railroad begins to appear elsewhere: e.g., V. A. Sollogub's "Adventures on the Railroad," a piece published in *The Dawn* (*Utrenniaia zaria*) for 1842. See Baehr, "The Troika and the Train." The train also plays a role in other works by Dostoevsky: see, e.g., its function in the pseudo-travelogue framework of *Winter Notes*. It of course begins to appear most prominently in works with a travel theme, such as Turgenev's *Smoke* (1867). For more on the railroad as a symbol of revolutionary change, see Al'tman, "Zheleznaia doroga."

²⁹ As one contemporary expressed it, this first railway was a "toy of the idle" going from "the capital to the pub [i.e., the 'Vauxhall' adjacent to the station in Pavlovsk]" (letter from N. N. Muravyov to Nicholas I of December 5, 1838, in M. Krutikov, ed., "Pervye zheleznye dorogi v Rossii," *Krasnyi arkhiv* 74 [1936]: 87, 127; cited in Baehr, "The Troika and the Train"). This *voksal* (later spelled *vokzal*) in Pavlovsk becomes an important part of the setting in *The Idiot*. Some of the nineteenth- and twentieth-century literary subtexts for the *vokzal* (leading up to Mandelshtam's poem "At the Station") are discussed in Ronen, *An Approach* xvii–xx, 290.

rail in 1851 (while Dostoevsky was still doing hard labor in Siberia). But it was only under Alexander II (ruled 1855–81) that Russian railroading developed in earnest. In 1856 construction was undertaken to extend rail lines from Petersburg both westward (to Europe) and eastward (to Siberia). In James Billington's words, "for Russia, the new railroads brought the first massive intrusion of mechanical force into the timeless, vegetative world of rural Russia, and a great increase in social and thus class mobility throughout the empire. . . . Railroads . . . became a symbol of progress to the new materialistic and egalitarian students of the sixties" (*The Icon and the Axe* 384).

We get some sense of the liberal intelligentsia's early naive faith in the machine (*mashina* meaning both "machine" in general and train in particular) and their attachment to it on the semantic level of such notions as "progress" and "usefulness" (*pol'za* was a term of special odium to Dostoevsky) from a lead essay written in 1839 by a certain A. Bashutsky for the journal *Notes of the Fatherland*:

> The application of steampower to movement over water and dry land, [and] the railroads, which are obliged to the steam engine for their miracles . . . these are the great forces stimulating growth in the physical and rational capabilities of man. . . . Movement is a given [*dvizhenie dano*], and the enlightened world cannot stop; it must continue always to move forward; success is essential; its is a status that is compulsory [*vynuzhdennoe*], already unalterable, a basic condition for existence.
>
> It is in vain that we would begin now to judge and pontificate at random—this is not the time to heed the cries of fear and indignation, the gloomy predictions of old men, the irrational assumptions of the short-sighted and the ignorant: the shining core [or nucleus: *svetiashchee iadro*] has been set in motion, it flies on, swallowing space and illuminating cities, seas, and deserts beneath itself. And peoples, who have been separated from one another for a long time and perhaps at odds, can [now] be tightly joined together by the bonds of fellow-feeling and mutual interest" ("Parovye mashiny" 6).

This view of the train as a vehicle capable of penetrating not only hitherto unreachable geographical but also social or class boundaries will be taken up from the first pages of *The Idiot*, where a prince, a merchant's son, and a down-and-out government official meet in a third class coach of the Warsaw-Petersburg express. Here high class meets low, East (Russian native traditions) meets West (Poland, Europe, Dostoevsky's hated Roman Catholicism) in that raucous, melting-pot atmosphere of "polyphony" described by Bakhtin (*Problemy* 5–53).[30] The literal terminus for all this movement, both physical and dialogic, is the station, the place in *The Idiot* that frames or is the site of numerous scandal scenes.

The railroads became then a question of vital interest to the liberals of the 1840s (Belinsky being their chief spokesman) and, more centrally, to the "enlighteners" of the 1860s (Chernyshevsky, Dobrolyubov, Pisarev).[31] In his memoir of Belinsky, Dostoevsky recalled how the famous critic met him once in the late 1840s near the Znamenskaya Church and led him to the construction site of the new Nikolaevsky Station (XXI: 12). The two talked about the future of railroading, about how trains would change the economic face of Russia through their rapid and cost-efficient distribution of commodities such as timber. But the context and setting of this remembered conversation are curious. As the same episode is recounted in the drafts of *The Devils* (X: 73), it is Belinsky's atheism, his sarcastic attempts to "convert" the young Dostoevsky, who was still impressionable and deeply attached to his naive ideal of Christ, that triggers the recollection of the talk about railroading, which follows immediately.[32] In this respect, Belinsky's (and the young Dostoevsky's) "progress" from church to station

[30] A good example of the social and linguistic melting-pot associated with first-, second-, and third-class railroad travel is found in a "physiological sketch" published by an anonymous author ("S") in vol. 54 of the journal *The Contemporary* (*Sovremennik*) for 1855: "The Railroad between Petersburg and Moscow" 43–71. Here the train is repeatedly referred to as a new and potentially perilous *mashina*; there is a sense of bustle and rapid mindless movement as the passengers board the train at the station and say farewell to friends and relatives; and within the different class coaches social boundaries are continually threatened and traduced. Confusion reigns above all in the second-class coach because the passengers don't know how to deal with competing views of difference/equality: one woman, for instance, is angry because she is forced to occupy space that is shared by charwomen, whereas a man nearby complains that, though "we are all equal here" (51), a young dandy has taken the liberty to smoke.

[31] As Nikolay Kibalchich, one of the technophiles of the 1860s who would eventually become a revolutionary and plot the 1881 attempt on Alexander II's life, exclaimed: "For Russia railroads are everything. This is the most necessary, most vital problem of our time. *Covering Russia by sections with an interconnected network of railroads* such as exists for example in England, we shall prosper and blossom forth [with] unheard-of progress" (cited in Billington, *Icon* 383; my emphasis). Cf. this passage with the digression by Lebedev (VIII: 305–16).

[32] For Dostoevsky's very ambivalent feelings toward Belinsky, see Frank, *Seeds* 172–98. "If Belinsky had not really introduced Dostoevsky to Socialism, he had introduced him to *atheistic* Socialism—and this was the only kind that the Dostoevsky of the 1870s believed to be spiritually honest and intellectually self-consistent. . . . The mechanical 'scientific' materialism that Belinsky admired in Littré did succeed in becoming the philosophical dogma of the Russian Left for much of Dostoevsky's life. And moral values were derived from a utilitarian egoism which, if it stemmed more directly from Bentham than from Max Stirner, fully shared the latter's supreme contempt for all sentimental humanitarianism. . . . Dostoevsky thus had good reason to regard his disputes with Belinsky as having foreshadowed the major issues posed by the later development of Russian socio-political and cultural life; and his encounter with Belinsky certainly colored his own reaction to such changes" (196–97).

may be relevant, suggesting that homage at a traditional temple was being undermined and replaced by homage at a new and more modern place of worship. Whatever the precise meaning of these events, after his years in Siberia and his genuine conversion (in a direction that would have made Belinsky turn in his grave), Dostoevsky did come to associate the railroad with the spread of atheism and the spirit of the Antichrist. This new awareness is demonstrated in *The Idiot* on many occasions.

At the same time that the train as a symbol of progress and mechanical force was being viewed with an optimism bordering on euphoria by Belinsky and his followers, it was being viewed with anxiety and skepticism by those of a more conservative stripe (the *"old* men," with their *"irrational* assumptions," in the passage quoted above).[33] If the horse had ties to an older agrarian or nomadic view of the world, one in which the controlling hand, either at the plow or in the saddle, belonged to an *individual*, then the train had ties not only with the concept of newness and progress but with that of *collective* movement. The reins of fate, as it were, were taken out of the individual's hands and given back to the (mechanical) beast; the lone rider on his steed or the lone peasant urging on his work horse in the field became the group of passengers, the societal microcosm, being driven by the train. As Prince Vyazemsky, Pushkin's old friend, wrote in 1847, "Railroads have already annihilated, and in time shall completely annihilate, all previous means of transportation. *Other fires, other steams have long ago put out the fire of the winged horse"* (PSS II: 353). Dostoevsky himself, in a heavily satiric piece entitled "On the Road" (1874), made the mythic connection between the folkloric steed that was by then all but extinct as a major mode of public conveyance and the iron steed that had come to replace it: "I have in mind the road [traversed by means] of steam, [that of] the train and the steamship. As one peasant recently expressed it, we, the inhabitants of capitals, have begun to forget completely the roads of former times, the roads 'driven by horse' " (XXI: 159).[34]

It is also true that Dostoevsky was never narrowly consistent. His view of the railroad could be either xenophobic and negative or jingoistic and positive, depending on whether he was looking toward Europe, where, as

[33] In order to calm the fears of those who felt that this mechanical intrusion would destroy faith, Russian railway officials were compelled to hang icons in terminals, to build railroad lines to or near monasteries, and, in the case of the Trans-Siberian Railway, to include a church car with bells and a cross on top (Baehr, "Troika and Train"; see also Massie, *Land of the Firebird* 174, 376).

[34] Cf. Gleb Uspensky's article on the "Suburban Peasant": "Yes, doesn't the same fate sooner or later await the most remote Russian backwater [*medvezhii ugol*] that has already happened in these parts [i.e., the Novgorod province]? Sooner or later a stone and, perhaps, an iron road will proceed through these quiet parts where recently a witch was burned" (PSS VI: 469–70).

we learn from an important passage in *The Idiot*, the network of railroad lines was poisoning the "waters of life" (Revelation 7:17, 8:10, 21:6), or whether he was looking toward home, where for political reasons the training of "practical" railroad personnel and the construction of more efficient and extensive lines needed to be made a national priority.[35] Still, Dostoevsky's letters and journalism, while often supplying the source material and point of departure for a theme, are not the same as his art, where that theme may be reworked according to a wholly new set of demands. What, on balance, can be said is that the "Slavophile"[36] Dostoevsky of the late 1860s and 1870s was genuinely concerned by the inroads of Western materialism into the "organic" world of the *narod*, and that he "novelized" this abstract fear with the help of a concrete image for time (inroad = railroad). His thoughts would probably have been very close to those of a rector of the Riga Theological Seminary, who when asked in 1872 to bless a new railroad bridge expressed the following doubts: "Will it [the new route] not be in part the expeditor of that would-be civilization, which under the guise of false all-humanity and common brotherhood of all . . . destroys . . . true humanity, true brotherhood?" (cited in Billington, *Icon* 382.)[37]

No discussion of railroading in the context of *The Idiot* would be complete without brief mention of that other great novel of the period in which the contest between competing loves (erotic-maternal) launches the heroine on an "iron path" to suicide.[38] *Anna Karenina* (1873–77) was written just a

[35] See letter of March 20, 1868 to A. Maykov in Dolinin II: 96–103. Cf. beginning of Part Three of final version of *The Idiot* (VIII: 268–70), where the narrator bewails the lack of "practical" railroad men and extends the analogy to families (e.g., the Yepanchins) who have "slipped off the rails."

[36] Although Dostoevsky could not be called a Slavophile in a narrow chronological sense, he did derive a number of his most cherished ideas from their movement and came to see himself, as letters to Maykov indicate, squarely within their tradition. His hatred of Roman Catholic authority ("unity without freedom") in the West and of the Roman juridical tradition that had developed there into "legalistic" niggling over rights ("individual over community") as well as his advocacy of the "Russian idea" of *sobornost'* ("free unity") and of Russia's privileged position in history owe much to the writings of Ivan Kireevsky, Khomyakov, and others. On the difference between Dostoevsky and the traditional Slavophiles, see Kirpotin, *Dostoevskii* 73–90.

[37] Apparently the Metropolitan of Moscow had a similar reaction to the proposed railroad line from Moscow to the Trinity-Sergius Monastery: "Pilgrims would come to the monastery in railroad cars, on which all sorts of tales can be heard and often dirty stories, whereas now they come on foot, and each step is a feat pleasing to God" (Del'vig, *Vospominaniia* III: 29; trans. in Westwood, *A History of Russian Railways* 45). Cf. the conservative Leontiev's fear of corrupt Western values as expressed in a train metaphor: "And may the raging and thundering train of the West hurtle past us into the abyss of social anarchy" (cited in Levitskii, *Ocherki* 126).

[38] Both the train ride and steeplechase scenes in *Anna Karenina* have been discussed often. See, e.g., Al'tman, *Chitaia Tolstogo* 111, and "Zheleznaia doroga"; Browning, "The Death of

few years after *The Idiot*, and it is noteworthy, if not remarkable, that Tolstoy resorts to precisely the same symbol complex (the train, the horse) to prefigure Anna's ruin. Although the styles, subjects, and worldviews implicit in the "realisms" of Tolstoy and Dostoevsky are versts apart, the great chronicler of Russia's aging patriarchal order and aristocratic *moeurs* was as deeply concerned as Dostoevsky about the erosion of traditional values and as anxious to find a way, in novelistic terms, to express the momentum of this deterioration. Tolstoy's remarks to Turgenev, in a letter of April 1857, show to what extent his feelings toward the railroad anticipate the ideational structure of both his and Dostoevsky's novels: "the railroad has the same relationship to travel as a brothel does to love: just as convenient but just as *inhumanly mechanical* and *murderously monotonous*" (Tolstoi, *Perepiska* 95; my emphasis). Like Dostoevsky, Tolstoy frames his heroine's story, the beginning and end of her "journey," with pivotal scenes at the train station. Anna first meets Vronsky at the station in Moscow and is frightened ("It is a bad omen" [Maude 60]) by the death of the watchman that anticipates her own. On her return trip to Petersburg, she falls into a dangerously impressionable state in which the snowstorm raging outside the coach mirrors her inner turmoil and, pursued by Vronsky, gives him the hope he seeks; on this same trip she also has her first dream of the peasant who is associated with a dreadful squeaking and clattering sound and with someone "being torn to pieces" (93) and who reappears at the rails at the moment of her suicide. Even her son Seryozha, the chief victim of the affair, is figuratively drawn into it when, abandoned by his mother, he is told by his tutor not to play the "dangerous game" of railways (658).

As in the case of Nastasya Filippovna, there is something both noble and pathetic in Anna's dilemma; she too is a victim of her own life force and sexuality, of a "fall" that divides her biography into a once meaningful "before" and a now unanchored, chaotic "after." In some sense she is the embodiment of Russia herself, with her "excess vitality" (56), at a crossroads of history, but this same vitality becomes her undoing when its sole outlet is mediated by the Western values of Petersburg high society. Tolstoy's placing of *French* words, the language of Anna's circle, in the mouth of the terrifying *native* peasant of her dreams is additional evidence of how confused her value system has become. In the moments leading up to her suicide Anna's eyes are riveted to one image: the large iron wheels (692, 694, 695), which, moving pitilessly along the rails, are both the instrument of her death and a constant reminder of the vicious circle of her love ("Then, realizing that in her attempts to quiet herself [in Vronsky's absence] she

---

Anna Karenina"; Christian, *Tolstoy* 204–7; Jahn, "The Image of the Railroad"; Muchnic, *Russian Writers* 134; and Wasiolek, *Tolstoy's Major Fiction* 134ff.

again *completed the circle* she had gone round so often, and had returned to her former cause of irritation [i.e., jealousy], she was horror-struck at herself" [671]).

This confusion as to the past, tradition, "Russianness" itself, is further reinforced in the famous episode at the races. Here, rather than Levin's massive, plodding work horses, we find highstrung thoroughbreds gathered for society's entertainment. These latter perform no vital function in Russia's agrarian life, but, for the sheer sport of it, are made to endanger themselves and their riders by leaping a series of artificial obstacles along an elliptical track. Vronsky's horse, a mare, is given the French name Frou-Frou (which, in terms of sound repetition, suggests a foreign version of *Anna*)[39] and several other traits (unruly mane, excitability, sparkling eyes, "thoroughbred quality" [166]) obviously reminiscent of the heroine. Vronsky breaks the back of his favorite horse just as his self-centered Western values, his relentless amorous attentions followed by his equally inevitable cooling, will eventually crush Anna. In various ways, he is unable "to keep pace" (Blackmur, "The Dialectic" 907). Although he tries to legitimize their relationship as best he can given the fact that he knows only how to run "unalterably and inevitably along . . . [the] customary rails of social and regimental connections and interests" (158), his love affair with Anna is no more than an exhibition, a thrilling contest set in a closed, and ultimately deadly circle with no other goal in sight save an arbitrary finish line. Thus Tolstoy, like Dostoevsky, prefigures his heroine's doom through a series of mechanical and equine images of relentless movement in a novel far more symbolically patterned than earlier works. For manifest aesthetic and philosophical reasons, he does not mention the apocalypse in this context, nor does his novel in any explicit way suggest a transfiguration of the biblical plot. Nevertheless, the structural parallels between *The Idiot* and *Anna Karenina*, especially the way in which a thematic motif is gradually transformed into a "world picture" of Russian history in crisis, are profound and worthy of closer study.

The scene that opens *The Idiot* is sufficiently dramatic to attract the attention of any reader, and one must assume that this was Dostoevsky's primary intention.[40] But the drama here, involving Myshkin, Rogozhin, and Lebedev, also sets up a metaphysical pro and contra that the author, a past

---

[39] As Eikhenbaum (*Lev Tolstoi* 190) has shown, the name Frou-Frou appears to have originated from a popular French play of the same name by Henri Meilhac and Ludvic Halévy. Published in 1869, it dramatizes the plight of a heroine who abandons her husband and son for a lover.

[40] See R. Miller's perceptive comments on Dostoevsky's various narrative strategies in *Dostoevsky and "The Idiot"* 11–45 and 223–31.

master of the use of mystery and tension in narrative form, knew he would
have to resolve at some later point. The visual field of the narrative is immediately dominated by Myshkin and Rogozhin, who are seated "opposite
one another" (*drug protiv druga*) at the same time that they are bound by
a hidden kinship through the anaphoric use of "both" (*oba*):

> Two passengers had found themselves sitting *opposite one another*
> by the window of one of the third-class compartments since day-
> break—*both* of them young men, *both* traveling light, *both* far from
> fashionably dressed, *both* of rather striking appearance, and, finally,
> *both* anxious to start a conversation *with one another*. Had they
> known what was so extraordinary about them at this moment, they
> would no doubt have been surprised that chance should have strangely
> placed them *opposite one another* in a third-class compartment of the
> Warsaw-Petersburg train (Mag 27; VIII: 5; my emphasis)

Here at the very outset we find an unmistakable shaping of the story to
come. The narrator's admission that "Had they known what was so extraordinary about them at this moment" and that "chance should have strangely
placed them opposite one another" implies that the meeting is pregnant
with possibility and that significant happenings are in store. The superficial
comparison of these young men, so alike at the first sweep of the narrative
eye (the "both"), will soon recede before the more important *differences* of
character that set the story in motion. The arrangement of Myshkin and
Rogozhin in the space of the coach suggests what the narrative will soon
bear out: they are, as it were, metaphysical Siamese twins, unable to move
without straining the painful integumentary seam of their different loves
for Nastasya Filippovna. They want to talk, to enter into discourse "with
one another," but a communality of words will always elude them. In this
sense, their stance will remain, as Bakhtin would argue, dialogic, "one
against the other" (*drug protiv druga*).

Nevertheless, the function and ultimate purpose of this dialogic relationship is *not* to keep conversation (and narration) "open." It is an "opening"
and "openness" only *for a time*, since what begins here starts the process
toward the closure, the total blackout and eerie silence, of Nastasya Filippovna's death. In this initial meeting of the heroes, as in the final one at her
deathbed, the heroine is mentioned in absentia. And indeed, the Nastasya
Filippovna for whom Myshkin and Rogozhin compete will never be fully
present either as her "ideal" or as her "real" self, but will always be caught
somewhere in between. Perhaps most telling, the bustling, volatile movement of this beginning, which the train embodies ("The Warsaw train was
approaching Petersburg at full speed" [Mag 27; VIII: 5]) and by which Nas-

tasya Filippovna comes to be constantly driven,[41] disappears in the end of the novel: the terminus so painfully sought after will at last be reached, and the heroes, this time with desperate gestures revealing the failure of words, will once again sit down "opposite one another" (Mag 652; VIII: 503) to contemplate the fate of their sleeping beauty. All this is not of course to suggest that Dostoevsky had the ending of his novel in mind when he wrote the beginning. Such an argument would be another instance of literally "getting ahead of ourselves" where the history of the text does not warrant it (see Hollander, "The Apocalyptic Framework" 123–31). It would be more accurate to say that the relationship between Myshkin and Rogozhin initiated on these rails is bound to lead somewhere, and, as the narrative progresses, a conclusion, not inconsistent with what has come before, gradually emerges.

The role of the train in this opening scene is first of all realistic. It provides a place for these three characters to meet and carries them to Petersburg, one of the novel's two primary settings. Along with other features, it also gives the novel a stamp of "modernity." But its figurative function for the novel's subsequent development is no less important. It brings a Russian who knows nothing of his country's present into contact with a Russian who lives fully in, and is a product of, that present. (Lebedev's role in the opening is significant, as indeed it will be later on, for as go-between and "know-it-all" [vseznaika] he is able to supply information of which the innocent Myshkin is unaware and which the sullen Rogozhin would be apt to withhold.) The prince comes from a romantic Switzerland—not the object of derision found in Dostoevsky's letters, but a land of waterfalls, mountain vistas, and the pathetic "fairy tale" about Marie.[42] Dostoevsky thus creates the narrative effect of dropping a hero onto earth from another planet. An orphan in various senses, Myshkin has no past continuous with the present—his bout with epilepsy and gradual recovery in a foreign country constitute a temporal vacuum which others might fill with memories of youth. He is, we might say, a character of beginnings (he offers Nastasya Filippovna "new life") and ends (he is obsessed by thoughts of execution and death), but never of any continuous middle. He cannot "develop" in any traditional sense because he is Christ-like and "positively beautiful" to begin with.[43] Also, because he is the last of an aristocratic line without any

[41] When outlining in his notebooks scenes involving Nastasya Filippovna, Dostoevsky returns repeatedly to the word beg—"flight"—and its variants.

[42] On a possible Rousseau connection in The Idiot, see Ar. Kovac, "Genezis."

[43] It is one of the fascinating vagaries associated with this novel, which went through eight drafts, that the "Idiot" of the early versions had a cruel and vindictive streak not inconsistent with the character of a typical Dostoevskian anti-hero. These traits were later dispersed among other characters, including Ganya Ivolgin, Rogozhin, and Ippolit, while the idea of a troubled

means—that is, sexual potency—of extending it, his very genealogy, and
the historical future of his kind, must be brought in question. Like Christ
who is sent into time by God, the prince is sent into the "moment" of the
story by his author to explain to the other characters that there are meaningful beginnings and ends beyond the aimless flux of the middle. That is
to say, Myshkin, according to our typology for apocalyptic fiction, is that
"messenger" figure come, as it were, from another space-time to deliver his
"revelation" to those trapped in this world (see Introduction).

Rogozhin, on the other hand, is the essence of the struggling middle that
Dostoevsky identified with human nature at the bier of his first wife. His
family has links with the Old Believers, those vociferous advocates of religious tradition and opponents of the Petrine Antichrist.[44] Moreover, the
greed of the father is visited on the son in the form of possessive sexual
passion. The father's death, retold in the context of Rogozhin's attempts to
buy Nastasya Filippovna with diamond earrings, inspires no real change in
the status quo but only effects a transfer of money from one generation to
the next. Taken together, these legacies serve to mire Rogozhin in the continuous present. Both as actual mode of conveyance with a geographical
destination and as chronotopic symbol for movement with no higher goal
beyond itself, the train is a logical site for this confrontation. Not only does
it join opposing concepts of space (the prince's idyllic Switzerland versus
Rogozhin's capitalistic Petersburg), but, more significantly, it joins opposing concepts of time (the beginning and end beyond history versus the middle that is synonymous with it).

Throughout Part One the train continues to be used as a framing device
with thematic import. As we learn from Myshkin himself when he retells
his experiences in Switzerland to the Yepanchin sisters, the period of his
"new life" began the moment he left the waterfall, the children, and the
memories of Marie behind and boarded the train for Russia: "As I sat in the
train [*vagon*], I thought: 'Now I'm going among people; I may not know
anything, but a new life has begun for me.' . . . When I had taken my seat
in the carriage and the train started, they [the children] all shouted 'Hurrah!' and stayed on the platform until the train was out of sight" (Mag 102–

---

but at heart magnanimous youth would have to wait for the character of Arkady Dolgoruky in
*The Adolescent*. For a full and informed treatment of the notebooks, see R. Miller, *Dostoevsky
and "The Idiot."*

[44] The name "Rogozhin" suggests "burlap" or "burlap sack" (*rogozha*), perhaps an allusion
to the character's working class origins. See Peace's interesting observations on the link between Rogozhin's name and the sect of schismatics (*Dostoyevsky* 86). I disagree with Peace
that the clues to a Castrate-inspired fanaticism within the Rogozhin family imply *sexual* sterility. There is the implication of sterility to be sure; however, what is sterile is not the passion
*per se*, but rather its possessiveness, its underlying spiritual greed, and its ultimate self-de-
structiveness.

3; VIII: 64–65). And as he goes on to exclaim in almost the same breath, "Listen, when I came in here a short while ago and looked at your dear faces . . . and heard your first words, I couldn't help thinking that perhaps I am lucky, for, you see, I know you don't often meet people to whom you take a liking at once, but I met you as soon as I left the train" (Mag 103; VIII: 65). In this rapid file of impressions, the train functions as a kind of time machine, moving the hero from an idyllic[45] and now separate past of happy endings (the children shouting "Hurrah!") to an uncertain, but still hope-filled present (the "new life" associated with the Yepanchin daughters and the child-like Lizaveta Prokofyevna). It is also noteworthy that the story of Marie, with its disturbed and guilt-ridden heroine finally finding forgive-ness through Myshkin, is an obvious template for the story of Nastasya Filippovna to come.[46] Here difference seems to outweigh similarity, how-ever: the setting (time-place) of the new heroine's tragic story will be con-temporary Petersburg. When later in Part One the prince meets Nastasya Filippovna face to face, he is drawn to recount, in the manner of a preface, how her story first came to his attention *on a train*: " 'Early this morning, in the train, before I arrived in Petersburg, Parfyon Rogozhin told me a lot about you' " (Mag 134; VIII: 89). The end of one love story and the begin-ning of another are therefore fused in the motif of the train.

The image of the apocalyptic steed also makes its first elliptical appearance in Part One. The heroine's full name is Nastasya (from Anastasya— "woman returned to life") Filippovna (daughter of Filip—"lover of horses") Barashkova (from *barashek*—"lamb"). She is, furthermore, the only major character whose story remained essentially intact from Dostoev-sky's various plans to the final version, a fact indicative of the author's sharply focused and unwavering conception of her from beginning to end (Wasiolek, *The Notebooks* 10–12). As it turns out, her given name involves a bitter irony: like the Mary Magdalene on which she and Marie are mod-eled, she wants desperately to be returned to (prelapsarian) life, to that in-nocent condition existing at Otradnoe before the "fall" at the hands of Totsky[47]; her patronymic, however, binds her to an inherited passion for horses, that is, to an urge to incorporate into her life story the speedy and

---

[45] This is not to say that nothing "evil" happens in the story of Marie. She is ostracized by the moralists of the village and taunted (at first) by the children. But, against the background of the Swiss countryside, this story comes to have a happy ending—Marie's fallen state is redeemed by her prince's kiss; both are united with the children; and she dies in a state of bliss.

[46] For more on the similarities and differences in the *telling* of the Marie and Nastasya Filip-povna stories, and the implication this has for the dialogic structure of the novel, see Ar. Kovac, "The Poetics of *The Idiot*."

[47] The estate has definite associations with an Edenic paradise. See Holquist, *Dostoevsky* 115.

inevitable means to its apocalyptic end.[48] Unlike Marie, Myshkin's other heroine cannot separate the guilt of her past from the continuous present. And so, like the lamb of her surname, she remains forever a sacrificial victim awaiting Rogozhin's knife.[49] When, at the conclusion of Part One, she refuses the prince's proposal (the "new life" she desires), leaves her birthday party (an occasion signifying a return to origins and lost innocence), and flees with Rogozhin in a flurry of troikas to a "terrible orgy at the Yekaterinhof Station" (Mag 208, 210; VIII: 148, 150), her future assumes a definite shape for the first time. The repeated references to her as a "lost" or "doomed" woman (*pogibshaia zhenshchina*)[50] make the connection clear. Thus while the favorite animal of the "Prince Christ" is the ass (*osel*), the alter-ego in the animal world for the frantically driven and ultimately suicidal Nastasya Filippovna is the horse.[51]

The first half of Part Two (Chapters 1–5) takes place in Petersburg; the second half (Chapters 6–12) takes place in Pavlovsk, a "green world" of dachas and country living outside the city. In each of the first three parts of the final version of the novel Dostoevsky begins with prominent mention

[48] See Peace (*Dostoyevsky* 84) on the connection between the Flagellants and her patronymic. She is referred to always by her given name *and* patronymic, whereas Aglaya is referred to simply by her given name. It may seem at first glance far-fetched to interpret the *Greek* etymology of the heroine's patronymic (see note 25 above). What meaning could that have for Dostoevsky and his reader? On the other hand, Nastasya Filippovna is repeatedly associated with a carriage drawn by white horses (VIII: 250, 253–54, 262), Ippolit in his doomed life appears to be living up to the activities of his namesake (see note 65 below), and Ivan Filippovich, the leader of the Flagellants mentioned in *The Devils*, is reported to have been seen ascending into the sky in a chariot: all this suggests that Dostoevsky may well have been aware of the etymology. A decoding of Stavrogin's name (Gr. *stavros* = "cross" + Russ. *rog* = "horn") also involves a Greek etymology.

[49] As early as Part One Nastasya Filippovna says that Ganya would "slit her throat like a ram" (VIII: 137); in Part Two Rogozhin speaks of Nastasya Filippovna's marriage as "going under the knife" and laughs convulsively when he hears Myshkin's anecdote about the peasant who "butchered his friend like a ram" over a gold watch (VIII: 179, 183). See below.

[50] See VIII: 148–49. It is intriguing that Myshkin is also alluded to in this context as "a man [who is] cultured, but doomed" (Mag 201; VIII: 142).

[51] Also offering additional grounds for assuming a proto-apocalyptic framework for the novel *before* Part Two is the presence of the secondary character Princess Belokonskaya ("White Horse"). First referred to in the notebooks innocuously as "the aunt" (IX: 354), and remaining offstage in the final version until near the end of the novel, where she passes judgment on the prince (VIII: 459), she is seen as the chief patroness of the Yepanchin family and guiding spirit of the *beau monde*. It seems more than chance that the author, who was sensitive to the nomenclatural level of his art, would choose a character with this name to be society's keeper. It is Belokonskaya's daughter whom General Ivolgin, a notoriously unreliable narrator, claims to have insulted while traveling on a train, and it is this same little anecdote, told by the general, that provokes his cry of *svetoprestavlenie* (literally "doomsday" [VIII: 94]) and that initiates the scandal scene culminating in Ganya Ivolgin's slapping Myshkin in the face.

of the train, but it is in the early chapters of Part Two that the image and its surrounding context take on marked apocalyptic overtones (Hollander, "The Apocalyptic Framework" 131). Now, prepared by the wild conclusion to Part One, the reader witnesses a tangible *foreshortening* of those options only recently open to Myshkin and the other characters. If the effect of his Christian goodness and unwillingness to judge was heretofore an "open book," from this point on we can sense a definite and ominous narrowing in his story. In addition, the ending, with explicit reference to Rogozhin's knife, is alluded to for the first time.

This new narrowing of possibilities is most keenly felt when the hero, having visited, in a six-month interval, other parts of Russia and mixed with the *narod*, begins to act in a manner qualitatively different from what we have come to expect. Suddenly he is given an all-too-human trait—he is able to judge. In his mind he imputes evil intentions to Rogozhin that then—quite in accordance with the law of the Dostoevskian world which stipulates that the reality of thought is prior to that of action—materialize. The fact that Myshkin does not *want* to judge his "brother" and indeed tries every means to repress his fear is of no matter, since the thought *exists*. It is as if the two temporalities associated with Myshkin and Rogozhin, which in Part One were perceived as separate and counterbalancing, have been conflated within one consciousness, brought together and applied as a dual optic through which to interpret the meaning, the *causality*, of events. The result is a combined sense of prescience and modal disorientation (a "revelation") as to which point of view should be determining our response. This disorientation begins at the train station and thereafter continually reasserts itself there. Hence rather than the distinct messenger of biblical revelation who delivers knowledge of a higher design to a member of the elect, Myshkin becomes both messenger from beyond *and* victim (and *victimizer!*) within history. This is an extraordinary gambit on Dostoevsky's part, for now his "positively good" hero, without any particular motivation, is seen as not only incapable of healing those sick at heart but as actually contributing to their affliction with his benignly discontinuous spatio-temporal model. In fact, he himself seems strangely prone to ambient infection. (The prince's sudden vulnerability to the wages of a continuous, postlapsarian temporality is most obvious, as shall be seen, in the first appearance of his special affliction, the "falling sickness.") To be sure, Myshkin is not now, nor will he ever be, fully dimensionalized as a fallible human character; it is simply that an important, if incremental, first step has been taken in that direction. In any event, while the question of causality remains moot, one could argue that the hero's flawed perception, his "judgment" of his friend, is brought on by the excitability preceding an epileptic attack. As Dostoevsky explained to his niece in an oft-quoted letter written on the eve of his work on Part Two, "The main idea of the novel is the depiction of a positively good man. There is nothing on earth more difficult than that, and especially *nowadays*" (letter of January 1, 1868 in Dolinin, II: 71; my emphasis). It is at this juncture in the novel that the "nowadays," the forceful and combative voice of the 1860s, begins to take the upper hand in its dialogue with the positively good Myshkin and his ecstatic temporality.

The change in the prince's character generates an attendant shift in narrative momentum, and this shift is in turn announced through a constellation of interrelated motifs. These motifs are not merely atmospheric; they attach themselves to specific temporal categories (past, present, future) and to their narrative counterparts (beginning, middle, end). They can be summarized as follows: the garden (*sad*)—past/beginning; the railroad (*zheleznaia doroga*) and the machine (*mashina*)—present/middle; and the station (*vokzal*) and the knife (*nozh*)—future/end. As the temporalities represented by Myshkin and Rogozhin meet once more and clash, there is, not unexpectedly, a certain semantic overlap. The machine, for example, can suggest both the engine/train motif *and* the guillotine/knife motif. That is to say, it can serve to introduce the meaning of future/end into the context of present/middle. Or the knife can be of the "garden" variety, thereby fusing in one semantic unit notions of past/beginning and future/end. This obviously makes for a difficult and in some ways confused narrative, but one entirely adequate to the larger task of "revealing" the hero's dilemma in terms of temporal disjunction—both we and the hero must ask: in *which* time is my story unfolding? Dostoevsky often returns to these motifs to create a sense of mounting tension; they will culminate in Rogozhin's attempt on Myshkin's life at the conclusion of Chapter 5. With regard to narrative structure, the attempt to end Myshkin's life is also coterminous with a temporary end to the Petersburg chapters—immediately thereafter the story resumes in a strikingly different setting, at Pavlovsk.

Part Two begins with a brief recapitulation of the happenings at Yekaterinhof Station that framed the climax of Part One (VIII: 151).[52] In this prefatory first chapter we also learn of the existence of a suitor for Adelaida Yepanchina, a certain Prince Shch., who pursues what is "useful"—*poleznyi*, always a suspect word in Dostoevsky's vocabulary—and who has been engaged in the "planning of one of the most important of the newly projected railroad lines" (Mag 216; VIII: 154, 155). Just a few pages later the generation of the 1860s is caricatured in the person of Lebedev's nephew:

[52] Dostoevsky enjoined himself repeatedly in his notebooks to resume the narrative "at the station." See IX: 220, 224, 228, 230, 234, 356, 360. It seems significant that his first mention of the Apocalypse in the notebooks takes place on the next page of the same March 11, 1868 entry in which the "scene at the station" is outlined (IX: 221).

this peevish young man turns out to be an outspoken atheist who supports himself by working on the railroad (VIII: 162). The third such occurrence takes place two chapters later when Myshkin explains to Rogozhin how an atheist he met on a train managed to miss the point in his condemnation of religion: "he didn't seem to be talking about that [i.e., God]" (Mag 251; VIII: 182). Thematically interrelated, these three episodes establish a kind of genetic bond in the reader's mind between the religious (i.e., atheistic) and political (i.e., rationally self-serving) ideas of the 1860s, on the one hand, and the spatio-temporal metaphor for their dissemination, on the other.

As soon as the prince returns to Petersburg at the beginning of Chapter Two, he feels a strange, piercing glance coming from somewhere in the crowd at the station:

> Two or three days after the Yepanchins had left for Pavlovsk, Prince Lev Nikolaevich Myshkin arrived from Moscow by the morning train. No one met him at the station, but as he left the train, the prince suddenly became aware of two strange, burning eyes staring at him. . . . When he looked more attentively, he could no longer see anything. Of course he had only imagined that he had seen those eyes, but it left a disagreeable impression. Besides, the prince, as it was, was pensive and sad and seemed to be worried about something (Mag 220–221; VIII: 158).

What is curious about this passage is that the eyes, which seem to burn into Myshkin's soul and read his thoughts, are present *before* he actually judges Rogozhin (cf. VIII: 171). They are evidence both of his coming guilt and impressionable pre-epileptic state (the two, to repeat, are not mutually exclusive, but may be seen as different, contemporaneous aspects of the same phenomenon—Myshkin's imminent "fall"). Equally noteworthy is the setting of this inchoate guilt and physical affliction. Unlike the motif that brought Myshkin and Rogozhin *together* at the outset of Part One, the station is now the location where *alienation* between friends, brought about by the prince's rival love for Nastasya Filippovna and Rogozhin's jealousy, is underscored. It is no longer the place for a *first* entrance from afar, but is the frame for an arrival with an existing "pre-history"; the hero's notion of time, with its a priori rejection of judgment and of a present continuous with the past (the eyes are "of course . . . only imagined"), has become implicated in the time of his foil, with its rejection of forgiveness and of a present without prior, ulterior motives (the actual awareness of the "strange, burning eyes"). Depending on *whose* eyes are viewing this return, Myshkin's appearance at the station is either innocent or cynical, disarming or threatening.

From the station Myshkin proceeds to Lebedev's house. There he meets the entire Lebedev household, including the buffoonish widower himself. Lebedev's role appears to have expanded since Part One. Now, despite his constant lying and pulling of faces, he makes statements that must, in this context, be taken seriously. He claims that the nephew's insistence on personal rights rather than on mercy is tantamount to committing the Zhemarin murders, for that is where such logic leads. Then he speaks, in another access of seriocomic hyperbole, of the death of Countess Du Barry on the guillotine. These comments are particularly telling: they recall Myshkin's story of the condemned man in Part One, when the Yepanchin sisters were told how it would feel to experience time at the moment of death and to hear overhead "the iron come slithering down." At this moment, Myshkin had mused, one's brain operates like "an engine [literally *mashina*— 'machine'] going at full speed" (Mag 92; VIII: 56). Lebedev's reading of this experience is remarkably similar to that of the prince: "Seeing that he [the executioner] was bending her neck down under the knife and kicking her from behind . . . she began screaming: '*Encore un moment, monsieur le bourreau, encore un moment!*' . . . And for that little moment the Lord will perhaps pardon her, for a greater *misère* than that it is impossible to imagine for the human soul" (Mag 228; VIII: 164).

It is directly after this outburst that Lebedev accompanies the prince into the garden[53] and tells him of the present condition of Nastasya Filippovna:

> "Tell me, how did you leave her?"
>
> "She was after something." ["*I-iskatel'na.*"]
>
> "After something?"
>
> "I mean, she seemed to be looking for something, just as if she had lost something. [. . .] She's restless, sarcastic, double-faced, short-tempered. . . ."
>
> "Double-faced and short-tempered?"
>
> "Short-tempered, for she nearly seized me by the hair last time because of something I said. I was quoting the Apocalypse to her."
>
> "What do you mean?" the prince asked, thinking that he had misheard him.
>
> "I was reading the Apocalypse. [. . .] She agreed with me that we've arrived at the time of the third horse, the black one, and of the rider who has a pair of balances in his hand, for everything in our present age is weighed in the scales and everything is settled by agreement, and all people are merely seeking their rights: 'A measure of wheat for a penny, and three measures of barley for a penny.' And, on top of it,

---

[53] The motifs of garden (*sad*) and bench (*skam'ia, skameika*) will be taken up later in the summer garden and in Pavlovsk. See VIII: 166, 189, 301, 351.

they still want to preserve a free spirit and a pure heart and a sound body and all the gifts of the Lord. But they won't preserve them by seeking their rights alone, and there will therefore follow the pale horse and he whose name was Death, and after whom Hell followed" (Mag 231–32; VIII: 167–68).

This heavy-handed passage indicates to what extent the author has, as it were, laid his Tarot cards on the table. Clearly Dostoevsky knew that only a character such as Lebedev, performing in the tradition of the Shakespearean "wise fool," could manage such a balancing act between high seriousness and comic bathos. Suddenly the little narratives (Lebedev's argument with his nephew, the anecdote about Countess Du Barry) within the larger narrative (the story of Myshkin, Rogozhin, and Nastasya Filippovna) make sense. The references to death (the Zhemarin murders), the guillotine (a knife-like engine of death), and fear of the end (the *un moment* of Du Barry) can be decoded in terms of Nastasya Filippovna's frantic search "for something" and Lebedev's unorthodox exegesis of the Book of Revelation.[54] According to Dostoevsky's *porte parole*, the plot being worked out in contemporary Russian history and in the fate of Nastasya Filippovna, a victim of that history, is equivalent to *the distance traveled between the third and fourth horses of Apocalypse*, between a society increasingly atomized by its insistence on "rights" and the actualized impulse to self-destruction implied in such a human-centered system of justice (see Girard, *Deceit* 256–89).

Myshkin's next visit is to Rogozhin's. He proceeds to the *crossroads* (*perekrestok*)[55] of Gorokhovaya and Sadovaya Streets where, full of agitation, he looks over the facade of his friend's house (Mag 235; VIII: 170).[56] The prince pauses for a moment as if to take in not only the meaning of the building but the spatio-temporal choice, the "fall" into history, involved by crossing its threshold. He is entering into this "temple" of tradespeople and money-changers, as Christ once did, to make his case for a higher currency of exchange among human souls. Once across the threshold, Myshkin is met by Rogozhin, who recalls the time before their rivalry in terms of the *first* train ride: "Remember how we traveled in the same coach from Pskov last autumn—me coming here and you—you wearing that cloak and gaiters—remember?" (Mag 237; VIII: 171–72) But Myshkin can only think of the burning eyes of *the present* that betoken his coming fall: "When I got

---

[54] The black horse has traditionally symbolized famine.

[55] Information about the reputed location of Rogozhin's house in nineteenth-century Petersburg is provided in IX: 440. According to G. A. Fyodorov, the house originally serving as the source for Dostoevsky's description was #33.

[56] For Dostoevsky and other romantic realists the physical appearance of a dwelling often offers clues to the psychology of the dweller. See Fanger, *Dostoevsky* 195–98.

off the train this morning, I saw a pair of eyes that looked at me just as you did a moment ago from behind. . . . I think I must have imagined it all. . . . I'm afraid, brother Parfyon, that I feel almost as I did five years ago when I still used to have my fits ['pri*pad*ok'—literally 'a falling down']" (Mag 235; VIII: 171).

What is implied at this point is that the *horizontal* train ride stands in for the *vertical* motion of the guillotine (the *mashina*) mentioned earlier. *Nozh* (knife), *mashina*, and *zheleznaia doroga* (iron road) are kindred symbols for a time that, if not already fallen, is in the process of falling, a time which cannot be turned back. Myshkin fully understands the force and trajectory of what has been set in motion when he exclaims, "If she marries you [Rogozhin], she will certainly perish [*za toboiu ei nepremennaia gibel'*]" (Mag 239; VIII: 173). As a possible ending to the love story, the version feared by the prince is still, for the moment, only an uncut page—hence the image of the *garden* (*sadovyi*) knife in the volume of Solovyov's history that is presented to Rogozhin as a gift by Nastasya Filippovna.[57] But as the strained exchange between Myshkin and Rogozhin continues, the motif of the knife is invoked so frequently and pointedly as to seem hypnotic in its gathering momentum. Rogozhin tells Myshkin that Nastasya Filippovna wanted at one point, in a fit of anger, to kill him with a knife; Myshkin speaks agitatedly of his premonition that Rogozhin will slit Nastasya Filippovna's throat; in her thoughts of marriage, Nastasya Filippovna is described by Rogozhin as going, like a sacrificial victim, "under the knife"; Myshkin recounts an anecdote (directly after that of the atheist on the train) of a man who "butchered his friend like a ram" over a gold watch. Hence by now there can be little doubt that someone, probably the heroine, will eventually be driven to fill that uncut page of history not with a comic epithalamium but with a tragic bloodletting. Any other ending would frustrate expectations and make this momentum and its shaping ironic in a way that is inconsistent with what has come before. Dostoevsky is here bound to follow the logic of his fictional method, to see what must happen as he transposes the idea of (wo)man as "transitional being" in history to narrative form.

The final episode in this drama takes place between the time the prince leaves Rogozhin's and the time Rogozhin tries to kill him on the hotel landing. When Myshkin goes to "The Scales" to find Kolya Ivolgin, he begins

---

[57] It seems likely that Dostoevsky was consciously singling out Solovyov. More than any other historian in the 1870s, he advocated *linear* history, the glories of material *progress*, the indispensability of Peter the Great (see, for example, his public lectures on Peter given in 1872 for the bicentenary celebrations at Moscow University), and the statist worldview. In other words, what Solovyov stood for was the very opposite of Dostoevsky's apocalypticism.

to move mechanically, "like a machine" (*mashinal'no*) (VIII: 186).[58] He senses that he may be to blame for something and, as he loses himself in thought, he notices that he has turned up on the platform of the Tsarskoe Selo railroad. After deciding to buy a ticket for Pavlovsk—and thus *not* to go to Nastasya Filippovna's and to arouse Rogozhin's jealousy—he prepares to board the train, but then suddenly, for no apparent reason, he tosses away the ticket and leaves the station. From there he walks on in a daze, driven forward by an "unconscious impulse" (*bessoznatel'noe dvizhenie*) (VIII: 187), until he feels the urge to verify an item that recently attracted his attention in a shop window. This urge also provokes more anxiety and confusion about time, since now Myshkin realizes that he has definitely entered his "pre-epileptic stage" ("pri*pado*chnoe vremia"), a time when the categories of past, present, and future interpenetrate and lose their distinct boundaries. The *idée fixe* is of course a knife, and in the prince's disoriented mind the potential murder weapon is associated with the train station and Rogozhin's accusing eyes:

> That object, consequently, had impressed him so much that it had attracted his attention at a time when he was in a state of utter confusion just after he left the train station. He walked back, looking in anguish to the right, and his heart beat with uneasy impatience. But there was the shop—he had found it at last! . . . He now clearly remembered that it was just then, while standing in front of that shop window, that he suddenly turned around, as he had done only a short time before when he caught Rogozhin's eyes fixed upon him. . . . He felt that he must think it all over very carefully; it was now clear that he had not imagined it at the railway station, that something had really happened to him that was most certainly connected with all his former uneasiness (Mag 257–58; VIII: 187).

It is of no little significance that only now, shortly before the murder attempt by Rogozhin, does Myshkin have his dramatic monologue about the positive and negative effects of his (and his author's) falling sickness. The sense of higher life, of harmony, joy, and other-worldly synthesis, that the hero experiences during a moment of the aura before the onset of the actual seizure is, he surmises, worth an entire lifetime. The price of this gift, this escape from the chains of history, is the stigma(ta) of "idiocy." At this point Dostoevsky offers one of his most vexing paradoxes, for the reader's praise or censure of the prince now depends entirely on whether the "idea" he

---

[58] Rogozhin, who is caught in the same ineluctable forward movement, but from "the other side," is also described as shaking Myshkin's hand *mashinal'no* (VIII: 182).

embodies is in any way "tellable." After all, is it possible to tell the story of a character willing to trade his role in a continuously developing plot for an ulterior, extra-narratorial vantage that undermines the temporal reality of that plot? How can a fictional hero *in the middle* of a life, or a reader in the middle of a text, pose questions that can be answered only from *beyond the end*? The author seems to be saying that to look at Myshkin *within time* (narrative, biographical, historical) is to judge him a sick man and a failure: "Reflecting about the moment afterwards, he often said to himself that all those gleams and flashes of the highest awareness . . . were nothing but a disease" (Mag 258; VIII: 188). But to look at him *outside of time*, when all the struggle that comes between life's beginnings and endings collapses into an instant, is to see only his spiritual beauty: "a great calm . . . full of understanding and the knowledge of the final cause" (Mag 258; VIII: 188).

Yet because such spiritual beauty exists, as Myshkin himself says, quoting Revelation 10:6, when "there shall be no more time" (VIII: 189), this paradoxical knowledge is also, as it were, his cross, his "rood of time." It is the burden that must be shouldered because he has been blessed (cursed?) with *both* viewpoints—life before and after the fall—and is unable to superimpose the one on the other. The central contradiction of Myshkin's character brought into focus is that the moment of his salvation and the moment of his fall are simultaneous.[59] Any attempt to join them in a temporal causality (the euphoria is posterior to, and hence derives from, the sickness, etc.) is to fall back into the "error" of the novel form, with its *différance*, its story of the relation over time between contiguous moments. Here as elsewhere, Dostoevsky shows a remarkable sensitivity to the competing, and, as it were, self-canceling narrative modalities associated with developing or retarding a story, on the one hand, and ending it, on the other. And yet, while his "dialogic" imagination never ignores the opposing elements of an argument, there should be little doubt on which side of the pro and contra his sympathies lie.[60]

The prince awakens from his reverie to find himself sitting, not fortuitously, on a bench in the Summer Garden. In the hot and heavy air that

[59] Cox implies something like this with his notion of "completeness within flux" (*Between Heaven and Earth* 172). This in turn sounds close to the condition of transcendent breakthrough à la Shelley, of "the loss of the individual self in oneness," described recently by Jay Clayton in *Romantic Vision and the Novel* 19–26, 160–74. The core texts treated by Clayton are: *Clarissa, Mansfield Park, Wuthering Heights, Little Dorrit, Adam Bede*, and *Women in Love*.

[60] As Strakhov once related Dostoevsky's words on the nature of the aura: "For several moments I experience a happiness that is impossible in a normal condition and that other people can have no understanding of. I feel complete harmony in myself and in all the world, and this feeling is so strong and sweet that for several seconds of such bliss one could give ten years of one's life, perhaps one's entire life" (cited in *PSS* IX: 441–42).

bodes a thunderstorm, he quickly returns to his former "train of thought."
He leaves the garden where he had his vision of harmony and, overcome by
the temptation to see Nastasya Filippovna, proceeds along "almost without
noticing his way" (*pochti ne zamechaia svoei dorogi*) (Mag 260; VIII: 189).
Once more the magnetized topoi converge, but now with even greater in-
tensity, like musical motifs intertwining in a final crescendo:[61]

> "Isn't it criminal, isn't it base of me to assume such a thing [i.e., that
> Rogozhin would murder] with such cynical frankness?" he exclaimed,
> his face flushing all over with shame. He was amazed, he stood still in
> the roadway, as though rooted to the spot. He remembered all at once
> the Pavlovsk station that afternoon and the Nikolaevsk station in the
> morning, and the question he had asked to his [Rogozhin's] face about
> those *eyes*. . . . The prince wanted to turn back to his hotel at once; he
> did, indeed, turn back and go the other way, but a minute later he
> stopped, thought it over, and went back again in the first direction [*po
> prezhnei doroge*—literally "along his former way"] (Mag 261–62;
> VIII: 190–91)[62]

Clearly the hero is being drawn toward Nastasya Filippovna (who is not at
home) and toward the lapse in faith and brotherly love that a visit to her
represents *as if along rails*. Having fallen victim to the strange temporality
of what he will later call "double thoughts," he has no strength to turn back.
He believes he is going to save Nastasya Filippovna from history *at the
same time* that his judgment of Rogozhin causes him to fall back into history. This is presumably what Myshkin means when he acknowledges that
a demon of doubt "whispered to him in the Summer Garden" and that this
doubt led by its own logic to the picture of Rogozhin standing in the station
"like an accuser and judge" (Mag 265; VIII: 193). The distance between the
garden and the station, between the aura and the convulsions, between life
"in" and "out" of history is equal, in the collapsed and hopelessly ambiguous time-space of Myshkin's present state, to the path of tragic contradiction covered en route to Nastasya Filippovna's. It is her residence (as it will
be Rogozhin's at the end of the novel) that is the psychological "terminus"
for this section of the narrative.

Finally, this duel of temporalities is brought to a momentary climax when
the prince, having failed to locate Nastasya Filippovna, arrives at his hotel.
He spots Rogozhin in a niche on the landing, and, as the latter emerges from
the shadows with a knife in his hand, shouts, "Parfyon, I don't believe it!"

---

[61] Cf. "For some obscure reason he kept remembering Lebedev's nephew . . . just as some-
times one cannot help remembering some persistent and stupidly tiresome musical motif"
(Mag 260; VIII: 190).

[62] Cf. the same motifs in Mag 264; VIII: 193.

(Mag 267; VIII: 195) The pun is more obvious in the original, where Myshkin's exclamation is rendered literally as "I don't believe" (*ne veriu*). The
verb phrase suggests both that the speaker does not believe his friend is
capable of murder *and* that the speaker simply does not believe. In the paradoxical temporality of this confrontation, Myshkin has at once kept and
lost his faith. Although the first (sanguine) meaning is more in keeping
with the character of the hero, both are possible. And as might be expected,
it is immediately after his outcry, *in the same instant*, that Myshkin has his
fit ("pripadok") of *falling sickness* ("*paduchaia*") which, ironically saves
him "from the inevitable blow, already *falling* [*padavshego*] at him, of the
knife" (Mag 268; VIII: 195). Dostoevsky manages to spare his favorite hero
and continue his story about the end by a kind of optical illusion. By eliding
the notions of salvation and judgment, and by describing with the contiguity of words what has just happened simultaneously, he arrests the narrative in mid-step and shifts the setting to the green world of Pavlovsk.

The shift in setting from Petersburg to Pavlovsk is a fact of considerable
importance. Here the story will remain until the very end, when the three
lovers return to the city for the novel's climax. As numerous commentators
have noted, the structural waywardness of *The Idiot* derives in large part
from these very Pavlovsk chapters, since it is in them that the author seems
to lose his way. The Myshkin-Aglaya-Radomsky triangle and the impending fate of Ippolit gradually come to the fore just as the original story re-
treats backstage, creating the impression that the entire artistic enterprise
has been bereft of a center. One possible motivation for this sudden atomi-
zation of the plot is its hitherto rapid forward movement and eschatological
impulse: from this point forth Nastasya Filippovna must remain mostly in
the background because her story has progressed *too far*; as was remarked
earlier, its ending is in sight and would be difficult to retard convincingly if
she were constantly under scrutiny. On the other hand, the Pavlovsk chapters manage to sustain, however circuitously, the relentless momentum begun in the Petersburg chapters. They do so by a sort of narrative detour, a
switch to different, but parallel tracks. The obsession with endings characterized earlier by Nastasya Filippovna's constant flight between lovers will
be transferred to other characters, most notably to Ippolit. In spite of our
expectations, the rustic surroundings of Pavlovsk[63] will not function to dis-
arm the tension between competing egos, to offer a brief "whistle stop" in

---

[63] The potentially regenerative powers of Pavlovsk are mentioned several times in the text.
Ippolit, for example, is attempting to rely on them when, at the prince's prompting, he trades
the urban anguish of "Meyer's wall" (VIII: 321–22) for Pavlovsk's trees. Yet as it turns out,
Ippolit comes to the country not to restore his hopes but to parade the bitter irony of his
imminent death in these surroundings.

the middle of history's ride. Once the human being has entered history there is no way back to Otradnoe. Hence Dostoevsky is able to write his large novel about the End only by *postponing* the climax and inserting in the middle a series of subplots that, while interrelated thematically, have little direct impact on the main plot. The greatest "structural flaw" in *The Idiot*, if it is helpful to pose the problem in such terms, is that the narrative, being concerned with ends, points too soon to its own without being ready to fulfill it. Without diversions, "a story about the End" can become a contradiction in terms.

If Nastasya Filippovna is fated to disappear for much of the last half of the novel, then the author needs an additional cynosure in order to keep his apocalyptic design in plain view.[64] This new focus falls on Ippolit, whose strange and poignant confession constitutes the emotional climax of Part Three. Ippolit has much in common with Nastasya Filippovna (see Skaftymov, "Tematicheskaia kompozitsiia" 149–54). In fact, one might go so far as to say that in the story of the consumptive boy Dostoevsky has, *mutatis mutandis*, reincarnated the story of Nastasya Filippovna. Both characters are "condemned persons" who lash out—the one physically, the other verbally—at an intolerable status quo; both are morbidly consumed by thoughts of impending death; both are volatile mixtures of kindness and cruelty, self-abnegation and self-absorption; and, most revealing, both are forced to choose between the temporalities and attendant moralities embodied by the Christ-like Myshkin and the Antichrist-like Rogozhin. Dostoevsky then had ample reason for calling Ippolit "the main axis of the entire novel" (IX: 277). In this "unleasher of horses"[65] he had found a way to start over and continue an apocalyptic story that had "gone too far." Correspondingly, in neither the notebooks nor the final version is there a character (except for Nastasya Filippovna) more closely associated with apocalyptic motifs, and, indeed, one whose narrated life is more apocalyptically shaped than that of this embittered adolescent.

Like Nastasya Filippovna's outburst at her own birthday party, Ippolit's rambling *cri de coeur* is set at a similar occasion—this time Myshkin's. The chief difference, one reflective of how far we have progressed from Part One, is that the heroine's hope for a new beginning is now countered by Ippolit's urge to make an appropriate end. The only activity of any signifi-

---

[64] For Dostoevsky's mention of the Apocalypse in his notebooks, see IX: 221, 253, 262, 269, 277.

[65] Ippolit's name is a russified version of Hippolytus, the bastard son of Theseus and the Amazon Hippolyta. Hippolytus was thrown from his chariot and dragged to death when a monster sent by Poseidon (one of whose names was *Hippios*) frightened the horses. Dostoevsky could also have in mind Hippolyte, the innocent victim in Racine's *Phèdre*. See note 25 above.

cance left open to him by the advanced state of his illness is suicide. His confession is preceded by Lebedev's longest and most pointed seriocomic digression. Once more Dostoevsky's fool returns to his favorite topic, the Apocalypse, and to the lines about the polluted waters of life that, when read through the prism of modern life, yield up an image of the railroad.

> "Our question is whether the 'waters of life' have grown weaker or not with the increase of . . ."
> "Railways?" cried Kolya.
> "Not of railway communications [. . .] but of the whole tendency, of which the railways may serve, as it were, as an illustration, as an artistic expression. They hustle, they roar, they rend the air with their noise, they hurry, they say, for the happiness of mankind. 'People are getting too noisy and commercial,' some recluse of a thinker complains, 'there is little spiritual peace.' 'That may be so,' triumphantly answers him another thinker, who is always on the move, 'but the rumble of the carts bringing bread to starving humanity is perhaps better than spiritual peace,' and he walks away conceitedly. But, vile man that I am, I do not believe in the carts that bring bread to humanity! For carts bringing bread to all humanity without a moral basis for that action, may quite deliberately exclude a considerable part of humanity from the enjoyment of what they bring" (Mag 412–13; VIII: 311–12).

This is as close as the reader will come to a full disclosure of the railroad motif. Lebedev (and his author) question the moral and psychological motivation for material progress. His remarks become more obvious when viewed in the context of a polemical exchange that took place between V. S. Pecherin and Alexander Herzen in 1853 (see IX: 393). Pecherin wrote Herzen of his fear that the rising tide of commercialism would engulf the spiritual calm and harmony within the *narod*; but Herzen, a representative of the liberal generation of the 1840s for whom the later Dostoevsky felt only scorn, retorted, "What are you afraid of? Can it be the noise of wheels bringing daily bread to the starved and half-clad masses?" (*ss* XI: 402.) By parodying this argument in the pages leading up to Ippolit's confession and by closing the tirade with a lament over the loss of a "binding idea" ("Show me anything resembling that force [i.e., of the 'binding idea'] in our age of vice and railroads" [Mag 417; VIII: 315]), Dostoevsky lays the tracks, as it were, for the response of the young nihilist who must face the injustice of his own end.

With the possible exception of Kirillov in *The Devils*, there is no other character in all of Dostoevsky's fiction more obsessed with the *now* of his end than Ippolit. This sense of urgency is generated in the very patterns of his language. Over and over again he resorts to some form of *chas*, the Russian word for "moment," "hour," and (in the plural) "watch/clock," until the time has arrived, by his calculations, to shoot himself.[66] He begins his last will and testament with a series of precise temporal phrases, at least one of which is a familiar allusion to the Apocalypse:

> "What time is it? [*Kotoryi chas*] Don't bother; I know what time it is. The hour is at hand [*Prishel chas*]. Now is the time [*Teper' samoe vremia*]. . . . Tomorrow 'there shall be no more time.' . . . But don't worry. It won't take me more than forty minutes to read—oh, an hour [*chas*] at most" (Mag 420–21; VIII: 318).

Between the biblical "hour at hand" that gets Ippolit's story underway, the sixty minutes that it takes him to narrate it, and the "now" ("seic*has*"— literally "this moment") that serves as the mnemonic prod to pull the trigger (VIII: 348), we witness the full range of how he, and by implication his generation, experience life by the biological clock. All the apocalyptic motifs with which he invests his narrative, including the melodramatic breaking of the seal, the prophecy of universal catastrophe in the pathetic "*Après moi le déluge*," and the image of the scorpion (see Hollander, "The Apocalyptic Framework" 134), suggest that Ippolit wants his passing to be a genuine threshold, something memorable and full of high drama, not, as his nihilism would dictate, "in the nature of things." It is his passionate wish that the time he has chosen—the sunrise following Myshkin's party—be "final" or "ultimate" (*poslednii*). During the hour allotted he vows to speak "only the truth, ultimate and triumphant" (VIII: 322) and to demonstrate how he came to his "ultimate conviction" (VIII: 337).

What Ippolit rebels against is the *injustice* of his early dying, the traducing of his *right* to a longer life. But in Dostoevsky's world it is never justice that bestows grace.[67] Hence the use of an apocalyptic framework for Ippolit's story is primarily ironic. That is to say, this story avails itself of familiar topoi from the Book of Revelation, but not with the aim of telling about the vindication of the righteous. Like the Underground Man, whose tone may be alternately sincere and sarcastic or indeed both at the same time, the youth does not fully believe in what he is saying. Rather, he uses the occasion to create good theater. On the other hand, as Dostoevsky's ingenious method of narration ensures, it is not for us—just as it is not for the other characters—to judge (see R. Miller, *Dostoevsky and "The Idiot"* 90–222). The Apocalypse is, first and foremost, about judgment, and Ippo-

---

[66] See, e.g., VIII: 318, 321, 322, 333, 337.

[67] Cf. the very different deaths of Marmeladov and Katerina Ivanovna in *Crime and Punishment*.

lit's story, ostensibly following yet at a more basic level subverting the logic of the biblical text, is about the judgment of one who wants to die having *earned*, through his torments, the good judgment of others. That, however, according to his author's version of theodicy, is impossible without a prior desire for Christian forgiveness and mercy. Ippolit wants to forgive the others their good fortune, but the others deny responsibility for this turn of events. The others (rather haughtily, to be sure) want to forgive Ippolit his embarrassing display of emotion and pathetic suicide attempt, but he refuses "to be judged." For this story to have a "happy ending" the forgiveness would have to come *before* the right to judge, which again implies a totally different and "ahistorical" temporality, not after, as a result of, or reward for, one's tribulations. In the end what emerges from the "Necessary Explanation" is a second version, or cynical parody, of the Book of Revelation. Its "ghost writer" would not be Christ, but Antichrist, and its sense of overwhelming bitterness and futility accords perfectly with the "just punishment" of its participants, especially Ippolit, who are judged by the implied reader in inverse proportion to their ability to forego judgment (see R. Miller, *Dostoevsky and "The Idiot"* 205–19).

Ippolit has two visions that open and close his narrative. The first is the dream about his dog Norma and the second is the imagined visit of Rogozhin set within a delirious recollection of Holbein's painting "Christ in the Tomb" (1521). As becomes clear, not only are these episodes powerful indices of psychic health (or disease) and subconscious motivation; more importantly, they offer a precise reckoning of the changes wrought in Ippolit over time by his rebellion and loss of faith. In the dream about the now dead Newfoundland, a younger Ippolit is trapped in his room with a "terrible creature, a sort of monster" that "looked like a scorpion, but was . . . more hideous" (Mag 427; VIII: 323). Because of its trident-like shape and resemblance to a scorpion, this monster has been identified with the Antichrist (Hollander, "Apocalyptic Framework" 135).[68] Yet Norma, though fully aware of the danger ("There was something . . . almost supernatural in Norma's terror" [Mag 428; VIII: 324]), saves the child from the sting of death he so fears. What is significant about the scene is that she too is afraid and that, in saving the child, she is destroyed. At the end of this passage, as if to link the waking and dreaming worlds and to reinforce the analogy with Christ-like self-sacrifice and a human (here the child's) triumph over death, Ippolit declares, "Then I awoke, and the prince came in" (Mag 429; VIII:

---

[68] Cf. this scorpion and the tarantula of the second vision with the apocalyptic *piccola bestia* of *Diary* (September 1876): "Everyone is waiting, everyone is alarmed, over everyone there hangs a nightmare, everyone has bad dreams. Who or what this *piccola bestia* is that produces such turmoil it is impossible to determine because a sort of wholesale insanity has set in. . . . And yet, it is as if everyone had already been stung" (XXIII: 107).

324). Subconscious feelings have intuitively chosen the logic of a wisdom tale/parable and a non-verbal image from the animal world to express what would be inadmissible to the logic of positivism or materialism.

The second vision is a mirror opposite of the first. Describing Holbein's painting of a mutilated and all too human Christ, it is totally dominated by the spirit of death:

> Here [i.e., in front of the painting] one cannot help being struck with the idea that if death is so horrible and if the laws of nature are so powerful, then how can they be overcome? . . . Looking at that picture, you get the impression of nature as some enormous, implacable, and dumb beast,[69] or to put it more correctly, as some *huge engine* [lit. "machine"—*mashina*] of the latest design, which had senselessly seized, crushed, and swallowed up—a great and priceless being, a being worth the whole of nature and its laws, worth the entire earth, which was perhaps created solely for the coming of that being! (Mag 447; VIII: 339)

Now the laws of nature, which dictate that all must die, even he who was "most beautiful," are in control. Instead of Norma catching and crushing the beast in her mouth, it is the beast that seizes, crushes, and swallows the "priceless being." And the *mashina* which Magarshak translates nicely as "engine" (in various senses) is the root image for this cruel, inhuman force. Furthermore, as if to complete the mirror symmetry, Ippolit associates the end of the vision with the entry of Rogozhin, the incarnation of the all-powerful spirit of death. The moment of truth is made more forceful by the knowledge that the latter's house, with its links to commercial Petersburg, is the setting for the Holbein copy which earlier had captured Myshkin's attention. Thus the "progress" narrated by Ippolit's story is from a meaningful end (Norma/Myshkin) to an end without meaning (machine/Rogozhin). After the boy's suicide attempt, little more can be done to squeeze additional drama from his story; like Nastasya Filippovna, its overplayed hero must dwell in the shadows for much of the remainder of the novel.

By the last chapters of Part Four, the narrowing of options once open to the prince has reached its outer limit. There is no longer any doubt that his good intentions weigh cruelly on those around him. The prince loses control of himself in a rambling monologue made during a party in his honor and

---

[69] Cf. this beast and the fourth and most terrible beast from Daniel 7:7 (one of the major Old Testament apocalyptic texts): "And behold, a fourth beast, terrible and dreadful and exceedingly strong; and it had *great iron teeth* [bol'shie zheleznye zuby]; it *devoured and broke in pieces* [pozhiraet i sokrushaet], and stamped the residue with its feet. It was different from all the beasts that were before it; and it had ten horns [a motif also associated with the beast/Antichrist of Revelation]" (my emphasis; *Oxford Annotated Bible* 1078/*Bibliia* 1055).

then, in the initial stages of a fit, breaks a Chinese vase, a Yepanchin family heirloom that perhaps symbolizes the artistic sense of proportion and grace which he lacks. When the party is disrupted on Myshkin's account, the formidable patroness Princess Belokonskaya (*belyi kon'*—"white horse") judges him a "sick man" and a social misfit (Mag 596; VIII: 459). He is further isolated from "proper society" when pity forces him to choose the fallen Nastasya Filippovna over the virginal Aglaya in the dramatic confrontation between heroines. The implied irony is that Myshkin, in following his best Christian instincts, can do nothing to avert the coming tragedy. Quite the contrary, his efforts to move upstream against the powerful current of historical time seem now only to redouble the forces converging rapidly on the climax. The end of the novel becomes not only inevitable, as indeed it has been for several hundred pages, but at last imminent when the author breaks off the Myshkin-Aglaya-Radomsky subplot and returns the major characters and their triangle to center stage.

The novel's final scandal scene takes place on Myshkin's and Nastasya Filippovna's wedding day. Like the birthday parties that earlier played a strategic role in the apocalyptic subtext, this festive occasion might be seen as a fresh start, another new page in the story of life. But Nastasya Filippovna, in her last change of heart, refuses to make such a start. Once again, her story has progressed too far to be rewritten with a happy ending. As she leaves for the church, she catches sight of Rogozhin in the crowd of admirers and screams, "Save me! Take me away! Anywhere you like— now!" (Mag 638; VIII: 493) Rogozhin responds by seizing her in his arms, passing a hundred ruble note to the nearest coachman, and urging on the latter with, "To the station [*na zheleznuiu dorogu*], and if you catch the train [*a pospeesh' k mashine*] there's another hundred for you!" (Mag 638; VIII: 493) With this final convergence of money, speed, and iron force, the apocalyptic race, as it were, enters its last leg.[70] The couple returns to the city by train, and Myshkin follows the next day. Perhaps most intriguing, the neutral word for train—*poezd*—that Dostoevsky had employed from the first sentence of the novel is now nowhere to be found.[71] Instead these two return trips are repeatedly described in terms of the *mashina*, a word rich in nineteenth-century folklore and the popular belief/fear that the train

[70] This scene is presented in terms that imply flight and hot pursuit: Rogozhin's command *na zheleznuiu dorogu* means literally "onto [i.e., get going to] the iron road"; the coachman whips his horses on to the station; Keller and Burdovsky want "to give chase" (*brosilis' bylo v pogoniu*), but realize they have fallen too far behind; the fleeing couple "gallop to the station on time," etc.

[71] Up to this point in the novel, Dostoevsky has used the term *poezd* five times (VIII: 5, 158, 186, 210, 268) and the term *chugunka* once (VIII: 303). His only use of *mashina* with the precise meaning of train comes at the end (VIII: 493, 495, 504), where it appears five times.

is the ultimate "machine" (VIII: 493, 495, 504). This reading is further corroborated by the notebooks, which show a marked role for the word in a
scene following the wedding fiasco: originally there was to be, *in the presence of Ippolit*, a "lecture on *machine production* [*mashinnoe proizvod-
stvo*]" and its ability to "swallow everything"; and the prince himself was
supposed to speak (deliriously?) "about machines" (IX: 284). The implication is that Dostoevsky, recalling the implacable machine of Ippolit's second
vision and intent on working the motif into the narrative, transformed these
planned conversations into the actual images of locomotion that accompany
the three principals back to Petersburg and the novel's dénouement.

The final scene is the most powerful in the novel. It is so not only because
that which has been dramatically retarded for hundreds of pages is at last
accomplished, but also because the poetics of space and time employed earlier to suggest precipitous forward movement is now used to depict its utter
absence. The reader experiences a macabre sense of dejà vu precisely because all this has happened before, but in altered circumstances. Again
Myshkin and Rogozhin sit down "opposite one another" (*drug protiv
druga*) (VIII: 503); again we realize that the pro and contra of their respective temporalities have been the source of all tension, conflict, movement.
Only now there is no tension, as there is nothing for these temporalities to
compete for. Neither the "ideal" nor the "real" Nastasya Filippovna is present. The Petersburg station, their initial destination, has been replaced by
the morgue-like house at the crossroads of Gorokhovaya and Sadovaya
Streets.[72] The heroine has merged into a tragic composite of the two temporalities—the *dead bride*. Her death epitomizes the curse of judgment, of
past lapses forbidding present change, while her wedding dress shows how
much she longed for a new beginning. At last she has fully traversed the
distance between the black horse and the pale horse. From her hysterical
movement *na mashine* ("on the train") (VIII: 504), she has, on this *white
night* in Petersburg, come to rest against the pale immobility of the setting:

> The prince's heart beat so violently that it seemed it could be heard in
> the room, in *the dead silence* of the room. But his eyes had already got
> used to the dark, and he could make out the whole bed; someone lay
> asleep on it in an *absolutely motionless* sleep; not the faintest rustle
> could be heard, not the faintest breath. The sleeper was covered, from
> head to foot, with a *white* sheet. . . . All around . . . clothes were
> scattered—a rich *white* silk dress, flowers, ribbons. On the little table
> at the head of the bed diamonds, which had been taken off and thrown
> down, lay glittering. At the foot of the bed some sort of lace lay in a

---

[72] As might be predicted, Myshkin and Rogozhin meet each other for the last time *at a
crossroads* before proceeding on to Rogozhin's house (VIII: 500).

crumpled heap, and on the *white* lace, protruding from under the sheet, the tip of a bare foot could be made out; it seemed as though it were carved out of marble, and it was *dreadfully still*. The prince looked, and he felt that the longer he looked the more *silent* and death-like the room became. Suddenly a fly, awakened from its sleep, started buzzing, and after flying over the bed, settled at the head of it. The prince gave a start (Mag 651–52; VIII: 503; my emphasis).

All these images of whiteness and stillness surrounding Nastasya Filippovna's nuptial bier reveal to what extent she has realized her personal mythology. The whiteness of virginity is now at one with the paleness of death. Her ride on history's train is over. Whatever motion is left in this *nature morte* is provided ironically by the hovering fly, one of those insects that in Dostoevsky's world are sooner associated with death and physical corruption than with buzzing biological life (see Tate, "The Hovering Fly" 17–23). And if Dostoevsky's roots in nineteenth-century realism would not permit such a naked analogy, this heroine, as Vyacheslav Ivanov first noted, also in some sense symbolizes Russia the bride, who must choose *in time* between Christ and Antichrist as suitors. Dostoevsky often expressed exaggerated hopes for his homeland in his correspondence,[73] yet in the honesty of his art, where time must have its own reality, those hopes were transmuted into tragic insight.

In a celebrated recent study of Dostoevsky's fiction, Michael Holquist has argued that the central idea of *The Idiot* is "an inspired moment that subsequently fails to change anything" (*Dostoevsky* 104). This perhaps most difficult of Dostoevsky's major works is primarily, as Holquist continues, about the inability "of *kairos* to affect *chronos*" (122). Such a line of reasoning has its cogency, for it posits a certain tension and dialogic openness characteristic of the *middles* of Dostoevsky's novels. Moreover, Holquist is correct to identify chronos, time in history, as the force capable of undoing whatever kairotic ends the prince might insert in the story of his and the others' lives. It is true that Dostoevsky's view of human life in time is tragic ("der Christ muss scheitern" ["the Christian must run aground, be wrecked"], as the Swiss theologian Walter Nigg once said),[74] and therefore to state that in this story of clashing temporalities the idea of time as inev-

---

[73] E.g., "All the world is being prepared for a great regeneration through the Russian idea (which, as you rightly say, is inextricably bound with Orthodoxy) and this will take place in some century—that is my fervent belief" (letter of February 18, 1868 to A. Maykov in Dolinin II: 81).

[74] See Nigg's fine essay on *The Idiot* in *Der christliche Narr*.

itable continuity comes to dominate the idea of time as radical change is logical, even self-evident, inasmuch as it allows that story in the first place.

But Holquist's reading does not adequately account for the final scene at the bedside of the heroine. Here one finds it difficult to argue that "discourse is open." The dark forces of history without God may have defeated this Ivan Tsarevich and his sleeping princess, but it would be almost perverse to claim that the chief implication of the silence and immobility is ongoing dialogue, continued movement, never-ending struggle. What one can say is that the end of this novel is appropriate to its beginning and middle. It is the end that we knew would come and that now has. To imply that it is another failed epiphany is to see it *within history*, that is, to judge it through the eyes of the characters (and narrator) who ostracize Myshkin. But this death, after all, comes *at the end*, at that privileged moment when the reader leaves the temporality of the narrative to enter the temporality of his/her world. As we know from the notebook entry written on the occasion of his first wife's death, Dostoevsky was painfully aware of the difference between life "in the middle" and life "at the end." In this sense, the viewpoint of his implied reader, who judges the novel's meaning *from the end*, from a temporal vantage above or beyond that which generated the plot, may be taken a step further. A study of the interrelation between aesthetics and metaphysics in Dostoevsky would begin with the assumption that any reader's life is in turn part of a larger plot whose meaning is evaluated by its reader only at the appropriate "Finis." Perhaps then it is not reading too much into this ending to reverse Holquist's conclusion and suggest that Nastasya Filippovna's death *does* represent qualitative change and *is* meaningful in its silence. It is a meaning that is implied rather than stated. It symbolizes the end of the ride, the pale horse whose name is death, the Apocalypse that has come for these people personally and, by an associative logic of which Dostoevsky was certainly aware, *will* come for their country. If it is not a sanguine meaning, it is a meaning nonetheless.

Bakhtinian theory can, like any body of thought, impose its own orthodoxy. What is *only* open can also be closed. To Bakhtin and his followers Dostoevsky's works are best characterized by the sound of competing voices.[75] And in terms of narrative time, this means that the Dostoevskian plot "is set up to do nothing else so relentlessly as to dramatize the absence of essence in chronology, the separation of moment and sequence" (Holquist, *Dostoevsky* 110). Yet such a viewpoint, apt for a plot in progress,

[75] "In the Dostoevskian novel there is no causality, no genesis, no explanations based on the past, on the influence of environment, upbringing, etc. Each action of the hero is entirely in the present, and in this regard is not predetermined; it is conceived and depicted by the author as though it were free"; "The polyphonic novel is throughout dialogic"; "All in life is a dialogue, that is, dialogic opposition," etc. (*Problemy* 35, 49, 51).

cannot adequately respond to the sense of an ending, where silence and the discontinuation of dialogue obtain—be it Raskolnikov's conversion or Stavrogin's suicide. For Dostoevsky death and rebirth are not merely convenient ploys with which to end a story. They become meaningful when placed in the larger context of God's plot. Apocalypse, lest we forget, means an "uncovering" or "disclosing," and, depending on how one views human history and one's place in it, its revelation can be positive or negative, justificatory or retributive. An end, therefore, may involve a tragic and just punishment, as it does for Stavrogin, or it may involve a new beginning, as it does for Raskolnikov, but both possibilities have their place in the higher design. The forces of history would be victorious and the dialogue would remain open in the event that such characters as Stavrogin and Svidrigaylov went "unpunished." Then we might indeed say that an ending is nothing more than a convention, a literary whistlestop. Yet that is not the case. So it seems only fair, in the ongoing pro and contra generated by Dostoevsky's art, to balance the scales by proposing that he was at least as concerned with giving appropriate artistic form to what he felt was the end of discourse as he was with keeping that discourse open. What lies beyond that end, whether it be of a novel, a life, or a history, was not, as we noted at the outset, within his purview as an artist or an Orthodox believer.

# TWO

## ———

### *Petersburg*:
### The Apocalyptic Horseman, the Unicorn,
### and the Verticality of Narrative

> Turning and turning in the widening gyre
> The falcon cannot hear the falconer;
> Things fall apart; the centre cannot hold;
> Mere anarchy is loosed upon the world,
> The blood-dimmed tide is loosed, and everywhere
> The ceremony of innocence is drowned;
> The best lack all conviction, while the worst
> Are full of passionate intensity.
>
> Surely some revelation is at hand;
> Surely the Second Coming is at hand.
> —W. B. Yeats, "The Second Coming"

> I am the white horseman sent by Someone to fulfill a command.
> —Andrey Bely,
> letter to Alexander Blok, December 1905

Certain novels, as was suggested in our Introduction, can be termed "apocalyptic fictions" because their stories not only have an end in sight, as all stories tend to do, but, more basic, they are actually *about the End.* Such works, at least in the Russian context: (1) invite the reader to interpret current events (a time of crisis) through the prism of Revelation; (2) create an intentional modal confusion, one that cuts across the grain of novelistic realism, by introducing a character who comes from a temporality *beyond* and who presents a revelatory message to other characters still trapped *in history;* and (3) use as their primary means of moving their stories forward, to the end, the apocalyptic images of horse and train (iron horse). All of these qualities were seen to be present in *The Idiot;* in this chapter an attempt will be made to demonstrate how they generate the "deep structure" of Bely's *Petersburg. Petersburg,* a novel that has moved still farther from the guiding ethos and pathos of nineteenth-century realism, was written between the revolutions of 1905 and 1917—the gathering crisis alluded to in *The Idiot* and *The Devils* is now at hand. Consequently, that sense of crisis is much closer to the surface of Bely's artistic manifold, permeating every level of expression, including that of plot. Indeed, nowhere in Russian literature has the idea of apocalypse entered so fully into its own artistic presentation as in this novel.

Although all the works discussed in these pages are about the shaping of contemporary history by apocalyptic (or utopian) expectations, one should not lose sight of the fact that only *The Idiot* and *Petersburg* were written *prior* to 1917. More than the others, these novels actually seem inscribed, "stigmatized" structurally (Bely in particular was obsessed with the christological paradigm), with the anxiety and suffering produced by living "under the shadow of the End." The dialogue between text and context that generates an ominous foreboding in Dostoevsky and Bely and a distanced, even serene retrospectivism in Bulgakov and Pasternak[1] cannot then be separated from the knowledge of *which side* of 1917 these authors wrote from. The very form of *The Idiot* and *Petersburg* reflects their authors' feelings of combined dread and fascination in the face of imminent revolution. They are written by individuals who have lifted personal experience (a difficult father, a harrowing prison term in Siberia, and a trying first marriage in Dostoevsky's case; a tortured family life and ambivalent feelings toward his own sexuality in Bely's) to the level of generational, societal, and national conflict. It is enough to point out, on the other hand, that Bulgakov and Pasternak insist on an individual—as opposed to collective—salvation through art and that Platonov dwells on the obstacles in the path from revolution to utopia to confirm that these writers are writing *after* the long awaited *transitus*. In other words, the aesthetic fields of their postrevolutionary novels are *prefigured* by the knowledge that the so-called *political* apocalypse of 1917 has *not* resulted in a mass transformation of old to new. Because *The Idiot* and *Petersburg* are conceived on this side of the epochal event by authors representing societal groups under siege—the conservative "saving remnant" and the liberal intelligentsia deserving the scourge of the *narod*, respectively—Dostoevsky and Bely invest their narratives with a *negative* apocalypse of judgment and retribution rather than with a *positive* apocalypse of universal reconciliation. In terms of the triadic pattern of crisis-judgment-vindication found in the biblical plot of Revelation, the accent in these works is decidedly on the second stage, but that does not mean, as shall be seen, that the third stage is not *implied* in the first two (McGinn, "Early Apocalypticism" 9). This is the Christian message that,

---

[1] I have in mind here especially the *endings* of *The Master and Margarita* and *Doctor Zhivago*.

despite the openness of the novel form and the many *unorthodox* elements in these works (especially *Petersburg*), cannot be written out of their plots.

Numerous literary historians have maintained that Blok's *The Twelve* (1918) is *the* poem of the revolution, representing an ultimate—for the poet's generation—dovetailing of Russian millenarianism and symbolist aesthetics. Certainly this became the accepted view at the time, when Blok, after months of silence, and lifted to a state bordering on Pythic possession by the sights and sounds of October, came forth with the last great flourish of his destructive music—the stark street medley of political sloganeering, incessant rifle fire, and snowy whirlwind. Here, after all, was what the symbolist poetic word had come to: from the assonance, vague lexicon, and prescient outline of an otherworldly harmony in turn-of-the-century poems to the Beautiful Lady to a work that on every level of discourse had turned to chronicle its own demise. Figures from different social classes, words from different lexical categories, meters (and non-meters) from different poetic genres all competed in a carnival of verbal and psychic carnage until the last moment when, miraculously, Christ (who was "with them"—the revolutionaries) initiated his *Parousia* and led his Bolshevik apostles out of the snowy mayhem and, *presumably*, into the people's New Jerusalem.[2] That Blok soon fell victim to a mystical deafness and that the New Jerusalem *implied* by the appearance of Christ in the poem's closing lines never materialized only added to the poet's legend and the tragic finality associated with this work.

Time has also shown that *The Twelve*'s status as exemplar of symbolist millenarianism should be shared with a prose work—Bely's *Petersburg*.[3] The threads linking Blok and Bely, these two major and in some sense competing voices of an era, stretch deep into the enchanted labyrinth of symbolist myth-making. Despite numerous misunderstandings, fallings-out, and near duels, Bely can only be called Blok's "soul-mate," one whose restless intellect and mathematical yearning for abstract pattern complemented the other's intuitive sensibilities and "pure" lyricism in a way reminiscent of the two halves searching for the whole—"the yolk and the white of the one shell," as Yeats put it—of the Platonic parable. Knit from a vast canvas of intertextuality implicating many of the major figures of Russian and

---

[2] The ending of *The Twelve* is one of the most disputed passages in all Russian literature.

[3] This is in some ways ironic, since the Symbolists were known primarily for their poetry, for their return to lyricism, aestheticism, and to what Merezhkovsky hailed as a "new idealism" following the age of the realist novel, with its "positivist" and "materialist" orientation and socially *engagé* reading public (see "O prichinakh" 209–305). Still, Bely's prose is anything but "prosaic," a fact of which he was well aware; in *Petersburg* especially the spectral presence of both Pushkin's *Bronze Horseman*, the most famous narrative poem in the Russian language, and Gogol's *Dead Souls*, a novel subtitled *poèma*, looms large.

Western literature, thought, and culture; looking back on the past and forward to the future in terms at once autobiographical, historical, and aesthetic; and cast in a narrative prose framework sensitive to its own poetic elements, *Petersburg* fully deserves its reputation as symbolist novel par excellence. Moreover, it is a work as conscious of its position *at the end* of an historical and artistic tradition as is Blok's poem, and what it achieves for the genre of prose fiction is equivalent to what *The Twelve* achieves for the genre of the *poèma* (see Anscheutz, "Bely's *Petersburg*"). Hence there is a certain "bio-aesthetic" rightness to the fact that, though both were consumed by their own brands of millenarianism, Bely, with his expansive intellect, gravitated toward the genre that best accommodated his artistic gifts, while Blok, who was not particularly disposed to a narrative story-line, gravitated as far as he could in that direction (the *narrative* poem) without sacrificing entirely his gifts as lyricist.

But before telling more of this story, it would be well to look at the context out of which Bely's novel grew. One might begin with the statement that from the early 1890s until the October Revolution of 1917, a period roughly contemporaneous with the reign of Nicholas II (1894–1917) and known to literary historians under the suggestive name of "the Silver Age," there was an explosion (Bely would have used the term) of apocalyptic literature (poems, novels, plays), painting, music, and essay writing unlike anything hitherto or thereafter seen in the annals of Russian culture.[4] While even a scholar as astute as M. H. Abrams has argued that "the nation possessed of the most thoroughly and enduringly millennial ideology is . . . America" and that "the period of English and German Romanticism . . . is the most apocalyptic of cultured eras" ("Theme and Variations" 357, 358), one can only suppose that this hyperbole is driven by a certain West European/American cultural bias. For the fact remains that, due to a constellation of factors—agrarian Russia's position on the verge of the industrial age, political and social tensions both internal (periodic famine) and external (a powerful Japan on the Eastern front), and an intellectual community long obsessed with a messianic urge to expiate its guilt before the long-suffering *narod* and insecure about a past unworthy of Western standards of "history"—eschatological literature in Russia seemed ready to burst into rich and exotic bloom.

The coming of the new century was viewed by neo-idealists as a millennial date, the dawn of a new era (see Merezhkovskii, "O prichinakh" 209–305). Vyacheslav Ivanov, a leading theorist of Symbolism, exclaimed that "the period of crisis and the Last Judgment is beginning" (Blok, *ZK* 169);

---

[4] On the various sources for the apocalyptic theme in Silver Age thought and writing, see Hackel (*A Poet* 1–48) and Rosenthal ("Eschatology").

in his famous study of Tolstoy and Dostoevsky (published 1901–02) Merezhkovsky wrote that "the principal thought of Christianity is the thought
of *the end of the world*" (*Tolstoi i Dostoevskii* 528); Blok wrote a friend in
the summer of 1901 that "the end is already near, the unexpected will soon
take place" (*ss* VIII:18); and Bely linked the "end" of poetry with "the approaching End of Universal History" in an article provocatively entitled
"The Apocalypse in Russian Poetry" (*Lug zelenyi* 246). Over and over
again in their early work and correspondence Bely and Blok returned to this
theme of the imminent apocalypse. Not only did they work it into their art,
they also found occasion to work it into the emerging legends of their
lives—Bely in particular saw himself as a Christ figure, as the "white horseman" who, as offspring of the "Woman Clothed with the Sun" of Revelation, had come to reign victorious over the new era.[5]

   [5] Bely from early on saw his art and his age as poised on a *rubezh* (hence the title of one of
his books of memoirs), a "borderline" separating all spatio-temporal world (and artistic)
models as they had been viewed up to then and the totally new and different one that was
about to arrive. This eschatologism entered into Bely's personal mythology, including his view
of himself (often parodic but nonetheless at some level serious) as a Christ figure. As he wrote,
not inappropriately, at the *end* of *On the Border of Two Centuries*, when recalling the birth of
the new century and his transformation from Boris Bugaev into Andrey Bely ("Andrew the
White"), "Thus did I approach the border (January 1901) with the real knowledge of an in-
credible, unheard-of crisis—entailing both future wars and revolutions and unprecedented
construction—in all of culture, but without a precise knowledge of the causes shaping the
picture of the future" (486). See also Cioran, *Apocalyptic Symbolism* 27, 38; Lavrov, "Mifotvorchestvo 'argonavtov' " 137.
   Nearly every writer of note at some point during the first two decades of the century paid
tribute to the theme of the apocalypse. To some, such as Valery Bryusov, whose poem "The
Pale Horse" (1903) caused Bely and his friend Sergey Solovyov to leap from their chairs at a
first reading, the apocalypse was more pyrotechnics and stage decorations—the background to
political and social tensions—than part of a clearly articulated philosophy of history. Others,
such as Merezhkovsky, Alexey Remizov, Vasily Rozanov, and Maximilian Voloshin, used the
theme of the apocalypse in a conscious effort to telescope patterns in biblical and national
history. In his trilogy *Christ and Antichrist* (pub. 1896–1905), Merezhkovsky (who probably
had greater impact on the young Blok and Bely as a biographical figure than as literary mentor)
began his post-Nietzschean critique of historical Christianity. His efforts were directed toward
the inauguration of a neo-Joachimist "Third Testament," a future time when all the dualities
(pagan-Christian, Dionysus-Apollo, East-West, male-female, etc.) that had produced tension
and conflict in the past would be unified. Remizov's elaborate use of the *skaz* technique and
his striking blend of orality and lyricism in *Sisters in the Cross* (1910), his playing of the
*skoromokh* (minstrel/clown) "at the margins" of discourse, his portrayal of the Bronze Horseman as a "giant fireman" come to haunt a modern Evgeny (Marakulin), and his interest in
cyclical time at the expense of a linear plot suggest that this novel may have had a considerable
impact on Bely's *Petersburg*, which was begun shortly afterward (see Slobin, *Remizov's Fictions* 8–24). Rozanov, who insouciantly demolished generic boundaries, mixed fact and fiction,
and placed statements of the most intimate lyrical pathos alongside statements of riotous buf-
foonery worthy of Karamazov *père*, became the Bakunin of Silver Age prose. Perhaps better
than anyone it was this combination of philosopher and *pater familias* in soiled dressing gown

While this apocalypticism was certainly "in the air," it had to have some
concrete point of origin, and evidence indicates that in the cases of Blok and
Bely, as well as in those of other symbolist colleagues, this source was
largely the life and work of Vladimir Solovyov (1853–1900).[6] Solovyov,
who has been called Russia's first genuine philosopher, and his foil, the reactionary but equally eschatological Konstantin Leontiev, together formed
a living bridge from the thought of Dostoevsky to that of the "younger"
symbolists. That he died like Nietzsche,[7] the other *predtecha* (precursor)

---

(in one revealing metaphor he likens his soul to goldfish frolicking in the sunlight while
trapped in the fetid water of an aquarium) who epitomized the sense of simultaneous anarchy
and faith, "openness" and "closure," hanging over his generation. Rozanov's last work was
significantly entitled *The Apocalypse of Our Time* (1918–19), and its fascinating view of the
End predicated not on humanity's failure to live up to Christ's message in the New Testament
but on Christ's inability to be sufficiently human has been shown to be a source for *The Twelve*
(Hackel, *The Poet* 166–71). And with themes reminiscent of Blok but framed in a distinctly
new post-symbolist idiom, Maximilian Voloshin made the transition from pre-Raphaelite aesthete to philosopher of history in his poems on the First World War and Revolution. These
poems, some of the most striking ever written on the horrors of those times, make periodic
allusion to Russia's Armageddon and Last Judgment and, without taking sides, draw parallels
with other apocalyptic moments in history (e.g., the French Revolution). In "Russia" (1915),
for example, Voloshin invokes the battered mare of Nekrasov and Dostoevsky, whereas in
"Wild Field" (1920) he traces the spectacle of national chaos to the folkloric stallion of the
Asiatic horde. (Intriguingly, with his emphasis on femininity, this had been a mare in Blok's
"On the Kulikovo Field" [1908].) As shall be shown in our discussion of the equine motif in
Bely, these two sides of the Russian popular character—victim and avenging judge—represent
an objectification of history's final movement. See below.

  [6] To be sure, the influence on Bely's writings of *a number* of philosophers (Nietzsche, Kant,
Schopenhauer, Hegel, Comte, Bergson, Skovoroda, Steiner, etc.) has been duly noted. In addition, Bely seems in later life to have had at least some mixed feelings about his early infatuation with the "eternal mystic" (*Stikhotvoreniia* 38). On Bely's changing view of Solovyov
(as well as of Rudolph Steiner), see Elsworth, *A Critical Study* 7–53; and Cassedy, "Bely the
Thinker" 316–20. Perhaps Cassedy expresses it most succinctly: "In spite of the number and
great diversity of systems that Bely passed through, the central principle remained in force,
and that principle was the incorporation of Kantian criticism into Orthodox theology (or Orthodox theology into Kantian criticism) in a manner that resembles the structure of Solov'ev's
thought" ("Bely the Thinker" 319). For more on Solovyov and his influence, see Cioran, *Vladimir Solov'ev*; Levitskii, *Ocherki* 190–202; Walicki, *A History* 371–405; West, *Russian Symbolism* 35–42; and Zenkovsky, *A History* II: 469–531.

  [7] On the Nietzschean connection in Bely, see Anscheutz, Bennett, and Gerigk. It should be
stressed at the outset, however, that, despite the undeniable attraction that both Solovyov and
Nietzsche held for the young Bely, these two thinkers were, in his case, more *symbols* than
objects of scholarly study. Solovyov was seen as a precursor (*predtecha*), one who sounded the
horn of a new era about to begin; Nietzsche the prophet (*prorok*) represented the essential
anti-positivist mind turned in on a world-in-crisis. In other words, while what Solovyov and
Nietzsche said was important to Bely, perhaps more important was how their works (and,
equally important, their lives) could be applied to the context of Russian and world history
coming after them. See Lavrov, "Mifotvorchestvo" 141–42.

who was a rival for the young Bely's attention, in the year 1900, at the watershed of the new century, was understood by those who came after to be predestined. Simply put, Solovyov represented the final stage of a confluence of German idealist philosophy (Hegel and especially Schelling) and Russian messianism (the Chaadaev of *Apologie d'un fou*, Khomyakov and Ivan Kireevsky, the Herzen of "Russian socialism," Dostoevsky, Danilevsky) that had been active in Russian thought for much of the nineteenth century. But unlike the Slavophiles and more like the Dostoevsky of the Pushkin speech (whom he anticipated by several years with his 1877 speech entitled "Three Forces"), Solovyov saw Russia's manifest destiny and role as world exemplar in a turning away from the spirit of nationalism and a move toward the spirit of ecumenicalism. He was, furthermore, an avid student of mystical thought (here the links with Bely become most obvious), and in his eclecticism he seems at one time or another to have made forays into the writings of the Jewish *Cabala* and the works of Jakob Boehme, Swedenborg, Saint-Martin, and Baader (Walicki, *A History* 381). Solovyov has been described as a man of contrasts, an enigmatic figure whose physical and metaphysical stature was somehow upstaged by a light, puckish humor and an almost childlike laughter. Although there is an erotic streak running through much of his lyric poetry (which Bely and his friends knew by heart) and his philosophy,[8] he was also plainly uncomfortable with the notion of sexual intercourse (again prefiguring Bely). Especially meaningful for the impressionistic and speculative Bely was the fact that the older philosopher and father figure discerned a hidden movement and meaning in history, one seen first as evolutionary but near the end of his life as violent and apocalyptic, and recast the now tired East-West debate in terms at once provocative and "prophetically" appropriate to the times.[9]

[8] See, e.g., *The Meaning of Love* (1892–94).

[9] It might be said that Solovyov's abstractly synthesizing cast of mind was, if transposed to the Western European cultural context, essentially anachronistic, even "medieval" (see Alexandrov, *The Major Fiction* 191–93, as well as Solovyov's own "On the Decline of the Medieval Worldview" [1891]). After all, the crisis of transcendent faith brought on by the constant intrusion of humanistic values, values which Dostoevsky, Solovyov, Bely, and others were trying to oppose, suggests a return to a much earlier time in the West—not that of the post-Enlightenment but that of the emerging Renaissance (which Russia largely missed), when Dante, as Bakhtin has pointed out, was building his elaborate cosmology and Rabelais, with his human-centered *joie de vivre* and carnivalesque laughter, was dismantling it concentric brick by brick. Solovyov's mystical view of history as tripartite progression toward reintegration (Moslem East → Western civilization → Slavdom) is not so much reminiscent of the Hegelian dialectic as of Joachim of Fiore's break with Augustinian tradition and his assertion that a third, and last, *status* of history (that of the Holy Spirit) is yet to come. And to compare Bely's earlier and later literary descriptions of Solovyov, say those in the Symphonies and those in *The First Encounter*, is to see an evolving mythical kinship between the philosopher in his role as John the Baptist and the young poet in his role as Christ figure of Symbolism.

Solovyov's urge to achieve a *vseedinstvo* (all in one) of absolute and relative, God and creation, Eastern and Western churches sounds curiously like the apocalyptic marriage of word and world associated with Wordsworth's generation of English and German Romantics at the time of the French Revolution. The principal difference between the pre- and post-revolutionary phases of English Romanticism lies, as Abrams has shown, in a shift from socio-political to artistic apocalypse, from a massive, revolutionary restructuring to a private, imaginative *revisioning* of reality. For Solovyov, however, who still describes Sophia as "the Bride of Christ" and "the image of the transformed world" (Levitskii, *Ocherki* 192), the apocalyptic marriage is something to be approached primarily through mystical rather than aesthetic terms (although the two are not mutually exclusive, and the possibility of metaphorical transference is present because Sophia is also the source of human *creativity*). His apocalypticism, even its "pessimistic" variant in *Three Conversations*, lies on *this* side of both revolutions, and hence is characterized by a more "naive" faith in the actual restructuring of reality. It would take Bely of course, with his exclusive insistence on the theurgic power of language, to extend the process begun by Solovyov, to "metapoeticize" the latter's religious philosophy, and to seek a logosemantic basis for the ties between revolution and revelation.[10]

---

One could in fact extend the anachronistic analogy farther still: just as Dante became a "lover of wisdom" through his study of Boëthius' *Consolation of Philosophy*, where the condemned author is rescued from despair by a *dialogue* with Lady Philosophy, so too was Bely introduced to the notion of mystical knowledge through the Solovyovian ideal of Holy Wisdom, Sophia, and through the dialogic form of Solovyov's most influential work, *Three Conversations* (1900).

[10] If, in the early and middle stages of his career, Solovyov expressed faith in Sophia—or the transfiguration of humanity that will come to pass when we live up to the divine potential in each of us—then at the end of his life he was consumed by the counter-notion of apocalypse, or the *initia dolorum* that will come in its place precisely because what was hoped for previously has failed to materialize. And whereas in early works, such as *Philosophical Principles of Integral Knowledge* (1877), the stress had been laid on a three-part integration at the levels of creativity (theurgy), knowledge (theosophy), and social practice (theocracy) (Walicki, *A History* 376), in *Three Conversations* the stress is laid on the historical *disintegration* of humanity. A similar pattern of faith (or perhaps "hope" is the more operative term) in the promised coming of Sophia followed by a period of frustration, despair, and apocalyptic foreboding is found in the works of Bely and Blok, who called their versions of *Das Ewig-Weibliche* "the Woman Clothed in the Sun" and "the Beautiful Lady," respectively. The chief difference is that the younger Symbolists, worn out by waiting and caught up in the ferment of the times, thoroughly "Russianized" and "revolutionized" their feminine ideals. So much in fact did they alter Solovyov's original notion that, in the later works of Blok especially, Sophia/Beautiful Lady, rather than the spirit of harmony, has become just the opposite—the spirit of popular and elemental chaos, of bleeding *Rus'* itself (see, e.g., "On the Kulikovo Field" [1908]). This might lead one to the hypothesis that what are essentially separate concepts in Solovyov (Christ/Sophia) are somehow combined or blurred in the subsequent generation, and that the

*Three Conversations* (1900) is an often witty but ultimately serious presentation of history's confrontation with the active powers of evil: from the "down-to-earth" approach of the general, the leader of the first conversation, who in his earlier life fought evil with the sword (the "past"); to the "progressive" approach of the statesman, the leader of the second conversation, who advocates negotiation and ameliorative measures as the best antidote to evil (the "present"); to the "unconditional" approach of Mr. Z. (clearly Solovyov's mouthpiece), the leader of the last conversation, who suggests in his story-within-a-story ("The Short Tale of the Antichrist") that the Tolstoyan concept of passive resistance to evil is itself a weapon of the Antichrist (since evil must be *actively* confronted and since there is no such thing as Christianity without the divinity of Christ) and thus a sure sign that the "last days" are upon us (the "future"). Following the philosopher Nikolay Fyodorov, Solovyov is essentially arguing that there can be no "progress" (the "religion" of the statesman) where there is death, and a society or nation that so fears a physical end to life that it sacrifices its soul for a safe spot in the here and now is on the verge of disaster.[11]

Mr. Z's "short tale," borrowed from a monk with the suggestive name "Pansophius" and strongly reminiscent of Dostoevsky's "Legend of the Grand Inquisitor" in *The Brothers Karamazov*, is a visionary, highly far-fetched account of what history has in store for the doomed modern world: the twentieth century, a time of "last great wars, civil strife, and revolutions" (*Tri razgovora* 193), will be marked by a Japanese-led emergence of "Panmongolism." (Solovyov's implication, to be taken up by Bely and Blok, is that history has come *full circle* from the time of the Tatar Yoke in medieval Rus'.) This united Asiatic assault on Russia and Europe will result in a fatal intermingling of blood,[12] an ultimate loss of faith in both positivism and religious truth, and conditions fertile for the appearance of the "man of the future" (*griadushchii chelovek*). When he does appear, the Antichrist will be a kind of photographic negative of Christ—a thirty-three year old *sverkhchelovek* (*Übermensch*), a "great thinker, writer, and public figure," who *believes* "in good, God, and the Messiah" but *loves* "only

---

strangely androgynous figure at the end of *The Twelve* is at once Sophia, inasmuch as it is the objectification of popular hopes for a different world order, *and* Christ himself, inasmuch as it has come out of the pages of Revelation to signal the End. For Blok's "understanding" of the difference between Christ and Sophia and their role in the End, see Orlov, *Perepiska* 34–37, and my "Blok, Bely, and the Poetics of Revelation."

[11] This sounds very much like Lebedev's message in *The Idiot* (VIII: 309–16). In general, the intertextual connections between *The Idiot* and *The Devils*, on the one hand, and *Three Conversations*, on the other, are obvious and rich.

[12] Konstantin Leontiev, in many ways Solovyov's foil, also had strange forebodings about the dangers of a universal racial intermixing (*vsesmeshenie*). See, e.g., his "Nad mogiloi Pazukhina," *s* VII: 425.

himself" (*Tri razgovora* 199–200). His father is not God, but the latter's distorted image (Satan), whom he encounters in a revelation, and his mother is not the Virgin, but a "woman of easy virtue" (i.e., the Whore of Babylon). The Antichrist seems poised to achieve the theocracy of which the author—now apparently parodying himself—only dreamed, including the unification of the Catholic, Protestant, and Orthodox churches. And he will do so by using the ethic of this fallen world against itself ("In order to be accepted [*priniatyi*], one has to be pleasant [*priiatnyi*]" [*Tri razgovora* 206]) and by plying his connections as military man, capitalist, and *littéra-teur*. The theocracy, whose only article of faith is an allegiance to the man-god on earth, is held together by the conditions of a self-imposed slavery: peace (*mir*), satiety (*sytost'*), and spiritual entertainment (*chudesa*—"mir-acles").[13] However, the supremacy of the Antichrist is finally challenged by a multi-denominational saving remnant that makes its way into the desert to await the End.[14] The Jews revolt when it is discovered that the Antichrist is not circumcised. Shortly thereafter he and his armies are swallowed up by a lake of fire, and the remnant is rewarded for its faith by a vision of the returned Christ descending to the now transfigured city of Jerusalem. So it seems that Solovyov, even in his modern parable of humanity's *failed* mission in history, could not avoid a Christian version of deus ex machina and what is basically a triumphant or "happy" ending to the biblical plot.

I have chosen to dwell on *Three Conversations* not because of the work's speculative interest and charm (which are considerable) or because of its literary merits (which are not) but because many of its ideas and even images make their way into the *aesthetic* shape of *Petersburg*. Whereas a connection between these two works on philosophical grounds has been posited more than once, no one has demonstrated how Bely actually "meta-poeticizes" the concepts of his first and most influential father figure. I would begin by suggesting that *Petersburg* can be read as Bely's *long* tale about the Antichrist and that the entire question of authorship and narra-tive hierarchy (Pansophius—Mr. Z.—Solovyov) that is raised rather super-ficially in *Three Conversations* can be seen as a central issue in Bely's novel. The point is that, for the "prophetic" consciousness, the formal expression of revelation is not the same as its source, which comes from another, higher order. Prophets (who literally "speak before") do not control the voice from beyond but are controlled by it; they are *pierced* (one of Solo-vyov's and Bely's favorite words in this context) by sights and sounds *from above* which they pass on to those *below*.

After his epiphany, the Antichrist gains control over the public through

---

[13] Once again, note that these conditions are very close to the ones of which Dostoevsky warned in the "Legend."

[14] The Orthodox contingent is led by the elder John, who legend maintains is the still living author of Revelation.

the writing of a book, *The Open Way to Universal Peace and Welfare*, which reveals "the unprecedented power of genius" (*Tri razgovora* 205). This "all-encompassing" and "all-reconciling" work is of course not the Bible but its Satanic counterpart. Rather than pointing the way, as does the New Testament, to the Heavenly City and salvation, it points the way to temporal power and to the dark capital of this world (the Antichrist eventually moves his residence from Rome to Jerusalem). In *Petersburg*, Bely will also focus on a "profane center" doomed for its history of denying transcendent faith. And he will do so by *"Russianizing"* the context and writing his own version of the last book of the Bible. But just as the destruction of the faithless necessarily implies *vindication* of the saving remnant in Solovyov, so too will the destruction of the old order imply the eventual appearance of a totally purged and restored new order in Bely. What this means *on the narrative level* is that the Antichrist figures in both works (the *sverkhchelovek* in Solovyov, The Bronze Horseman in Bely) *appear* to control their stories when in fact they are tools in the hands of a higher author/narrator. It is their role to bring judgment, punishment, retribution: only through and after these trials can the other, "happy" side of God's ending be reached. This is another way of saying that the christological pattern of trial-crucifixion-resurrection and the apocalyptical pattern of crisis-judgment-vindication are analogous, since the latter recapitulates on a universal scale the central event of Christian history—the victory of one human being over death—presented in the former. Thus it follows for Solovyov as for Bely that the way *out* of God's plot is not the way back into this world, and that in troubled times one has to read the signs carefully in order to glimpse the watermark of divine intentionality in the destructive activities of an awesome imposter.

Before leaving Solovyov I would like also to propose that Bely drew from the description of the revelation of Satan to his son for his (Bely's) treatment of the climactic confrontation between Peter and Dudkin in *Petersburg*. Satan appears as a "metallic" figure shining with a "misty, phosphorescent" radiance and his eyes "pierce" the Antichrist's soul (*Tri razgovora* 203). Likewise, his spiritual essence (an icy stream rather than the molten lava of Bely) flows into his son (Dudkin is also a "son" by Peter) before the latter goes out to do his bidding (in Bely the murder of Lippanchenko). These and other points of contiguity, numerous enough not to be happenstance, are, to repeat, "Russianized" by Bely, translated into what he took to be the *sound* of revolution/revelation in his language (see below). That is to say, Bely clearly borrowed from Pushkin for his literary description of the Bronze Horseman,[15] but he also superimposed on that description the

---

[15] Which is, to be sure, full of ambiguity and tension though not yet "apocalyptic" (see Introduction).

biblical nexus, mediated by Solovyov, joining Satan to Antichrist, father to son, spirit of death to act of destruction, etc.

The events surrounding the Russo-Japanese War (1904–05) and the Revolution of 1905 provided the necessary context for the rather vague millennial hopes expressed in the early works of Bely and Blok.[16] What had conspired to frustrate the personal lives of the two friends in the years leading up to 1905 (e.g., Sophia had failed in her hypostasis as Blok's wife Lyubov Mendeleeva) was now coupled in their minds with the indignities suffered by the Russian people. In short, Bely and Blok gradually became aware of how personal trials could be emblematic of popular ones. This in turn lent a new sense of urgency to their "maximalist" logic: the change symbolized by the coming of Sophia was no longer to be passively awaited, but *actively induced*. As Blok put it many years later, the poet's *podvig* (feat), his sacred responsibility, was *"to remake everything*. To organize it so that everything becomes new; so that our false, filthy, boring, and ugly life becomes a just, pure, happy, and beautiful life" ("Intelligentsiia i revoliutsiia," *ss* VI: 12).

To invest their potentially anarchistic impulses with historical legitimacy, Bely and Blok did not draw on the time-honored image of the patient, self-sacrificing, traditionally Orthodox *muzhik*.[17] Rather, they were attracted to the tradition of sectarian movements. Since the time of the Schism in the last half of the seventeenth century, when the Old Believers (*starovery*) split from the established Orthodox faith on ritualistic (and other) grounds,

[16] Both of these violent episodes—the decimation of the Imperial navy by the Japanese at Tsushima Strait in May 1905 and the brutal suppression of Father Gapon and his fellow demonstrators by tsarist soldiers on "Bloody Sunday" (January 9 [22], 1905)—were marked by disastrous lapses of judgment on the part of Nicholas' government. The tsar was no longer seen in the popular imagination as an essentially innocent but misinformed *batiushka* (little father). The literary community (most of the Symbolists were left-leaning) also seized on these happenings to confirm their belief in the rightness of popular rebellion and in the inevitable overthrow of the corrupt Romanov dynasty. To cite only the most famous Decadent of the time, Valery Bryusov declared a death sentence on Imperial Russia and its pretensions as the "Third Rome" in his poem "Tsushima" (1905)—

> And on that day, when in fire and tempest
> It [the Imperial fleet], innocent, went down
> We [also] fell from the azure heights into the abyss
> and drank the deadly wave.

—and he called for a barbaric bloodletting, an unleashing of nomadic hordes into the tired centers of civilization, in "The Coming Huns" (1905):

> Like a drunken horde come crashing
> In on us from your dark encampments—
> To give new life to our decrepit body
> In an ocean of burning blood.

[17] See, e.g., the Lukeria of Turgenev's "Living Relics" or the Alyosha of Tolstoy's "Alyosha the Pot."

Russians had perceived a close connection between times of popular unrest and apocalyptic prophecies regarding the Antichrist (see Introduction, and Hackel, *The Poet* 40). This was especially true of the reign of Peter, a seminal figure in Bely's novel, who, because of his westernizing ways and desire to reduce the role of orthodox tsar to that of worldly emperor, was widely regarded by the Old Believers to be the Antichrist.[18] Elsewhere it has been alleged that the Old Believers played an underground role in the uprisings of Stenka Razin (1667–71) and Emelyan Pugachyov (1773–75) (Hackel, *The Poet* 36–41). In 1907, Blok vowed to study "this phenomenon of sectarianism" (*ss* v: 215), and at some level he took himself quite seriously, as his growing infatuation with the following figures suggests: the novelist Melnikov-Pechersky, who wrote about the Schismatics in his work *In the Forests*; the poet Mikhail Kuzmin, whose parents were Old Believers; the decadent Alexander Dobrolyubov, who left his private world of the aesthete to disappear "into the people"; and most importantly, the peasant poet Nikolay Klyuev, a favorite correspondent of these years, whose mother had been a *khlystovka* (a member of the sect of Russian "Flagellants"). It is presumably not coincidental that Bely wrote his first novel, *The Silver Dove* (1909), during roughly the same period, and that this work centers around a young man (Daryalsky) who, weary of his civilized past, goes into the country, where he is caught up in a sect of *golubi* ("Doves"—an offshoot of the Flagellants) and ritually murdered when he fails to fulfill his role as groom to their demonic popular version of the Woman Clothed in the Sun (Matryona). Furthermore, the only character migrating from *The Silver Dove* into the text of *Petersburg*, Bely's next novel, is Styopka, a sectarian apocalypticist who fills Dudkin's head with cryptic allusions to the Second Coming.

The revival of the revolutionary movement caused Bely and other intellectuals to rethink the essential tenets of Marxism, to examine the parallels between the latter's version of violent change in history and that outlined by the apocalypticists (Solovyov, Leontiev). This process of reevaluation reached a fever pitch in the famous debate over *Landmarks* (*Vekhi*, 1909), a collection of essays by such leading cultural and religious thinkers as N. Berdyaev, S. Bulgakov, and S. Frank, among others. Rejecting materialism as a useful platform for change (and thus in effect condemning much of their own youthful activity on the fringes of the Marxist left), these individuals urged the intelligentsia to work instead for the *spiritual* life of the

---

[18] One of Bely's contemporaries, Ivan Konevskoy, described Peter in a turn-of-the-century poem ("Sreda") as a Demon, "the Antichrist of native lore" (*Stikhi i proza* 119–21). This poem in turn made a deep impression on Blok, who in his own "Petersburg Poem" portrayed the conflict between Petersburg and Moscow in terms of an Antichrist–St. George opposition. See Hackel, *The Poet* 41.

people—to "turn from political struggle to constructive intellectual work" (Brooks, "The *Vexi* Dispute" 28). On the other hand, at this same time a number of influential Marxist intellectuals were shrewdly secularizing ready-made patterns from the biblical plot and tapping into their emotionally charged language.[19] In *Mother* (1907), one of the prominent texts of his "God-building" phase, Gorky repeatedly describes his revolutionaries as latter-day Christian martyrs, whose enlightened Marxist values are the equivalent of a new faith.[20] Presumably Bely could not have missed the obvious: Solovyov's vision of theocracy, of a world transfigured through the agency of Sophia and based on *sobornost'* (the Slavophile notion of "free unity"), had been redefined in economic and political terms and presented as world without class strife. By 1908, as N. Valentinov has attested, Bely had advanced to the point where he was at least investigating the possibility of proceeding from Symbolism to Marxism (*Two Years* 12, 17, 48–49, 61–67).

Yet Bely could never accept the most basic tenet of Marxism—that history is not governed by an abstract authority (God) but *determined* by immanent laws, "definite relations that are indispensable and independent of [one's] will" (Marx and Engels, *Selected Works* 1: 362). One has only to acknowledge the reality of these relations, the fact that it is impossible to live *outside* them, in order to be enlightened. If this determinism had a surface resemblance to divine authority, it differed on the more fundamental grounds that the historical process was now seen as inscribed with, and ultimately circumscribed by, such laws. They were the "given," what Fredric Jameson has called the "untranscendable horizon" of Marxist thought. There was nothing beyond or prior to them. Their "plot," whose image in time was the Hegelian-Marxian spiral of dialectical forces, was said to culminate in a classless paradise *in this world*:

> For Hegel, the notion of reality unfolding through its contradictions and rising to ever-higher levels until Spirit at last becomes conscious of itself constituted no new Revelation but only (and here was the originality of Hegelian philosophy as he saw it) Revelation in its *immanent* form, History discovering its own meaning *from the inside* [my emphasis], humanity grasping itself not as the arbitrary creation of some

[19] Background to this question is provided by Rosenthal, "Eschatology" 111–12. For additional historical context, see Tucker (*Philosophy and Myth* 22–25, 222–26) and Ulam (*The Unfinished Revolution* 113–19), and for the literary links, see Clark and Holquist, *Bakhtin* 156ff.

[20] Cf. the case of Trotsky, who could do without the world beyond, but could not dispense with the notion of a classless paradise, the "end" toward which the dialectical process was relentlessly moving: "Let the priests of all confessions tell of a paradise in the world beyond—we say we will create a true paradise for men on this earth" (cited in Cohn, *Pursuit* 312).

absent sky-deity but as the Spirit gradually becoming manifest to itself (Dowling, *Jameson, Althusser, Marx* 45).

For Solovyov, however, it was the transcendent, not the immanent, that was foremost, and herein lies the central difference (leaving aside such obvious but not unrelated matters as language) between the Bely of *Petersburg* and the Gorky of *Mother*.

These two works, written within a few years of each other, represent the ultimate irreconcilability of the Christian and Marxist plots of history in their novelized forms. There is no dramatic irony in *Mother* precisely because there is no sense of epistemological disjunction between author, narrator, and character. The story is told in the third person, and what the hero Pavel knows to be true (the Marxist view of history) within his space-time is *self-contained*, leaving no room for doubt. That is to say, with the help of a naive and straightforward narrative tone we are lead to believe that what Pavel thinks is identical to what his author/narrator thinks. In Gorky, therefore, there is no sense of narrative hierarchy, of one figure (the narrator) knowing more than another figure (the character). But, as we shall see in more detail shortly, Bely's novel is structured throughout on dramatic irony and narrative hierarchy: the narrator, playful yet at some level serious, knows more than Apollon Apollonovich, and his knowledge begins with the fact that he accepts the possibility of higher forces and willingly assumes his role as *another's* voice. Thus, while Bely's importance as a master stylist is well-established, his single greatest contribution to the "counter-tradition" of modern Russian novel as Christian history may be his insistence on the essential *verticality* of narrative discourse, which, to repeat, opposes the essential *horizontality* of the Socialist Realist exemplar.

The underlying differences in the thought systems of Solovyov and Marx lead us to the question of how indeed did Bely visualize the course and climax of the historical plot at the time of the writing of *Petersburg*. Like Blake and Yeats, both Bely and Blok were intrigued by the form of the spiral, and it is arguable that they saw the development of history in general and of their own artistic development in particular in helical or conical terms. Blok, for example, remarked to Nadezhda Pavlovich near the end of his life that "if one views my oeuvre as a spiral, then *The Twelve* would be on the top loop, [at a point] corresponding to [that on] the lowest loop, where *The Snow Mask* [would be located] (Pavlovich, *Vospominaniia* 487). And Bely reassessed his own work prior to *Petersburg* in a letter of 1915 to Ivanov-Razumnik in this way: "Here I come to the question posed by you—did I not [at that time] *return* to the period of the *Symphonies*, not however, by way of a circle, but by way of a spiral? Yes, of course" (Dolgopolov, "Dopolneniia," in *Peterburg* 520).[21] The spiral of history most often associated with Hegelian dialectic and the Romantic period entered Western thought as a marriage of the Neoplatonic "circle" (the theory of cycles and eternal recurrence coming largely from Chrysippus, Aristotle, and Posidonius; the idea of the "great circle" from Plotinus and Proclus) and the Christian "line" (Christian history's sharply defined forward movement coming primarily from Augustine's assertion in *The City of God* that the Christ example is unique and unrepeatable).[22] The Romantics saw the spiral as an elegant way of incorporating continuity in change, of moving through the flux of history to a "recovered unity" and higher level of consciousness. "In the most representative Romantic version of emanation and return . . . the recovered unity is not, as in the school of Plotinus, the simple, undifferentiated unity of its origin, but a unity which is *higher*, because it incorporates the intervening differentiations" (my emphasis; Abrams, *Natural Supernaturalism* 183–84). Or, to recast the Hegelian dialectic of history becoming pure spirit in terms of the original biblical plot, the Heavenly City that opens its gates to the righteous at the end of Revelation differs from the Edenic paradise of Genesis not in the quality of its bliss (both are *beyond* history in the sense that they are *pre*lapsarian and *post*parousial), but in the price of entry—the one was given freely to our first parents, the second is to be *earned* through the trials of time.

It is difficult to say precisely where Bely found his image of the spiral. The Hegelian/Marxist view of history was certainly "in the air," and, what is more, Hegel's statement at the end of his *Logic*—"We have now returned to the notion of the Idea with which we began," but "this return to the beginning is also an advance"—sounds curiously like Bely's escape from the "eternal return" of Nietzsche (see below). On the other hand, Bely may have been trying to counteract the influence of Schopenhauer (who also envisioned the natural order in circular form) on the work of other Symbolists, most notably the misanthropic escapist Sologub, whose work he knew well (see Dikman, in Sologub, *Stikhotvoreniia* 53). Even more likely is the possibility that Bely came to the idea of spiralate evolution through his study of Rudolph Steiner (begun in 1909), whose elaborate schematization of the history of the universe in anthroposophical terms recalls certain aspects of Solovyov's philosophy.[23] This master plan, which included

---

[21] Other examples include Blok's comparison of life's transitions to a series of "tormented returns" (zк 304) and his ruminations on the conical form of *Retribution* (ss iii: 397). See Maksimov, "O spira leo braznykh obrazakh."

[22] For more on the complex issue of the circularity versus linearity of history, see, e.g., Abrams (*Natural Supernaturalism*), Arendt (*Between Past and Future*), Cullmann (*Christ and Time*), Eliade (*The Myth of the Eternal Return*), and Starr (*History and the Concept of Time*).

[23] It should be stressed that the precise extent of Steiner's influence on the conception of

the individual ego's helical odyssey through seven planets, seven races, and seven sub-races, is laid out in Steiner's *Occult Science: an Outline*. As John Elsworth has demonstrated, there are significant parallels between Steiner's notion of the process of initiation into true cognition, which leads the ego *back* through three stages (imagination-inspiration-intuition) to a psychic unity since lost, and Solovyov's tripartite cosmology. Moreover, the idea of a triumphant or higher return, found in both Solovyov and Steiner, hints at, once again, something more familiar—the re-enactment in history of the birth, crucifixion, and resurrection of Christ (see Elsworth, *A Critical Study* 38–45).

But regardless of the specific provenance of the spiral in Bely's case, there is sufficient evidence to suggest that he had this geometrical form in mind as he worked on *Petersburg* and that it is implicated in the shape of Russian history as presented in the novel's plot.[24] Two little-known articles, written by Bely for the Moscow journal *Works and Days* and entitled "The Line, the Circle, the Spiral—of Symbolism" and "Circular Movement (Forty-Two Arabesques)," provide important clues to his thinking at the time (1912). Many of the symbols that come to play a central role in the novel appear here in passing: a horse and rider,[25] the Sphinx and Pyramids, a map,

---

*Petersburg* is still very much open to question. Maguire and Malmstad ("*Petersburg*" 97) point out several parallels between lectures given by Steiner in August and September 1912 (and attended by Bely) and two contemporaneous articles ("Circular Movement" and "The Line, the Circle, the Spiral—of Symbolism") that were to play a significant role in the conceptualization of time/history in *Petersburg*. See below.

[24] On the circle or spiral of time in *Petersburg*, see Berberova, "The 'Circle' of *Petersburg*"; Cioran, *The Apocalyptic Symbolism* 147–48, 154–55; Dolgopolov, *Na rubezhe vekov* 169, 182; and *Peterburg* 603–4. See also Janecek, "The Spiral": this short article is helpful for its identification of spiralate images in other works by Bely (including the *Third Symphony* and *Kotik Letaev*). As the present study was going to press, I discovered the fine article by Robert Maguire and John Malmstad ("*Petersburg*," in *Andrey Bely: Spirit of Symbolism* 96–144), in which considerable discussion of "The Line, the Circle, the Spiral—of Symbolism" and "Circular Movement" is found (see below). The conclusions drawn by Maguire and Malmstad from these two articles (and applied to *Petersburg*) are interesting and defensible, but differ from my conclusions in several important respects. Perhaps the most basic difference is their emphasis on the *circular*, as opposed to my emphasis on the *spiralic*, shape of the novel. See, e.g., their analysis of Dudkin's role (125–35), where they speak of Peter's impact on his "son" as representing "a triumph of circularity" (133). Only at the end of the article do they make the point which, in my judgment, should underlie any comprehensive reading of *Petersburg* as *symbolist* novel: "In reading . . . we create the spiral that pulls us out of ourselves, detaches us from the fate of Nikolay, Apollon, Dudkin, Petersburg, and Russia" (143).

[25] Belyi, "Liniia, krug, spiral' " 13: "At the last instant (of experience) we sense the entire line of time. It seems that we have taken a position over time, but in fact we are only *riding* on time. Our standing over time is a reining in (*prinuzhdenie*) of time: time is a horse without a bridle—it races, races, races ahead." This joining of the image of the horse with the notion of time has important implications for *Petersburg* (see below).

rhinoceros, coat of arms, word as anagram, the crucifixion, and lines, circles, and spirals. In both articles Bely returns to one concern: as cognitive models for understanding our position in the time-space of history, the line (viewed as an evolutionary series of moments) and the circle (viewed as an endless turning in place that opposes qualitative change) are only half-truths. The former is a perspective too mired in the here and now; the latter is a perspective too disengaged, abstract, and finally "motionless."[26] Only when these two perspectives are conflated, only when progress through time is somehow reconciled with the stasis of eternity, will revelation and deliverance ensue. And for Bely the way out of this dilemma presented itself in the shape of a spiral. In "Circular Movement," for example, he argues that Nietzsche's emphasis (in *Thus Spake Zarathustra*) on the "return," rather than the "eternal," of his famous formula had been both the source of his madness (i.e., he was trapped in a vicious circle) and a *sign* to those coming after him.[27] He urges his reader, including presumably the reader of his new novel, to see that the tragedy of the circle must be overcome and that a simple "return" to Nietzsche is impossible. All of world culture, exclaims Bely, has been possessed by circular movement, and what is needed is a new metaphysical compass and walking stick: "We should have understood that the path described [by Nietzsche] is a spiral, yet we hastened to enclose our line. . . . The *Übermensch* has become the cretin. Let us *once again* take up our staffs and—upward, upward! But this time along the spiral" ("Krugovoe dvizhenie" 68).

It seems almost fated that Bely would eventually transpose this metaphysical model to the act of artistic creation itself, to the novel he was then writing. And so he does. In a passage of the same article he compares the form of a book to the shape of a spiral. This is perhaps as close as the reader comes to actually witnessing Bely's remarkable mind in the act of "border-crossing," in the acrobatic leap from philosophy and historiosophy to aes-

[26] Cf., e.g., Henri-Charles Puech, "La Gnose et le temps" 60–61: "The circular movement that ensures the maintenance of the same things by repeating them . . . is absolute immobility. According to the celebrated Platonic definition, time, which is determined and measured by the revolution of the celestial spheres, is the moving image of unmoving eternity, which it imitates by revolving in a circle. . . . Certain thinkers of declining antiquity—Pythagoreans, Stoics, Platonists,—reached the point of admitting that within each of these cycles of duration, of these *aiones*, of these *aeva*, the same situations are reproduced that have already been produced in previous cycles and will be reproduced in subsequent cycles—*ad infinitum*. . . . Cosmic duration is repetition and *anakuklosis*, eternal return" (cited in Eliade, *Myth* 89n). For Bely's links with Platonism, see Cioran, *The Apocalyptic Symbolism* 48–52.

[27] The height of Bely's infatuation with Nietzschean metaphysics was reached in his *Third Symphony* (1905), whose title (*Vozvrat*—"The Return") was taken from *Thus Spake Zarathustra*. See note 7 above.

thetics. It is also as good a point as any for making our own leap from the context surrounding the novel to the text itself:

A book is indeed a four-dimensional being—this is obvious to the point of banality. The fourth dimension, intersecting three-dimensionality, describes, as it were, a cube in the shape of a booklet in octavo, where the page is a plane, and the line time in its most linear form.

The transition of one line [to the next], forming the plane of the page, is a joining of circular movement to straightforward movement: from line to line the eye describes a circle. The joining of page to page, which combines circular movement with movement along a line, forms a spiral. The truth of a book is spiralate; the truth of a book is the eternal change of changeless positions ("Krugovoe dvizhenie" 58).[28]

One final word needs to be said on "this side" of the text. Bely's use of the apocalyptic horse and rider (in all its possible incarnations—phonetic, semantic, visual, etc.) turns out to be an extremely productive marker in a novel crowded with both symbols and mare's-nests. It joins what is more properly context or "intertext" (the *theme* of the apocalypse in Silver Age literature) to what is more narrowly text (the visual and acoustic images of the horse and rider as they appear idiosyncratically in the work itself). And while there are numerous such potential "points of entry," this particular image cluster may have been uppermost in Bely's mind as he rendered the "thought trains" (*khod myslei*) of Solovyov, Nietzsche, Steiner, and others into novelistic terms. For both Bely and Blok the horse was, from their earliest works on, a convenient, visually compelling meeting place for the chivalric, folkloric, and religious traditions.[29] Like other Symbolist col-

---

[28] Bely's somewhat impressionistic argument here for a book's "four-dimensionality" anticipates the pioneering work on space-time relations in art made by other Russian philosophers and aestheticians, including Pavel Florensky, V. A. Favorsky, and L. Lisitsky. See V. V. Ivanov, "The Category of Time" 34–35.

[29] The horse and rider is a notable leitmotif in the early Bely and Blok. It shows up in three of Bely's symphonies, including an important and probably self-regarding allusion to the white horseman (actually it is the horse that is white) of Revelation 6:2 in *The Second Symphony* (written in 1901): " '5. The times of the four horsemen—white, red, black, and deathly [i.e., 'pale']—are approaching.' [. . .] 1. The prophet said, 'And the spirit and the bride say—come. 2. I hear the clatter of horses' hoofs—that is the first horseman. 3. His horse is white, and he himself is white; and he wears a golden crown. He has come out to conquer. [. . .] 5. This is our Ivan Tsarevich, our *white* standard-bearer. 6. His mother is the Woman Clothed in the Sun [see Revelation 12:1]. And she has been given wings in order to save herself in the desert from the dragon. 7. There a *white* child will grow up in order to shine at the sun's rising. And the spirit and the bride say—come' " (*Simfoniia* [2-aia dramaticheskaia] 212–13; see also 248). The ecstatic young Bely shares much with the prophetic speaker of these lines, Sergey Musatov. That from early on he both saw himself as a Christ figure/conquering white horseman

leagues, these two were consciously working in a belletristic tradition that invoked such "polygenetic"[30] symbols to make statements about Russian history. The horse became one of the most powerful shorthand expressions in all Russian literature for telescoping various notions of history: poised in uneasy balance (the statue of Peter on his mount), moving at breakneck speed (Chichikov's troika ride), and falling into ominous decline (the same Petrine steed, now *overdriven*, in Dostoevsky's *The Adolescent*). In other words, the horse came gradually to be associated with, indeed was a metaphorical equivalent of, the passage and shape of historical time.

That Blok and Bely were aware of these allusions is repeatedly borne out by their choice of imagery to express the historical crisis facing their generation. In fact, it is difficult to find a Symbolist poet or prose writer who did *not* at some point write a piece centering around a horseman of doom (usually linked to Peter) and the fate of the imperial city and, by analogy, the empire (see Antsyferov, *Dusha*; and Ospovat and Timenchik, *Pechal'nu povest' sokhranit'* 110–93). In his article "Stagnation" (1906), Blok concludes with the picture of a rider driving his tired steed around a swamp—a simultaneous allusion to the Pushkinian and Dostoevskian texts mentioned above and to Gogol's "A Terrible Vengeance." And in another well-known

---

(thus the link here with his name) *and* undermined his grandiose visions with self-parody is borne out by the fate of Musatov in *The Second Symphony* and in a number of works thereafter, including *Petersburg*. As the ever-effusive Bely unburdened himself to the more passive Blok in a letter of December 1905, "You will see me flying along the horizon radiating joy . . . my joy will give birth to swift white steeds. I gather lonely fliers, and on our white steeds we race along the horizon . . . describ[ing] circles around a cloud that is quietly sailing by. . . . *I am the white horseman who was sent by Someone* [my emphasis] to fulfill a command. . . . Perhaps I have betrayed Him who sent me for the sake of the cloud, but I will not be a traitor a *second* time" (Orlov, *Perepiska* 162). For more on Bely's interpretation of the Four Horsemen of Revelation, see his review of N. A. Morozov's *Otkrovenie v groze i bure* (*Revelation in Storm and Tempest*), in *Pereval* (*The Divide*) 6 (1907): 56–57.

In Blok, the horse is also often white and may be associated with death and (later) Russia's national tragedy: see, e.g., "I went into the night to learn, to understand" (*ss* I: 215–16), "The evening was late and crimson" (*ss* I: 222), "The Statue" (*ss* I: 310), "My beloved, my prince, my groom" (*ss* I: 315), "The distances are blind, the days are without anger" (*ss* I: 319–21), "The white steed barely moves at its tired pace" (*ss* II: 18), "In October" (*ss* II: 193), "The Fire" (*ss* II: 201), "She has appeared . . ." (*ss* II: 254), "On Death" (*ss* II: 295–96), "Along the swampy, deserted meadow" (*ss* III: 203), "On the Kulikovo Field" (*ss* III: 249–53), *Retribution* (*ss* III: 295–344; see esp. 329). For additional discussion, see Dolgopolov, *Na rubezhe vekov* 177–78; and Mints, "Blok i Gogol' " 157–58.

[30] Z. G. Mints's definition of the "polygenetic" symbol in the later Blok might be applied to Bely's use of the Bronze Horseman in *Petersburg* as well: "One ought to remember especially that 'another's word' in the work of the later Blok is, as a rule, 'polygenetic' (V. M. Zhirmunsky['s terminology]), that is, it traces back *simultaneously to several* different sources, acquiring its overall meaning only in relation to all of them (and in the full range of intertextual links)" ("Blok i Gogol' " 129).

article, "The People and the Intelligentsia" (1908), he refashions the Gogolian troika into an icon of destruction: "what if the troika . . . *is flying
right at us?* Rushing to the people, we [in fact] rush right under the legs of
the mad troika to certain death" (*ss* v: 328).[31] Likewise, in a letter of December 1905 to Blok, Bely went so far as to describe himself as "the white
horseman [of Revelation] sent by Someone to fulfill a command" (Orlov,
*Perepiska* 162), an image that, combining the biblical text with the imperial
and popular traditions of St. George/Yegory Khrabry, would be taken up
again in his *Fourth Symphony* (The Goblet of the Snowstorms, 1908) (see
Levinton and Smirnov, " 'Na pole Kulikovom' Bloka" 94). It is accurate to
say, therefore, that by the time *Petersburg* was being written the equine
image, while still "tethered" to its literary and folkloric past, had definitely
become colored by current apocalyptic overtones. Yet Bely, who saw the
path of spiritual transcendence and the verticality of narrative discourse as
calques for the same higher unity, could not content himself with this symbol of the End. As we shall presently see, there had to be, within and
*through* such a symbol, a way out—of the text, of life, of history.

Bely called his novel *Petersburg* because he conceived of that city not only
as the capital of the Russian Empire but as the symbolic center of a generational strife that had marked Russian history from the moment Peter I, a
baffling combination of authoritarian father figure and rebellious son, first
laid the cornerstone to his massive project.[32] According to Bely, this generational strife was now eventuating in the Revolution of 1905, the inci-
dents of which supply the background to the novel. *Petersburg* begins as the
story of one father figure, Apollon Apollonovich Ableukhov, and his fear of
the growing number of revolutionary plots that are shaking imperial Russia
to its foundations. Some of Russia's most notable political figures (von
Plehve) have fallen victim to terrorist bombs, and Apollon Apollonovich, as
a high ranking official, is rightly concerned about his own safety. Apollon
Apollonovich's obsession with order and regimentation has led, on a per-

[31] See also as possible subtext Nekrasov's poem "Troika," and Blok's *ZK* 117–18.

[32] The Russian edition used throughout this chapter is that of Dolgopolov; the English translation is that of Maguire and Malmstad. Although they represent separate editions (Maguire
and Malmstad have translated the rare but textually preferred 1922 edition, while Dolgopolov
bases his scholarly "Literary Monuments" volume on the longer but in many ways "rough"
1916 Sirin edition), both texts have been prepared with care and are provided with extensive
notes. The textual history of *Petersburg* is complex and need not be examined here (for more,
see Dolgopolov 624–40, and Maguire and Malmstad xxiii–xxvii). Page numbers for citations
are inserted parenthetically, with those keyed to the Russian-language text coming first.
Where necessary, slight changes in the interest of clarity have been introduced into the translation; interpolations from the longer Dolgopolov text are made in square brackets, and the
translations of these interpolations are mine.

sonal level, to the loss of his wife Anna Petrovna, who abandoned him for a romantic "Italian" before the action of the novel begins, and the estrangement of his son Nikolay Apollonovich, who secretly despises his father and has great difficulty communicating with him. On a national level, this same passion for bureaucratic order has generated an offspring very much its opposite—the counter-force of strikes, subversive leaflets, acts of anarchism, and imminent revolution.

Most of the novel's "plot" (Bely would have enjoyed the pun) is devoted to the sensations of madness and phantasmagoria surrounding the activities of the two son figures, Nikolay Apollonovich and Alexander Ivanovich Dudkin (the "Elusive One"), one of the terrorists. In a fit of spite following a failed romance with Sophia Petrovna, the wife of a friend, Nikolay has agreed before the novel's opening to carry out a plot to murder his father. Now, as the action begins, he is repulsed by this idea, but is unwittingly drawn further into the plot when Dudkin arrives at his home with a bomb concealed in a sardine tin. Nikolay does not know the contents and absent-mindedly starts the mechanism ticking. It also turns out that Dudkin, who is pushed to the brink of insanity by alcoholism, insomnia, a Nietzschean will to power, and popular notions of an apocalyptic end, has also been embroiled in the affair against his wishes. When he discovers that Lippanchenko, the notorious agent provocateur and terrorist father figure, has been manipulating him to get at Nikolay Apollonovich and the latter's father, he rebels. Soon thereafter, the spirit of Peter—a "truer" paternal model—appears in the doorway of his flat, pours his destructive essence into him (Dudkin), and bids him kill Lippanchenko. Thus, Dudkin carries out his execution of Lippanchenko under the guidance of the Bronze Horseman at the same time that Nikolay, overcome by a sort of abulia and also "doomed irrevocably" by the presence of Peter, allows the bomb to tick on. Ironically, when it finally explodes, it kills no one: Apollon Apollonovich, who has stepped down from his post and is no longer a worthy target, is merely frightened. Anna Petrovna has reappeared to look after her husband in his childlike dotage. The novel ends with a profound change in Nikolay: after doing research in Egypt, he returns to his homeland much chastened. Instead of studying the ultrarational Kant, he gives his time over to studying the mystical *Russian* philosopher Skovoroda. His parents are dead, and he is left alone to solve the Sphinx-like riddle of his, and his country's, feelings of generational strife. In the coda-like epilogue, 1905 seems only an afterglow, but there is also reason to suppose that its dying embers contain the spark that will ignite another conflagration (that is, 1917) (see Alexandrov, "Unicorn Impaling a Knight" 43).

With this rough plot summary in mind, let us now take a closer look at how the elements of Bely's apocalypticism—specifically, his view of history as spiraling toward an end—are inscribed in the structure and ultimately the very language of his narrative discourse. For the time being at least, logic would dictate that we start with the role of Apollon Apollonovich, who as seriocomic father figure *appears* to be the prime mover of the plot.[33] On a literal level, every action that moves the work *forward* in terms of narrative time and space is attributable, that is, *returns* to Apollon Apollonovich's repressive nature. Dudkin's appearance with the terrorist bomb is, as Bely's narrator presents it, a direct reaction to Apollon Apollonovich's powerful "thought trains" (*khod myslei*), his urge to bind inchoate Russian space (typified by Vasilevsky Island and other outlying workers' haunts) with the pinching lines of his intellect, and his lack of sympathy for the common people. From Dudkin's appearance soon issue the fuzzy shapes of Lippanchenko, the double agent Morkovin, and the subplot associated with them. Apollon Apollonovich recalls Dudkin's face in the context of his home, where the stranger had visited his son, and this memory links the terrorist subplot to the domestic subplot, bringing us full circle by the end of Chapter I, when Apollon Apollonovich *returns* home from the office and Nikolay Apollonovich, in red domino costume, leaves to terrorize Sophia Petrovna. Nikolay Apollonovich's desire to avenge himself on Sophia Petrovna by donning the red domino, which parodies both his role as terrorist and that as romantic clown, is generated by his sexual ambivalence, which again has its origin in his father's repressive nature. And to close the circuit once more, Nikolay Apollonovich made his fateful promise to Lippanchenko and the terrorists in the wake of his disastrous affair with Sophia Petrovna. In a word, everything in the narrative is interconnected, and all the interconnections, if pieced together, ostensibly lead back to Apollon Apollonovich.

What emerges from even this cursory glance at the work's opening is a certain dramatic rhythm. In fact, it seems that each chapter proceeds toward and ends with a narrative "bang" that closes one circle of action at the same time that it adumbrates the explosion that will end the story at large. This echo of the bomb-to-come is usually associated with death or retribution in some form and with significant mention of the Book of Revelation and its symbolism. To summarize: the end of Chapter I recapitulates all that has been set in motion by Apollon Apollonovich's thought trains; Chapter II concludes with the return of Dudkin, set around the famous lyrical aside to

[33] The protagonist's name, *Apollon Apollonovich Ableukhov*, suggests that he is: (1) the "alpha" of the plot, (2) a parody of Apollonian order, and (3) a relative of Apollyon, Satan's agent, in Revelation 9:11. Maguire and Malmstad (*Petersburg* 300) also link him with Apollonius, the Antichrist of Solovyov's "Tale of the Antichrist," in *Three Conversations*. See in addition Bennett, "Echoes" 249; Burkhart, "Leitmotivik" 302; Carlson, "Coat of Arms" 164; Cioran, *Apocalyptic Symbolism* 149n; Dolgopolov, *Peterburg* 642–43; and Steinberg, *Word and music* 172–74.

the Bronze Horseman, to his room on Vasilevsky; the final section of Chapter III describes Apollon Apollonovich's dream of a "second space," wherein he hears the sound of approaching hoofbeats that grade into the clicking noise made by a threatening Mongol (his son Nikolay); at the end of Chapter IV Sophia Petrovna returns from the masquerade ball to the attempted suicide, intimated by the presence of the Flying Dutchman,[34] of her husband. The end of Chapter V is a mirror image of the end of Chapter III: Nikolay's dream vision is called the Last Judgment, and within it the young hero is portrayed as an avenging horseman arriving from the East. Chapters VI–VIII all conclude with an atmosphere of mounting tension and climax: at the end of Chapter VI, Dudkin returns home to his terrifying encounters with Shishnarfne and the Bronze Horseman, then afterwards goes out to buy the scissors he will use to murder Lippanchenko; at the end of Chapter VII, Dudkin carries out his plan under the aegis of the Bronze Horseman; and at the end of Chapter VIII, the bomb, the detonation of which has been awaited almost from the beginning, finally explodes.

Hence the composition of *Petersburg* might be said to resemble a series of expanding circles (a figure mentioned at the end of the Prologue), whose center is the *roditel'* (parent, "genitor") and *praroditel'* (progenitor) of this chaos, Apollon Apollonovich, and whose outer circle or ultimate circumference is the exploding bomb at the end of Chapter VIII. However, in the eyes of the characters, all of whose actions are determined by their proximity to the End, these circles lead back to the repressive nature of the senator and forward to death, revolution, and the exploding bomb itself. They seem, in other words, *closed, charmed*. As the narrator says of Apollon Apollonovich's thoughts of Dudkin, "And one fugitive thought was the thought that the stranger really existed. The thought fled back into the senatorial brain. The circle closed" (35/21). This image of violent and senseless recurrence,[35]

---

[34] The important leitmotif of the Flying Dutchman (Der fliegende Hollander), with its implication of stormy voyage and death at sea, functions—and often appears—in tandem with the apocalyptic symbol of the Bronze Horseman (recall, e.g., Peter's admiration for Dutch shipyards). The Flying Dutchman is to motion over water what the Horseman is to motion over land: the ship, like the steed, acts to "materialize" the swift epochal passage of time that takes place in Petersburg, locus for spatial and temporal border-crossings. The associations of the Dutchman with Heine and Wagner (and, through Wagner, Nietzsche) were of course not lost on Bely.

[35] Two important symbolist sources on life in *this* world as a closed and moribund circle are Innokenty Annensky and Fyodor Sologub (Bely would have been especially familiar with the latter). Annensky wrote in his poem "The Anguish of a Mirage": "And in the anguish of an endless cycle [*bezyskhodnyi krug*] / I drag along my hateful path" (*Stikhotvoreniia* 211). See as well his "May" (*Stikhotvoreniia* 69–70), with its reference to "eternal transformation" (*vechnoe prevrashen'e*), and "To Another" (*Stikhotvoreniia* 156–57), with its lament over the "circling of existence" (*kruzhen'e bytiia*). Sologub wrote in an untitled poem of 1907 that "What was will be once more,/What was will be more than once" (*Stikhotvoreniia* 345); he

of a world possessed by Nietzschean madness, has led most commentators to the conclusion that Bely's overall design is circular and ironic, that the "apocalypse" in *Petersburg* consists exclusively in a negative judgment, a death sentence, passed on the city and its inhabitants.[36] But what is overlooked in this view is the "profoundly teleological" element in Bely's thinking and his efforts, in this novel and indeed in many other works, to "transvalue evil into something closer to good" (Alexandrov, *Major Fiction* 131). So the question, to be answered by Bely's readers at various "turning points" in the novel, is *how* might these circles take on depth, how might they become a spiral with a way out, how might they rise out of the notion of apocalypse as end?

In the article on circular motion Bely argued that a flat page can be dimensionalized when pierced with a certain understanding. What appears at each level of perception (character, narrator, reader) as a vicious circle of death, revolution, and historical time can change its epistemological shape if one admits the possibility that there are greater forces orchestrating human affairs (Alexandrov, *Major Fiction* 109–12). This accounts for the grotesque deflation and distancing in Bely's characterization and for his narrator's conspiratorial efforts to implicate the reader in the circle of terror— what is "real" is not the rounded portrait of a hero but the thoughts that, appearing to have originated in his brain, take on a life of their own. Everything that seems "playful" and "idle" (the senator's thoughts, the narrator's chatter) is not that at all, and the butt of Bely's irony is directed precisely at those who read the novel in such terms. Hence the only way out of the circle of history and into the spiral of which it is part is to remain *open* to the intrusion of the fourth dimension into the three-dimensional realm of habitual cognition, to intuit, as it were, the fingers of one's author turning the pages of the book that is one's life.[37]

To read *Petersburg* in these terms is to see immediately that Apollon Apollonovich is not the *praroditel'* of the plot—he is only the literal point

---

also entitled one of his collections "Fiery *Circle*" ("Plamennyi krug") and in general avoided datelines because he did not want to give the impression of "developing over time." For more on the Symbolists' perception of an "evil eternity" (durnaia beskonechnost'), see Maksimov, "Ideia puti" 25–121.

[36] Thus Anscheutz's otherwise perceptive discussion of Nietzschean aesthetics in *Petersburg* may be overstated, just as Maguire and Malmstad may be only partially correct when they argue that "the structure of the novel as a whole is circular" (xxi).

[37] This metaphor ("life is a book") would not be at odds with the symbolist position—basically romantic in origin—on the function of art. As Lavrov points out, "The most characteristic trait of the symbolist worldview was the perception of the world as an 'art-like' [iskusstvopodobnyi] phenomenon, the ascription to reality of the qualities of the artistic text" ("Mifotvorchestvo 'argonavtov' " 140). See also Mints, "Poniatie teksta i simvolistskaia èstetika" 134–41.

of departure, an origin chosen by convention. For standing behind or above Apollon Apollonovich is the shadowy presence of far more ominous father figure. It is this presence, that of course of the Bronze Horseman, which must be taken as the true point of departure. Yet curiously enough Bely does not attempt, *in terms of a strict narrative causality*, to identify the Horseman's origins as prior to those of Apollon Apollonovich. These origins, while alluded to elliptically, are of another order, lying, as it were, *beyond* the boundaries of the printed page. To borrow a theatrical metaphor, they belong to the script of a drama whose stage machinery creaks and rumbles behind the scenes. The epiphany-like moments when the Bronze Horseman moves into action do not really make him a character, a "limited partner," in the story. Quite the opposite, his role is to remove the story of the Senator from its element—narrative chronos. Together with his apocalyptic steed, the equestrian figure of Peter is the embodiment of the End that appears, anachronistically, when characters, still caught "in the middle" of their story, are forced to confront turning points which they are in no position to understand (see Brown, "Turning Points" 19–22). He is not simply a multiple literary allusion but a *symbolic prime mover*, the genuine "author"—once removed, spatially and temporally, from his "plot"—of the chaos. His viewpoint, if it can be called that, is relentlessly "meta"; his mystery is that no amount of psychological realism can adequately account for the causal link that exists between his invisible (yet real) influence and the marionette-like actions of the lesser characters. To claim that he is a "projection" of the characters' anxiety and madness is to reverse Bely's equation, for the characters are functions of the Bronze Horseman, not vice versa. And in the sense that death and the end of world history cannot be narrated but must be shown as a limit, border-crossing, or threshold of some sort, the Horseman seems to wait, all-powerful, beyond the edge of the story, intermittently crossing its threshold for the sole purpose of reminding others of the ultimate threshold that is his meaning.

If Bely had simply written about the apocalypse rather than written his version of it, there would be little difference between his prose and that, say, of Merezhkovsky. But his entry into the world of eschatological thinking was not through the portal marked "theme" but through the one marked "the word." As he theorized in his article "The Magic of Words," any revelation or "piercing" of time begins at the fundamental level of language, in the interplay of sound and sense (*Simvolizm* 429–48).[38] The Pro-

---

[38] Bely's most extended study of sound patterns as they relate to meaning is found in *Gogol's Mastery*, but see also his "poem on sound" *Glossolalia* (1922). Steinberg, for example, argues that Bely strove for "the penetration of the semantic dominant of one or several words by a specific sound or digraphs for the purpose of creating a symbol"; and "if music was for

logue, that which precedes the logos of the narrative, already introduces, in numerous guises, the prefix *pro-* (motion through) which will become perhaps the most important semantic field in the novel.[39] That *Petersburg* was actually conceived by Bely as a kind of logosemantic echo chamber originating in these and other sounds is borne out in the later *Gogol's Mastery*: " 'pp' is the pressure created by covering surfaces (walls, the bomb)" and " 'rr' is the energy of the explosion (beneath the covering surface): [thus,] *prr-o-rryv v brred* ('a breakthrough into delirium')" (*Masterstvo* 307). There are, to be sure, many such stylistic and structural keys (e.g., the use of apostrophe, indented text, narrative digressions) to the seemingly hermetic inner realm of this novel, but none is more basic or widespread than that of sound (see Alexandrov, *Major Fiction* 100–52). On the other hand, this aspect of sound has not been adequately elucidated within the overall structure of *Petersburg*, although numerous commentators have noted Bely's wordplay. I focus on the *pro*-unit to begin with because it brings together the tension of opposing forces (the "p"), the explosion resulting from that tension (the "r"), and the spatio-temporal point (the vocalically bonding "o") where this happens.

It can be assumed that Bely's paronomastic design (which, he would contend, is being worked out not *by* him but *through* him) is already very much in evidence as we follow Apollon Apollonovich's forward movement in Chapter I from home to office. The hero proceeds through the physical space (*prostranstvo*) of his household and the streets (*prospekty*—"prospects") and through the metaphysical space of his dreams of portioning out and controlling Russia. "And he passed into [*proshel*] the dining room to partake of his coffee"(12/4); "And immediately, without awaiting an answer, he looked at the clock and proceeded [*proshestvoval*] to his coffee"(12/ 4); "Apollon Apollonovich raised his bald head and departed [*proshel von*] from the room"(17/7). This movement forward through time and space reaches its apogee in Apollon Apollonovich's musings as he speeds to his office in the carriage prior to the appearance of Dudkin: "And he wanted the carriage to fly forward [*chtob vpered proletela kareta*], the prospects [*prospekty*] to fly to meet him—prospect after prospect [*za prospektom prospekt*] [. . .] so that all the earth, crushed by prospects [*prospektami pritisnutaia*], in its lineal cosmic flight should intersect, with its rectilineal principle, unembraceable infinity; so that the network of parallel prospects [*set' parallel'nykh prospektov*], intersected by a network of prospects [*pe-*

---

Wagner a language, and a leitmotif a word in this language, then for Bely language was music and the leitmotif a sound (or digraph) in this music" (*Word and music* 239).

[39] In the Prologue, for example, we find the first marked references to "*prostranstvo*" (space) and "*prospekt*," words which are one of the sources for the geometrically contrived "idle thoughts" to ensue.

resechennaia set'iu *prospektov*], should expand into the abysses of the universe in planes of squares and cubes"(21/11).[40]

All of this protrusion of one man's physical and intellectual energies into the surrounding world is futile, however. Apollon Apollonovich is simply the agent of a larger divine—or for the time being demonic—dispensation. He is *not* in control, as is soon made clear when the intellectually piercing *pro-* of his gaze encounters the anarchistically expanding *shir-* of Dudkin's eyes at, significantly, a crosswalk (*perekrestok*) on Nevsky Prospect. This is the lowest level of piercing in the novel. Bely seems to be saying that our attempts to control our inner and outer worlds through intellect alone do not lead to deeper understanding and resolution. Instead, they generate the antipodal image of expanding circles (i.e. the bomb) and of a world reeling out of control (the "*provokatsiia*" [provocation] of terrorist acts). In this regard, it is not surprising that Apollon Apollonovich and Lippanchenko, the two father-figures who in purest grotesque fashion embody the Western (i.e. "straight-laced intellect") and Eastern (i.e. "gut instinct") principles here at war, are the least susceptible to the presence of the Bronze Horseman. And just as the one's piercing intellect will be undone by the expanding circles of the bomb, so will the other's rounded belly be ripped open by Dudkin's scissors.[41]

The next level of piercing or dimensionalized meaning is connected with the Bronze Horseman, whose polysemous character, as we noted, unites a conscious return to the atmosphere of Pushkin's *poèma* and an obvious contemporary allusion to the apocalyptic horse and rider.[42] The silhouette of the steed and its master coalesce for Bely into one potent image—the extended ("*prostertaia*") arm of Peter that points the way into the future (i.e., it is the hand of fate) and lets the city's inhabitants know that they are "doomed irrevocably" (i.e., *bez vozvrata*—"without return").[43] This *pros-*

[40] There are many more examples of this. See, e.g., "Edva Apollon Apollonovich *proshest-*voval mimo, kak dva iurkikh lakeichika zataratorili bystro" (17) ("Hardly had Apollon Apollonovich passed by when two sneaky little flunkies set up a brisk chatter" [deleted from 1922 edition]); "Apollon Apollonovich, vziav tsilindr, *proshel* v otkrytuiu dver' " (18) ("Apollon Apollonovich, having picked up his top hat, proceeded through the open door" [deleted from the 1922 edition]).

[41] Bely himself saw Apollon Apollonovich and Lippanchenko as phonetic mirror images: "The leitmotif of a provocateur is inscribed in the name 'Lippanchenko': his 'lpp' is the reverse of 'pll' (of Ableukhov)" (*Masterstvo* 307).

[42] Again, for more on the horse and rider in Bely and Blok, see note 29 above.

[43] The motif of the extended arm appears to go back to Bely's Argonaut days. As Ellis (L. L. Kobylinsky) wrote Bely in fall 1903, "A symbol is a landmark of experiences, it is a conventional sign saying 'Remember that which was revealed to you then' . . . That's how I look on my own symbol—the golden fleece. It is a conventional sign, *an arm pointing to the entrance to a house* [note both the pointing arm and the idea of threshold], a phonograph shouting 'rise up and go' " (GBL, f. 25, kart. 35, ed. kh. 46; cited in Lavrov, "Mifotvorchestvo" 140–41). Thus the image of the "pointing arm" (*ruka ukazyvaiushchaia*) and sounding horn (rog) join

*tertaia ruka*, normally appearing in verb form ("extending [*prostiraia*] a heavy patinated hand, the enigmatic Horseman . . ." [99/64]), constitutes a sort of magnet for all manner of *pro*-prefixed verbs, which seem to gather in the narrative vicinity of the Horseman and even, one might say, to assemble his contour around the imperious arm.

There are many instances of this, a number coming at climactic moments at the ends of chapters, but for the sake of brevity I shall mention only the first. In the section entitled "Thus It Is Always," which serves as the first chapter's emotional climax, Nikolay Apollonovich puts on the red domino for the first time and sets out to terrorize Sophia Petrovna:

> Above the empty Petersburg streets there flew [*proletali*] vaguely illumined forms.
>
> A phosphorescent blot [a leitmotif associated with the Bronze Horseman] raced across [*pronosilos'*] the sky, misty and deathlike. The heavens gradually misted over [*protumanilas'*] in a phosphorescent glow, making iron roofs and chimneys flicker [ot togo *problistali* zheleznye kryshi i truby]. Here flowed [*protekali*] the waters of the Moika. [. . .] There, against the bright background of a bright building, Her Majesty's cuirassier slowly paced [*prokhodil*]. He had on a golden, shining helmet.
>
> And a silver dove extended [*rasproster*] its wings above the helmet.[44]
>
> Wrapped in furs, and scented and shaven, Nikolai Apollonovich was making his way [*probiralsia*] along the Moika, his head sunk in his overcoat but his eyes strangely aglow. Nameless tremors arose in his heart. [. . .]
>
> A shaft of light flew by [*proletel*]: a black court carriage flew by [*proletela*]. Past window recesses of *that very same house* [emphasis in the original] it bore [*pronesla*] blood red lamps. They played and shimmered [*proigrali* i *problistali*] on the black waters of the Moika. The spectral outline of a footman's tricorne and the outline of the wings of his greatcoat flew [*proleteli*], with a light, out of and into the fog. [. . .]
>
> Higher up, ragged arms mournfully stretched [*prostirali*] vague outlines across the sky (53–54/33–34).

The ultimate intrusion of this symbol into the narrative comes at the end of Chapters VI and VII: in the first instance, Dudkin is visited by the Bronze Horseman, who turns white hot ("*prokalias'* "), flows over his victim

---

in *Petersburg* in the symbol complex of the unicorn (see below). For another possible subtext, see Bryusov's influential 1906 poem "To the Bronze Horseman" ("K Mednomy Vsadniku"), which ends with the lines "Only you, unchanging, crowned, with an extended arm [s rukoiu *prostertoi*] fly through the centuries on your steed" (*Stikhotvoreniia* 317).

[44] This is an obvious allusion to Bely's first novel.

("*protek na sklonennogo Aleksandra Ivanovicha pepeliashchim potokom*"),
and pours himself into his (Dudkin's) veins ("*prolilsia v ego zhily*") (*Peter-burg* 307); and in the second he is directed by the *prostertaia ruka* to Lip-panchenko's bedroom, where, after committing the murder, he ends up in
the pose of his apocalyptic father figure: "the man had mounted the dead
body; in his hand he was clutching a pair of scissors; he had extended [*pros-ter*] that arm" (386/264).

The highest level of penetration, however, does not belong to the Bronze
Horseman. As Apollon Apollonovich is the stalking-horse of a higher order,
which in this context points to the Antichrist whose reign is about to begin,
so is the Bronze Horseman part of a higher order still, one whose function
is to turn personal and national endings into beginnings. This metaphysical
*esprit d'escalier* culminates of course in the *edinorog* (unicorn), emblem of
Christ, Eastern mysticism, and unity (*edino-*) through piercing death (*rog*)
(see Alexandrov, "Unicorn" 44; Burkhart, "Leitmotivik" 286–87; and es-pecially Carlson, "Coat of Arms" 160–67).[45] Here too, in the Ableukhov
coat of arms, we find the prefix *pro-* with all of its connotations: "Gray
dappled horses bounded forward and drew up to the entrance a carriage on
which was depicted a coat of arms: a unicorn goring [*probodaiushchii*] a
knight" (19/9). The mention of horses is not fortuitous,[46] for the unicorn
ties together in *one* symbol-complex the apocalyptic horse and the instru-ment of death. Each level of penetration has brought the reader closer to
the central equine image. Apollon Apollonovich, surrounded physically by
the walls of his carriage and metaphysically by the walls of his logic, is
separated from his horses but driven by them; the Bronze Horseman, still
a human figure who straddles the roles of autocrat and rebel, father and son,
rides the steed of time; and the unicorn, purged of human frailties, has
merged with the steed itself.

Thus for Bely the unicorn is another, higher version of the Bronze Horse-man: the coppery steed has become white and the penetrating arm has be-come the horn. This horn has apocalyptic associations (the archangel's
trumpet) which extend across the author's oeuvre: it first surfaces in the
*Second Symphony*, where Solovyov, Bely's spiritual father, plays the in-

[45] This notion of piercing death can also be found in Bely's first novel, *The Silver Dove*
(1909). In that work the hero Daryalsky, who is eventually murdered by members of the Dove
sect, has a vision during which the bird (changing from dove to hawk) tears open his chest with
its beak (*Serebrianyi golub'* II: 153).

[46] The web of equine (and equestrian) motifs is extraordinarily dense in *Petersburg*. It runs
the gamut from the horse-hair that Nikolay nervously plucks from his divan to the awesome
figure of Peter himself. See, e.g., in Dolgopolov, *Peterburg*: 16, 19, 20, 26, 47, 49, 53, 61, 63,
75, 76, 86, 97, 99–100, 107, 111, 114, 120–21, 125, 138, 141, 174, 203, 214–15, 224, 238, 244,
256, 266, 289, 301–2, 305–6, 324, 345, 347–48, 361, 386.

strument as a distant summons; it appears again in Bely's early lyrics as a
call for otherworldly departure to his Argonaut friends; it serves as climactic symbol in the article "The Magic of Words," where it is also joined with
the color white and reference to a mystical beast; and in *The First Encounter*
it is linked with the young Bely's first glimpse of Sophia (Margarita Moro-
zova), a version of the New Jerusalem, a sacred bull, and the familiar verb
"*prosteret'*."[47] What all this means for the text of *Petersburg* seems clear—
the *rog*, like all of Bely's genuine symbols, combines more than one meaning. It produces both the sound, that is, the language of the end that is the
beginning, and the image of the physical cross on which the characters must
die—at least figuratively—in order to be reborn on the tree of life (see Carlson, "Coat of Arms" 165).

The ways in which Bely inscribes this highest level of penetrating sound
and sense in his narrative are too numerous to detail here. Suffice it to say
that all the factory chimneys and schooner stacks (*truby*), smoking pipes
(*trubki*)—including those of the Bronze Horseman and Flying Dutchman,
gramophone speakers (both *truby* and *roga*), hunters' horns (*roga*), and
flourishing trumpets (*truby*) fall within this semantic field, defined roughly
as "announcement of the revelation at hand."[48] Equally significant are all
the allusions to horned or tusked beasts—rhinoceros (*nosorog*), bull (*byk*),
wild boar (*kaban*), and deer (*olen'*).[49] These animals serve as parodic surrogates for the *edinorog*, hints of a metaphysical penetration beyond a brute
physical one. Here no doubt Bely was playing with his own real surname—
"Bugaev" comes from the Ukrainian for "bull" (*bugai*)—which he replaced
early on with a pseudonym (*Belyi*, "White") signifying purity of intention
and unity of being (see Bely's note to *Stikhotvoreniia* 439; *Na rubezhe* 486–
87; Lavrov, "Mifotvorchestvo" 169; and note 5 above).

The figure in the novel most closely aligned with the "monoceros" and
Bely himself is Nikolay Apollonovich. If Dudkin comes to assume, on a
parodic level, the equestrian pose of his apocalyptic maker, then so does
Nikolay Apollonovich, in his mask of death, become a debased version of

[47] See *Simfoniia* (2-aia geroicheskaia) 215 (this image—both the horn [*rog*] and the trumpet
[*truba*]—appears often in the symphonies); "Zolotoe runo," *Stikhotvoreniia* 74; "Magiia
slov," *Simvolizm* 446–47; and *Pervoe svidanie, Stikhotvoreniia* 425. Bely connects the trumpet of judgment (*sudnaia truba*), his own origins, the theme of borders, and the Apocalypse in
*Na rubezhe dvukh stoletii* 72–73. For the horn and trumpet in Blok's work, see, e.g.: "Na
strazhe" (*ss* II: 215), where the *truba* appears together with the verb *prosteret'*; "Kogda ia
prozreval vpervye" (*ss* III: 71); and *Vozmezdie* (*ss* III: 305). The horn, one should also not
forget, is an important Wagnerian motif associated with Siegfried.

[48] See, e.g., Dolgopolov, *Peterburg*: 43, 62, 66, 102–4, 111, 145, 169, 205–6, 208–9, 216,
306, 315–16.

[49] See, e.g., Dolgopolov, *Peterburg*: 19, 43, 72, 163, 183, 186, 188, 192–93, 212, 217–18,
274, 277, 280, 363, 373, 374, 382, 395–96.

the unicorn.[50] At the ball, Nikolay's father perceives the approach of the red domino as that of a "one-horned being [that] hurled itself upon the little knight and broke off the knight's luminous phenomenon" (112).[51] The transfiguring *rog* of the mythical beast is more powerful that the little knight's *mech* (sword) of logic. But Nikolay Apollonovich, as agent of the unicorn, does not understand his purpose; indeed, he too senses that he is being gored by a higher force even as he does his goring. The repeated nursery rhyme which represents the call of his origins catches the young hero in a familiar pose:

> Durachok, prostachok
> Kolen'ka tantsuet:
> On nadel kolpachok—
> Na kone gartsuet.[52] (120–21, 224, 330)
>
> (Noodle-doodle, dummy-wummy,
> Little Kolya's dancing,
> On his head a dunce-cap wears,
> On his horse he's prancing. [81, 155, 228])

Although Bely's intention is clearly to deflate his split and imperfect hero, the combination of equine image and pointed object protruding from the head (the dunce-cap) resurrects unmistakably the symbol of the unicorn and its spiritual harmony. Thus the penetration of this symbol into the flat and circular narrative that is the characters' (and readers') lives is another, perhaps ultimate, means by which Bely dimensionalizes his text.

Not unexpectedly, it is at a "point" such as this, when one recognizes the similarity within the difference, and the essential seriousness within the parody, that the various linguistic "seams" of Bely's prose are brought most vividly to the fore. The fine line dividing sound from sound, sense from sense, suddenly "materializes." The reader of this apocalyptic fiction must be able to apprehend *both* points of view, the lower and the higher, Nikolay's and the unicorn's, simultaneously.[53] The various phonetic, morphological, and semantic borders are thereby made palpable even as we are

---

[50] In fact, Bely is saying that at some level *all* of his characters are masks for transcendent forces: recall, for example, that "[Apollon Apollonovich's] cerebral play is only a mask. Under way beneath this mask is the invasion of the brain by forces unknown to us" (56/35).

[51] For an extended Freudian treatment of *Petersburg*, see Ljunggren, *Dream*.

[52] Bely used the motif of the dunce-cap in several of his early works. See, e.g., "Vechnyi zov," *Stikhotvoreniia* 80; *Simfoniia* (2-aia dramaticheskaia) 244; and *Vozvrat* (III simfoniia) 31–39.

[53] In this sense, *Petersburg* can be read *both* as a text that "deconstructs" itself (cf. the pervasive image of the bomb, which on a stylistic level can be equated with the subversive function of parody) and that "transcends" its various possible literal meanings. See below.

urged to cross them, to see that Nikolay *is* the unicorn when of course he is not, and to look back at the text from *the other side*, where the long hidden mystery has at last been made manifest (Gr. *apokalūpto*). From one angle, the plot brings no resolution: Dudkin kills a too Eastern father who he fears may already be compromised; Nikolay Apollonovich mentally murders his too Western father who has been removed from his post before the bomb goes off. From another (more privileged) vantage, however, the death and chaos *are* necessary, a step closer to the final explosion of the revolution, the millenarian reign of the Antichrist, the *Parousia*, divine judgment and the end of time. And finally, it may be significant that at the conclusion of the article on circular movement Bely makes an allusion to a coat of arms: "On the wall [of a Basel building] a knight, bound in his armor, was frozen in attack of a dragon" ("Krugovoe dvizhenie" 73). In *Petersburg* all these terms are shifted with dramatic results: the frozen conventions of Western intellect, including those of art itself, are not on the attack but on the re-treat, and what they have to fear is the Eastern beast's assault, the "horned word," as Bely might say, as it enters the flesh of the printed page. For the symbolist punster and prophet (*prorok*), there is a secret bond joining *rok*, or human fate, and *rog*, the horn of Christ's *logos*.[54]

Everything suggested thus far supports the conclusion that there exists, or there was *thought* to exist, a higher movement inscribed within the lower movement of Bely's narrative, and that this movement has meaning and direction, although those trapped "in the middle" may not be aware of it as such. The fact, however, as the modern reader would argue, is that the novel can still be read *either* way, that is, its narrative shape can be seen as circular and senseless (the end everyone keeps returning to is simply that) *or* spir-alate and open (only *through* the End can we make a genuine Beginning). It all depends on who and where the guiding intelligence is. The neo-Kant-ian epistemological tradition, against which Bely, like his character Nikolay, rebelled, would consider the identification of history and story, life and art, subject and object, as a gross intermarriage of systems, a flagrant infraction of the rules.[55] Yet to Bely, whose symbolist prose strikes one as the artistic equivalent of bending over and trying to lift oneself up by the feet (gravity only exists in the mind!), such an identification was the only way of posit-

[54] Both *rog* and *rok* have, at least in the nominative and accusative case singular, the same pronunciation (the "g" of the former is devoiced). Bely joins the notions of *prorok* and *rog* in his description of Vladimir Solovyov in the *Simfoniia* (2-aia dramaticheskaia) (214–15), and he includes *rog*, *prorok*, and *prostertaia ruka* in, significantly, his cycle of poems to Blok (*Stikhotvoreniia* 146–48).

[55] Of course much modern critical theory is an offshoot of the neo-Kantian tradition. On Bely's understanding of Kant, see Cassedy, "Bely the Thinker" 313–22.

ing a unity beyond the "before" and "after" of a text, a life, a history. In this respect, there are no two thinkers whose aesthetic priorities are more different than Bely and Mikhail Bakhtin. The first is obsessed with apocalypse and closure, with at least implying the possibility that there is a viewpoint on the outside giving meaning and ending to everything within; the second is obsessed with ongoing history and openness, with the patterns that we project onto time from the inside if only, for the moment, to give it a semblance of meaning.[56] Bely, for example, would certainly have reversed Bakhtin's formula for the chronotope: the latter is not the "world picture" (Clark and Holquist, *Bakhtin* 278) of space-time relations binding him to the symbolist tradition on the eve of the revolution, but the *threshold* through which he is to leave behind historical time altogether.[57]

Lest we forget, *Petersburg* is an *apocalyptic* fiction: it is about the end of the road. Its idea of space-time relations cannot be stretched out indefinitely, but must be collapsed toward a world picture implying closure. And as in the other works included in our study, the End, while perceived spatially, is really about an end in—and of—time. That is why, for instance, the iron road in *The Idiot* takes Nastasya Filippovna back to Rogozhin's house and death; or the hippodrome's circular track in *The Master and*

---

[56] In fairness to Bakhtin, he too was a devotee of "outsideness" (*vnenakhodimost'*), and said often that all aesthetic experience requires the genuine externality of the creating consciousness. What one cannot get outside of, in Bakhtin's understanding, is *the time* in which one writes.

[57] "Sound unites space and time, but in such a way that it *reduces spatial to temporal relations*. This newly created relation liberates me, in a certain sense, from the power of space" (Bely, *Selected Essays* 94). For more on the chronotope, see the Introduction, and Bakhtin, "Forms of Time"; Clark and Holquist, *Bakhtin* 278ff.; Emerson, *Boris Godunov* 5–6; Medvedev, *Formal Method* 129–30.

In his study, Bakhtin identifies three ancient proto-novelistic forms (Greek romance, adventure novel of everyday life, and biography/autobiography) which are in turn structured by three times (adventure time, everyday time, and biographical time). Although each form is dominated by a certain time, that time does not exist in isolation, but is engaged in a constant tug-of-war with its counterparts. Bakhtin is especially interested in what he sees as the first glimmers of novelistic time in the adventure novel (Petronius' *Satyricon*, Apuleius' *The Golden Ass*), when a character, Lucius, descends into everyday life as an ass and when elements of everyday time begin to seep into the fabric of adventure time. What distinguishes then the chronotopic configuration of the adventure novel is that Lucius' life is presented as a pattern of significant metamorphoses and that these turning points take place during the course of travel, on *the path of life*. To be sure, Bely is a long way from Apuleius, but what Bakhtin is proposing is that the chronotope of the open road (so vital to writers such as Gogol and Platonov) has an ancient origin and that from the beginning the tension between mythical time (e.g., the ideal Russia that Gogol's narrator is searching for) and flawed, quotidian time (e.g., the Russia that Chichikov and his colleagues actually inhabit) has been with us in the form of a spatial relationship. The way in and out of Gogol's provincial city is not simply the way in and out of space but, more importantly, the way in and out of (everyday) time.

*Margarita* only reminds Pilate of Yeshua's crucifixion (see Chapter Four). In other words, apocalyptic visions in literature tend to be governed by what one scholar has called a poetics of the center: that is to say, they resort to a kind of "cross-over zone" where the narrative line along which a life or history unfolds suddenly collapses into a point of almost absolute mass and where two qualitatively different temporalities (the mythical and the profane times of Bakhtin) are seen to intersect and interpenetrate (see Fletcher, *Allegory* 349–59). This special zone is the secularized and novelized equivalent of what structural anthropologists, such as Edmund Leach, call the "betwixt-and-between" places set aside for prophetic utterances in biblical texts (Noah in his ark, Isaac on the altar, Jesus on the cross). Prophecy "nearly always takes place in the wilderness or on a river bank away from human habitation[58]—the point being that, in a cosmic sense, such places stand at the boundary between The World and The Other and are therefore appropriate places for a meeting between the natural and the supernatural" (Leach, *Structuralist Interpretations* 16).

In the tradition of the Christian epic, the center from which the human journey began or toward which it was destined to return was uniformly *sacred*—its models being Dante's glimpse of Earthly Paradise (*The Purgatorio*), Spenser's Garden of Adonis (*The Fairie Queene*), Milton's sylvan haven soon to be lost (*Paradise Lost*). It also tended, in Eliade's archetypal definition, to be located along an *axis mundi*, or "gateway" to heaven and hell (Eliade, *Myth* 12). The forms of the Christian epic are thus seen to hark back to an archaic, pre-Christian consciousness, which made the temple's sacred space, with its altar located at the center (the omphalos) of the universe, the site for year-end rites. These rites functioned to ban the immediate (profane) past and return the human being to a Great Time of universal harmony. It is this version of a Great Time that, *mutatis mutandis*, Eliade says structured the Christian epic about the Fall, since in the latter the "way back" has been cut off. After Augustine and his interpretation of the Christ example, history could only move *forward*. What happened, therefore, in the Christian version of history was that the *in illo tempore* of an ideal past was projected into the future, to be restored *at the end*.[59]

In the modern fictional depiction of apocalypse, including its Russian variant, the situation is reversed. Here the center is often a city (Petersburg, Moscow), a place "magnetized" by history and steeped in legend, where characters *within* everyday time (Nastasya Filippovna, the Master and Margarita) are put in touch with messengers from a seemingly different, biblical

---

[58] Cf. the oft-cited example of Raskolnikov's conversion in the epilogue of *Crime and Punishment*.

[59] Eliade's formulation has some fascinating implications for the history of Soviet literature and the doctrine of Socialist Realism. See Clark, *Soviet Novel* 39–41, 146.

or fairy tale time (Myshkin, Woland; see Introduction). Instead of the talking hen that saves the day in a fairy tale, or the divine envoy that straddles the horizon line of a sacred text, these miraculous mediators are usually human and, in Myshkin's case at least, potentially fallible.[60] Whatever their human (or inhuman) faults or modal ambiguity as novelistic heroes, it is through them and their betwixt-and-between zones that the "uncovering" or "disclosing" rooted in the idea of apocalypse takes place. But this same notion of apocalypse, inasmuch as it is still bound by the shape of the original biblical text, is a vindication "from the other side" only for the chosen few.[61] For the majority living in this inverted model of the Heavenly City, the center does not provide an escape from chronos, but rather places them in history's death-grip. According to this notion of time the biblical plot is now coming to a close, and the focus is on God's judgment: Peter (the Antichrist) "split" the Russian character and started his people on the path to destruction when he built his city; Moscow has not lived up to its role as the "Third Rome" but has become the fallen Whore of Babylon.

Bely's novel, as was noted earlier, seems an clear avatar—via Solovyov—of medieval thinking within an ironic modern context.[62] The Dantesque uniting of cyclical motion with the beginning and end of time in a vision of painful progress toward the center leads us back to the image of the spiral, where we began. Bakhtin is correct in identifying Dante's work with *the end of an epoch*, with "an image of the world structured according to pure verticality," and with the urge "to synchronize diachrony" (Bakhtin, "Forms of Time" 157). He is in his own way also correct to say that "after Dante, the most profound and consistent attempt to erect such a verticality was made by Dostoevsky" ("Forms of Time" 158).[63] Yet, perhaps because

---

[60] That is to say, the novel form must still in some sense pay its respects to the "reality principle."

[61] It is conceivable that the "saving remnant" might include, in an extreme case, only the reader(s).

[62] Bely had occasion to mention the ties between his epoch and that of Dante. Indeed, he once suggested that his generation's search for an ideal form of love (symbolized by Blok's Beautiful Lady and his own Woman Clothed in the Sun) was analogous to Dante's service to Beatrice. See his "Vmesto predisloviia," *Kubok metelei* (Chetvertaia simfoniia) 3; "Na perevale," *Arabeski* 289; "Emblematika smysla," *Simvolizm* 79.

[63] For Bakhtin (see "Form of Time" 156–206), Dante is the culmination of a Middle Ages worldview whose syncretic eschatology concerned itself with vertical time and the end, while Rabelais was the spirit of the emerging Renaissance artist whose urge it was to dignify and heroicize *all* of the world, including one's own body and one's own inevitable death. Dante's work is thus "filled with a powerful desire to escape this world" (157): like *Petersburg*, *The Divine Comedy* is permeated with the "struggle between living historical time and the extratemporal worldly ideal"; it is poised on "the boundary line between two epochs" (158). For Rabelais, on the other hand, the metaphysical hierarchy of Dante must be destroyed and deheroicized: "The whole man is brought out on the surface and into the light, by means of the

he himself was located so closely in time and space to Symbolism and its heirs, he neglects to mention authors like Bely who were most concerned with the relation between vertical form and an apocalyptic vision of the End. In terms of the Bakhtinian world picture dictated to (or through) him by his understanding of the historical moment, Bely stands Dante's cosmology on its head.[64] The sacred center, the idyllic garden outside history, has become the demonic city pursued by the past; its position at the beginning of time has been transposed to the end; instead of cosmos (creation) and meaningful archetype one finds chaos (destruction) and meaningless repetition. And whereas Dante-protagonist wends his way down through the narrowing circles of Hell to the profane center of the earth and there views Satan frozen in isolation at the farthest point from God's Empyreum, he still has a way *out*. His journey is not over until he reaches the *other* side and the mountain top (the tip of another cone), where Eden, the atemporal Paradise of humanity's beginning, meets Purgatory, the atemporal limbo of humanity's end. Bely, on the other hand, who was just as obsessed with the geometry of salvation, has his characters proceed from a prosaic *dot* (Petersburg's lack of dimensionality on a map and the "arbitrary" point of the author's own pencil) in ever-widening circles of anxiety and thoughts of death.

Yet even Petersburg, this ultimate threshold city and dark parody of the New Jerusalem, holds in its explosive center the seeds of spiritual regeneration. They are found on those very *thresholds* that transform narrative time, in Bakhtin's words, into "the fourth dimension of space" (Bakhtin, "Forms of Time" 84). The word *porog* (threshold) conceals the *rog* on which various characters are gored as they pass into the fourth dimension or it passes into them. Bely was conscious of this word-play; he employs it often in important contexts as the primary semantic source for all the other

---

word, in all events of his life. . . . Rabelais must portray, finally, a death that—even in this world—is not an *absolute* end for anyone, or anything" (192–94).

[64] Although Dante and Bely were separated by centuries and cultures, the similarities in their art and worldviews are striking. Both embarked on "paths" of life and work that turned out to be "triadic": youthful idealism—abstract philosophy—syncretic works of major period. Both had a series of metaphysical teachers whose ideas fed (but were always uniquely "digested" by) their work: for Dante it was Boëthius, Aristotle (above all), and the models of scholastic thought (Avicenna, Averroes, St. Albert of Cologne, and St. Thomas); for Bely it was Solovyov, Nietzsche, Kant, Skovoroda, and Steiner. Both fervently embraced a feminine ideal, with obvious autobiographical grounding, as the centerpiece of their personal mythologies. Both employed a knowledge of mathematics to develop cosmologies that were governed by geometric figures (notably the concentric circle and the helix or cone). Both were obsessed with the revealed word of God and a vision of all-encompassing unity. And both ended their masterpieces with revelatory flashes (Dante's "sublime" in tone, Bely's undercut by irony and parody but at some level serious) of cosmic magnitude. See the excellent discussion in Boyde, *Dante Philomythes* 1–40, 57–73, 84–87, 109–11, and 132–71.

threshold images.[65] The end thus makes its presence felt whether we observe Nikolay Apollonovich, clad in his domino, at the threshold of Sophia Petrovna's apartment; or the Christ-like White Domino that meets Sophia Petrovna as she crosses the threshold and leaves the Tsukatovs' ball; or the encounter between father and son, in the presence of the unicorn, at the threshold of their home; or the Bronze Horseman as he passes over the threshold into Dudkin's room; or Lippanchenko's hesitation as he crosses the threshold to his room and the death awaiting him there.[66]

Perhaps one concluding quotation will suggest how the author sought to incorporate all these meanings—worldly chaos, otherworldly order, and the *limen* where the one enters the other—at the sacred center, the word, where his art began:

There, there the prospects stretched out [*prosterlis' prospekty*]. [. . .]

The Admiralty presented [*prodvinulo*] one eight-columned facade. It glowed pink [*prorozovelo*] and disappeared. [. . .]

Apollon Apollonovich, having seen [*provodivshii*] a young girl home, was now hurrying to the threshold [k *porogu*] of his yellow house. [. . .]

Apollon Apollonovich heard the rumble of a carriage [*proletka*] at his back, and when the driver had drawn abreast of the senator, the senator saw, sitting inside, a misshapen [*urodlivyi*] young man, hunched up, his great coat wrapped aroung him in a most unpleasant manner. [. . .]

When they caught sight of him, the eyes of the unpleasant young man began, in the blink of an eye, to dilate, dilate, dilate [*shiritsia, shiritsia, shiritsia*]. In the blink of an eye they dilated [*rasshirilis'*] unpleasantly, fixing in a look full of horror. In horror Apollon Apollonovich halted before the horror. That look had been pursuing him more and more often. It was with that look that subordinates looked at him, and it was with that look that the mongrel breed of passers-by [*prokhodiashchii ubliudochnyi rod*] looked at him. [. . .] And he glimpsed the number plate [of the carriage]: 1905.

Nikolai Apollonovich sprang out of the carriage [*proletka*] and [. . .] tugged at the door bell. [. . .] And over the griffins [depicted on the walls of the porch] the Ableukhov coat of arms was sculpted in stone. The coat of arms depicted a long-plumed knight, surrounded with ro-

---

[65] The word *porog* appears on the following pages of the Dolgopolov edition: 22, 53, 90, 102, 131, 135, 153, 173, 191, 196, 216, 217, 230, 266, 283, 286, 302, 305–6, 363, 383, 389, 391.

[66] A "fatal threshold" (*rokovoi porog*) is also associated with the death of Daryalsky in *The Silver Dove*: it is crossed by the members of the sect as they enter the room to murder the hero. See *Serebrianyi golub'* II: 243.

coco curliques, being gored [*pronizannogo*] by a unicorn [edino*rog*om].
A thought passed through [*proshla*] Nikolai Apollonovich's head like a
fish skimming the surface of the water: Apollon Apollonovich, who
lived [*prozhivaiushchii*] beyond the threshold [za *porogom*] of this
door, himself was the knight being gored [*probodaemyi rytsar'*]. After
this thought another glided dimly by [*protemnitsia*], without rising to
the surface: the old family coat of arms applied to all the Ableukhovs,
and he, Nikolai Apollonovich, was also being gored [*probodaem*]. But
by whom [no kem *probodaem*]? (215–17/149–50)

In the year 1905, in the city of Petersburg, a father (*roditel'*—"parent")
and son (u*rod*livyi iunosha, ubliudochnyi *rod*—"a misshapen young man,
a mongrel breed") have just crossed paths. The unexpected and unwanted
meeting produces the psychic equivalent of a small electrical storm, and the
sparks that fly raise the question of the ultimate why, the origin, the birth
(*rod, rozhd*enie) of this conflict. The answer is of course "by Christ," by the
point of his logos, though Bely leaves this unsaid.

This constant crossing of borders was meant to suggest not lateral, but
*vertical* movement. Here again, in an almost Dantesque typology, the various levels of meaning and interpretation (literal, allegorical, moral, and
now anagogical—or, as Bely would redefine the highest medieval category,
mystical, "symbolical") show forth in an elusive staircase that is the verbal
analogue to an Escher print. The intersection of transcendent movement
(*pro-*), object of fate (*rog, rok*), and point of crossing (*porog*) was the writer-
prophet's (*prorok*) world-picture and *word-picture* for the space-time relations characterizing the story. It was his way of verbalizing the impossible—the outside from within, the end from the middle. "Petersburg" was
not simply a window to the West, as it had been for its founder, but a window to the beyond. Each epiphany in the novel is a small-scale template of
the cosmic revelation at hand. The bomb is the final such template, but even
it, considering the consequences, is a grotesque parody of the end that Bely
felt was bearing down on his generation. Indeed, as I have tried to demonstrate, the End (*and* Beginning) that lay beyond these personal endings
could not be narrated, could not be incorporated into a story unfolding over
time. "The novelist . . . cannot hope," Walter Benjamin once mused, "to
take the smallest step beyond the limit at which he invites the reader to a
divinatory realization of the meaning of life by writing 'Finis' " (*Illuminations* 100).

Hence the most that can ever be said is that the much desired step beyond
"Finis" exists by implication, "symbolization." The spiral of Euclidean geometry is open-ended, yet Bely insists that that which has a point of origin
must also, in some fourth dimensional space and time inaccessible to human

figuration, have a point of destination. In this sense he takes the novel form of his time to the limit, fully acknowledging in the process that, except with hints of a symbolic penetration, this limit is not to be broached. Without ignoring the injunctions of a specific age, Bely brings his generation closer to the threshold of pure verticality than ever before. In the end, his time was not the ultimate border he hoped and feared it was, and his identification of revolution with revelation was not borne out in the years ahead—though there are those, especially among émigré philosophers and theologians, who would say that we are still living through the reign of the Antichrist in the Soviet Union. Be that as it may, Bely's apocalypticism has its own historico-literary vindication. *Petersburg* can still be seen as a uniquely Russian reworking of John's text, a swansong to a city and its *genius loci* whose end had been prophesied almost from the time of its foundation (see Antsyferov, *Dusha*). For after Bely the myth of Petropolis became the myth of Necropolis, and in Soviet times this demonic/sacred center, now the city of Lenin, has been invoked more as a cultural monument, a Bronze Horseman *tout court* fixed in a modern tourist's consciousness, than as a living presence.[67] And it is on these last grounds that Bely and his novel would, one has to believe, rest their case.

[67] Joseph Brodsky has written in one of his recent essays that "In the national experience, the city is definitely Leningrad; in the growing vulgarity of its content, it becomes Leningrad more and more. Besides, as a word, 'Leningrad' to a Russian ear already sounds as neutral as the word 'construction' or 'sausage' " ("Less Than One" 4).

# THREE

—

## *Chevengur*: On the Road
## with the Bolshevik Utopia

The railroad has changed the entire flow, the entire construction,
the entire rhythm of our prose.

—Osip Mandelshtam,
*The Egyptian Stamp*

The idea of paradise is the logical end of human thought in the sense
that it, that thought, goes no further; for beyond paradise there is
nothing else, nothing else happens. It can safely be said, therefore,
that paradise is a dead end; it's the last vision of space, the end of
things, the summit of the mountain, the peak from which there is
nowhere to step. . . . [And] in general, it should be noted that the
first casualty in any discourse about utopia—desired or already attained—is grammar.

—Joseph Brodsky,
"Catastrophes in the Air"

The utopian urge, as has often been asserted, is essentially a "secularization," a placing within a human-centered *saeculum*, of the original apocalyptic urge to see the end of time.[1] These two urges are of course not distinct, but genealogically bound; indeed, in one important respect they may
be viewed as the *same* urge as it has developed through history. The millennium, or the thousand years of harmonious rule on earth that, according
to Revelation 20:1–6, is said to precede the final battle between the forces
of Christ and Antichrist, gives way to Utopia, that "no place" which, *thus
far*, has eluded embodiment in history, but which, if *only* human beings
would change their nature, *could* become a heaven on earth. Commentators

---

[1] An excellent recent study of the utopian urge in Western thought, which I have made
broad use of in the present chapter, is Manuel and Manuel, *Utopian Thought*. See Lasky (*Utopia and Revolution*) as well. For the utopian model, both in its popular and literary variants,
within the Russian context, see Baehr ("In the Name of the Father"), Chistov (*Russkie narodnye sotsial'no-utopicheskie legendy*), Khlebanov (*Narodnaia sotsial'naia utopiia*), Morson
(*Boundaries of Genre*), Stites ("Fantasy and Revolution" and "Red Visions"), Striedter
("Three Utopian Novels"), and Sviatlovskii (*Russkii utopicheskii roman*).

from biblical exegetes to social historians are quick to point out the unhappy historical circumstances that gave rise to similar revolutionary movements otherwise separated by centuries and continents. And thus the chief difference in this vast historical marriage of millennial hopes and all too militant failures is finally one of *narrative viewpoint*: what is the actor's role in the plot we call history, and where is the guiding intelligence that gives this plot a meaningful shape—a beginning, middle, and, most important, an end?

In Christianity's first centuries, the actor's consciousness was informed primarily by Intertestamental Jewish and early Christian apocalyptic thinking—the human being was free to act out a positive or negative role in the unfolding of God's "end-determined" plot, the conclusion of which was imminent. The crucifixion and resurrection of Christ, as Oscar Cullmann has written, formed the central turning point in the Biblical plot and conferred meaning both "backward" (to the Creation) and "forward" (to the *Parousia*) on the economy of salvation (*Christ and Time* 32). One could look ahead to a general End predicted by the narrative rhythm of the Christ example, but equally important, one now had a "covenant" with a viewpoint outside of historical time, *beyond the plot*, that granted tragic or unintelligible events a higher meaning.[2]

What tends therefore to make so much of the history of apocalyptic sects in the Middle Ages alike is their leaders' repeated insistence on being God's chosen agents for hastening the plot to its conclusion. Whether such leaders were simply mad or charismatically self-promoting; whether they called themselves Aldebert, Peter the Hermit, Eon the Breton Christ, or the Master of Hungary; whether their often extravagant actions were provoked by the deteriorating economic and social conditions in feudal Europe (Taborites), by fear of the Black Death (the revolutionary Flagellants), or by the religious fervor of the Crusades (the Tafurs)—the overriding conviction propelling their movements and allowing followers to believe in their righteousness in the face of much evidence to the contrary was that God was guiding their hands and singling them out—usually the poor "destined" to inherit the kingdom of heaven—as the ones whose role it was in this plot to usher in the end.[3] It matters little that time and again these movements confused the pope with Antichrist or a secular ruler with the Emperor of the Last Days. What is more striking than the historical record of failure is the resiliency of the paradigm, the need to have God speak from His future to our present and to enjoin humanity, in terms often murky but no less

---

[2] This linear pattern was of course already present in the Old Testament view of history, with the important difference that the Jews as yet had no crucial turning point equivalent to the Christ appearance. See Cullmann, *Christ and Time* 82.

[3] For more on the social history of millenarianism in medieval Europe (primarily Northern), see Cohn, *Pursuit*.

compelling, to bring that future to pass as soon as possible. As early as the fifth century many were perplexed that the end promised in Revelation had *not* come to pass, a fact which led Augustine to declare that the millennium was now coterminous with the reign of the Church and that any sectarian movement arguing otherwise would be contradicting history's meaning and thwarting God's plot. But one feature of Christian eschatological thinking remains constant: it is *God* that endows human history with meaning; it is only He who knows when and how the plot which He oversees is to be fulfilled, although there is ample room, according to His word, for interpreting the shape of that end from within history and within a limited human viewpoint.

Perhaps more than any other Russian writer, Andrey Platonov represents the collision of the Christian apocalyptic and Marxist utopian models, of meaning coming from "without" as opposed to from "within" history. And nowhere is this collision more apparent than in *Chevengur* (wr. 1928–29), Platonov's most complex and provocative work. This chapter is a study of *Chevengur* within the context of Russian utopianism and apocalypticism.

When translated into narrative form, the utopian urge gives rise to a range of conceptual paradoxes. If a utopian fiction does not question its own aims, and if it advances a viewpoint that is obviously privileged,[4] then the ideal

---

[4] It is also true that the experience of reading a utopian fiction can never be removed from the context, the actual historical space-time, in which it is written. Thus when we speak of a text that does not question its utopian pretensions, we are, in context, only speaking of a tendency, not an absolute position. Striedter ("Three Utopian Novels" 198) points out that the decision to classify a novel as utopian "depends primarily on the relationship to the context, to the cultural and political reality. This does not make a discrimination between utopian and anti-utopian novels, between positive and negative utopias, worthless, but it does force the critic to remember that any kind of utopia has a negating aspect." Morson devises a third term, "meta-utopia," to describe the authorial position which calls into question the pretensions of *both* the utopian and anti-utopian (dystopian) fiction: "A type of threshold literature, meta-utopias are designed to be interpreted as dialogues between utopia and the parody of utopia. One side of the dialogue—usually utopia—may seem to predominate, but that predominance is inconclusive and never free from the possibility of reversal. In some works, large sections may exhibit the *topoi* of utopian literature so well that, when considered separately or excerpted for anthologies, they appear to be utopian without qualification. Read in the context of the complete work, however, these works are framed by others that do qualify them and may even make them seem to tend toward self-parody" (*Boundaries* 146). Morson offers, as examples of the meta-utopian strategy in the Russian context, Herzen's *From the Other Shore* and Dostoevsky's *The Diary of a Writer* (among others). Finally, it is worth recalling the presence of *irony* in More's original conception: his hero, Hythloday, *does* seem to feel that too much emphasis is placed by the pre-Christian Utopians on a hierarchy of pleasures. This is of course More the *Christian* humanist—whose highest good was still the contemplation of God—interjecting his slight caveat into the scheme and creating a sense of dialogue and "many-voicedness" even in this monolithic and influential first paradigm. See Manuel and

community it describes is as a matter of course separated from the contingent here and now by centuries of time or by oceans, mountain ranges, or galaxies of space. This special polis should not be contaminated by too much proximity to recalcitrant, open-ended "reality." Thus what often happens in the classic utopia such as More's is that a representative of a time and space in flux (the Portugese mariner Raphael Hythloday) *goes to* that isolated but hopefully expandable time and space where utopia has been achieved and where utopia's spokesman (King Utopus) can educate the naive visitor. The difficulty in the telling of utopia in story form is, of course, that the guiding viewpoint is not really *outside* the text, but inside it, belonging not to God the author, but to an enlightened character.[5] As interlocutor, Ambassador More is still entirely distinct from the obsessed voyager, and yet he rarely questions or argues with the latter. He too, for example, in a statement sharply condemning the materialism of the time, is presumed to agree that the Utopians' use of gold (for chamberpots) is appropriate. The ideal of utopia is further complicated by the fact that it is, by definition, static—it is *already* achieved and fixed. Problems arise, however, when readers, located outside the text and constantly vulnerable to the *context* of their unfolding time and space, are forced to engage the validity and persuasiveness of the ideal *from the middle* and not *from the end*, with its customary narrative flourish of climax, resolution, and closure. This is why the classic utopia is often, at least to a later more secular and skeptical audience, better read as political or philosophical essay than as compelling fiction. As Frank Kermode has said, we want our fictions to end where our expectations, conditioned by centuries of knowing what is "real" and fictionally allowable in terms of the current deformation of the biblical plot, tell us they should.

In anti-utopia, the setting of the "model" polis may have parallel fea-

---

Manuel, *Utopian Thought* 129. Also significant is the fact that "More's *Utopia* is *inconceivable without a belief in the immortality of the soul* and *in rewards and punishments in the next world* [my emphasis]" (Manuel and Manuel, *Utopian Thought* 125).

[5] In More's work Utopia was *not* a replacement for the original "garden east of Eden" (which the author, like many of his contemporaries, felt still existed somewhere on the face of the earth) or for the Heavenly Kingdom, but simply the most humane and convenient model for governing one's activities on earth. As converted spokesman for this model polis, Hythloday begins to take on the psychological lineaments of the beloved "other," becoming in a way as "gentle, merye, quycke, and fyne wytted," as "delytynge in quyetness" (Robinson's 1551 Tudor translation; cited in Manuel and Manuel, *Utopian Thought* 122) as the Utopians themselves. In any event, despite much dialogic juxtaposition of the lamentable state in sixteenth-century England (Book I) and the ideal state on the ahistorical island (Book II), in *Utopia* there is not the kind of purely metapoetic play with narrative levels (God-author-character) that becomes commonplace after the birth of romantic irony.

tures,[6] but the viewpoint of the enlightened alien speaking to socially imperfect humanity from a "beautiful afar," as Gogol would say, is undercut.
There is a disparity between the ideal life advocated by the spokesman and
a real fear of parting with life "in process." This disparity emerges most
clearly through an author's use of dramatic irony. What D-503 assures us
is wonderful about the One State of Zamyatin's *We* is precisely what we,
from our position beyond the "Green Wall" of the text, should take to be
"inhuman." The past that the protagonist repeatedly suppresses by denying
the atavistic hair on his hands is exactly what the author would have the
reader affirm. The anti-utopian fears the inhuman ends promised by utopia
and the violent means often used to achieve those ends, and hence will opt
for the openness of "being human" over an ideal that is either utopian (per-
manently achieved within history) or apocalyptic (resolved by God the
"Other" at the conclusion to the biblical plot). That is to say, the authorial
viewpoint guiding anti-utopia is fervently *human*, but not necessarily
hopeful. It is not coterminous with that of a leading character: D-503 is
limited by his conscious desire to be "machine-like," while Winston Smith
in Orwell's *1984* is limited precisely by his "human" weakness, by his refusal to recognize that all control is already in the hands of O'Brien. Nor
does this viewpoint imply that there may be a higher viewpoint still—that
of God. Ultimately, it rejects the desirability of any polis governed by authority, patriarchy, *order from above* (the Well-Doer) in favor of fraternity
or sorority—a freely chosen, loosely organized, even anarchistic kinship.[7]

Apocalyptic fiction offers a third, in some ways inverted alternative to the
conceptual problem of "telling the end."[8] Its focus is not *the earthly tran-*

---

[6] Often it is futuristically oriented, emphasizing what the Manuels call "euchronia" at the
expense of "eutopia," that is, the model for social life in which "good place gives way to good
time." "In the bosom of a utopia of agrarian calm felicity, a utopia of endless, dynamic change
in science and technology was born," beginning with "the awakened sleeper of Sébastien Mercier's *L'An 2440* and with the utopian projections in the Tenth Epoch of Condorcet's *Esquisse*"
(*Utopian Thought* 20).

[7] A good recent example of this rejection of patriarchal hierarchy in favor of sororal equality
is found in the Strugatsky brothers' eerie tale *Snail on the Slope* (1966). See Greene, "Male
and Female in *The Snail on the Slope*" (forthcoming).

[8] Morson's argument with regard to the meta-utopia (see note 4 above) is pertinent here,
but with one qualification. For him, the meta-utopian author (Herzen, Dostoevsky) questions
the authority underlying both positions—that of the utopian and that of the anti-utopian. We
know that irony or parody is present in the meta-utopia for *formal* reasons, the most obvious
being a boundary or frame with other material (often less than reverent) that causes the "serious" statement to be upstaged or critically commented upon. In this respect the meta-parodic
viewpoint has much in common with the aesthetic logic of the romantic ironists (Solger, Friedrich Schlegel, Tieck, Hoffmann, Heine: see Muecke, *Irony* 78). The principal difference between the "meta-utopian" and "apocalyptic" fiction is that the latter, while acknowledging the
full irony of any absolute (i.e., ethically self-enclosing) truth and any higher author, never-

*sition* to a state variously interpreted as perfected humanity or inhuman perfection, but *the divinely induced end* of personal and universal history as prophesied in the Book of Revelation or other apocalypses. In this fictional model, the uninitiated one does not go to utopia, nor does the benighted hero write back to us from a vantage of "happiness without freedom"; rather, a force from beyond *comes to* the hero, who is living under the shadow of the end, in this case an ultimate and long-promised revolution. Moreover, this end, either in genuine or parodic form, is closely associated with death and comes *at the end*: the death of Nastasya Filippovna, the bomb that explodes in the Ableukhov household, the deaths of the Master and Margarita, the death of Yury Zhivago. It is the end we have been waiting for; the end that has finally come; the end that, in terms of the apocalyptic subtext, presumably gives meaning and shape to all that has come before. If an apocalyptic fiction is about the end, then its narrative tension, its interest as story, arises from the various ways that this end can be inscribed throughout the text yet staved off until "its time has come."

This, to be sure, is what is usually meant by being "end-determined." Yet even if all fiction can in some sense be read "backwards," from its prefigured end to its as yet uncoded beginning, these fictions, which openly allude to the Book of Revelation as a key to understanding Russian history in crisis, are more consciously and boldly modeled on the climax of the biblical plot than others. Authors of apocalyptic fiction, like those of anti-utopian fiction, fully understand that there is a disjunction between the knowledge available to their characters and that available to them, standing—safe, "ulteriorized," potentially ironic—beyond their texts. However, authors of apocalyptic fiction go one step farther. Because they are believers, or at least *want* to be, they imply that there is a viewpoint wholly independent of their time and space, one that sees human life as a text bounded by a beginning and end. To put it in Belian terms, these authors see their texts as "flat," two-dimensional objects that, with the proper volume of imaginative empathy or "inspiration" breathed into them, can take on an added dimension, a third one that comes from "beyond." Likewise, God, from his vantage, can interpose into the three-dimensional, apparently "open" and forever contingent time-space of the author's life signs that there is yet another dimension, out of reach of habitual cognition, but

---

theless implicitly posits their existence from *within* the formal boundaries of a text and within that text's representation as history. This optical illusion makes the artist's ability to *imagine* what "might be" more significant than the historian's ability to record and reconstitute what actually was and, in terms of the conceptualization of time-space, often builds upon what the philosopher Florensky would call the *coincidentia oppositorum* (the "circle that opens")—the artist's escape route from the necessity of history and the inevitability of closure.

nevertheless operative and capable of conferring meaning and eventually *ending* on the "text" of that life (see Chapter Two).

Hence the author of the apocalyptic fiction, located on a spectrum of religious belief somewhere between fervent affirmation and doubt (but never outright or categorical denial), inserts into the text signs that a parallelism does, or *may*, exist between the "sense of an ending" available to each level of perception (character—author/reader—God). If, therefore, in utopian fiction the author's and character's viewpoints are coextensive, and in anti-utopian fiction these same viewpoints are at odds, "resolved" only by a radical undermining of the utopian order and a return to historical flux and irresolution, then in apocalyptic fiction there is a third voice, not that of the author but that of a Bakhtinian "other," which in an un-Bakhtinian manner *implies*, without saying so explicitly, that history *does* have meaning because God speaks into it from beyond the end. It is of course an optical or verbal illusion to claim that this other voice belongs to an intelligence distinct from the author's. On the other hand, authors such as Bely, Bulgakov, and Pasternak are intent on finding narrative structures that suggest that other powers are working *through* them, their narrators, and their narrator's words. In short, they consciously play with the illusion of author qua prophet and of his text qua revelation.

What all this means for our discussion is that the patriarchal order affirmed in classic utopia and undermined in anti-utopia is *reaffirmed* in the literary representation of apocalypse by placing the source of that order, God the Father, *beyond the text*. At the same time, the symbolic plotting of a life and a history within that text is imbued with a meaning not simply "aesthetic." Aesthetic shape for the author of apocalyptic fiction is the most appropriate surrogate at hand for suggesting a divine shape to human history. Regardless of the valence of these intrusions from beyond—whether they are positive, as in the concatenation of "coincidences" or the appearance of the fairy tale Evgraf in *Doctor Zhivago*, or negative, as in the threat of an imminent end announced by the Bronze Horseman in *Petersburg*—they bespeak a chiaroscuro balance of light and shade, of meaning as viewed from the other side of history's "Finis." The voices in an apocalyptic fiction are, therefore, not all equal, if by "equal" we mean that the other collocutor/interlocutor implied by a given utterance is always on the same level of contingency and openness as the speaker. These authors encourage their readers to see a hierarchy of utterance whose highest level is, as Bakhtin would hold, the novelistically impossible—"dialogism," or the full awareness of life's competing voices, *within* "monologism," or the hope that, despite the fragility of paradigms, there is an order outside it all. Therefore, apocalyptic fictions can be said to forestall the threat of "utopian pretension" because (1) they do not claim that this order can be fully embodied in the text (it can only be *implied*), just as, moving one step higher, they do not claim that God's kingdom can come to earth; and (2) they reserve their most powerful statements about how the apocalyptic urge is to be translated into narrative form for the *ends* of their stories—it is here that the optical illusion of a divine resolution to open-ended history finds its most ingenious expression.

How does Platonov's *Chevengur* fit into the dialectic between utopianism and apocalypticism standing at the center of much modern Russian fiction? To begin to answer this question we might look briefly at the utopian sources—biographical, popular, and literary—that influenced the young Platonov. Then we might proceed to a closer examination of the text of *Chevengur* by showing how this "naive" utopianism is challenged in the later work and how, ultimately, the result, both in terms of structure and guiding philosophy, differs radically from the responses of other authors, such as Bulgakov and Pasternak, who also saw the revolution as an apocalyptic event but who found a way out of the "failed" millennialism of the post-revolutionary era through their renewed faith in the artist's transfiguring vision.

Nearly every aspect of Platonov's background prepared him for the role he was to play in the dizzying atmosphere of the first post-revolutionary years, during what is now referred to as the "proletarian episode" in Soviet Russian literature. Born in a suburb of Voronezh (an area known to have the highest mortality rate in European Russia) to a working-class family, and compelled by his family's size and poverty to enter the labor force at a young age, Platonov came to see the machine as the potential savior of the down-and-out urban proletariat.[9] His generation was nurtured in the belief that if the "means of production" could be placed in the hands of the workers and if technology could be allowed to develop without the element of capitalist greed, then a communist paradise could become a reality. The machine of machines for the young Platonov was the locomotive, whose motion he soon likened to the unswerving course of history: "In addition to the field, the village, my mother, and the sound of church bells, I also loved (and the longer I live the more so do I love them) locomotives, the machine, the singing whistle and sweat-filled work" (cited in Geller, *V poiskakh schast'ia* 13). Much of his childhood and adolescent experience took place around the railroad tracks and workshops where his father was employed as a machinist. This autobiographical element would enter directly into the characterization of Zakhar Pavlovich, the foster-father figure and train enthusiast of *Chevengur*, and of Sasha Dvanov, the young hero who has a

[9] The writer's real surname was Klimentov.

brief and calamitous ride at the controls of the "locomotive of the revolution." After participating in the civil war, and while still studying at the
Voronezh Polytechnic Institute, Platonov began to publish articles and verse
which were heavily influenced by A. A. Bogdanov's views on proletarian
culture and by the work of the "Smithy" poets, including A. K. Gastev,
M. P. Gerasimov, and V. T. Kirillov.

It cannot be stated too strongly that Platonov's coming of age belongs to
the time when utopian enthusiasm in Russia was reaching its high water
mark. [10] Many people fervently believed that the new Soviet state was the
laboratory in which their cherished dreams of social and economic harmony
would pass through the alembics of futuristic technology to become reality.
Platonov felt that the creator of this new Russia would be "not that one
[tot], the former, the old, but one resurrected, happy and unique" ("Vospitanie kommunistov"). And he was far from alone when he rhapsodized
in a poem of his cosmist phase, significantly entitled "The Last Day" (1919),
that "we are the coming truth, / The truth of an earth under which [sic] /
All secrets of the heavens will come crashing down . . . / O, we will crush
this world, will explode it with dynamite,/ Will turn it into sand!/ And we
will dictate to the comets/ And colossal distant worlds/ The will of machines,/ The truth of burning hearts" (Plamia #69: 16). This was, after all,
the period in the late teens and early twenties when, like a new god, Lenin
was promising to galvanize the country with a mythical jolt called "electrification"; when Bogdanov, already the author of Red Star (1908), a Bolshevik utopia set on Mars, was speaking of art as a means of mobilizing the
collective labor force; when Vladimir Tatlin's famous "productivist" monument to the Third International was being designed to blend form and
function and, by actually moving its spiral-shaped ribs, to imitate the Marxist dialectical climb toward communism; when Gastev, in his role as head of
the Central Institute of Labor, was praising in Whitmanesque fashion the
liberating nature of labor and the machine and seeking to create, with the
help of Frederick Winslow Taylor's time-motion studies and Henry Ford's
assembly line, human automatons out of ill-disciplined work recruits; when
P. Kerzhentsev's "League of Time" was ferreting out workers who did not
use their minutes and hours efficiently; when a number of writers, including V. Itin in The Country of Gonguri (1922) and Ya. Okunev in The Coming World (1923), were projecting in fictional models how the new utopia
might look, while others, such as Gastev and Platonov, were attempting to
live out their cosmist dreams in the factories and countryside; and when

[10] "The ideological genesis of 'proletarian art' in Russia lay in the materialistic hypostasis of
Russian utopian-religious thought at the turn of the century, with all its ethical maximalism
and definite syncretism" (Tolstaia-Segal, "Ideologicheskie konteksty" 237).

various "social engineers" were looking for new civic rituals (Lenin's public funeral and internment in a mausoleum being the grand archetype) and places of worship (palaces of labor) to replace those of the traditional church and were heatedly discussing the expanded size and configuration of the family in a society which advocated sexual freedom and communal living.[11]

Most of these utopian projects, these quixotic attempts to legislate a future of liberty, equality, and fraternity within the present, came to naught. All too soon they would be dismissed, then actively suppressed, by the centralized, "patriarchal" order of high Stalinism. Be this as it may, Platonov and his generation of cranks and geniuses were, for the most part, sincerely motivated and therefore genuinely disenchanted when the new bureaucracy—the entropic "crust" forming over the molten energy of the revolution, as Zamyatin would say—began to thwart their undertakings. Platonov himself, who worked as an "ameliorator" (one who endeavors to irrigate the steppe) from 1922–27, was profoundly shaken and embittered when one of his projects was undermined in 1926 by the corrupt establishment of Tambov. It is not surprising, then, that soon after this difficult period of "living down" his youthful utopian plans Platonov turned his whole attention to writing, creating the major product of his early mature period, *Chevengur*.

In addition to personal involvement with the proletarian experiment, there are at least three other sources that together exerted a profound influence on Platonov's early utopianism: the literary tradition of Russian utopian fiction, the popular legends about a distant peasant paradise, and the all-encompassing philosophy of Nikolay Fyodorov.[12] Of these, the first, the *literary* tradition, seems paradoxically least formative. Although Platonov was certainly not unaware of his country's belletristic past, and in fact writers such as Pushkin, Dostoevsky, Saltykov-Shchedrin, and Korolenko figure prominently in the plots and themes of a number of his works, he had little patience with narrow aesthetic concerns per se (what Russians call *literaturnost'*—"literariness") or with the tastes of an elitist readership.[13] His

---

[11] For more on this period, see Fitzpatrick, ed., *Cultural Revolution*.

[12] Fyodorov's thought, especially in its futuristic aspects, finds a close parallel in that of Bogdanov, Gastev, and the Smithy poets, with whom Platonov was also clearly infatuated in his early years. On the various points of contiguity between the ideological systems of Fyodorov and Bogdanov, see Tolstaia-Segal, "Ideologicheskie konteksty" 238ff.

[13] Despite the fact that " 'sincerity' for Platonov was tightly linked with his departure from the position of professional man of letters" (Tolstaia-Segal, "Ideologicheskie konteksty" 236), he obviously did not create his work in a vacuum. The influence of Boris Pilnyak, for example, is an important chapter in any study of Platonov's formative years. Pilnyak's *okhlomony* (from *Mahogany*, 1929) and Platonov's Chevengurians, as representatives of an obsolete revolutionary fervor in a time of consolidation and bureaucratization, seem especially close in conception. It was during this time (late twenties) that Pilnyak and Platonov worked together

keen empathy with the laborer and peasant "orphaned" by society and worn out by a daily life of toil place him squarely in the "humanitarian" tradition of Russian literature. Nevertheless, inasmuch as the utopian visions that lure Platonov's heroes onto the "road of history" seem on one level to be unmistakable calques of Dostoevsky's "Golden Age"[14] and Korolenko's vision of a relenting God in *Makar's Dream*, this tradition deserves some mention.

As suggested earlier, literary versions of utopia can be, given the *context* in which they are intended to be read, positive or negative: herein lies the essential *generic* distinction between utopian and anti-utopian fiction. From the late eighteenth century (but especially after 1850) through the 1920s Russian literature yielded a rich utopian lode, with the anti-utopian element being a relatively late development. When such early exemplars as Mikhail Kheraskov and Pavel Lvov began to experiment with the genre, they applied its stabilizing worldview to the task of reinforcing the tsar's authority: "*This*," they seemed to be saying, "is the best of all human societies—look at it in admiration." Kheraskov's novel *Polidorus, the Son of Cadmus and Harmonia* (1794), makes transparently clear that the tsar as wise father is preferable to an anarchistic brotherhood and that a strong centralized government is the Russians' best defense against the chaos of the French Revolution.[15] And in Lvov's *The Russian Pamela* (1789), which takes place on

---

on the essays in *Che-Che-O* (1929). For the Pilnyak connection in Platonov, see Tolstaia-Segal, "Stikhiinye sily." Elsewhere ("Ideol. konteksty" 234ff.) Tolstaia-Segal posits the presence of other contemporary writers and thinkers in the early Platonov: Balmont, Bryusov, Remizov, Lyashko, Neverov, Khlebnikov, Gastev, and Bogdanov. See also Teskey, *Platonov* 50.

[14] I.e., the prelapsarian period evoked in "Stavrogin's Confession" and *The Adolescent* and based visually on Claude Lorrain's "Acis and Galatea." See also the blissful state before the "fall" brought on by the hero in "The Dream of the Ridiculous Man." (This same Golden Age [*Zolotoi Vek*] as presented in the Russian popular consciousness is discussed in Chistov, *Russkie narodnye sotsial'no-utopicheskie legendy* 15–23. See below.) As Joseph Brodsky writes in *Less Than One*: "There is a sense of terrific autonomy to this man [Platonov], and much though I'd like to link him to Dostoevsky, with whom he perhaps has more in common than anyone else in Russian literature, I'd rather refrain from doing so: it would illuminate nothing. Of course, what screams to be pointed out is that both *Chevengur* and *The Foundation Pit* thematically, at least, can be regarded as sequels to Dostoevsky's *The Possessed* because they represent the realization of Dostoevsky's prophecy" (291).

[15] See also Kheraskov's earlier novel *Numa, or Flourishing Rome* (1768), where parallels are drawn between Russia under Catherine and a flourishing Rome under Numa. As the author says in the preface, "If all people had the kind of thoughts as the author of this book, then the human race would not be unhappy, because truth, virtue and justice would have triumphed on earth. They are now beginning to triumph in Russia. May heaven grant the completion of this" (*Numa* v–vi; cited in Baehr, "From History to National Myth" 6). In general, this was a period (second half of the eighteenth century) when a number of writers were translating the notion of Third Rome into Russian terms. Other allusions to indigenous Slavic utopias, which were perceived as no worse than their Greek and Roman antecedents, are found in M. D.

an "Island of Prosperity" (i.e., an idealized, traditional Russia) ruled over by a patriarchal government (i.e., a perfected version of the tsar), the utopian urge is not directed à la More toward contemplating an ideal painfully distinct from the status quo, but, more in keeping with the tradition of Fénelon and Montesquieu, at establishing the correct rules for conduct within an already existing society (see Baehr, "In the Name of the Father"; Sviatlovskii, *Russkii utopicheskii roman*). This use of the utopian form to legitimize the status quo predominated in the Russian context until the post-Decembrist period, despite some irreverent fillips aimed at the establishment in the "projects for the future" chapters of Alexander Radishchev's *Journey from St. Petersburg to Moscow* (1790). One source of the Slavophile/Westernizer debate over appropriate models for the future was Vladimir Odoevsky's "novel" *Russian Nights* (1844); this work both conceals a response to the pro-Western, anti-Russian message of Chaadaev's *Philosophical Letters* and, in its epilogue especially, urges the citizen of the West to get a transfusion of Slavic blood, to join in Russia's emerging sense of love, unity, and "musical harmony," and to experience its ideal of happiness "for one *and* all" (*dlia vsekh i kazhdogo*) (*Russkie nochi* 182).[16] Not only would these ideas eventuate in the following generation in several of Dostoevsky's most famous texts, they would, as the germ of Slavophilism, help provoke the rise of a largely antithetical tradition, the one led by Nikolay Chernyshevsky and his quasi-utopian novel *What Is to Be Done?* (1863),[17] with its ideals of a Saint-Simonian brotherhood and sisterhood. The appearance of Chernyshevsky's highly influential work signaled the full legitimization within Russian "progressive" circles of a post-enlightenment, post-1789, Western European utopian paradigm.

Thereafter until the October Revolution (and in fact in many cases well into the 1920s) a lively dialogue took place between the utopians on the one hand and the anti-utopians on the other. Important milestones in the reigning realist tradition are Dostoevsky's recurrent dream of an agrarian Golden Age and his influential "Legend of the Grand Inquisitor." The first, which to some extent recalls Goncharov's idyllic patrimony "Oblomovka" (*Oblomov*), but without its feudal trappings, is clearly positive and devoutly to be

---

Chulkov's *The Mocker* (1766) and Kheraskov's *Cadmus and Harmonia* (1789). See Stephen Baehr's fine article "From History to National Myth: *Translatio imperii* in Eighteenth-Century Russia."

[16] See also Odoevsky's utopian tale *The Year 4338* (1840), in which the government, in a most un-Platonic twist, is ruled by "the leading poet of our time" (cited by Maimin, "Vladimir Odoevskii," in Odoevskii, *Russkie nochi* 269).

[17] Other examples of native Russian utopian fictions which space does not allow a discussion of here are Vladimir Odoevsky's *The Year 4338* (1840) (see note 16) and Vladimir Taneev's *The Communist State of the Future* (1879).

wished; the second, on the other hand, which served as a subtext for Zamyatin's *We*, reveals the danger of bartering freedom for happiness and of granting all social authority to an atheistic patriarch (i.e., a future socialistic "vanguard"). With the increasing industrialization, urbanization, and interest in technology of the 1890s, the debate took on the classic contours of what the Manuels have defined as the inevitable shift from "eutopia" (good place in the past) to "euchronia" (good time in the future; see notes 6 and 10 to the Introduction). Although the balance of persuasive power, at least within the literary establishment, seemed gradually to tilt in favor of the anti-utopians, the utopians had an immensely talented and—to judge by the number of printings of *Red Star*—popular spokesman in the indefatigable Alexander Bogdanov. Particularly in the ominous pre-revolutionary years, the symbolist Valery Bryusov's stories about the revenge of the machine age ("The Revolt of the Machines," 1908?) and the epidemic of self-contradiction that destroyed an otherwise "perfect" Platonic republic ("Republic of the Southern Cross," 1904–05) were accurate reflections of public anxiety.[18] And there were other anti-utopian works, such as L. B. Afanasyev's *Journey to Mars* (1901) and Nikolay Fyodorov's *An Evening in the Year 2217* (1906), which called into question the urge to achieve the end of communism through the Bogdanovian means of scientific discovery, tectology ("systems thinking"), and social engineering. All these anti-utopians found their most eloquent and prophetic voice in Evgeny Zamyatin, whose *We*, while written only in 1921 as a warning of what *might* happen if those like Gastev were given free reign, became a hauntingly accurate blueprint for Stalinist excesses.[19]

[18] But reflections, to be sure, which the author's "decadent" aesthetic certainly intended to capitalize on.

[19] In fairness to Bogdanov, however, who as a utopian was also aware of the weakness of human nature, it should be said that he did not depict his Martian polis as flawless. Unlike Gastev, whom he ultimately opposed, he did not want his comrades to ape the efficiency of machines in mass tableaux of synchronized motion; and whereas most burning social questions (e.g., monogamy versus polygamy) are resolved on his "red star," there is still room for a child to senselessly mutilate a frog and for one of the planet's patriarchs (Sterni) to contemplate the annihilation of earthlings. In other words, there is more dynamism and "dialogue" in Bogdanov's pre-1917 utopia than in the many utopian novels of the twenties, including Alexey Tolstoy's *Aelita* (1922–23), where socialism is treated as an established (or soon to be so) good, one that is *already* anchored to an historic time and place (the Soviet Union).

*Aelita*, by the way, turns out to be a kind of Siamese twin to *Red Star*. The main difference between the two works can be attributed to their respective ties to the historical context: in *Red Star*, written after the failed revolution of 1905, Bogdanov compares the desired Martian model to the chaos on earth (but with the promise, to be sure, of another revolution very much in the offing). *Aelita*, written after 1917 with the express purpose of showing the émigré author's change of heart toward the Soviet state and his new found loyalty as a *smenovekhovets* (member of the "changing landmarks" group soon to be repatriated), compares a corrupt and

Platonov's position in this tradition is peculiar: his mature works, such as *Chevengur*, are neither fully utopian nor fully anti-utopian. His sympathies are clearly on the side of the *duraki*, the simple folk and peripatetic visionaries (e.g., Foma Pukhov in "The Hidden Man") who are the post-1917 equivalent of the traditional Russian truth-seeker (*strannik*) and fool-in-Christ (*iurodivyi*). But his actual experience of the manifest failures of utopianism as worldview tell him that in reality history's road may not and probably does not have a terminus. In this sense, Platonov is a logical descendant of Dostoevsky, who at the bier of his first wife debated the irreconcilable paradox of human life as constant process and divine viewpoint as harmonious and meaningful end (see Chapter One). Like Dostoevsky, Platonov was obsessed with the vision of a Golden Age but honest enough to show what happens when human beings attempt to incorporate that vision in multifarious, ever-changing history. And unlike both Bogdanov and Zamyatin, the mature Platonov could not, however he may have wanted to, give his full allegiance to the one's utopianism, which claimed that an intellectual model of perfection could satisfy the more basic human need for brotherhood, or to the other's anti-utopianism, which satirized the regimentation of a future urban paradise, but which offered no counter-model save for a return to nomadic hordes, sexual freedom, and permanent revolution.

Equally powerful as a shaping force in Platonov's early utopianism were the popular legends—the "good places" in a distant land rather than the "good times" in an urban future—that sustained the Russian peasant during periods of misfortune.[20] As a number of folklorists have amply demonstrated, these legends usually involve some sort of popular savior (the iconic Lenin was later cultivated for this role) who founded a kingdom in a faraway region where his peasant following could live in righteousness and

senescent Mars ripe for socialist revolution to the implied better world that is a *fait accompli* at home. In the first the hero Leonid goes to Mars to observe the utopia that could come to earth (and Bogdanov believes will); in the second the heroes Los and Gusev also go to Mars, but with the purpose of spreading the revolution beyond the borders of Russia into the universe. The shift in *locale* of the ideal from Bogdanov's to Tolstoy's work is a telling detail in the history of utopian literature before and after 1917. After 1917, despite the great blossoming of the genre in terms of sheer numbers (there were, according to Stites ["Fantasy and Revolution" 14], approximately two hundred works of revolutionary science fiction written in Russia in the 1920s), almost all preempted the possibility of anti-utopian dialogue by either eulogizing the technological feats of the communist future (e.g., Okunev's *The Coming World*) or totally criticizing the capitalist model, with its greed and dehumanizing potential (e.g., A. Paley's *Gulfstream* [1928]).

[20] Here it should be emphasized that the droughts that drive the peasants to the towns and cities in *Chevengur* were a real threat to survival in Platonov's childhood surroundings.

plenty.[21] Perhaps the best-known folk versions of an ideal Russian monarch and a peasant paradise are Tsar Gorokh (to whom both Pushkin and Dostoevsky allude) and the underwater city of Kitezh. In Platonov's case, however, it was probably the so-called Zadonskaya Doroga ("The Road Beyond the River Don"), which passed by the suburb of Voronezh where he was born (Yamskaya Sloboda), that brought a host of regional legends to feed his youthful imagination and utopian dreams for a better life. These included such colorful names as the "Whitewater Region" (*Belovod'e*), the City of Ignat, the River Darya, Anapa, "New Islands" (*novye ostrova*), "Land of Nuts" (*orekhovaia zemlia*), and the Eternal City on the Distant River (*Vechnyi-Grad-Na-Dal'nei-Reke*) (Vasil'ev, *Platonov* 7). It is the last of these, the Eternal City on the Distant River, that becomes the Siberian utopia ruled by Ivan Zhokh in the story by the same name—Platonov's first attempt at the plot that would be fully realized in *Chevengur*. Thus from the rebellions of Ivan Bolotnikov (1606), Stenka Razin (1670–71), Kondraty Bulavin (1707), and Emelyan Pugachyov (1773–74), to the utopian movements that sprang up at the time of the October Revolution, such as the Tsardom of Ur and Nestor Makhno's "Republic on Wheels,"[22] Russian history has been punctuated by attempts of the lower classes to translate indigenous legend into reality. Platonov was as conscious of this tradition as that of Gastev's proletarian urbanism, and many of his works can be neatly divided into those that experiment with a utopia achieved through science and those that project what might happen if the peasants are given their dream of a land of milk and honey.

The last and strongest influence on all of Platonov's works, including *Chevengur*, is the philosophy of Nikolay Fyodorov (1828–1903), a highly eccentric but seminal figure whose ideas, *mutatis mutandis*, made their way into some of the most important monuments of modern Russian literature and thought. Among the works that attest to the vitality of Fyodorov's metaphysical system are Dostoevsky's *Brothers Karamazov*, Solovyov's *Three Conversations*, Nikolay Berdyaev's *The Meaning of History*, Konstantin Tsiolkovsky's *The Investigation of Outer Space by Means of Reaction Apparatus*, Mayakovsky's *About That*, Nikolay Zabolotsky's *The*

---

[21] Note here the link with many of the medieval sects studied by Cohn and the need, even if he emerges from the peasantry itself, for a patriarch figure. Pugachyov, for example, was not satisfied with simply being the ruler of his peasant band, but had himself called *batiushka* ("little father") and played the role of resurrected Tsar Peter III within his rag-tag marauding court. For more, see Chistov, *Russkie narodnye sotsial'no-utopicheskie legendy* 147–74; Geller, *V poiskakh schast'ia* 91–92; and Stites, "Red Visions."

[22] The Tsardom of Ur was a remote Siberian pine forest where a new monarchy was briefly established and the "Republic on Wheels" was a short-lived anarchist substate in the Ukraine. See Stites, "Red Visions."

*Triumph of Agriculture*, and Pasternak's *Doctor Zhivago*. Although it is difficult to determine precisely when Platonov read Fyodorov's central work, *The Philosophy of the Common Cause* (1906, 1913), the writer's widow has attested that this study took place early and was thorough. The reason why Fyodorov appealed to the idealistic but non-believing Platonov was that the former's highly unorthodox "Christianity" was first and foremost practical or applied (though not necessarily pragmatic).

To put simply what is stated in many complex permutations over more than a thousand pages, Fyodorov believed that a negative apocalypse of divine judgment, a decision by God to enter history because humanity has not been able to live up to its Christian duty toward itself and its members, could be averted if we turned our energies toward the proper task. He called the apocalypse of judgment a "transcendental resurrection," or a punishment that would occur when "the resistance to the divine will have reached its ultimate degree" (*Filosofiia obshchago dela* 1: 187). But this sort of apocalypse was not inevitable; if we could join in viewing history differently, with genuine Christian imagination, it would give way to an "immanent resurrection." "History is always [the process of] *resurrection*, not *judgment*, because the subject of history is not *the living*, but *those who have died*, and in order to judge, it is first necessary to resurrect . . . those who have already borne the supreme punishment—the death penalty" (*Filosofiia* 1: 129). Fyodorov's "common cause," which would have struck a kindred utopian chord in Platonov, was nothing less than the literal resurrection, from the molecules up, of our dead, dispersed ancestors and the Edenic "greening" (cf. Platonov's work as an "ameliorator") of the universe's vast pockets of aridity and uninhabitability through the miracles of modern science. Thus, practical Christianity and scientific technology would go hand in hand to the altar in an apocalyptic marriage worthy of William Blake.

Only a task such as this, reasoned Fyodorov, could succeed in harnessing the "blind forces of nature" and fostering in humanity a sense of genuine brotherhood. "The common cause is not limited simply to the living; it is the unification of the living for the resurrection of those who have died, that is, it is a [process of] resurrecting that demands a universal joining together, not only of external, but of internal, real brotherhood, a brotherhood based on fathers, on a fatherland, and not one of citizenship" (*Filosofiia* 1: 194). On the other hand, any scientific endeavor whose incentive for advancement is based on the Darwinian greed of capitalism or on the envy-driven "brotherhood" of socialism could not, according to Fyodorov, bring us closer to the goal of true filial respect and sibling love. The beneficiaries of such endeavor are the triumphant and self-promoting "children," not the forgotten and too easily replaced parents.[23] But if the sexual urge could be channeled into resurrecting our ancestors rather than preparing a place for our descendants, then the chief evil in human history, that is, death, could be overcome. Heaven could then come to earth (and the universe) and be embodied *in* history without God having to resort to what Rufus Jones once called "an apocalyptic relief expedition from the sky" (Jones, *Eternal Gospel* 5). This *homo ex machina*, therefore, was Fyodorov's way of "secularizing" the last book of the Bible and of making a narrative detour away from the idea of Endtime as *ekpyrosis* instigated from above.

Even a cursory reading of *Chevengur* reveals that many of Fyodorov's cherished ideas enter into the themes and structure of the novel: the emphasis on genuine brotherhood, the (from our viewpoint almost morbid) preoccupation with death, the positive sublimation of the sex drive ("positive chastity"), the responsibility toward parents, the seemingly congenital[24] need for movement toward a worthy goal, the skepticism toward any society that separates the "thinkers" from the "doers," the belief that Russia provides the ideal historical and geopolitical setting for an undertaking of the grand task. For Fyodorov, as for Platonov after him, the Christ example was important not because it showed the way to otherworldly time, but because it was a model of ideal filial devotion and a sign that human beings must seek to resurrect themselves *in this world*. And even if all these ideas do not find positive expression in *Chevengur*, since Platonov's own fondest dreams for a better world were frustrated by reality and this frustration could not help but inform the tone (often wryly ironic) of the novel, Platonov never ceased to have a profound affection for the sincere good will and quixotic ingenuity of Fyodorov's project.[25] "Satire," at least in the sense of a narrative tone that questions and undermines a given version of societal order (*We*, say, is satirical), is not a term one feels comfortable applying to the utopian projects of Platonov's cherished *duraki*, Nikolay Fyodorov included.

To sum up our findings, much of modern Russian fiction can be seen as a dialogical tug-of-war between the opposing urges of utopianism and apocalypticism. The view of history as meaningful from within, according to its own *immanent* laws, has led in the Soviet context to the raising of the So-

---

[23] The notion of "progress" as a self-serving improvement on, and therefore denigration of, the life and work of one's parents was anathema to Fyodorov (see, e.g., *Filosofiia obshchago dela* 1: 191). It would be taken up again in such works as Solovyov's *Three Conversations* and Berdyaev's *The Meaning of History*. For more on the Fyodorov connection in Platonov, see Teskey.

[24] Cf. in this context the many images of throbbing blood in *Chevengur*.

[25] Fyodorov himself, by the way, throughout his life as modest librarian, seemed by all accounts to have lived up to the ideal of brotherhood he set for others.

cialist Realist novel to the status of orthodox canon. The view of history as meaningful from without, according to God's laws of *imminence*, has led in the broader context of *Russian* literature (prerevolutionary and postrevolutionary, Soviet and émigré) to the valorization of an entirely different canon, an object of intense study in the West. It is precisely works like Bely's *Petersburg*, Bulgakov's *The Master and Margarita*, and Pasternak's *Doctor Zhivago* that, while modernizing the biblical plot and raising the same questions of historical causality as do their Socialist Realist counterparts, have attracted the most attention in Western academic circles. This attention, furthermore, has less to do with politics than with the "aestheticization" of history. These writers do not argue for a "closed" view of history, just as their narrators do not usually feign "omniscience," and yet they do not imply that history is meaningless. Quite the opposite, they imply, through various narrative sleights-of-hand, that aesthetic shape is the closest we can come to a mimicry of divine purpose.[26] Unlike the novels of Dostoevsky and Bely, *Chevengur* does not, as we shall see, *look forward* with a millennial enthusiasm colored by fear and anxiety to the approaching end of God's plot. By the late twenties the revolution is an acknowledged *fait accompli*. Nor does *Chevengur* possess the fundamental optimism of the novels of Bulgakov and Pasternak, which proceed from the philosophies of Pavel Florensky and Nikolay Fyodorov (among others) to texts in which life's symbolic patterning is glimpsed as if "from beyond" and in which, ultimately, the mistakes of history can be "unwritten." Platonov differs radically from these authors in that he had no allegiance to the aesthetic object as such and because once the epochal end (and beginning) of 1917 had been corrupted by the concessions of the New Economic Policy (NEP) (1921–28), he had little else on which to rely.

As M. H. Abrams has eloquently demonstrated, when the English and German Romantics, led by Wordsworth, were faced with the excesses of the French Revolution and the manifest failure of their chiliastic designs for the future, they began to strip themselves of their former commitment to political apocalypse and to reinvest their fervor in an "apocalypse of consciousness." The process of re-education was successful: it created some of the greatest works of Romanticism (e.g., Wordsworth's *Prelude* and Shelley's *Prometheus Unbound* in the realm of literature, Hegel's *Phenomenology*

---

[26] Even Vladimir Nabokov's elegant deployment of inserted texts in *Despair, Invitation to a Beheading, The Gift*, and other works and his insistence on the roles of author as chess master and character as pawn partake of this hierarchy of viewpoints, this play of "meta-," that constantly posits a higher order. If, to cite just one example, Cincinnatus as character can be allowed to walk away from the mock apocalyptic ending of *Invitation*, then why cannot his author, in the realm of biography he was so cryptic about, be freed to enter a higher order by *his* creator at the climax of the other "story"?

in the realm of philosophy). Abrams concludes that Romanticism triumphed because of its ability "to save the overview of human history and destiny, the experiential paradigms, and the cardinal values of [its] religious heritage, by reconstituting them in a way that would make them intellectually acceptable, as well as emotionally pertinent, for the time being" (Abrams, *Natural Supernaturalism* 66). The goal, thus redefined, was "to achieve a New Jerusalem not by changing the world, but by changing the way we see the world" (Abrams, "Theme and Variations" 363). This is essentially the route taken by Bulgakov and Pasternak, who see the artistic consciousness as privileged and prophetic in a world where political revolution has not brought the desired result. But Platonov, with his working class origin, his profound suspicion of intellectualism, and his equally profound commitment to the brotherhood of humanity, was not free to opt for an aesthetically elitist re-visioning of reality. Above all else, Platonov is a *failed utopian*, not a confirmed apocalypticist. But as he uses many of the same space-time symbols found in other works of apocalyptic fiction (road, horse, train, etc.), it is important that we examine how these economies make for an entirely different yet equally compelling novelistic structure and meaning.

*Chevengur* is one of the strangest novels ever to appear in the Russian language. From its very first sentences, which depict Zakhar Pavlovich as living "in nature," placing burdocks over his eyes prior to sleep to protect them from the morning sun, and building a wooden clock that is supposed "to run without works, powered just by the rotation of the earth" (Olcott 3), the reader feels the presence of a powerful, fresh, yet highly disquieting intelligence. For the individual schooled in a tradition of aesthetic sophistication, there is something too "raw" about Platonov's prose. Just as Zakhar Pavlovich the inventor loves to tinker with mechanical things, so does his author love to tinker with words, bring images and sensations together in unlikely metonymic marriages, as if they are the wooden clock without parts, the linguistic perpetuum mobile that runs by itself, "powered just by the rotation of the earth." "The whole point about Andrei Platonov," writes Joseph Brodsky, "is that he is a millenarian writer if only because he attacks the very carrier of millenarian sensibility in Russian society: the language itself—or, to put it in more graspable fashion, the revolutionary eschatology embedded in the language" ("Catastrophes" 283). Platonov's work is difficult for an academic audience precisely because of its revolutionary newness, its stepping out of tradition. Moreover, it tends to avoid assiduously its own being as a phenomenon of "literariness"—rather than "baring the device" (*obnazhenie priema*), as the Formalists would say, its purpose is to show language as a mechanism alive with movement yet oblivious to its own inner workings. Add to this perplexing use of language a loose, episodic plot (suggestive of a modern picaresque) and fragmented character- ization, and the reader is soon faced with what in some circles is called ar- tistic experimentation and, in others, artistic failure.

These were some of the issues, together with the novel's ambiguity and ideological "unreliability," that Gorky had in mind when he told Platonov that *Chevengur* was "of course unacceptable to our censorship" ("Pis'mo Platonovu" 313) and that he did not feel justified in using his patronage to place the work at a publishing house. Consequently, the novel's shadowy generic status has been reinforced by its equally shadowy status as historical and textual fact. As has so often happens with important but officially trou- blesome works of Soviet-Russian literature, we do not to this day have a complete and definitive edition of Platonov's Russian text.[27] Instead we have an abbreviated (or perhaps earlier) version that has appeared in the West (Paris, 1972) along with separate Soviet editions of the opening section (*The Origin of a Master*). The only apparently complete text now available is Anthony Olcott's English translation (1978). Yet despite these real obstacles to its reception at home and abroad, *Chevengur* has recently begun to at- tract a lively following among Western and (more reluctantly) Soviet schol- ars.[28] Now it is considered by specialists to be one of the most important works of the twenties, having at last crossed over, on the Foucaultian map of geo-aesthetics, from the "excluded" to the "included," from the "out- side" to the "inside." Quite apart from its topical appeal as political satire, this novel has made a place for itself by blending a startling stylistic origi- nality with profound metaphysical speculation in the spirit of Tolstoy and Dostoevsky, and it has done so by *remaking* for its time and place the ex- pectations of its genre. How this happens, and what it means for the *à re- bours* tradition in which Platonov was writing form the subject of the re- mainder of this chapter. Before proceeding further, however, it may be well

---

[27] Portions of *Chevengur* have appeared over the years under at least seven different titles, but no complete edition has ever been published in the Soviet Union. The most substantial portion to appear there is *The Origin of a Master* (1929), which has come to be accepted as a novella in its own right. In this study citations from the Olcott translation, which have been checked where possible against the Russian and are at times slightly modified, are indicated by page number(s) inserted parenthetically in the text. For more on the publication history of *Chevengur*, see Olcott, "Foreword" xv–xvi; and Geller, "Ob Andree Platonove" 9–22.

[28] The best overall study of *Chevengur* is found in Geller, *V poiskakh schast'ia* 173–253. Articles which either focus on *Chevengur* or provide helpful introductions to Platonov's lan- guage and worldview include: Brodsky, "Catastrophes in the Air"; Dryzhakova, "Andrei Pla- tonov"; Karlinsky, "Andrei Platonov"; Tolstaia-Segal, "Stikhiinye sily" and "Ideologicheskie konteksty"; Striedter, "Three Utopian Novels"; Varshavskii, "Chevengur"; and Yakushev, "Platonov's Artistic Model" and "Struktura khudozhestvennogo obraza."

to reformulate, in the context of the novel, several assumptions about Platonov's thought.

Why did Platonov write a novel so obviously at odds with prevailing literary canons? Our answer here should be predicated not simply on the absence of something (talent, education, taste) but rather on the presence of something else (a deeply held view of the world and the function of art in that world).[29] Platonov, to reiterate, was not writing to please the *umniki*, the elite of "thinkers" as opposed to the majority of "doers." His experience as a failed utopian during the years of NEP had taught him that the use of aesthetic shape (including the pathetic idiom of his cosmist phase) to suggest that personal and national histories have coherent and meaningful beginnings, middles, *and* ends was dishonest.[30] The mature Platonov, to cite Brodsky again, "simply had a tendency to see his words to their logical— that is absurd, that is totally paralyzing end. In other words, like no other Russian writer before or after him, Platonov was able to reveal a self-destructive, eschatological element within the language itself, and that, in turn, was of extremely revealing consequence to the revolutionary eschatology with which history supplied him as his subject matter" ("Catastrophes" 287). Likewise, he saw the kind of character study which focuses on one unique and fully realized individual (the traditional "hero" of the "bourgeois" novel) at the expense of the rest of humanity to be selfish, "unbrotherly."[31] Following Fyodorov, Platonov would say (and does so often in *Chevengur*) that the *umnik* spends time in devising abstract schemes of human engineering that have no practical relevance for the worker, while the worker, worn out by labor, has no time or energy to "think." Hence words, according to Platonov, like all tools of human en-

---

[29] Russian literature, to be sure, from Pushkin's novel-in-verse *Eugene Onegin* and Gogol's subtitle to *Dead Souls* ("long poem"—*poèma*) to Dostoevsky's "unmotivated" epilogue in *Crime and Punishment*, Tolstoy's disquisitions on history in *War and Peace*, and Pasternak's use of a poetic cycle at the end of *Doctor Zhivago*, has remained remarkably open to what is generically eccentric in the novel form. If Platonov belongs to any literary "tradition," it is this one. A good recent article on this unorthodox aspect of the Russian novelistic tradition is Fanger, "Influence and Tradition."

[30] "In a sense, one can see this writer [Platonov] as the embodiment of language temporarily occupying a piece of time and reporting from within. The essence of his message is LANGUAGE IS A MILLENARIAN DEVICE, HISTORY ISN'T, and coming from him that would be appropriate" (Brodsky, "Catastrophes" 288).

[31] As Katerina Clark writes of the period in the late twenties when Platonov was drafting *Chevengur*: "In the new concept, literature had to become part of the general mobilization for industrialization. It had to be integrated into the broad-based cultural revolution. It had to be of, by, and for those 'little men' and their 'great deeds.' This meant the rejecting as 'bourgeois' the old concept of literature as aesthetic, literature as the product of individual genius, literature as a privileged or distinctive language. It also meant rejecting as light-minded the notion that literary works should entertain their readers" ("Little Heroes and Big Deeds" 194).

deavor, should be wielded in the service of a higher goal, that of bringing the *umnik* and *durak* together in linguistic "brotherhood." Here, however, in a thoroughgoing democratization of narrative voice,[32] the point of departure is almost exclusively that of the *durak*: better to begin the search for utopian unity by plumbing the inchoate *feelings* of the simple people than to attempt to raise those feelings into the bright glare of articulate *thought*. The result of this democratization, as shall be seen, is the simultaneous demotion and promotion of the hero, and the genre he represents, to the story of *everyman* on the circuitous road to a better life.

The plot of *Chevengur* is as simple as its "retardation" and intentional incoherence are complex. It is the search for a utopian "city of the sun" undertaken by the generation coming of age at the time of the revolution.[33] This generation is represented but by no means dominated by Sasha Dvanov, an orphan boy who has no surname of his own, but who takes the one belonging to the family who raises him. That this family is dominated by economic worries (failed harvests), disrespect toward weak and weary parents, and sibling rivalry (Proshka insists that his foster brother's mouth is one too many to feed) provides the Fyodorovian twist that gets the plot started and Sasha on his way down the road of life and history. The figure of Sasha and the devastating circumstances surrounding the impoverished peasantry are, one recalls, largely autobiographical: Platonov himself had to face life's difficulties at a young age, and the frequent sight of starving peasants forced to migrate into the city in search of work was a real part of his childhood memories. Nevertheless, it is significant that the author, again following Fyodorov, has chosen to underscore the metaphysical orphaning of *all* human beings by making it literal in Sasha's case.

Once alone and out "on the road," Sasha is raised to maturity by Zakhar Pavlovich, himself a character without roots and accustomed to constant movement. Zakhar Pavlovich's interest in machines, especially the train, dominates the first part of the novel and has an influence on Sasha's early

---

[32] Platonov takes the by then oft-used technique of *skaz* to its logical conclusion, removing any evidence of an "I" and dissolving, as it were, the strangeness of the verbal presentation directly into the consciousness of his *duraki*. In this respect it could be said that the author wishes to avoid, as "uncomradely," a separation of narrator and character. Any such distancing between "I" and "they" would imply an ironizing aspect, a view from "without," which Platonov feels to be dishonest when depicting the dilemma of those caught "in the middle." As Tolstaya-Segal remarks, "In Platonov's prose it is nearly impossible to distinguish between the 'material' [of the text] and the 'position of the author.' . . . Thus, it is difficult to decide immediately, if not at a second reading, how, for instance, Platonov relates to the heroes of *Chevengur*—is he mocking their utopia, is this utopia a tragedy or a satire?" ("Ideologicheskie konteksty" 233)

[33] The link between Lenin's interest in the utopian project outlined by Campanella in *Civitas Solis* (1623) and the epithet Platonov gives to Chevengur is presumably not accidental.

development: Sasha takes part in the revolution and in a highly charged episode briefly becomes the engineer of a Red Army troop train. But when this period of war communism ends, and with it the enthusiastic hope that time can be conquered by the machine, Sasha must return "home" to Zakhar Pavlovich and to the recognition that his dreams of finding a meaning to history's movement have not been realized. It is at this point that a "romantic" element enters the plot in the person of Sonya Mandrova, a sweet but strangely distant girl with whom the chaste Sasha never consummates anything, but who nonetheless represents the focus of an impossible desire—the successful "quest" for a nondestructive embodiment of the sex drive.

The road, "iron" and pursued along inexorable rails in the first part of the novel, is then gradually transformed into the more common country variety; what seemed governed by purely political and ideological concerns gives way to the deeper, more basic question of how to turn primitive human drives onto a path leading neither to anarchy nor to bureaucracy but to utopia. In this part of the novel, covering a period of history roughly equivalent to the post-revolutionary years and the establishment of NEP, Sasha and his new companion Kopyonkin embark—now, significantly, *on horseback*—along Russia's backroads and sprawling countryside (the steppe) to discover what the revolution has wrought and to find where, if anywhere, the people have formed a community based on true brotherly love ("communism"). Like Sasha, Kopyonkin has his feminine ideal (the *dead* revolutionary Rosa Luxemburg), who will be resurrected and re-embodied in history at the coming of communism. He is carried down history's road on the Soviet equivalent of the epic hero's steed—the powerful and ever-loyal work horse "Proletarian Strength."

After much searching and many futile (and hilarious) attempts to spread the gospel of communism, the heroes seem no closer to their goal. What they constantly meet "on the road" is the next setback, often the result of good intentions gone awry, and revolutionary idealism corsetted into a reductio ad absurdum, which only means that their job is not yet done and that their next stop beckons. Sasha (Platonov's chief raisonneur) is deeply disenchanted by the concessions to the old made by NEP. Finally, Kopyonkin, in the absence of a now road-weary Sasha, makes his way to Chevengur with the help of Chepurny the Jap, the nominal leader of the new Soviet utopia, who assures his traveling companion that "we already have communism" (156). The entire last half of the novel is given over to various descriptions of what it is like to live in a state of *realized* communism. It is most telling philosophically as well as structurally that Platonov places his utopia not at a novelistic end but *in the middle*. Here we meet all the *duraki* who are trying to live *at the end of history*, in a completely brotherly fashion, but who are still caught in the middle. After numerous attempts to cleanse their community of bourgeois elements, prevent a relapse into sedentary, acquisitive habits, free themselves from the presence of death, and live in harmony with nature, these Soviet Don Quixotes (Kopyonkin in particular is an unmistakable allusion to Cervantes' hero) are massacred in a parody of Armageddon, at the hands of a well-disciplined Cossack patrol—presumably a Red Army detachment sent by Moscow to quell this anarchistic state-within-a-state. Sasha, who by now has himself come to see Chevengur, is a lone, Ishmael-like survivor of the debacle. (Only his foster-brother Proshka manages to save himself as well by lagging *behind* and "organizing" for the battle rather than participating in it.) Profoundly torn by the events and especially by the death of his best friend Kopyonkin, Sasha rides Proletarian Strength back to his "hometown," where he finds Lake Mutevo, the site of his father's suicide and the novel's opening. He concludes his and his generation's story by entering the water and taking "the same road along which once his father had passed in his curiosity about death" (332).

This schematization of the plot of *Chevengur* does not do justice to the baffling texture of Platonov's language, but does tell us several things. To begin with, the novel is, compositionally, the opposite of a *Bildungsroman*: the temporal unfolding of Sasha's life is *not accompanied* by a growth in knowledge, a sense of domestic or societal "fitting in," a slow but ultimately triumphant groping for the "truth." Sasha does not become a parent, nor does he resurrect one; the secret of death to which his father once laid claim and which made the son an orphan remains just that. Furthermore, this absence of substantive change has important implications for the way pertinent (aesthetically marked) information is conveyed to the reader: Boris Tomashevsky's well-known distinction between *fabula* ("story": the arrangement of events in their temporal succession) and *siuzhet* ("plot": the freeing of these same events from temporal/causal contiguity and their rearrangement for artistic purposes) does not seem illuminating in this context. Plot and story appear to coalesce largely because of the similarity posited between a chain of events "united" by a picaresque character (pure narrative contiguity) and the agglutinative, non-teleological nature of history as viewed from within one life-span (historicism). The plot has a beginning (the death of Sasha's father), a protracted middle (the search for communism), a premature end (Chevengur), and an end "whose time has come" (the routing of the utopians and Sasha's suicide)—but all this gives the appearance of being the most unregenerate contiguity. If plot means authorial design *from without*, there is none. Movement in *Chevengur* is *only* spatio-temporal; "meaning" is part of a process leading not *out* of itself, to the *end* of history, but back *into* contingency, openness, failure.

Nevertheless, Platonov's conscious sabotaging of the idea of plot as an aesthetic reordering of reality does not make his novel's stubborn charm unknowable, the artistic equivalent of a screw with stripped threads. One should investigate *Chevengur* not in terms of a circularity writ large (suicide to suicide), or of a plot about the "dead end" of "openness," but at closer range, in terms of those narrative tropes whose function it is to move the process along. Such tropes—the interlocking images of the road, the train, the horse, and the terminus/destination—constitute the real "story" behind *Chevengur*. It is at their level that Platonov's mythopoesis of linguistic material takes place and his radical play with setting comes to the fore. The interplay of these elements shows Platonov was trying to visualize the rapid passage of time in space and to give form to the quixotic idea that his generation could, from the new vantage offered by the revolution, vault "over the middle." In this context "setting" is not a passive grid of time-space coordinates within which the peripeties of plot take place, but an active opponent (the "blind forces of nature," in Fyodorov's words) to Sasha's and Kopyonkin's utopian quest. These knights of the revolution must joust with time and space and subdue them *before* they can arrive at communism and be rewarded with the maidens of a higher order (Dulcinea = Rosa Luxemburg). Hence what seems, and ultimately becomes, the blind contiguity of the picaresque is to these riders looking for the future in the present merely a time-space to be quickly and violently reconstituted and *passed through*.[34] Time, as Bakhtin would say, "thickens" into space as the broad expanse of the Russian steppe dissolves into the mythical "no-place" of Chevengur. Such are the principal categories with which Platonov was working as he depicted his Soviet paladins in their struggle to transform movement and process, which plague all humans in history, into Fyodorovian progress—movement in the right direction, towards resolution and the End.

The most striking pieces of information provided by the novel's opening are Zakhar Pavlovich's love of tinkering and the fisherman's (Sasha's father's) suicide. The rootless Zakhar Pavlovich fills up his time making things because gadgets run by themselves (thus the human being seems like God in giving movement and purpose to something outside itself) and because they possess nothing extraneous in their *raison d'être*. However, Zakhar Pavlovich's inventions may possess movement but their purpose is another matter: a wooden frying pan that succeeds "in bringing water to boil over a slow fire" (4) is a *utopian* project, for it goes against the laws of nature, one of the most basic being that wood is a source of fuel, not a

---

[34] "What changed historically [in the tradition of utopian literature] was the growing emphasis on the second, more dynamic aspect [i.e., the 'journey' as opposed to the description of a static 'polis']. The description of utopia became a journey to and *through* utopia" (my emphasis; Striedter, "Three Utopian Novels" 189).

domestication of it. Zakhar Pavlovich tinkers then "for his own pleasure," and much of this first section is devoted to the shift in Sasha's foster father from a playful and self-indulgent love for machines to a purposeful one—the tending of the locomotives whose movement symbolizes the coming revolution. Zakhar Pavlovich's story is typical in that it shows a man in search of a goal which, *in the process of attaining*, he can appear to control and, in the case of the locomotive, actually accelerate. Logically enough, this search leads Zakhar Pavlovich, who had been residing "in nature," to the city, where trains are the focus of attention and the prime source of employment. In short, Zakhar Pavlovich's "road" is one of the only ones (perhaps *the* only one) open to a person in his time/place who wishes to feel in touch with the course of history.

The fate of the fisherman, however, offers quite another possibility:

Zakhar Pavlovich had known one man, a fisherman from Lake Mutevo, who had questioned many people about death, and was tormented by his curiosity. This fisherman loved fish most of all not as food, but as special things that definitely knew the secret of death. He would show Zakhar Pavlovich the eyes of a dead fish and say, "Look—there's wisdom! . . . It already knows everything." Contemplating the lake through the years, the fisherman thought always about the same thing, about the interest of death. . . . After a year the fisherman couldn't stand it anymore and threw himself into the lake from his boat, after tying his feet with a rope so that he wouldn't accidentally float. In secret he didn't even believe in death. The important thing was that he wanted to look at what was there—perhaps it was much more interesting than living in a village or on the shores of a lake. He saw death as another province, located under the heavens as if at the bottom of cool water, and it attracted him (6).

This individual (called "Mitry Ivanovich" by the other muzhiks) is in every respect the opposite of Zakhar Pavlovich: he is Sasha's natural, not adoptive, father; his path leads him into the water and death rather than over land and through life; he passes his time not by making things whose purpose it is to run but by catching living organisms that already "know" the secret of death; rather than a city governed by the movement of trains, his cherished destination is a version of Kitezh, a utopian "province located under the heavens as if at the bottom of cool water"; for him death is not something to be avoided ("Zakhar Pavlovich tried to talk him out of it, saying, 'There's nothing special there, just something tight'" [6]), but something to be explored. The path of the fisherman, here in the novel's opening, is the ever-present alternative to a realization of the utopian urge in history; it forks away from the other overland roads as an option to be taken when all else fails. As readers we cannot know, and the author cannot say, what the fisherman found in his underwater kingdom. All that is presented from *this side* of the boundary separating life and death is that he was dragged from the water after three days and buried in the village graveyard. Like Kirillov in Dostoevsky's *The Devils*, he tried to overcome death through death, and in so doing left his son an orphan on the road of life. Sasha must now try to discover how, by taking the route of his foster-father (life), he can eventually be reunited with his dead natural father.

The road is a ubiquitous image in *Chevengur*. Anyone with hope of a better life is always on it. In this regard Platonov very much belongs to the tradition of Russian *strannichestvo* ("wandering" or "searching" for the truth). Nikolay Berdyaev, the Russian religious philosopher, once remarked that

> [The medieval tradition of] chivalry did not develop on the spiritual soil of Russian Orthodoxy. In the martyrdom of Saints Boris and Gleb there is no heroism; [instead] there dominates the idea of sacrifice. . . . Also characteristic of Russian religious thought is *iurodstvo* [condition of being a "holy fool"]—the acceptance of ridicule from people, a feeling of mockery toward the world, a challenge to the world. . . . Russians are *beguny* [a religious sect called "Runners"] and bandits. And Russians are *stranniki* [pilgrims] searching for God's truth (*Russkaia ideia* 9–10).

Whether or not Berdyaev is correct to speak this categorically about a phenomenon called the "Russian character" is, as was noted in the Introduction, ultimately beside the point, since here as well his perception of an East-West opposition[35] belongs to a belief system largely shared by Platonov. Berdyaev goes so far as to call all great Russian writers "spiritual pilgrims," and one has to assume he would have included Platonov in this group. What he says about the Schismatics could be applied with startling validity to Platonov's *duraki* and Pilnyak's *okhlomony* (in *Mahogany*) in their search for truth after 1917:

> The Schism was a withdrawal from history because history was controlled by the prince of this world, the Antichrist, who had penetrated to the top of the church and the government. . . . From the year 1666 there commenced in Russia the kingdom of the Antichrist. The true kingdom had to be sought in a space under the earth [Kitezh], in a time of the future colored with apocalyptic overtones. . . . And [as a result] an extraordinary characteristic of the Russian people was disclosed—

[35] "Western people are much more sedentary [*osedlye*], more attached to perfected forms of civilization, more apt to value the present [than Russians]" (*Russkaia ideia* 199).

its endurance to suffering, its urge toward another world [*k potusto-ronnemu*], toward the ultimate (*Russkaia ideia* 16–17).

All that needs to be amended in Berdyaev's formulation are the details surrounding the *raskol*, not its principal motivation and expression: instead of 1666, we find 1921; instead of the Antichrist leading the church and government, we find the bureaucracy of NEP that has corrupted the true faith embodied by the revolution; instead of an underwater kingdom, we find Chevengur in the nowhere of the steppe; and instead of an Old Believer's apocalypse, we find the worker's solution to the plot of history.

It might be argued, therefore, that *strannichestvo* is the Russian equivalent of chivalry: a quest without its grounding in the lore of courtly love, but with its attachment to high ideals and a better, nobler world. Rather than Spenser's Red Crosse Knight, defender of Una, or Cervantes' knight of woeful countenance, Platonov gives us Bolshevik *stranniki* whose code of honor, like Quixote's, is out of place in this world. A quest requires some means of transport to move people down the road faster than they can take themselves: Don Quixote's aging steed Rosinante is replaced first by the train, the "iron steed," during the period of war communism, and then by Kopyonkin's Proletarian Strength and Sasha's pacer during the time leading up to the discovery of Chevengur. That Platonov actually had the chivalric tradition in mind as a foil for his *duraki* is suggested by the figure of Pashintsev, one of the eccentrics met by Sasha and Kopyonkin on their travels, who wears a coat of armor (but is virtually immobile because he has no horse), hoards blank grenades, and announces that "I maintain the revolution in its untouched, heroic category" (116).

Platonov's *stranniki* are constantly confronted with new roads which must be traversed before all of Russia can be brought into the future. The first and most obvious means of accelerating this process is the train, that ultimate machine which Belinsky, Herzen, and later radicals saw as Russia's savior and which Dostoevsky and Tolstoy so feared. For Platonov, who at first followed Belinsky's faith in technology and modernization (but not his urge to westernize), the train is the emblem of his youth and cosmist phase. Zakhar Pavlovich becomes the chief focus of Platonov's machinophilia. Like a boy in love, he cannot "take his eyes from the engine" (27); "machines [are] his people, constantly arousing within him feelings, thoughts, and desires" (6). He fears the limits of space because he wants wheels always to be necessary. People are perniciously unpredictable, careless, and "beside the point" (7). These sensations lead to a deification of the machine, an infatuation with movement over destination, and a rhapsodic hymn (note Platonov's language) to the horse of the future:

The locomotive which they were warming up for the night express stood opposite the two people [Zakhar Pavlovich and the foreman]. . . . The locomotive stood magnanimous, enormous, and warm in the harmonious swales of its high majestic body. . . . The depot doors opened into the evening expanse of summer, into the roiled future, into that life which could be repeated in the mind, in the elemental speed of the rails, in the oblivion of night, risk, and the slight thrum of a well-tuned engine (28).

Platonov's lyrical appeal to speed, power, and freedom as he reproduces Zakhar Pavlovich's and the foreman's awe makes the train more alive, more like a horse, than the people who work or ride on it.

Yet Zakhar Pavlovich's love affair with the locomotive is fated to be short-lived. Two circumstances cause the realization that his energies are misplaced. First, he comes to see that his road is leading nowhere: "Amazing. I'm going to die soon, but everything's the same" (31). While walking along the tracks during the autumn holidays he decides to visit his mother's grave, where the words "sleep with peace, beloved daughter, until children and parents shall meet" (31) strike him with the full anguish of his orphaned state. Wheels continue to turn, but parents and children have not been reunited. It is at this point that Zakhar Pavlovich looks again at the tracks and at the poor people who gather alongside to watch the iron horses rumble past: "They saw how the triumphant locomotives led the trains with great speeds. However, not a single poor person knew why the engine itself went" (31). If the trains do not take the poor with them, and if they can provide no higher reason for the locomotive's furious movement, then how is this road a way out?[36]

The second sobering circumstance is the death of the foreman at the depot where Zakhar Pavlovich works. This is also the first death that Sasha witnesses, and presumably it has a decisive influence on how he is in later life to view the phenomenon of one's passage out of this world. The foreman dies as a result of his "own carelessness and failure to observe applicable rules of movement and usage" (41): he has suffered a fatal blow on the head from the support irons of an entangled lamp post while trying to move an engine with a steel chain. A loving father–figure to his engines but a harsh critic of his workers, the foreman perishes in the service of his mechanical child. Here the train does not save or resurrect the parent, but rather destroys him. Most ironic and baffling is Platonov's description of the death in terms of birth: "This had all happened to him before, but very long ago, and he could not remember where. . . . Then the foreman remembered where he had last seen this quiet burning blackness. It was simply the closeness within his mother, and now once again he was pushing against her parted bones. . . . 'Push me farther down the tube,' he whispered with

---

[36] Cf. the parallel here with Blok's poem "On the Railroad" (1910), where, after the revolution, the passengers have no energy to travel on.

childish and swollen lips" (40).[37] Death becomes a birth into another realm, but as in the case of Sasha's father, Platonov refrains from telling us whether this crossing-over is benign or evil, meaningful or senseless. It is death's secret, which only those on the "other side" have solved, but which we on "this side" are agonizingly puzzled with. After this episode, Zakhar Pavlovich concludes that this mystery is not to be unraveled by the train and its rails and soon loses interest in them altogether: "Thus Zakhar Pavlovich began to live peacefully, no longer hoping for a general radical improvement—no matter how many machines were made, neither Proshka, nor Sasha, nor himself would ever ride on them. . . . The machine itself is not a free agent, but only an unanswering substance" (41).

Sasha's love of machines differs fundamentally from that of Zakhar Pavlovich, and may suggest how Platonov himself saw the distinction between his generation of cosmists and the generation of his machinist father. "His [Sasha's] attraction [to the machine] was not curiosity, which ends with the discovery of the secrets of the machine. Sasha was interested in machines as he was in other moving and living things. He wanted more to feel them, to live their life with them, than to find them out" (38). Rather than curiosity, which is satisfied when one knows *how* something works, Sasha is moved by pity for all things—he wants to know *why*. He imagines what it is like to feel like a locomotive; for him the machine is a living being like everything else, while for Zakhar Pavlovich and the foreman it is a substitute for human, living contact. Sasha's aims are not yet focused ("He did not have his own goals, though he was past sixteen" [38]) because they are still dissolved in a pool of fellow-feeling for all the world. Yet this vague feeling, the premature rumblings of the quest, is already likened to the rush of sexual desire: "He was filled with that dark inspired agitation which adults have in their true love for one woman" (38). Platonov seems to be plunging deeper into the subconscious or pre-conscious as he tries to express the distinction, couched here in generational terms (the "before" and "after" of the revolution), between curiosity and pity, understanding and desire, movement and purpose.

Soon the revolution comes,[38] the hero finishes classes at the railroad school and polytechnicum, and the party orders him to the front. He is assigned to a troop train that comes under attack from the Cossacks; his job is to keep the fire box well stoked. But, as he tells the political commissar, he is "afraid about the road" (51), about the possibility that the "train's madly dashing body" will end in a wreck. In this context the train becomes

---

[37] Cf. Ivan Ilyich's struggle to get out of the black sack at the end of Tolstoy's story.

[38] Which Sasha, presumably as Platonov himself had once done, believes will be "the end of the world" (48).

an awesome symbol of revolutionary movement out of control: the engine "trembles[s] from the pressure, waving its entire body, seeking an opportunity to throw itself down some bank, away from the force which was choking it and the speed it couldn't expend"; it "*gallop*[s] over switches and crossovers," its "wheels smash[ing] out flames on the junction frogs"; and it plummets "into the murky thickets of its future path, into the frenzy of a machine at full throttle" (51; my emphasis).[39] Eventually the engineer disappears, and Sasha must drive the train on himself. Through no fault of his own he enters on a collision course with another train and tries to avoid the disaster by breaking on an incline. But the brakes fail, and he is thrown from the train amidst much carnage. At this point in the text, with the well-intentioned Sasha "engineering" death and destruction because of his inability to rein in the iron horse of the revolution, it becomes clear that Platonov is not only questioning the notion of mechanical force, as he was in the case of Zakhar Pavlovich, but showing its full implications and ultimate destination. Thereafter the train plays a less significant role in Platonov's narrative. Instead of rails and locomotives, the reader is more apt to meet marauding bands on horseback or *stranniki* on foot: "speed makes the force of gravity, the weight of a body and of life grow less, which was probably why in bad times people try to move. For the same reason Russian wanderers and pilgrims trekked continually, dissipating the weight of the people's grieving soul with their motion" (61).

Platonov's gradual substitution of flesh-and-blood horse for iron one is dictated by several considerations. First, on the simple level of verisimilitude, the author is taking his twin notions of revolution and communism, threshold and goal beyond, where the train cannot go—that is, into the vast Russian steppe, into "Russia" itself. Hence, the shift in narrative time (war communism → NEP) brings with it a shift in narrative space (urban centers → steppe).[40] Platonov is entering into dialogue with the Russian intellectual tradition, epitomized by the famous *troika* ride at the end of Gogol's *Dead Souls* (I), that questions the possibility of effecting *any* change over the expanse known as the steppe. Here space becomes the chief obstacle to the

---

[39] This view of the "locomotive of the revolution," mythologized in the negative, directly opposes the late twenties and early thirties portrayal of society as harmoniously moving train and of the Party as its "driving axle." See, e.g., V. Ilenkov's *The Driving Axle* (1931), as well as the discussion in Clark, "Little Heroes" 190–91. In Ilenkov's work there is also a giant crash, but it is not due to any inherent flaw in the revolutionary movement. Rather, it is due to the wholly rectifiable situation—discovered by the "little men" of the factory—of negligence and industrial sabotage.

[40] For the mythical border separating the urban center from the boundless steppe, see, e.g., Blok's "New America" (1913), in *Stikhotvoreniia* 507: "Here everything is of the steppe—without end, without issue, / The steppe, and the wind, and the wind again—Then suddenly / The many-tiered outline of factory buildings, / Of a city made up of workers' shanties."

apparent changes wrought in historical time by the revolution (see Cherniavsky, *Tsar* 168). Second, this shift in time-space coordinates may also be motivated by the author's wish to tap into an older and richer tradition, that of the Western knight errant (especially Cervantes' hero) and that of the Russian *bogatyr'* (folk/epic hero). As Kopyonkin and Sasha, the Russian Don Quixote and his faithful Sancho, try to transfer their quest from the trenches of the civil war to the economic front, we sense that we are moving back into the past at the same time that we are moving into the future. And consequently, when Sasha sets out *on foot*[41] "to look for communism in the initiative of the populace" (63), the novel slows down from a locomotive at full throttle to something closer to a snail's pace.

Out on the road Sasha has a series of adventures, including an encounter with a peasant called "God," and nearly loses his life when he chances upon a band of anarchists on horseback. The horsemen are passing through a ravine when Sasha shouts at them from the hill above. Nikitok, their marksman, shoots Sasha in the leg, whereupon the latter tumbles down into their midst. As Sasha, with his wounded leg, clings to the leg of one of the horses, Nikitok prepares to finish him off:

> . . . The leg trembled quietly from fatigue and smelled of sweat, the grass of many roads, and the stillness of life.
>
> "Nikitok, see if you can scare the flame of life out of him. The clothes are yours."
>
> Dvanov heard this. He grabbed the horse's leg with both hands, and the leg was transformed into the fragrant living body of that woman whom he did not yet know and would not recognize, but who became mysteriously vital to him now. Dvanov had understood the mystery of hair. His heart rose into his throat and he screamed into the oblivion of his liberation and immediately he sensed an unburdening, satisfied calm. Nature did not neglect to take from Dvanov that for which he had been born into the delirium of his mother, the seed of propagation, which would form of new people a family. Life's last minutes flowed on and Sonya prevailed deeply upon Dvanov's hallucinations. In those final moments, as he embraced the horse and the soil, for the first time Dvanov recognized a resonant passion for life, and was unexpectedly amazed at thought's insignificance before this immortal bird which now hushed him with its extended, trembling wing (71–72).

This bizarre and haunting passage shows to what extent the elements of Sasha's quest form a densely interwoven (though not necessarily logical) whole, and how Platonov's allusive language is able to convey meaning

---

[41] There is for a time a "horse shortage."

without the right angles of a systematically unfolding viewpoint.[42] Here
contiguity gives rise to great associative leaps (leg—sweat—road—life) that
are explainable in terms of the mythology of the quest but that seem almost
surreal when lifted out of context. Platonov does not fill in these synec-
dochic spaces (the horse's leg = fatigue of expended energy = time/space
traversed = stillness/end of life) with a tight causality, but allows them, as
it were, "free rein." The horse's leg, which is the source of beauty and
movement (now momentarily spent—"trembl[ing] quietly from fatigue"),
changes into the body of Sasha's phantom bride, the object of his desire, the
realization of his utopian search. As Sasha faces what he believes will be his
death, he feels that end in sexual terms (his orgasm), so that the horse, the
road, and the destination telescope into one harmoniously liberating moment. The means and the end, the movement and the goal, become indistinguishable aspects of each other. Life's last minutes (death) bring life's
first minutes (the seed of propagation), yet the sexual urge does not, in the
utopian dreamer, produce children. Sonya, the distant bride whom Sasha
never knows in this sense, is now only a vision. Sasha's rush of passion is
thus chastened and deflected—à la Fyodorov—back into the symbols of his
search. By embracing the horse and the soil, he is embracing his very urge
for fulfillment and his own genesis ("mother earth"). Platonov's concludes
this privileged and ostensibly ultimate moment by producing another magical synecdoche: the horse (movement on earth) turns into a bird (movement over/above earth) and the leg into a wing because Sasha is preparing
to leave this world, with its dirt roads and spatio-temporal limits, and enter
a realm of airiness and freedom. Ironically, however, as the reader has
nearly forgotten in the midst of Platonov's lyricism, this realized utopia is
none other than death.

Miraculously, Sasha is not killed by the anarchists: Nikitok feels a brotherly affection for him when he sees his wound and learns that this "communist" is "leaving parents behind." Sasha is soon rescued from his captors
by Stepan Kopyonkin, who becomes his closest comrade for the remainder
of the novel. Kopyonkin is a tragicomic figure combining the ridiculous and
poignant idealism of Don Quixote with the lust for death and retribution
associated with an apocalyptic horseman. Our first glimpse of him immediately brings to mind the Don's chaste love for Dulcinea, both as it exists
in Cervantes' original and in the Russian versions made famous by Pushkin
("There lived on the earth a poor knight") and Dostoevsky (*The Idiot*):

> Dvanov shouted from the porch and came back. Nikita came in, fol-
> lowed by another man, who was short, thin, and had eyes which lacked

[42] For more on the proto-surrealistic or illogical elements in Platonov's imagery and syntax,
see Yakushev, "Struktura khodozhestvennogo obraza."

attentiveness; although while still on the threshold he had seen a
woman and immediately felt an attraction toward her, not to possess,
but to defend her oppressed feminine weakness. His name was Stepan
Kopenkin.

Kopenkin bowed to everyone, lowering his head with a tensed dignity, and then offered Sonya a little barberry candy that he had carried
in his pocket for a couple of months, not knowing for whom (76–77).

Like Sasha's, Kopyonkin's attraction to women is not possessive. In the new
world women are not to be owned like other acquisitions of the bourgeois;
they are to be defended like the name of Rosa Luxemburg, the Marxist Joan
of Arc, who is the very embodiment of the future classless paradise. The
gift of candy is a gesture of pathetic kindness coming as it does from the
powerful hand of Platonov's quintessential Bolshevik warrior.

The difference of course between Don Quixote and his Bolshevik descendant is that, while the former projects his feminine ideal (Dulcinea) on
an all-too-real wench (Aldonza), the latter projects his ideal (realized communism) on a corpse moldering in the grave (Rosa Luxemburg). At some
point (unspecified in the time-space of the text) Kopyonkin's role veers
away from that of ridiculous knight errant to that of apocalyptic horseman.
Kopyonkin's quest leads not to a universal overcoming of death (the Fyodorovian model), but to death itself. From the best motives, yet ones that have
become hopelessly confused in the mind of this *durak*, Kopyonkin is ready
to slaughter all opposition in the name of Rosa. Unlike Quixote's opponents, Kopyonkin's are real, and, like Pilate's title "Rider of the Golden
*Spear*" his name is linked with an instrument of torture (*kop'e*) that reinforces this second, retributive role. Thus, as he hacks his way to communism, Platonov's brave horseman fully believes that his road will lead back
to Rosa's grave, to her resurrection from the dead, and to the apocalyptic
marriage of the knight to his ideal.

Kopyonkin's faithful steed Proletarian Strength combines the same tragicomic characteristics as does its master. Indeed, it could be argued that the
horse is an extension of its rider's urges. In several of the novel's most
humorous passages, Proletarian Strength understands and anticipates Kopyonkin's inarticulate desires. Here is how Platonov introduces the "steed
of the future":

Kopenkin went outside to his horse. The horse had a heavy build
and was more suited to carry logs than a man. The horse was used to
his master and the civil war, and he ate hurdles, thatched roofs, and
was content with little. However, to get sufficiently full, the horse
could eat an eighth of a young tree plantation, then wash it down with
the contents of a not particularly large steppe pond. Kopenkin re-

spected his horse and valued it third. Rosa Luxemburg, the Revolution, and then the horse (84).

Proletarian Strength is on one level a hilarious working-man's version of the epic steed of Russian folklore. His modest origins (the "heavy build," etc.) are joined with a larger-than-life appetite, the experience of many battles, and an uncompromising loyalty to his master. But whereas the epic steed is likely to be associated with the wind, thunder, lightning, or an arrow (see Lipets, *Obrazy* 146–56), this plodding beast keeps close to the ground. As we learn a little later, it is not apt to leap over obstacles, but to trample everything in its path.

Moreover, Kopyonkin's steed and the ideal of a resurrected Rosa become linguistically, and thus conceptually, "tethered," the clearest evidence yet that in their desire to bring about communism Platonov's utopian dreamers have confused the means with the end:

> "Greetings, Proletarian Strength!" Kopenkin hailed the horse . . . "Let's ride to Rosa's grave!"
>
> Kopenkin hoped and believed that all matters and roads of his life led inexorably to the grave of Rosa Luxemburg. This hope warmed his heart and evoked the necessity of daily revolutionary feats. Each morning Kopenkin ordered his horse to go to Rosa's grave, and the horse had become so accustomed to the word "Rosa" that it recognized it as "gee-up." After the sounds of "Rosa" the horse began to move its legs whether it was in a swamp or a thicket or a wasteland of snow drifts. . . .
>
> The horse felt gratitude and zealously crushed the grass in its path back into its earthly origins. Kopenkin didn't particularly direct the horse if the road unexpectedly parted in two. Proletarian Strength would independently develop a preference for one road over the other, and they always wound up where people required the armed hand of Kopenkin. Kopenkin himself acted without planned itineraries; rather he took action at random and according to the will of the horse (84–85).

The horse is prodded into movement simply by invoking the memory of the Marxist maiden. It matters not which road is chosen, for in an imperfect life they all lead to confrontations with the real.[43] In fact, Kopyonkin and

---

[43] Cf. Cervantes' original link between chivalric ideal and unsupervised equine motion: "He [Don Quixote] . . . went on his way, taking *whatever road his horse chose*, in the belief that in this lay the essence of adventure. . . . Almost all that day he rode without encountering anything of note, which reduced him to despair, for he longed to meet straightaway someone against whom he could try the strength of his strong arm" (*Don Quixote* 36–37).

Proletarian Strength are only happy when they are on the road, in the midst of combat. Because the ideal is impossible (and dead!), and because there is no meaningful connection between the name and the movement (the horse understands "Rosa" to be "gee-up"), the effort is futile. Ironically, it is the will of the horse (that is, pure motion without meaning) that guides the rider. Once again, all of this would be, and indeed is, humorous, save for the fact that Kopyonkin's Bolshevik chivalry is genuine and that his victims are more than windmills.

The inseparable images of horse and rider, with their inseparable meanings of movement and ever-retreating goal, dominate Platonov's narrative until Kopyonkin's arrival in Chevengur. Sasha has his "pacer" (*rysak*) to complement Kopyonkin's Proletarian Strength, and both riders are constantly described as "[feeling] easier when they [sense] the road and distance drawing them outwards from the crush of population" (100). Indeed, this chronotope of the open road reaches a mock apotheosis shortly before Kopyonkin meets Chepurny and goes to inspect a "Soviet government out in the open, without structures" (153). The great restless horse engages in a gargantuan fracas, tearing down an entire barn simply to have another chance to breathe in the expanse of the steppe and to feel its master on its back and "invisible roads beneath its feet" (154). And yet, significantly, the roads in *Chevengur do* eventually lead somewhere, although the destination and the town bearing the novel's title are not perhaps what the utopians have in mind (if it can be said that they have anything "in mind"). It is at this all important *transitus* in the novel—that is, once Kopyonkin and (later) Sasha cross the threshold of Chevengur—that Platonov begins to mix the generic expectations associated with utopian and apocalyptic fiction. Based on conflicting evidence supporting either view, the reader is asked to judge whether the *civitas solis* being described is located inside or outside of history. The result is what can only be called a modal grotesque—a climax that drags on into the anticlimactic, an ending that appears "before its time." The author of course is fully aware of the implications of this grotesquerie. With a restive curiosity not often found in Soviet literature, Platonov pursues the "anachronicity" and "anatopicity" of the utopian ideal to its logical conclusion. He now gives his *duraki* the communist paradise they have been longing for, and he experiments, in an appropriate artistic form, with what it might be like to *live at the end*.

By placing Chevengur in the middle of the steppe, Platonov is making a powerful statement about the primordial human urge to live "out in the open, without structure," and about the possibility of visualizing that urge in time and space. The town is so far away from the city and existing governmental structures, so far *out in the open*, that it is also, or at least appears to be, *beyond time*. There is a point, suggests Platonov, at which space becomes coterminous with time: if fences and boundaries seem an anomaly out in the steppe, so too do the categories of past, present and future. This is not to say that Chevengur is completely independent from Moscow (as is discovered at the novel's conclusion) or that the Chevengurians can completely break free from the patterns of thought they have imported from the *umniki*, but simply that the author has taken pains to describe this historical tabula rasa in terms of the space-time coordinates of the steppe. In other words, rather than the chronotope of the open road, with it embedded meaning of temporal flux, the reader is now confronted with what Mircea Eliade and Angus Fletcher would call a modern inversion of the "sacred center," with its embedded meaning of temporal stasis. "How then," asks Jurij Striedter in his assessment of *Chevengur* within the Russian utopian tradition, "is the city going to integrate dynamics and openness into a system which, due to its completeness, must tend toward the static and the isolated? This, indeed, is the problem which confronts completed utopias in general . . . how to sustain spatial dynamics inside such a utopian island" ("Three Utopian Novels" 192).

As was demonstrated in earlier chapters, the modern Russian novelists most likely to experiment with the generic identity of "apocalyptic fiction" are also the ones most likely to experiment with the poetics of the center. Where and when an apocalypse—a revelation from one spatio-temporality to another—takes place is bound to be perceived as "magnetized" within the force field of history-theodicy. According to Eliade's interpretation of the function of ritual in primitive societies, the sacred center is the site of a collective reintegration, a "navel of the earth," where heaven and hell meet, where "profane space" and "concrete time" become "transcendent space" and "mythical time" (Eliade, *Myth* 21). The ritual is performed in an ancient temple, which in turn is erected on another holy place (e.g., a mountain top); it allows the primitive society to exorcize the imperfections of the recent past ("contingency," "openness") and to reestablish contact with an epic *in illo tempore* or "once upon a time" when the world was in perfect harmony. As this urge for reintegration was transposed to the Christian epic traditon (Dante, Spenser, Milton), the *in illo tempore* was projected both *backwards* to an Edenic paradise and *forwards* to the Heavenly City of Revelation. In later versions of the tradition, however, the sacred center became urbanized, chaotic, and ironically inverted: for Dostoevsky and Bely, Petersburg is a demonic capital ripe for an apocalypse of judgment; for Bulgakov, Moscow like ancient Jerusalem is a "Whore of Babylon" destined for "the abyss." What all this implies for Platonov and his novel is clear. He is polemicizing with the same tradition when he sets his sacred center, a very un-Edenic worker's paradise, as far as possible from the city, with its bureaucracy and bad faith.

Into this communist *in illo tempore* comes Kopyonkin, the embodiment of the human desire for a better world. To those who question Chevengur's eschatological reality, Chepurny answers emphatically (though never with complete understanding of what he is saying) that "history has ended here" (164) and that "there are no more paths" because "the people have arrived" (163). Yet arrival does not mean cessation of activity. It is up to Kopyonkin the quintessential traveler—and not to Chepurny, who is apt to fall asleep on his horse—to decide whether this activity adds up to a resurrected Rosa. Chevengur, as it turns out, is still inhabited by a number of unreconstructed townspeople who are sedentary, acquisitive, and religious. Logic tells the new town "brothers" that there can be no communism until these vestiges of the bourgeois epoch are removed entirely. In one of Platonov's sharpest satirical assaults, the new people's government "out in the open, without structure" arranges a mass execution to correspond with the population's forebodings about a "Second Coming." It separates out all those who belong to a corrupt past ("your bourgeoisie aren't people" [181]) in the name of future solidarity; paradise ceases to be paradise if it admits the possibility of ambiguity, difference, otherness. Hence rather than forestalling an apocalypse of judgment "from without" through a joint Fyodorovian effort to resurrect all of humanity, Chepurny and his comrades manipulate the biblical plot to devise a shortcut out of their dilemma. They allow the older Chevengurians to believe that they (the communists) are the instruments of divine judgment at the same time that they tell themselves, the inheritors of utopia, that "the end of the world [is] a counterrevolutionary [i.e. anti-utopian] step. . . . It doesn't apply to us, you see" (162). In short, they use death to proclaim an end to death—a *contradictio in adjecto*. Death is death no matter whom it comes to: "when a bourgeois has a bullet inside him, he needs friendship and comradeship just like a proletarian" (184). The point of the author's satire is directed at the gross disparity between abstract Fyodorovian thought and the practice of translating brotherhood into reality through violent revolutionary measures, between Platonov's own youthful idealism and the realization that that idealism went wrong. The future, implies Platonov, is not to be inherited by disenfranchising the past; the end is either the End (Platonov does *not* suggest that there is a higher viewpoint governing the actions of the apocalypticists or the utopians), or it is a lapse back into the open middle.

Once the Chevengurians have killed off or driven away all the bourgeois or "semi-bourgeois," thereby shrinking their ranks to an apostolic dozen,[44] they are at a loss as to what to do with themselves. If history has indeed run its course, it would be counterrevolutionary to work, to create any ob-

---

[44] The number of Chevengurians reaches twelve only with the arrival of Sasha Dvanov.

ject or produce any commodity with an ulterior purpose. Likewise, it is considered a breach of faith to "own" anything inherited from the bourgeois epoch. The madcap, Swiftian routine that the Chevengurians follow by constantly relocating houses and even gardens suggests that they are trying to keep from falling into "sedentary" patterns.[45] And yet even in utopia these apostles of doom cannot do without movement, cannot refrain from filling time as if it were space. While it is claimed that under the new regime the sun is laboring in the people's stead and the snow will keep them warm in the winter, the people themselves are plainly uncomfortable with this arrangement. They compensate for the burdens of leisure time by making poignantly absurd presents to one another as tokens of their brotherhood (e.g., an iron flag, tin buttons, clay statues). They try to extend their brotherly feelings to other creatures of nature, including cockroaches, and ultimately to nature itself. Inevitably, however, these peripatetic well-wishers begin to doubt the efficacy and temporal reality of their gift-giving impulse: Kirey and Zheev want to get a windmill started in order to grind flour for soft buns that would be digestible to the ailing Yakov Tity, yet Yakov Tity is the only person capable of making a feed hopper for the millstones, and once he is able to do that, he will no longer need the soft buns! Thus Chevengur deprives its inhabitants of the purposeful conjunction *chtoby* ("in order to"), with its ties to causality and a temporally meaningful posteriority, but cannot take away the urge underlying it. At some level Platonov's utopians remain *stranniki* even if located "at the end," in a "no place" and a "no time."

We realize that the utopian experiment has brought an end not to history but to itself when its apostles must confront two realities that belie their gospel: the death of one of their own and the need to provide women for the "miscellaneous ones" (*prochie*: those exploited and exhausted by the capitalist epoch who have now come to inherit their kingdom). When Kopyonkin sees that a child for whom Chevengur should be an ideal "resting place" prefers to die and leave the misery of this world,[46] he begins to doubt whether this so-called communism has lived up to the ideal of a resurrected Rosa: "It's just the same here as it was under imperialism. . . . The weather carries on the same way, and not a shred of communism anywhere. . . . What kind of communism is this? . . . They couldn't make the boy inhale even once, and the boy up and died right *in the middle of it*! [my emphasis] Maybe it's a plague, but it isn't communism. Comrade Kopen-

[45] That is, to quote Striedter again, they are forced to maintain "spatial dynamics" within a "utopian island." As Chepurny first tells Kopyonkin, "No, comrade, Chevengur doesn't collect property, it destroys it" (156).

[46] Cf. the death of the little girl Nastya in Platonov's next major work *The Foundation Pit* (wr. early thirties).

kin, it's time you rode out of here, time you went off into the distance"
(248). And when asked straight out to choose between Rosa and Chevengur,
between the open road with its promise, however faded, and the destination
with its manifest imperfections, Kopyonkin does not hesitate: " 'Which is
dearer to you, Chevengur or Rosa Luxemburg?' 'Rosa is, comrade Dvanov,'
Kopenkin answered in fright. 'There was more communism in her than in
all of Chevengur' " (326). This is the moment at which the relationship
between inhuman ideal and human need to search, against all odds, for that
ideal becomes at long last painfully explicit. All human beings possess and
perhaps ever will possess to fill the absence of the ideal is the presence of
the road. In this we are no different than the hound in pursuit of the mechanical hare that, forever in sight, is also forever out of reach.

But the road for the utopians is by now no longer open with endless possibility. It is, therefore, directly after his confession that Kopyonkin and his
comrades are attacked by a crack outfit of "Cossack" (Red Army?) horsemen, who move in to kill their ill-equipped adversaries with the "mechanical strength of victory" (327). There is a grim symmetry to the reintro-
duction at this point of equine and equestrian images into the "fixed"
environment of utopia—the horse has undergone a complete shift in signi-
fication from one of movement to one of real and ineluctable end. Perhaps
the greatest irony is that Platonov has seen fit to conclude his elaborate
fiction about the impossibility of utopia and the failure of history to close
with a parodic version of Armageddon. Just as the older Chevengurians
were victims of a "Second Coming" arranged by Chepurny and Proshka, so
now the new Chevengurians, in an ultimate battle, fall victim to a power
greater than they. Nowhere does Platonov indicate that this power has any
higher moral authority: it is simply power come to claim what is its own
and to destroy, as Chepurny and the others had done before them, whatever
stands in its path. This, after all, is the judgment that a revolutionary (non-
Fyodorovian) approach to the attainment of utopia in history inevitably carries with it. Or to put it in Platonov's own haunting way, " 'Where there's
a beginning, there's an end too,' Chepurny said, *not knowing what he
would say after that"* (my emphasis; 239). Both the character's words and
the narrator's editorializing are true, yet, when taken together, self-canceling. The truth of the End is not a truth that can become knowledge. And
this process of linguistic self-cancellation, so characteristic of Platonov, captures better than anything else the ultimate spatio-temporal disjunction between 1917 and communism, between *revolution* and *revelation*. Small
wonder, then, that Sasha Dvanov ends *Chevengur* by *circling* back to Lake
Mutevo and taking the road into the water and death.[47] For this Telemachus

[47] Striedter is especially perceptive on the conceptualization of historical movement in *Che-*

in search of Odysseus, the Plotinian procession and epistrophe of a great circular journey lead to a homecoming that is more a failure than a triumph. Ashamed that his father still lies in the grave while he in his efforts to resurrect him remains "ever and the same" (332), Sasha opts for the road that, from the beginning, has constituted the other great alternative. And strange as it may seem in a work so apparently unstructured, *Chevengur* ends at the only place it could, where it began, with the same sense of mystery and awe in the face of death and of overwhelming pity for death's one unequal, yet noble rival—the historical imagination.

---

*vengur*: "When Platonov's revolutionary wanderer Dvanov is asked to invent a 'Monument of the Revolution,' he draws a 'figure' which consists of a 'horizontal figure eight' and a 'vertical arrow with two heads,' symbolizing together the temporal and spatial 'eternity and endlessness' of the revolution. The addition of the arrow is significant for the revolutionary aspect of this kind of romanticism. The figure eight in itself symbolized an eternal movement, but this movement remained self-reflected and closed in itself; it could, therefore, indicate both completeness and autonomy, as well as closedness and isolation. The same is true with regard to its symbolizing or structuring of romantic poetry (or of completed utopias). The arrow indicates the revolutionary movement away from self-reflection as well as the straightness of the revolution. But in addition to this the arrow, with two heads which point in two different directions, indicates a concept of revolutionary dynamics, which stands for more than pointing toward a fixed goal. And both symbols together indicate a problem, crucial for revolutionary utopias as well as for romantic poetry. How can one express infinity in a limited, closed form?" ("Three Utopian Novels" 194) Compare these comments to my discussions below of the "open circle" in *The Master and Margarita* and the circle, line, and cycle in *Doctor Zhivago*.

# FOUR

---

## *The Master and Margarita*:
## History as Hippodrome

How pleasant and liberating to die.
He raced his entire life with one persistent thought—
to come in first. And on a dead run
his horse, now out of breath, faltered;
there was no longer strength in its legs to hold the saddle,
and the wobbly stirrups flew into the air,
and he flew forward, thrown off by the jolt . . .
he struck his crown against the native,
vernal, pleasant earth,
and in that instant all possible necessary thoughts
passed through his brain. Passed—
and died. And his eyes died.
And the corpse looks up with a dreamy expression.
—Alexander Blok, "On Death"

And the waves foamed under the horses' maddened stampede. Thus
perished all of the horsemen, and with them, the centurion, Mar-
cellus.
—Fyodor Sologub, "The Young Linus"

Of the writers discussed in these pages, all of whom played major roles in
the self-conscious evolution of the modern Russian novel, none has had a
more "artistically contrived" fate than Mikhail Bulgakov. Had he never
written *The Master and Margarita* (1928–40), he would still be remembered as a prose writer of considerable distinction and as one of the leading
dramatists of the Soviet period. He once compared himself to a pianist who
needs both left and right hands, drama and imaginative prose, to be a complete artist. Yet during his lifetime, despite the fact that he published an
impressive first novel, *The White Guard* (1925),[1] and wrote many stories
and novellas, he was known beyond his immediate circle primarily as the
author of *The Days of the Turbins* (1926), a play about the civil war based

---

[1] Which was not, to be sure, published in its entirety during the author's lifetime. Bulgakov
had great difficulty in finding an outlet for much of his work.

on *The White Guard* that enjoyed an enormous run at the Moscow Art Theater. For most of his contemporaries—from the crowds who warmly applauded Bulgakov's autobiographically colored description of a family of White sympathizers trapped in war-torn Kiev to the orthodox critics and censors who took the opportunity to pillory the playwright for his ideological "unreliability"—drama was "the piano hand" on which the spotlight shone, and even then rather fitfully, during the two decades of Bulgakov's literary activity. Today, however, Bulgakov's posthumous fame rests almost entirely on his last work, over which he labored in the years of isolation, depression, nervous disorder, migraine headaches, and ultimately nephrosclerosis, and which eventually, more than two and a half decades after his death, experienced a miraculous second life. Indeed, to a public starved for romance and myth, it rose, like the proverbial fairytale princess, out of its desk-drawer coffin to the ministrations of a literary establishment which, if not a Prince Charming, was not entirely a Wicked Witch either. And so, for a writer who spent much of his career satirizing the lack of justice *in this world*, Bulgakov and, by association, his generation have begun to have their day in the higher court of literary history. What the dying author called his "sunset novel" has in the end provided its own epilogue, achieving the "immortality" which is also its central theme.

There is a great deal, in fact too much, that could be said by way of preface to our analysis of *The Master and Margarita*. This work has become one of the most studied of all twentieth-century Russian novels, surpassing in recent years even *Doctor Zhivago* in terms of Western and Soviet scholarly industry. Unlike *Petersburg*, whose intense verbal texture and arcane anagogic keys discourage the uninitiated, or *Doctor Zhivago*, whose intentional blurring of realistic and lyrico-symbolic modes has annoyed many of its readers, *The Master and Margarita* can be read and appreciated on various levels simultaneously: therein lies an important clue to the instant recognition of its special status by the reading public. Although it is true that Bulgakov is in many ways the quintessential "modernist," his interest in plot, on the one hand, and in the trio of satire, the grotesque, and verbal play, on the other, goes back to his two favorite Russian forebears—Pushkin and Gogol. What these two writers signified to Bulgakov and how they, as touchstones, made their way into his last novel is of no little consequence, and hence it is with them that we will begin our contextualization.

The son of a theology professor and member of the liberal democratic intelligentsia,[2] Bulgakov did not share Pushkin's aristocratic heritage, but

---

[2] The two most complete and up-to-date sources for Bulgakov's life are Proffer, *Bulgakov*, and Ianovskaia, *Tvorcheskii put'*. But see as well Belozerskaia, *O, med*; Chudakova, "Arkhiv M. A. Bulgakova"; and Wright, *Life and Interpretations*. An excellent recent article on the formative influence that Bulgakov's father, the church scholar Afanasy Ivanovich Bulgakov,

he did share the latter's fastidious regard for personal honor, his insistence that others respect—if not love—him, and his fervent belief in cultural values. Temperamentally, from the chilly formality that hid a basic shyness to the trenchant wit so dangerous to ideological foes, to the oscillating infatuation with scholarly and creative work, to the deep, but ultimately private belief in another world,[3] to the abiding love for the father of Russian literature, there is much to recommend a comparative study of Bulgakov and that other foremost modern Russian novelist-cum-Pushkinist, Vladimir Nabokov. From different sides of the Russian border, Bulgakov and Nabokov looked to Pushkin as a powerful beacon in the high seas of shifting values, tendentious ideological concerns, and historical turmoil. Just as in *The Gift*, Nabokov's last novel in Russian, Pushkin's shade shows Fyodor the way out of his "internal" and "external" exiles, so too does Bulgakov's considerable knowledge of Pushkin's life and work under a repressive tsarist regime help him to become the ultimate escape artist in *The Master and Margarita*. Here there can be no question of influence, but only of striking parallels that emerge when two writers of similar casts of minds look to the Pushkin icon, with all the latter represents for Russian literature and culture, and borrow some of its "bio-aesthetic" patina in order to deepen and enrich the colors of their own artistic universes.

From his first steps in the provincial literary world Bulgakov was drawn to defend Pushkin against the crude, ad hominem attacks of spokesmen and impresarios of the new proletarian culture. In Vladikavkaz in the Caucasus (1920–21), where he began his apprenticeship as a writer after renouncing his first profession of medical doctor, Bulgakov had occasion to discover how, under present conditions, one's social status could suddenly predetermine one's place in literary history. For Bulgakov, true culture could be embodied in national guises, but its essence was timeless and catholic. His starched collars in the midst of abject personal poverty and his later *épatage* with the notorious monocle were not simply anachronistic affectations, as his detractors argued, but an insistence that tradition and self-discipline are

---

might have had on his son's religious beliefs and ultimately on their refraction in *The Master and Margarita* is Haber, "The Lamp."

³ But a belief that coexists with a scorn for the historical church and its compromised priesthood. See, for example, his "Kiev Town" (1923) for a glimpse of Bulgakov's satirical view of the priesthood. As Haber points out: "Bulgakov's father's belief in the church was founded, in the tradition of Khomiakov, on the concept of Christian *sobornost'*: 'Created on earth precisely to unite all people into one [a quote from one of the elder Bulgakov's articles].' . . . In Bulgakov's artistic universe, in contrast, such mystical unity appears not within the organized church, but only among isolated beings, attracted to the person and vision of a single individual. . . . The only broader 'communality' that remains in the novel is state-enforced collectivism, fueled by selfishness and mutual animosity rather than Christian love and self-sacrifice" ("The Lamp" 349–50).

necessary in life as in art and that, in any event, to judge the quality of his work by the presence of an eyeglass was as ludicrous as to judge the quality of another's work by the presence of a leather jacket or a worker's cap. Near the end of his life, an old Kiev friend, Platon Gdeshinsky, wrote Bulgakov: "reading the lines you've written, I know that real culture exists [. . .] your every word, even pronounced casually, is an artistic work, no matter what you speak of" (Chudakova, "Arkhiv M. A. Bulgakova" 138–39; cited in Proffer, *Bulgakov* 492).

It is against such a background, then, that Bulgakov's life-long admiration for Pushkin must be seen. When, for example, on June 29, 1920, the proletarian writer G. A. Astakhov rose before a mixed audience at the Vladikavkaz Actor's House and roundly condemned Pushkin for dancing the mazurka while the Decembrists were being hanged, Bulgakov felt it a matter of honor to speak for the absent poet and to set the record straight. The Mayakovskian flourish in Astakhov's remarks—"We remember all of this and boldly toss Pushkin into the purifying fire of the revolution" (cited in Gireev, *Mikhail Bulgakov* 87)—must have also struck a dark, monitory note in the consciousness of Bulgakov, who had been attached to the Belgrade Hussars in World War I. Two days later he stood at the same podium and with quiet dignity and characteristic elegance reminded the same public of the other Pushkin, the one "who loved freedom . . . [and] hated tyranny, the humanist of high ideals" (Proffer, *Bulgakov* 37). This is the first appearance in Bulgakov's biography of a theme that would inform some of his most philosophically far-ranging works, including *The Cabal of Hypocrites* (wr. 1929) and *The Last Days* (wr. 1934–35), his plays about Molière and Pushkin, and *The Master and Margarita*: that of the artist's higher calling in a world relentlessly dragged down by Realpolitik and the base urges of a cynical ruling elite.

But the real meaning of the Pushkin legend, as far as Bulgakov was concerned, lay in its special status as both fully historicized tragedy and fully redeemed comic victory through art. As we learn in *The Last Days*, where Pushkin never appears in person yet manages to assert his ghostly presence all the more forcefully,[4] the fate of the artist—hounded by anonymous notes, cruel and envious denouncers, and an omnipotent tsar—is timeless. More importantly, the many parallels between this play and *The Master and Margarita* lend credence to the argument that not only his characters, Yeshua and the Master, but Bulgakov himself saw the conflict between manifest failure on a biographical plane and equally remarkable, though at the time unacknowledged triumph on a higher artistic/ethical plane as a

---

[4] The closest the audience gets to seeing Pushkin is when his *corpse* is quickly carried across the stage.

reliving of Pushkin's tragedy. Some of these parallels include: the snowstorm[5] in *The Last Days*, which is transformed into the apocalyptic thunderstorm in *The Master and Margarita*; the letter of the law (*zakon*) used to judge the poet in the play and the wandering philosopher in the novel; the thirty rubles, which, like the blood money paid to Iuda, is handed over to the informers Bitkov and Bogomazov by General Dubelt of the Third Section as compensation for helping to entrap Pushkin; the play's marvelous Aesopian scene, anticipating the shadow play between Pilate and Aphranius, in which the tsar enjoins Dubelt to treat the duel between Pushkin and D'Anthès under the existing law (dueling at the time was strictly forbidden), but in actuality is telling him to look the other way; Dubelt's perusal of "Earthly Power," one of the last poems to be written by Pushkin, which describes, in terms both savage and simple, how the common people were kept away from the site of the crucifixion, and which, in terms of the poet's own death and burial, turned out to be prophetic. Furthermore, these same parallels take on added poignancy when one is alerted to other details scattered throughout Bulgakov's biography. For example, once out of desperation the writer began (but never sent) a letter to Stalin in which he urged the General Secretary to serve as his personal censor, as Nicholas I had done for Pushkin a century earlier (Proffer, *Bulgakov* 329; see also 340).

Thus the chess game played out between Louis and Molière in one century, Nicholas and Pushkin in another, and Stalin and Bulgakov in still another is "timely," in the sense that then, as now, real people suffered specific moments of pain and humiliation in the name of their beliefs and values, and "timeless," in the sense that each different confrontation between "Caesar's law" and "God's truth" strikes some primordial chord in the human condition. The issue it raises is central to the apocalyptic conception and structure of *The Master and Margarita*—namely, the direction and meaning of human history, its end as divine plot, and the ultimate purpose of historical study. As the son of a person deeply committed to investigating historical truth within the framework of theodicy, Bulgakov in all likelihood did not come to this problem *through* Pushkin, who was notoriously irreverent in his younger years,[6] but it is equally true that he could not have solved it, or perhaps even have posed it in terms that made a solution *imaginable*, without the poet-cum-historian's model. By this one means that Pushkin, after 1825 increasingly obsessed with his country's history and the legacy of its tyrants, provided Bulgakov with an example at hand of the artist who tries, after faithfully poring over sources, to intuit what *might*

---

[5] Also to play an important role in *White Guard*.

[6] After 1826 there are few if any blasphemous remarks to be found in Pushkin's works.

have happened. Pushkin's own investigation of Russia's past eventuated not only in works of historiography (*The History of Pugachyov*), but, more telling for Bulgakov, in works of art (*Boris Godunov, Poltava, The Bronze Horseman, The Captain's Daughter*). And it was two of these latter, *The Bronze Horseman* and *The Captain's Daughter*, that were especially on the modern writer's mind as he drafted *The White Guard*, the novel in which he first alludes to and clearly foregrounds the apocalyptic subtext.

From Pushkin's last novel Bulgakov took the epigraph to his first—the lines referring to the onset of an ominous snowstorm.[7] But behind these lines lay the more famous dictum about Russia's potential for revolt, with its prophetic significance for the situation in war-ravaged Kiev: "God preserve us from a Russian revolt, senseless and merciless" (*PSS* VIII: 383). And from Pushkin's greatest *poèma* (narrative poem) Bulgakov did not take, at least directly, his second epigraph, with its message of apocalyptic judgment ("and the dead were judged out of those things which were written in the books according to their works" [Revelation 20:12]), but he did borrow and adapt the potent motif of the apocalyptic horseman (Petlyura) and equestrian statue (Bogdan Khmelnitsky), which Pushkin had made famous and which Bely had recently celebrated in his novel.[8]

These parallels point to a similarity which Bulgakov cultivated in his own research into Pushkin's life. By carefully reconstructing an individual's historical identity from the pages of primary sources, the artist penetrates to the *essence* of that identity and, in those instances where documentary sources are overly laconic or non-existent, extrapolates the essence into imaginary words, scenes, and actions.[9] The point is not that Bulgakov took liberties with his sources, which he was certainly willing to do as the occasion demanded, but that, with the tools available to him, including imaginative empathy or what Keats might call "Negative Capability," he arrived

[7] "A light snow began to fall and suddenly came down in large flakes. The wind began to howl; it worked up into a snowstorm. In an instant the dark sky became indistinguishable from the sea of snow. Everything disappeared. 'Well, sir,' shouted the driver. 'There's trouble—a blizzard' " (*Kapitanskaia dochka, PSS* VIII: 287). Cf. as well Pushkin's famous poem "The Devils" (1830), where the speaker and his driver get lost in a snowstorm that is likened to a swirling band of devils.

[8] On the connections between Andrey Bely and Bulgakov, see Proffer, *Bulgakov* 156–57, 177, 180.

[9] See, for example, the "game of grades" (Proffer, *Bulgakov* 490–91) that Bulgakov played near the end of his life: "An individual would be rated by all [friends] present, and the grade would depend not just on opinions, as Bulgakov explained, but on the entire complex of qualities which made up the human being, the sum total of what he was as a man, even if he were in some ways flawed. 'One must search for the pith, the deepest concentration of the human in this person.' " Elsewhere Proffer also argues that "with a firm belief in the talent of the artist to understand what was likely, given a person's situation or character, Bulgakov would take a small detail, a little anecdote, and draw his conclusions" (343).

at a dramatizable or narratable truth he believed more genuine than that sponsored by the "pure" historian, with the latter's arguments of contingency or causality. In short, Bulgakov was trying to wrest narrative authority away from those who place meaning (and ultimately justice), however defined, *within* the historical process, and to give it over to a "fate" that, doubtlessly tragic and infinitely mutable, could still preserve the integrity and freedom of the individual. Justice was never here and now, yet the fact that Pushkin (and Bulgakov) did not compromise himself in matters of personal and artistic conscience made vindication at a subsequent time, *in another court*, possible. It was precisely this approach to the facts of Pushkin's life to which Bulgakov's friend the writer and literary historian V. V. Veresaev objected, causing him to remove his name from what was originally conceived of as a joint undertaking (*The Last Days*) (see Proffer, *Bulgakov* 445–49). As Ellendea Proffer, the foremost Bulgakov specialist in the West, summarizes her subject's use of historical source material and its application to both *The Last Days* and *The Master and Margarita*: "Bulgakov's view, as seen throughout his works, as well as his notes and letters on the play about Pushkin, was that the artist divines a kind of truth which makes use of all the known facts about something, and in this lies real talent. The Master says that he 'guessed' the details of the Pilate story correctly. This kind of guessing is what Bulgakov considers the essence of art. In this sense, the Master's novel and Woland's are one. There is an ur-text which only the initiated can discover" (*Bulgakov* 636; see also 343).

The Gogol connection in Bulgakov is equally unmistakable. Like Pushkin, Gogol was a Russian classic that Bulgakov read in childhood and revered forever after. As he wrote to his friend Pavel Popov, "Of writers I prefer Gogol; from my point of view, no one can be compared to him. At nine I read *Dead Souls*. I considered it an adventure novel. I think Gogol had a second period in his work, when he had written himself out" (*Unpublished Bulgakov* 39; cited in Proffer, *Bulgakov* 178). This preference was grounded primarily in a stylistic and thematic communality that seems to have been stronger in the earlier than in the later Bulgakov, although it never disappears entirely: a fascination with the demonic and the fantastic ("Diaboliad," *The Heart of a Dog*, *The Fatal Eggs*); an interest—often dehumanizing—in the "little man"; an irreverent or deliberately unreliable narrator; a camera eye that lights with satiric ferocity on the backside of Soviet life ("The Adventures of Chichikov"); a playful style that revels in its own lack of logic and thwarts expectation with realized metaphors and bizarre juxtapositions ("The Crimson Island," "Diaboliad"). Again, as in the case of Pushkin, Bulgakov paid his idol the ultimate compliment by reworking for the stage or screen several of his works, among them *Dead Souls* and *The Inspector General*. Finally, the autobiographical element suggests that Bulgakov was consciously tapping into the Gogol legend as well: his own prolonged bouts of depression often ended in trips to the stove, which he wryly described to Popov as his "editorial office" (Milne "K biografii" 165; Proffer, *Bulgakov* 341); in another letter written in a moment of triumph he comically pleaded with his "teacher" to shield him from public view "with your iron overcoat" (Proffer, *Bulgakov* 337); he dwelt in his thoughts on Gogol's terrible last days during his own final bout with nephrosclerosis (Wright, *Life and Interpretation* 252–53); and perhaps most fitting of all, although the earthly Bulgakov had no knowledge of it, his last wife, Yelena Sergeevna, managed to acquire Gogol's first grave- stone, called "Golgotha," as a monument for her husband's final resting place in the Novodevichy Cemetery (Lakshin, "Èskizy k trem portretam" 219; cited in Proffer, *Bulgakov* 505). Be this as it may, the ties with Gogol may not run as deep as those with Pushkin. Bulgakov's lyrical flights and satiric strafing missions are always under the control of a restrained and calculating pilot. And his interests in history and philosophy are more pro- found and rigorous than those found in Gogol.

In Bulgakov's world, the forces representing historical necessity tend to be cruel, cynical, punishing, judgmental. The continuous tragedy he saw in the lives of Russian writers from Pushkin and Gogol to himself led him to seek out several economical, yet highly charged image clusters whose func- tion it was to bear the semantic weight of this tragedy. Among these the most prominent are the horse and rider. Let it be said at the outset that there is no single interpretation, no single blade, capable of severing the Gordian knot of *The Master and Margarita*. Still, as shall be shortly dem- onstrated, a fuller exfoliation of the genesis and later deployment of this image cluster goes far toward clarifying Bulgakov's use of the apocalyptic subtext in his last novel, and of the importance of this subtext there can be no doubt. As in the other novels we have been investigating, the horse and rider surfaces continually, almost as if it were an "Ursymbol" for Russian history at an epic crossroads, where chaos, suffering, revolution, and death gather under the forces of a dark cavalier. Bulgakov was clearly aware of these various connotations and carefully builds them into his works. They culminate in *The Master and Margarita*.

The importance that Bulgakov placed on the equine/equestrian motif seems to have been motivated, first of all, by actual experience. As already mentioned, Bulgakov was attached to the Belgrade Hussars during World War I; at this time he knew many cavalrymen, including the prototype for the Nay-Turs character in *The White Guard*, who distinguishes himself in the novel for his valor and self-sacrificing death. More significant was an episode involving Bulgakov's younger brother Nikolay (the Nikolka of *White Guard*), who had volunteered for service against Petlyura's forces, then suddenly—to the family's great consternation—disappeared without a trace, finally resurfacing in the Caucasus as a brave cavalryman. Bulgakov himself left Kiev and made his way to Pyatigorsk to fetch his brother; he could not convince the latter to desert and blamed himself when Nikolay returned wounded from battle: these events provided the source material for the plot of "The Red Crown" (1922) (see Gireev, *Bulgakov* 51; Proffer, *Bulgakov* 26). In this early story, the vision of the dead rider[10] constantly reminds the conscience-stricken narrator that he did not do his filial duty. The disfigured physiognomy, unseeing eyes, and bloodied dressing ("the red crown") drive the speaker insane. The only moments of respite come as the narrator dreams of an earlier time, when the old home, with its comfortable furniture and "Faust" score on the piano,[11] had not yet been disturbed, and the brother had not yet left and "become a rider" (*ss* I: 196). Here the ties to Pilate's guilty conscience, his desire to unwrite history, and his status as deadly horseman[12] are already obvious.

In *The White Guard* Bulgakov's deployment of the horse and rider motif takes on an added dimension. Still associated with death and still motivated by personal experience, it now enters a larger semantic field—that of the apocalypse and of Russian history in crisis (see Barratt, "Apocalypse or Revelation?"; Mann, "Path of the Bronze Horseman"; and Proffer, *Bulgakov* 135–61). The atmosphere of the novel is thick with apocalyptic allusions: the parish priest Father Alexander reads constantly from the Book of Revelation (hence the epigraph and the judgment of the dead "according to their works"); Petlyura's prison cell bears the number of the Beast, 666; as Petlyura's army makes its triumphant entry into the city, blind ballad-singers intone songs about the Last Judgment and the End of the World; and in the last pages of the novel Rusakov, a syphilitic poet and recent convert to apocalyptic thinking, has a vision of a new heaven and new earth. Yet Bulgakov was enough of a realist and ironist to acknowledge that no light brigade from the sky would restore justice and make things right *in this world*. With this in mind, one perceptive critic has developed the term "negative apocalyptic thinking" to define Bulgakov's attitude toward eschatologists in *The White Guard*. That is to say, the thought that God will intervene to judge and damn the forces destroying the comfortable, insulated life of the Turbins and others is parodied in the novel (Barratt, "Apocalypse" 12ff.). Yelena Turbin's cry ("Curse the Germans. . . . If God does not punish them, then he is not a God of justice. They must surely be made to answer

[10] Nikolay, it is worth recalling, did *not* die in real life, at least not at that point.

[11] The details are taken from the Bulgakov family home in Kiev and show up again in the Turbins' apartment in *White Guard*.

[12] With the important difference that here the rider *is* already dead, while Pilate's role is to bring death and judgment.

for this—they *must*" [169/158]) may reach the ears of Bulgakov's deity, but he will not act on it, since it is generated by thoughts of *personal* vengeance. And, in the heaven of Alexey Turbin's dreams, both Bolsheviks (Zhilin) and White officers (Nay-Turs) are present, since in God's view "One man believes, another doesn't, but the actions of everyone of you are alike . . . you are all equal in my eyes, all of you slain on the field of battle" (*Belaia gvardiia* 72; see Barratt, "Apocalypse" 18). Hence Bulgakov, not unlike St. Augustine himself, is not against the notion of apocalypse, of imagining the end of human history as it would look from God's "astral aerie,"[13] but he *is* against those who would manipulate such categories in order to justify their own action (or inaction).

Like its more famous sibling, *The White Guard* is essentially about judgment and mercy, law and grace, brute reality and miraculous dispensation. Not quite a "cathedral novel," it still asks the reader to enter its world through the dual portals of Old and New Testament thinking (see Weeks, "Hebraic Antecedents"). Because it chronicles the latter-day time of troubles between the collapse of Hetman Skoropadsky's[14] government in November 1918 and the arrival of the Soviet army in February 1919, when Petlyura's native forces carried out their brief but fierce reign of terror, the accent is more on punishment, retribution, and swift, almost casual death[15]—the "eye for an eye" that the long-suffering peasant has awaited. Paraphrasing the Pushkin of *The Captain's Daughter*, Bulgakov thus describes the imminent judgment day: "As the fall turned to winter death soon came to the Ukraine with the first dry, driven snow. . . . Death itself remained unseen, but its unmistakable herald was a wave of crude, elemental peasant fury which ran amok through the cold and the snow, a fury in torn bast shoes, straws in its matted hair; a fury which howled. It held in its hands a huge club, without which no great change in Russia, it seems, can ever take place" (72/73).

Yet while the Turbins are forced to make sacrifices and to give up their asylum of freshly cut flowers and favorite books smelling of chocolate,[16] they do not betray their principles or their basic decency ("the dead will be judged according to their works"), nor do they disintegrate as a family.

---

[13] The last sentence of *White Guard* reads: "Why, then, will we not turn our eyes toward the stars? Why?" (297/270). Henceforth, page numbers of *The White Guard* will appear parenthetically: the first number(s) will refer to the Glenny translation; the second number(s) will refer to the 1973 Soviet edition. Small changes have been made in the English translation where appropriate.

[14] Ironically, his name means "soon to fall." See the description of his ignominious escape in *White Guard* 109–10, 114/105–6, 110.

[15] With the Jews most often the victims—see, e.g., *White Guard* 289–90/263.

[16] One of which is *The Captain's Daughter*. Others, such as Dostoevsky's *The Devils* and Bunin's "Gentleman from San Francisco," have obvious apocalyptic overtones of doom.

Indeed, with savagery and carnage all around them, they persevere *miraculously*. Alexey (whose prototype was Bulgakov himself) is saved not only once but twice: Yulia Reiss, who is mysteriously connected with the diabolic Shpolyansky, rescues the elder Turbin brother from the Petlyurians' bullets; and his sister Yelena appears to break the death grip of his typhoid fever with her prayers at the icon of the Holy Virgin.[17] Hence, despite the fact that there is ample evidence—including Nikolka's ghastly descent into the morgue in search of Nay-Turs' corpse—to recommend a wholly tragic reading of the text, one that sees history as simply a hell with no master plan, this sort of deus ex machina suggests the possibility of another view. Out of the ashes of Nay-Turs' death comes Nikolka's romance with Irina, the colonel's younger sister; out of Alexey's close encounter with his own end comes his love for Yulia. Bulgakov's point is that there may well be a divine plot making sense of these "apocalyptic" happenings; however, it is not for the participants to hasten its dénouement, which in any event will never be clear from their position "within." The best that can be hoped for is that human beings will continue to act as ethical agents in this lower court even as they patiently await their time in the higher one. In this regard, Bulgakov remained, from his earliest work through *The Master and Margarita*, an evolutionist rather than a revolutionist.[18] The "astral" view, God's position "from beyond," is hinted at in the text, but it is always the domain of religious revelation, "understood" only by those "touched" (Rusakov)[19] or by those already dead or dying (Nay-Turs, Zhilin). Apocalypse is reflected in their eyes; the insight coming from those eyes is, on the other hand, no longer of this world.[20]

So it is against this context of apocalyptic thinking—which on one level is parodied and on another is taken seriously—that the author's return to the horse and rider motif stands out. For Bulgakov the quintessential instrument of war is the cavalryman, and nearly all the important martial

[17] Cf. Yury's near fatal bout with typhus, which brings him in touch with his half-brother Evgraf (the "spirit of death"), in *Doctor Zhivago*.

[18] In a draft of a letter to Stalin dated March 28, 1930 (we are not sure how much of the draft was actually sent), Bulgakov writes of "[his] profound skepticism about the revolutionary process which is taking place in [his] backward country, and the opposition to it of [his] favorite Great Evolution" ("Pis'ma protesty" 159). See discussion in Proffer, *Bulgakov* 316–22.

[19] Rusakov seems a likely prototype for Ivan Homeless in *The Master and Margarita*. Other parallels include: an imposing figure with different colored eyes (Myshlaevsky/Woland); the metaphor of life/history as a chess game; reference to Bald Mountain (Golgotha); a playful, gossipy narrator; a vision with grim eyes; an apparition in jockey's boots (Koroviev has a jockey's cap); vulgar, motley crowds; boys watching passing cavalry; witches or witch-like figures; a small cap belonging to the hero (Alexey/Master); mention of Abaddonna; a five-pointed source of light (Mars/Temple candelabra); and above all a fearsome horseman.

[20] Bulgakov's paradox here will resurface at the conclusion of *The Master and Margarita*.

figures[21] in *The White Guard* are alluded to either as horsemen or cavaliers (or chevaliers). In fact, it is the equestrian image that links the Hetman's regime on the way out and the Petlyurian regime on the way in: "you are all equal in my eyes, all of you slain on the field of battle." One prominent example involves an artillery battery of raw recruits which has mustered, under the portrait of Alexander I, in the grand assembly hall of the high school bearing that tsar's name. Unlike the reader, who is constantly made privy to a higher view (Barratt, "Apocalypse"), these young people do not know that the Hetman is about to betray them and flee across the border. Their allegiance is to an epic imperial past which no longer exists, a past which Pushkin celebrated in his introduction to the *Bronze Horseman*, and one which the portrait of Alexander is also obviously intended to invoke:

> Mounted on his pure-bred Arab charger, saddle-cloth emblazoned with the imperial monogram, the Arab executing a perfect caracole, with beaming and white-plumed tricorn hat cocked at a rakish angle, the balding, radiant Tsar Alexander I galloped ahead of the ranks of cadets and students. Flashing them smile after smile redolent of insidious charm, Alexander waved his baton at the cadets to show them the serried ranks of Borodino (94/93).[22]

Alexander's charm is "insidious" (*kovarnyi*) because by this time the last of the Romanov line is already dead and the Hetman himself is thinking only of escape. The ironic contrast between then and now, between "the man who beat Napoleon" (95/93) and this charming will-o'-the-wisp, is made clear when the narraror's camera eye lingers on those details which upstage and vitiate the myth: "As the gorgeous Tsar Alexander galloped onwards and upwards to heaven, the torn drapes which had shrouded him for a whole year since October 1917 lay in a heap around the hooves of his charger" (94/93). The *onwards* and *upwards* movement of the myth is ludicrous in light of October 1917 and the *fallen* shroud which, though removed momentarily to inspire these impressionable boys, is a fitting metaphor for eclipse. This first imperial horseman, from our privileged view, thus signifies both a dead past and a potentially deadly present to those who insist on following him.

The second major horseman is Petlyura, who is never seen in person but is reputed to be carried aloft the crowds by a white steed (246/226). As Barratt has indicated, Petlyura is a parody of "faithful and true," the sword-bearing instrument of God's vengeance in Revelation 19:12 ("Apocalypse"

---

[21] Mars is of course one of the stars ruling over this world of cavalrymen, whose number include Nay-Turs, Alexander I, Petlyura and his generals, and Bogdan Khmelnitsky.

[22] Cf. also *White Guard* 38/38.

22). He too is myth or impostor ("It was all a myth. Petlyura was a myth. It didn't exist" [73/73]), since he brings not the real End but only death and chaos. By investing this "accountant" with the lineaments of an apocalyptic horseman, by surrounding his triumphant entry with songs about "the end of the world" (246/225), by believing in his trumped-up role as ultimate liberator, the people absolve themselves of responsibility and abandon themselves to another bogus plot, with its bloody carnival atmosphere. This is of course why Bulgakov keeps Petlyura offstage, since he is not a genuine knight from beyond, but (in his mythical function at least) only a figment of the people's imagination. It is during the procession (a parody of Christ's *Parousia*) leading up to, but never culminating in, Petlyura's arrival that Bulgakov mounts his fiercest satirical attack on false apocalypticism. Here the Holy City and fairy-tale snowscape of Turbin memory becomes a ragtag band of pickpockets, prostitutes, fools-in-Christ, brazen orators, and gullible citizenry come to witness the spectacle—in short, the Great Whore (Barratt, "Apocalypse" 16). The procession breaks up, ironically, when a disguised Shpolyansky mounts a fountain near the statue of Bogdan Khmelnitsky (a kind of Ukrainian Bronze Horseman) and makes a plea for the Bolsheviks. His words have the effect of prophesying the arrival of new (iron) horsemen (Trotsky will make his entrance on an *armored train*) even before the Petlyurians have had, as it were, time to dismount.

At this point Bulgakov's lengthy description of the Bogdan Khmelnitsky equestrian deserves a closer look:

> Quite suddenly a gray patch between the domes of the cathedral broke open and the sun burst through the dull, overcast sky. The sun was bigger than anyone had ever seen it in the Ukraine and quite red, like pure blood. . . . The sun reddened the dome of St. Sophia with blood, casting a strange shadow from it on to the square, so that in that shadow Bogdan turned violet, and made the seething crowd of people look even blacker, even denser, even more confused. And gray men in long coats belted with rope and waving bayonets could be seen climbing up the steps leading up the side of the rocks and trying to smash the inscription that stared down from the black granite plinth. But the bayonets broke or slithered uselessly away from the granite, and Bogdan wrenched his horse away from the rock at a gallop as he tried to fly away from the people who were clinging on to the hooves of his horse and weighing them down. His face, turned directly towards the red globe, was furious and he continued steadfastly to point his mace into the distance (253/231–32).

This lavishly framed scene of a fearsome horseman casting his glance over a "sea" of unruly elements recalls not only *The Bronze Horseman*, with its

Petrine myth come alive, but also Bely's modern treatment of it in *Petersburg*, a novel whose themes, sound play,[23] and marked use of indentation seem to have influenced Bulgakov. What is more, the same scene anticipates in many ways the first Yershalaim chapter in *The Master and Margarita*.[24]

When seen from our ulterior vantage, the three riders—Peter, Bogdan, and Pilate—appear to converge in a noteworthy instance of what might be termed intertextual "parallax." They all represent a ruthless, martial approach to the issue of historical change versus stasis; they look out over a scene of chaos from their positions atop huge stone platforms (recall the gabbatha in *The Master and Margarita*); the sea they would feign to master is natural in Pushkin (though fraught with Decembrist undercurrents) and human in Bely and Bulgakov; they look into the distance (their future "immortality") and are moved to act when the authority of their realms is questioned;[25] and Peter and Bogdan point the way with their imperious arm and mace (*bulava*) respectively, just as, on a figurative level, Pilate indicates the limits of his Roman worldview through his constant attribute, the *pilatus* or lance (*kop'e* in Russian). It may also be significant that Bogdan becomes "violet" in the sunlight, again adumbrating the violet horseman who comes to visit Woland in an alternate version of *The Master and Margarita* (Chudakova, "Tvorcheskaia istoriia" 238). Finally, the blood red sun shining directly into the furious Bogdan's face will be the same pitiless source of light that causes Pilate such anguish when he squints at the equine statues on the hippodrome and that blinds him as he prepares to pass judgment on the

[23] A good example would be the way Bely and Bulgakov play on the sound of civil disorder and chaos: the words *revoliutsiia* (revolution) and "Petlyura," respectively. Both show how these words are distorted (revoliuuuutsiia, Peturrra) by the swirling of the leaves/revolutionary leaflets (Bely) and the buzzing of the crowd (Bulgakov). See also note 8 above.

[24] See Mann, "Path" 1–4. Another possible subtext for the notion of the punishing horseman is found in Sologub's "The Young Linus" (1906). In this story, whose pervasive imagery of the closed circle is quite reminiscent of *The Master and Margarita*, Sologub portrays a Roman view of history that is brutal, unforgiving, and dominated by the hooves of war horses. A group of Roman soldiers led by a centurion surround a group of children (who in Sologub are often specially endowed). One of the children, Linus, not wishing "to live on an earth which the horses of your frenzied army trample" (*Kiss* 102), raises his tiny fist in defiance of the soldiers (an allusion to Pushkin's Evgeny in *The Bronze Horseman*?). The child has the last word, however, since after he is killed his ghost proceeds to lead the soldiers around in a circle and then on to their deaths in the water.

[25] Cf. Peter's pursuit of Evgeny/Dudkin, Bogdan's flight from the crowd, and Pilate's sentencing of Yeshua. Peter was originally portrayed in Pushkin's poem as *subduing* the elements—his equestrian leap off the granite "cliff" was presumably motivated by the urge to keep the upstart Evgeny (and the Decembrist "undercurrents" associated with the latter) under control. Conversely, Bogdan's energies seem to be devoted to *escaping* from the hoi polloi. Finally, Pilate, in sentencing Yeshua, appears to be the master of his crowd, but in fact he is being forced by Jewish law to go against his better judgment and execute a man he would prefer to save (this is his "flight").

criminals.[26] At moments of historical crisis and transition the horseman, Bulgakov seems to argue, has always exacted his toll: he was present as the Roman *status* gave way to the Christian one; he was present as the Petrine colossus began to experience the clenched fists of its "upstart Evgeny"; and he was present as imperial Russia and its "White Guard" entered their final death throes.[27]

Perhaps the ultimate question to be broached before any reading of *The Master and Margarita* can be undertaken is that of the author's religious faith. From childhood on Bulgakov enjoyed the reputation of being a master bluffer and mystifier; with his considerable acting skill, he loved to shock or surprise relatives and friends into believing that they had witnessed bizarre or supernatural happenings. Yet whether what was at issue was a children's magic show or a spiritual seance for adults, the poker-faced Bulgakov could be counted on to pull the strings. Bulgakov, writes Proffer, "was a great mystifier—he always preferred people to believe in the supernatural. But like any good magician, he knew there was a logical explanation" (*Bulgakov* 180). This important side of his creative personality has led more than one critic to the conclusion that the christological conception of *The Master and Margarita* is at base parodic (as the "Gospel according to Satan," how, one asks, can it be taken seriously?), that Bulgakov is again pulling the strings of any reader who possesses a naive faith, be it Marxist or Christian. Such an approach has a certain cogency, since it helps make clear why Bulgakov borrows from, but at the same time ultimately distorts, such ancient sources as Flavius Josephus, Tacitus, and Philo Judaeus (Zerkalov, *Evangelie* 60–63).[28] Presumably the author wants the reader to sense that some code is there, but not be able to crack it. In other words, the allusions to Revelation may be planted by Bulgakov with the express purpose of trapping the reader who still believes that there can be a meaningful end to a life or a history and that a justice administered from beyond still exists.

Here, however, we are not dealing with categories susceptible of proof or disproof, a fact which could justifiably lead one to advance an argument from the opposite direction. The most accurate test for the presence of irony or parody is the *context* of style and tone in which an allusion or subtext is located, and in our case it bears repeating that the tone of the novel's dénouement, the section describing the now dead hero and heroine's flight

[26] As Mann ("Path" 3) points out, in *The Bronze Horseman* the statue of Peter, which should be surveying the world through his open window, is *nezriachii* ("unseeing").

[27] The threatening horseman also shows up in other Bulgakov works: see, e.g., *A Theatrical Novel*, where a golden statue of a steed figures prominently, and *Life of Molière*, where the dead writer sees a cavalier in black.

[28] It must be admitted that Zerkalov at times strains to provide a *realistic* motivation for Bulgakov's distortions of his sources.

beyond history and the release of Pilate, is one of ardent lyricism, radically different from the playful grotesquerie of the earlier Moscow chapters. Evidence suggests, therefore, that quite apart from making any apologia for the strict doctrinal teachings of Russian Orthodoxy,[29] the author very much wanted the "mystical" element in his novel to be seen as more than "mystification." Again, to invoke the shadow of Nabokov, Bulgakov's playful narrator and skewed codes do not necessarily imply that the mystery ends with him. The strings that refuse to be disentangled entirely in the novel are the same strings that refuse to be disentangled in life. Yet just as the Master, with Margarita's help, releases his tormented character, and just as the author releases his favorite hero and heroine, so too did Bulgakov believe, and structure his novel to reflect such belief, that he would eventually be released by his creator (see below). Indeed, he once wrote in a draft of a now famous letter (probably unsent) to Stalin: "I am a mystical writer" ("Pis'ma protesty" 159). Moreover, thoughts of his much admired father, the scholar of biblical history, were very much with him as he began work on his last novel—not, one suspects, an appropriate breeding ground for light-hearted parody or a debunking of Christian faith.[30] Bulgakov's final words, uttered less than a month after dictating corrections to the first part of the novel, were reputedly "Take me, forgive me" (Proffer, *Bulgakov* 500).[31]

On the other hand, one should not lose sight of the fact that Bulgakov was trained as a medical doctor and spent his early adulthood as a venereologist in the remote backwater of Nikolskoe. He possessed a precise knowledge of life's physical limitations and he had a discursive cast of mind. Thus his faith could never be described as naive; instead, it was a mysticism born of imagination, historical research, and natural science. Here it seems appropriate to mention Father Pavel Florensky, whose *Imaginaries in Geometry* (1922) Bulgakov read and underlined as he was working on *The Master and Margarita*.[32] A true Renaissance man whom fate preserved into the

---

[29] To reiterate, Bulgakov seems to have had only scorn for the historical church as such.

[30] "If my mother served as a stimulus for the creation of the novel *White Guard*, then according to my plans, the figure of my father is to be the starting point for another work I have in mind" (autobiographical notes, c. 1926, recorded by A. S. Popov; cited in Proffer, *Bulgakov* 178).

[31] Bulgakov felt a desperate need to complete his novel before the end of his life. In October 1934 he wrote a note to himself that read, "Finish this [*The Master and Margarita*] before dying" (Chudakova, "Arkhiv" 112); and in June 1938 he confessed that "A halt in the writing is like death. . . . I must finish the rewriting, no matter what happens" (Chudakova, "Tvorcheskaia istoriia" 248).

[32] "The special value of this work lies in the marginal marks, which are more numerous than in any other work [in Bulgakov's library], made as usual in thick colored pencil. According to E. S. Bulgakova's recollections, the book was treasured by its owner and reread more than once

Soviet period, Florensky ranged over a multitude of disciplines, at one time
or other working as a mathematician, physicist, philologist, art historian,
archaeologist, philosopher and theologian.[33] He was also an ordained priest
and a deeply religious man. His participation after the revolution on various
scientific and technical projects (such as GOERLO—the body responsible for
implementing Lenin's call for electrification) was, to his mind, only an extension of a higher calling. Even in the twenties Florensky continued to
provide the intellectual spark for such *sub rosa* religious groups as the
Brotherhood of St. Seraphim.[34]

Katerina Clark and Michael Holquist have recently characterized Florensky as a foil for Mikhail Bakhtin. These two seminal philosophers, they
argue, represent powerful antipodes in twentieth century Russian thought.
One could also add that the differences between them provide a valuable
epistemological key to the artistic world of Bulgakov and to the Florensky
connection in *The Master and Margarita*:

> Florensky, who was of a slightly earlier generation than Bakhtin, was
> generally closer in thought to both traditional Orthodoxy and pre-rev-
> olutionary thought, especially Symbolist. . . . [W]hile Florensky
> dreamed of *an end to time*, of a stasis that would come when we get
> *beyond the flux of this world and history ends*, Bakhtin believed that
> there should be no end to becoming, and he was an enemy of all that
> is finished (*zaveršen*). . . . He [Florensky] sought ways to make all
> contradictions between "I" and "not-I" fall away as both *transcend*
> themselves; he looked to a *One that would resolve all differences*. For
> Bakhtin, however, all that is living is alive precisely because of a non-
> correspondence with others (my emphasis; *Bakhtin* 136).

Like Florensky and unlike Bakhtin, Bulgakov too was "generally closer in
thought to both traditional Orthodoxy and pre-revolutionary thought"; he
too "dreamed of an end to time, of a stasis that would come when we get

---

in the years of work on *The Master and Margarita*, since Bulgakov saw *in the mathematical
and philosophical interpretation which the author of the brochure gives to Dante's journey
with Virgil . . . a certain analogue to the 'geometry' of the last chapters of his novel* [my
emphasis]. . . . It seems to us inescapable that the pages of the mathematician's book gave
impulse to the artistic thought of the writer. And without these pages the peculiarities of the
artistic time-space of the concluding chapters of Bulgakov's novel cannot be sufficiently com-
prehended" (Chudakova, "Condition of Existence" 80). See also Beatie and Powell, "Bulgakov,
Dante, and Relativity."

[33] For a good brief introduction to Florensky's life and thought, see Clark and Holquist,
*Bakhtin* 120–45, and the texts about Florensky cited by them.

[34] St. Seraphim, an early nineteenth-century Russian mystic, had spoken of another order
of time and had predicted in some detail how the revolution would be ushered in a century
later.

beyond the flux of this world"; he too "looked to a One that would resolve all differences." The "actual infinity" (*aktual'naia beskonechnost'*) and *coincidentia oppositorum* that are Florensky's quarry in his major work, *The Pillar and Foundation of Truth* (1929),[35] are accurate metaphors for that condition beyond history granted to the Master and Margarita by their author (*Stolp* 43).[36]

In *Imaginaries in Geometry*, Florensky adduces the latest theories in geometry and physics (including that of relativity) to make a statement about "actual infinity" or the world beyond three-dimensional space and time.[37] Dante's cosmology in *The Divine Comedy* provides Florensky his focus in those concluding sections that most intrigued Bulgakov:

> His [Dante's] journey was a reality; but if anyone should begin to deny this [assertion], then in any case it must be acknowledged as a poetic reality, that is, one accessible to imagination and thought [*predstavimym i myslimym*], which means that it contains within itself the givens for explaining its geometrical postulates. And so, *proceeding all the while forward along a straight line and having turned over [perevernuvshis'] once en route, the poet arrives back at his point of departure in the same position in which he left* (my emphasis; *Mnimosti* 47).

Florensky's ingenious argument is that the poet-Dante's journey into hell, presented as a spiralic descent to the center of the earth and that lowest midpoint (Satan's head) where the pilgrim and his guide finally *turn* and make their way *up* the path toward Mount Purgatory (see Canto XXIII, 74–94), is more plausibly conceived not as two Euclidean cones joined at their points but as a kind of Moebius strip.[38] What Virgil and Dante attain with their turn or transit (*perekhod*) is a piercing *through* conventional time and space *to the other side*, so that, "on the way back," the poet still appears to be moving forward along a straight line even while his legs are, paradoxically, turned in the direction of his recent descent (*Mnimosti* 47).

In such a state of absolute time travel, which Florensky likens to life on

---

[35] To be sure, we do *not* know whether Bulgakov read this.

[36] See also *Stolp* 44: "*All our efforts* will always produce only the synthesizable [*sinteziruemoe*], but never the completely synthesized [*osintezirovannyi*]. The Unity without End [*Beskonechnaia Edinitsa*] is transcendental in terms of human attainment."

[37] For more on the Florensky connection in Bulgakov, see Beatie and Powell, "Bulgakov, Dante, and Relativity." In general, while this article has much to say about Dantesque time (as viewed by Florensky) and its impact on the structure of *The Master and Margarita*, it suffers from a certain pedantry and literalism. Bulgakov, in my opinion, was not so much interested in Dante as an actual subtext, but in Florensky's provocative twist to the more traditional notions of spiralic space-time in *The Divine Comedy*. See below.

[38] Fyodor Godunov-Cherdyntsev, Nabokov's largely autobiographical hero in *The Gift*, also sees time as a Moebius strip. See Davydov, *Nabokov's Matreška Texts* 197.

the Kantian model as it might be re-imagined beyond the speed of light, all prior understanding of cause and effect, anteriority and posteriority, is reversed:

> Beyond the limit [of the speed of light], where $V > C$, time flows in reverse [*v obratnom smysle*], so that *result precedes cause.* In other words, at this point the operative causality [*deistvuiushchaia prichinnost'*] is—as the Aristotelian-Dantesque ontology demands—replaced by a causality of the end [*prichinnost' konechnaia*], a teleology. . . . At the same time, *the length and mass of bodies become imaginary* [*mnimye*] (*Mnimosti* 52).

In typical fashion, Florensky goes on to postulate that Dante, as artist, was "ahead of his time" because he intuited what modern science has gradually come to through logic and experiment. Rather than a space constructed according to the laws of Euclidean geometry, Dante's cosmos

> is very much akin to elliptical space. This throws an unexpected shaft of light on the medieval notion about the finiteness [*konechnost'*] of the world. But these universal geometrical concepts have recently received a suprisingly concrete interpretation in the principle of relativity, and from the viewpoint of modern physics universal space [*mirovoe prostranstvo*] should be conceived precisely as elliptical space, and [thus] acknowledged to be finite, just as time [should be acknowledged as] finite, enclosed in itself [*zamknutoe v sebe*] (*Mnimosti* 48).

Here we find the passionate search for "actual infinity" and the *coincidentia oppositorum*—the urge to close, through an optical illusion more "real" than reality itself, that which gives every appearance of being open, endless, and tragic—that lies at the center of Florensky's and Bulgakov's worldviews and that so clearly opposes Bakhtinian logic. What, after all, does it really mean to exist in a state *beyond* the speed of light? "It doesn't mean at all," concludes Florensky, "that speeds equal to or greater than C are impossible, but only that along with them [must come] completely new and as yet unclearly imagined—and, if you wish, transcendent to our earthly Kantian experience—conditions for life" (*Mnimosti* 50). In this too the philosopher-priest seems "ahead of his time," anticipating the "ultimate loop" in artificial intelligence theory that seeks to simulate human creativity by projecting "beyond" itself from "within" a finite storehouse of information. Thus, of all the possible sources that might have influenced the ending of *The Master and Margarita*, we as readers can be certain of the crucial role played by Florensky's little volume, with its highly unorthodox attempt to marry non-Euclidean geometry, relativity theory, and historical closure. The way time is constantly conflated and "pierced" in Bulgakov's text points directly to the viewpoint "from beyond" advocated by the author of *Imaginaries*. And most of all, the Master's (i.e., the creative artist's) unique ability to *unwrite* history and *free* Pilate from his bondage to a Manichaean prison of good and evil harks back to Florensky's description of the reversal of the laws of causality that takes place at the speed of light, at that moment when Dante's descent into hell and death becomes an ascendent and *trans*cendent "crossing-over."

As was intimated earlier, there is a special justice in the fact that a vast scholarly industry has been lavished on *The Master and Margarita*. No other work of imaginative prose written in the post-revolutionary era (and especially in the Stalinist thirties) has come to raise and satisfy so many hermeneutical expectations. Yet its essence remains indeterminate. Reflective of both a nineteenth-century tradition of realism and fierce ethical commitment and a twentieth-century tradition of post-symbolism and destabilizing irony, the novel seems a kind of marvelous stone that with each stroke of the critic's blade reveals a new facet but that for this very reason can never be apprehended in the totality of its lapidary brilliance. That Bulgakov managed to encode elaborate parodies of the Bible story and Goethe's *Faust* in his novel is by now critical commonplace;[39] that the fate of his hero and of his hero's manuscript is in many ways a fictionalization—even up to the point of that manuscript's secret vitality after its author's death—of Bulgakov's life with and through his novel has been corroborated by Marietta Chudakova's seminal research and commented on elsewhere as well.[40] Thus, with its deep interest in questions of good and evil (à la Tolstoy and Dostoevsky) meshed with an exceedingly complex structure (the baldly "realistic" inner text ramifying into a diabolically playful outer text suggests parallels not only with *Hamlet*'s play-within-the-play but also with Gide's *Les Faux-Monnayeurs* and several of Nabokov's novels), *The Master and*

[39] The fullest accounting of how, given the primary and secondary sources available to him, Bulgakov might have used the Gospel story is found in Zerkalov, *Evangelie*. The thematic parallels between the Gospel version of Jesus' life and *The Master and Margarita* are discussed in Beatie and Powell, "Story and Symbol." On Bulgakov's role as a writer in the Orthodox tradition, see Krasnov, "Khristos i master." The Faust connection is dealt with extensively in Stenbock-Fermor, "Bulgakov's *Master* and Goethe's *Faust*," while the function of the Goethe subtext—most notably its impact on characterization—in Bulgakov's larger text is given a fine analysis in Haber, "Mythic Structure."

[40] In her *Bulgakov* Proffer points out many of the details from the author's life that eventually made their way into his novel. Some of these include: his work as a master of ceremonies (*konferans'e*) at a small theater, the early pseudonym "Ivan Homeless," a cat named "Behemoth," and his burning of drafts of the novel (58, 62, 239, 316). Other good sources on the autobiographical nexus are Chudakova, "Tvorcheskaia istoriia"; Gasparov, "Iz nabliudenii"; and Lakshin, "Roman M. Bulgakova."

*Margarita* might legitimately be called the Soviet-Russian "modern" novel *par excellence*, an artistic first among a large group of artistically lackluster equals.

Attempts, some plausible and others less so, to define what kind of work Bulgakov wrote and what keys might underlie a successful reading of it have provided a lively, almost geometrically expanding forum for debate since the novel's appearance in the pages of *Moscow* in 1966–67. Whether a case can be made for some epithet *tout court*—Menippean satire, cryptotext for Stalinist Russia, comic epos, novel-myth, Gothic romance with a surrealist twist, gnostic allegory, or Bakhtinian carnival/medieval mystery play; whether Woland turns out to be primarily good or evil, the Master a Christ-like figure or an ally of Satan, Margarita the Russian incarnation of Gretchen, Faust, or both are all questions which defy neat solutions and which, as one critic has wryly pointed out, have come to be as slippery as the whereabouts of Woland and his retinue.[41] The best that has been written about *The Master and Margarita* has not failed to acknowledge its dimensionality, to argue for the necessity of its mystery and even its mystification,[42] and to proceed on the assumption that somewhere, somehow, it achieves a state of homeostatic balance and release, of "opposites coming in place."[43] Offering yet another reading of the text and focusing on the Book of Revelation, one of its most potent sources, the following analysis will investigate the novel's apocalyptic imagery, most notably that of the rider and the horse. Through an extended examination of this symbol cluster and the author's deliberate shaping of it toward the final haunting chapters we might come closer to an understanding of those themes—history and imagination, retributive and redemptive justice, religious and artistic mystery— that generate the elusive meaning of *The Master and Margarita*.

Although *The Master and Margarita* has been called "an apocalyptic fiction, one whose referential focus is, within its defined context, 'the end of all things' " (Beatie and Powell, "Story and Symbol" 237), relatively little has been said beyond this.[44] Only Edward Ericson has ventured further than

---

[41] See Haber, "Mythic Structure" 384. The various epithets for the novel listed here are found, respectively, in Proffer, "Genre and Motif" 616ff.; Lakshin, "Roman M. Bulgakova" 286; Gasparov, "Iz nabliudenii" 198ff.; Prizel, "The True Absolute" 110ff.; Krugovoi, "Gnosticheskii roman" 48ff.; and Milne, *Comedy of Victory* 2ff. The numerous attempts to see the novel as cryptotext for Stalinist Russia include Kovac, "The Problem"; Mahlow, *Text as Cipher*; Piper, "An Approach"; and Rzhevskii, "Pilatov grekh."

[42] On Bulgakov's intentional use of mystification as a narrative device, see, e.g., Kejna-Sharratt, "Narrative Techniques."

[43] As Irving Howe once remarked (*Harper's* [January, 1968] 71), "*The Master and Margarita* is a very difficult book. . . . It is as if all the pieces of the puzzle were there, but the pattern has not yet become visible."

[44] See Ericson, "The Satanic Incarnation" 35–36; Gasparov, "Iz nabliudenii" 218–19, 224;

casual allusion to claim, in the closing of his article, that "the ending of the novel is an elaborate parody of the last book in the Bible, the Apocalypse of St. John" (Ericson, "The Satanic Incarnation" 35–36). As we have already demonstrated, there need be no doubt of Bulgakov's knowledge of the text of Revelation and of his willingness to use that text as an artistic point of departure.[45] Furthermore, it has been argued that from the beginning of his career Bulgakov associated the horseman or knight (*vsadnik*)[46] with ideas of eternal judgment, the burden of conscience, and the futility of atonement. By the time he began work on *The Master and Margarita* in 1928 he had apparently discovered equine traits in his Satan, as indicated in several early variants of the title—"The Hoof of the Engineer," "The Consultant with a Hoof," "The Juggler with a Hoof," and "The Horseshoe of the Foreigner"—as well as a rich semantic field for further development.[47] What remains to be shown is how text and image are telescoped in the novel's form and composition. To this end we might best proceed from the explicit to the implicit, from the Yershalaim chapters, where horses and horsemen are an obvious and not unexpected feature of the setting, to the Moscow chapters, where horses and horsemen are much less obvious and more un-

---

Krugovoi, "Gnosticheskii roman" 60–61; Leatherbarrow, "The Devil" 42–43; and Wright, "Satan in Moscow" 1164, 1167–68. In the final chapter ("The Apocalypse") of an as yet unpublished manuscript, Ericson moves beyond his earlier reference to the role of the Apocalypse in *The Master and Margarita*, uncovering a number of thematic parallels between key passages in Revelation and the final chapters of Bulgakov's novel. The reader should again be reminded that at some level Bulgakov's interest in the Apocalypse was a natural extension of his upbringing. His father feared that the "materialists"—that is, those representing false enlightenment (cf. the novel's Berlioz)—would gain the upper hand in his country's struggle for spiritual values and declared: "With the spreading of such a view in the human race the death of people and the end of the world must come" (from the article "The Church and its Relation to Progress"; cited in Haber, "The Lamp" 346). This sounds very much like the Dostoevsky of the period of *The Idiot* who, like Bulgakov's father, owed much to the Slavophiles. See Haber, "The Lamp" 345–46.

[45] See earlier discussion in this chapter as well as Milne, *Comedy* 9–12, 26; Chudakova, "A Vital Necessity"; and Krugovoi, "Gnosticheskii roman."

[46] Piper ("An Approach" 157) sees the Master in chivalrous terms, as "an important knight in an age-old battle, whose role . . . is to assert spiritual values in the teeth of and because of an evil whose existence he knows full well." Here the traits, such as idealism and love of beauty, of the romantic knight (*rytsar'*) should not be confused with those of the rider (*vsadnik*). For Bulgakov, the rider is not a benign figure, but one (such as Pilate) associated with the ideas of guilt and death. On the function of the rider in the context of first century Judea, see Zerkalov, *Evangelie* 22.

[47] See Chudakova, "Tvorcheskaia istoriia" 219, 225, 233, 237. It might be argued, of course, that the "hoof" in these variant titles refers to the *cloven* hoof of Satan, and therefore an equine allusion should be ruled out. But the "horseshoe" in the fourth variant suggests that indeed Bulgakov was linking, rather than trying to keep distinct, Satan and the image of the horse.

expected, and finally to the concluding chapters, where the Yershalaim and Moscow subplots coalesce and the idea of the apocalyptic horse and rider is embodied most fully.

Bulgakov's picture of Jerusalem, or Yershalaim as it is called by its Aramaic name in the novel, is dominated from the outset by implacable sunlight, the sharp blade of legality, and Roman military might. Everything in the Yershalaim chapters (2, 16, 25, 26) appears to have a realistic motivation, with the implication that Bulgakov intended to strip away any mythic coloration from his utterly verisimilar account of the trial and sentencing of Yeshua (the "historical" Jesus: on the ancient sources, see Zerkalov, *Evangelie*, and Èl'baum, *Analiz*). Here Pilate is the cynosure; the exchange with Yeshua is seen through his eyes, for it is he who stands in judgment over this earthly court. It should thus come as no surprise that Pilate, as an extension of the Roman state and its temporal power, is given the attributes of a *cavalryman*[48]—after all, by the time of Christ horses had been an important element of strategic warfare for centuries. But even here Bulgakov's equine and equestrian allusions are so marked as to suggest the presence of some other code or subtext. Pilate walks with a cavalryman's gait; he is repeatedly referred to as a horseman (*vsadnik*: his most awesome title is "vsadnik Zolotoe Kop'e"—"Rider of the Golden Spear");[49] and he observes with pained interest a Syrian cavalry ala speeding to Bald Mountain (Golgotha) moments after he has read the death sentence.[50] Thoughts of simply hanging Yeshua and being done with him are accompanied by distressed looks at the sun, "which [is] relentlessly rising over the equestrian statues of the hippodrome" (33/24). When Pilate vehemently denies Yeshua's claim that the kingdom of truth will come, he does so with a thunderous voice like the one in which he once commanded his horsemen to "Slash them [the Germans]! Slash them!" (42/31) during a battle in the Valley of Maidens. In his feelings of wrathful impotence before Caiaphas (here Bulgakov follows the Gospel of John by having Pilate, who wishes to save Yeshua, yield unwillingly to the legal pressure of the High Priest and the Sanhedrin),[51] Pilate imagines his revenge in terms of a flood of Arab horsemen bringing "bitter

---

[48] Èl'baum (*Analiz* 58) indicates that Judaean procurators were always selected from among cavalrymen (the *ordo equester*).

[49] Mikhail Bulgakov, *Master i Margarita* (Frankfurt/Main: Possev) 64. This Russian language text is used throughout the remainder of the chapter. The translation, emended where necessary for precision, is Bulgakov, *The Master and Margarita*, trans. Mirra Ginsburg (New York: Grove, 1967). References to the Russian text will be separated from those of the translation by a slash: e.g., 64/37.

[50] Compare this mention of Bald Mountain to that in *The White Guard* 60/63–64.

[51] On the precise political and juridical role of the High Priest and the Sanhedrin during the time of Christ, see Zerkalov, *Evangelie* 11–23.

weeping and moans" (49/38) to the streets of the Holy City. And as Pilate emerges from the Palace of Herod the Great to preside over the sentencing, he again notices the equestrian statues over the hippodrome, then hears, en route back to the palace, hoofbeats announcing the approaching ala and shouts of children (from a street leading onto the Square of the Hippodrome) to "Look out [for the horsemen]!" (54/43).[52] The last image passing before Pilate's eyes as he leaves the gabbatha is that of a lone cavalryman who, bringing up the rear, "gallop[s] past . . . with a trumpet on his back, flaming in the sun" (55/43).

The execution of Yeshua takes place in the next Yershalaim chapter (16) and is also pervaded—or perhaps, more appropriately for what follows, "encircled" or "surrounded"—by images of the horse and rider. The first sentence of this chapter, marked by being a separate paragraph as well, makes pointed reference to the double cordon (one made up of cavalry) surrounding the place of execution: "The sun was already setting over Bald Mountain, and the mountain was encircled [otseplena] by a double cordon [otseplenie]" (217/182). There follows a detailed description of the ala and its route to Bald Mountain. Those charged with overseeing the execution, including the Centurion Mark, the chief of the palace guard, and Afranius,[53] the chief of the secret police, are distinguished by arriving at their destination on horseback (the century, on the other hand, which Mark commands arrives on foot). Scattered throughout the chapter are other references to the cavalrymen, the ala, the grooms, and their horses. Matthu Levi understands that the "joyful ending" (Yeshua's death) is near at hand by noticing the sudden activity of the grooms and horses preparing to depart. And when the cordon is broken after Yeshua's death and a massive storm breaks over Bald Mountain, we watch through a shroud of water as the cavalry (now the Russian konnitsa rather than the borrowed kavaleriia) rides back to Yershalaim.

The reader already alerted to the "magnetized" images of horse and rider cannot help but see the last two Yershalaim chapters (especially "Burial" [26]), as straining the stays of Bulgakov's carefully wrought verisimilitude. This is not to say that the author's design is somehow flawed (for the careful reader feels from the start that there is something more beneath the laconic and muscular surface of this realism), but only that the tenacious presence of the imagery cannot be accounted for merely in terms of realistic motivation. Chapter 25 opens with still another sinister allusion (among others) to the hippodrome. By now we should begin asking ourselves about the

[52] Since the same verb is used in both instances, this warning anticipates the "Beware of the tram!" sign that flashes before Berlioz moments prior to his death. See discussion below.

[53] For a fine discussion of the problematical character of Afranius, see Pope, "Ambiguity and Meaning."

historical existence of this hippodrome. Why is it constantly in the background? What meaning can it have for Pilate and his story? That the execution is over and Afranius has arrived is signaled to Pilate (as the arrival of the "joyful ending" was earlier signaled to Matthu Levi) by the movement of horses: "Now, breaking through the tapping of the thinning rain, the faint sounds of trumpets and the clattering of several hundred hooves reached the Procurator's ears" (380/314–15). Pilate and Afranius then plot, in a bravura performance of Aesopian language, the murder of Iuda (Judas).[54] At this point Bulgakov's deviation from the Gospels is most significant: rather than have Iuda kill himself, he has him killed by Afranius and his henchmen. Pilate, the avenging horseman, and Afranius, his agent, seek out their prey in a virtual flurry of equine and equestrian imagery. Afranius sends horsemen to see to the burial of Yeshua and the others; he then disguises himself by wearing an old chiton and riding a mule into the city (an ironic allusion to the Gospel's triumphant Christ?), where he meets Niza, his double-agent and Iuda's lover, and sets the trap for Iuda; after that he disappears into a stream of pedestrians and riders. In his eagerness to get to his rendezvous with Niza, Iuda curses a mounted patrol that has momentarily blocked his passage. And after Iuda is murdered, Afranius changes back into his genuine costume in a passage full of marked imagery and allusive perhaps of Christ's legendary entry (thus the earlier mention of the mule) into Jerusalem.

The retributive horseman, at least at this stage of the text, has totally superseded the Prince of Peace:

> No one knows where Yehudah's two assassins went, but the path of the third man in the cowl is known. Leaving the road, he walked into the thick of the olive grove, making his way south. He climbed over the fence far from the main gate, in the southern corner, where the upper stones had fallen out. Soon he was on the bank of the Kidron. He entered the water and waded for a time, until he saw in the distance the silhouettes of two *horses* and a man. The *horses* were also standing in the stream. The water washed around their *hooves*.[55] The *groom* [konovod] mounted one, the cowled man leaped upon the other, and the two slowly walked through the water, the stones crunching under the *horses' hooves*. Then the *riders* left the stream, came out on the Yershalayim bank and continued at a slow pace along the city wall. Here the *groom* separated, galloped ahead and disappeared. The cowled man stopped his *horse*, dismounted on the deserted road, slipped off

[54] Pope ("Ambiguity and Meaning" 6–10) is especially good on this.

[55] Just as these sinister horses have their hooves washed after the murder of Iuda, so did Pilate the rider earlier gesture as though washing his hands in anticipation of the execution of Yeshua (43/32). Nearly identical verb forms are used in both cases: *obmyvat'*, *omyvat'*.

his cloak and turned it inside out. From under the cloak he took out a flat helmet without feathers and put it on. Now the *horse* was mounted by a man in a military chlamys with a short sword at his hip. He touched the reins, and the *spirited cavalry horse* went at a trot, shaking the *rider*. The road was short—the *rider* was approaching the southern gate of Yershalayim.

Under the archway of the gate the restless flames of torches leaped and danced. The patrol of the second century of the Lightning-Swift Legion sat on stone benches, playing dice. Seeing the *military rider*, the soldiers jumped up. He waved to them and entered the city (400–401/332–33; my emphasis).

What should becoming clear by now is the symbolically charged role of Pilate: both as "Rider of the Golden Spear" responsible for the execution of Yeshua and as mastermind who uses Afranius (the imposing "military rider" on the "spirited cavalry horse") to murder Iuda, he stands at the center of this punishing, deadly serious horseplay. He is the judge; his verdict in both cases is death; and his method of carrying out these executions is marked by images of horse and rider. But this is only half, the most obvious half, of Bulgakov's design. How does the text of Revelation and its notion of secular history combine with Bulgakov's depiction of Pilate as the avenging horseman?

First of all, Bulgakov sets the stage for subtextual interplay by introducing motifs from the Book of Revelation into the Yershalaim chapters, usually in connection with Pilate's perception of the hateful city. These include the repeated image of the catastrophic storm (to spill over into the Moscow chapters), that of the abyss over which the city, like the "Whore of Babylon," seems to hang, that of destruction by demonic fire, and that of the ominous Temple, with its roof covered by dragon-like scales and its pair of five-point candelabras recalling the dragon and the beast of ten horns (Revelation 13:1, 4; 17:3, 7, 12, 16).[56] As particularly noteworthy in this context we might cite the opening passage of Chapter 25 ("How the Procurator tried to save Iuda of Kerioth"):

The darkness which had come from the Mediterranean shrouded the city hated by the Procurator. The hanging bridges connecting the Temple with Anthony's dreaded tower disappeared. The abyss that had descended from the heavens engulfed the winged gods over the Hippodrome, the crenellated Hasmonaean Palace, the bazaars, the

[56] The English text of the Bible used throughout this chapter is *The New Oxford Annotated Bible with the Apocrypha*, eds. Herbert G. May and Bruce M. Metzger (New York: Oxford, 1977). It has been checked against the following Russian text: *Bibliia ili knigi sviashchennago pisaniia vetkhago i novago zaveta* [The Bible] (Valley Forge: Judson, 1964).

caravansaries, the alleys, ponds . . . The great city of Yershalayim had
vanished as though it had never been. Everything was swallowed by
darkness that threw fear into every living heart in Yershalayim. . . .

   With its belly, [the storm cloud] had already covered the Bald Skull,
where the executioners were hastily piercing the hearts of the victims;
its weight fell on the Temple in Yershalayim; it crept down the hill in
smoking streams and flooded the Lower City. It poured into the windows and drove the people from the crooked streets into the
houses. . . . Whenever the black steamy mass was ripped by fire, the
great bulk of the Temple with its glittering scaly roof would fly up from
the solid murk. But the fire would go out in an instant, and the Temple
would sink back into a dark abyss. Over and over, it rose and dropped
again, and every disappearance was attended by the crashing of catastrophe (378/312–13).

To anticipate a little, while everything here is given the expected realistic
motivation (the storm), this cluster of apocalyptic motifs will be carried over
into the Moscow chapters and given a largely fantastic (Woland-instigated)
motivation.

   It is not difficult to see that the wrath of the storm falls chiefly on the
Temple, in Bulgakov's rendering the seat of Old Testament morality, retributive rather than redemptive justice, and of satanic literalism. As critics
have noted, Pilate is, for the most part, a sympathetic figure caught on the
horns of a dilemma, trapped by the letter of the law. Neither Yeshua's nor
Iuda's death brings him satisfaction, since he knows, all too painfully, that
the law in the first case is driving an innocent (and to Pilate most appealing)
man to his death and that his personal code of vengeance in the second case
is poor compensation—it cannot bring Yeshua back to life. Thus Pilate is a
tool of a system or intelligence (Roman and Jewish law) larger than himself,
just as the Satan of Revelation is a deadly force whose acts, though apparently self-motivated, actually fulfill a larger divine dispensation. Perhaps it
is in this respect that Pilate might be seen as Satan's deputy in a setting
overlaid with the gathering presence of the Antichrist. Pilate, like Satan, is
empowered to punish, but retribution alone cannot generate a genuine solution: so death in the Yershalaim chapters is relentlessly associated with
endings that refuse to become beginnings. If the horsemen of Revelation
bring destruction and judgment all according to divine plan, then some
other agency (that of the Lamb) is needed to bring forgiveness and redemp-
tion.

   More than one commentator has suggested that by the final chapters of
*The Master and Margarita* the image of the closed circle develops into a

significant element of the novel's structural integrity.[57] Yet the circle is not for Bulgakov necessarily benign, and if the ending in fact does somehow return to the beginning, it is an ending which stresses *change through continuity*, not the tracks of futile, predictable motion. This becomes more obvious when we consider the negative images of circular confinement in the Yershalaim chapters. When Pilate rages at Caiaphas, "What are you saying, High Priest? Who can hear us now in this place [the palace garden]? . . . The garden is cordoned off [*otseplen*], the palace is cordoned off [*otseplen*], so that not even a mouse could slip through a crack" (48/37), he uses the same verb form, the same image of a closed chain [*tsep'*], that will later appear several times to describe the execution of Yeshua and the setting of Bald Mountain, with its double ring of horsemen and cavalry.[58] Birds describe circles in the air over the dying Yeshua. And the cavalry ala, returning from the site of the execution, crosses the same square (of the hippodrome?) as it did in the morning, thereby completing the circle of its deadly day's work.

Here it might be fitting to recall the hippodrome and the metaphor of the horserace, to become in the Moscow chapters central to the spirit of their dizzying play. Needless to say, there is no place for the pure entertainment of a horserace in the serious atmosphere of the Yershalaim chapters. Bulgakov may have moved the description of the Moscow hippodrome, which he certainly knew well, into Yershalaim in order to suggest an absurdly finite model for Pilate's view of history; the sources—especially Brokgauz-Èfron—make scant mention of such a hippodrome and offer no clues to its appearance.[59] Bulgakov is perhaps saying that the goals of the "realist" or "materialist," of one who denies the realm of the spirit and acts only to guarantee success and security in this world, are nothing more than a race around the track of history's hippodrome. These goals lead inevitably back to the reality of death. However clever and ruthless Pilate is as a horseman,

---

[57] See, e.g., Beaujour, "The Uses of Witches" 695, 706–7; and Delaney, "The Reach" 99.

[58] The double cordon is also mentioned earlier in the chapter "Pontius Pilate" (44/33). It is of course Pilate who gives the order to form the cordon around Bald Mountain.

[59] The equestrian statues atop the hippodrome have, as far as I know, no basis in any historical description of ancient Jerusalem and must have been added by Bulgakov from his knowledge of the Moscow hippodrome, which was indeed (and still is) adorned with such statues. Josephus, a primary source for anyone doing research on ancient Jerusalem, makes only passing reference to the hippodrome: in *The Jewish Wars*, he says that during an insurrection of the Jews in 4 B.C. one of their camps was located to the south of the city, near the hippodrome. The only other mention of the hippodrome, in *The Jewish Antiquities*, is likewise uninformative. One of Bulgakov's leading sources, Brokgauz-Èfron (*Entsiklopedicheskii slovar'* XIII: 652–58), tells us merely that "During the reign of Herod the Great, Jerusalem again entered a period of flowering and became adorned with magnificent buildings (a theater, amphitheater, and *perhaps even a hippodrome*)" (657; emphasis added).

he can never break the chain of his personal history. As Aristotle states in the *Metaphysics*, history at any given moment is an infinite series of possibilities, only one of which can be actualized in the next moment. It is poetry's function—as he states further in the *Poetics*—to describe the possibilities that history in its inexorability has left out. Hovering with its equestrian statues at the edge of Pilate's thoughts, the hippodrome is Bulgakov's objective correlative for this idea of tragic inexorability: as the present unfolds, Pilate sees a future full of rich possibility (his walks with the wandering philosopher) retreating into a finite, guilt-ridden past that will, ironically, continue to haunt him forever.

To sum up our findings thus far, we have shown that Pilate's chief function as apocalyptic horseman is to bring judgment (both on others and, equally important, on himself) and death to Yershalaim. He incorporates not only features of the Four Horsemen and the locust-like horses whose king is Abaddon (Revelation 9:7–11),[60] but also those of the avenging Lamb—the magnificent field marshal, mounted on white steed and clad in white robe dripped in blood,[61] who has come to lead his heavenly cavalry against the troops of Satan (Revelation 19:11–16). Here as elsewhere, Bulgakov's view of Revelation does not appear to be canonical: he is willing to deviate from, or "polemicize" with, this subtext as he sees fit, reinterpreting its basic message within the philosophic and aesthetic requirements of his, the larger, text. His Christ figures, Yeshua and the Master, are much less avengers than forgivers. In this light, the meaning of one of Bulgakov's most puzzling apocryphal strokes becomes clear: Yeshua, the historical Jesus, denies any basis for the legend that he entered Yershalaim riding on an ass—"I have no ass, Hegemon. . . . It is true that I came to Yershalayim through the Susa Gate, but *I came on foot*" (37/26; my emphasis). Apparently Bulgakov chose to transfer the role of retributive horseman away from the Lamb entirely, making Pilate, the fifth procurator (when he should traditionally be the sixth), the fifth horseman as well (Krugovoi, "Gnosticheskii roman" 56–57).

Before turning to the Moscow chapters, a final element of Bulgakov's anagogic design for the Pilate story deserves special mention. This is his use of paronomasia, his broad deployment (a "cavalry," as it were) of words that suggest the presence of the apocalyptic horse and rider not only semantically, but on the basis of sound association.[62] Here his phonetic force-field

---

[60] There is also an Abaddon who shows up in the chapter "By Candlelight" (329/274–75).

[61] Pilate's cloak has a blood-red lining as well. See Gasparov, "Iz nabliudenii" 204, n.3.

[62] Although sound play is, to be sure, not so immediately obvious in *The Master and Margarita*, it is in *The White Guard* (see discussion above), where the presence of Bely's *Petersburg* as a model seems indisputable. My analysis of the sound patterns in *The Master and Margarita* that follows should not be read in isolation from related semantic, thematic, and structural

is polarized around two roots—*kon-'* ("horse") and *sad* ("garden," which with its primary meaning of seating or planting serves as the etymological basis for "rider"—"*vsadnik*"). Bulgakov's application of these roots and their phonetic echoes at vital points in the text seems too dense to be fortuitous. Thus, in the first Yershalaim chapter ("Pontius Pilate"), beyond the already mentioned incidence of "pure" horse and rider vocabulary ("*konnye statui*"—"equine statues" [2x], "*konnitsa*"—"horse troops" [1x], "*konskii topot*"—"hoofbeats" [1x], "*vsadnik*"—"rider" [4x]), we find a remarkable incidence of *sad* (23x) and of words, such as "*balkon*" ("balcony") (14x)[63] and "*konvoi*" ("convoy") (12x), that, while unrelated etymologically, serve as phonetic stand-ins for the original. Often, almost in a litany, the "*balkon*" or "*konvoi*" and the *sad* (the cryptogram for horse and rider) appear in the same sentence or in close proximity: "Prokuratoru kazalos', chto rozovyi zapakh istochaiut . . . pal'my v *sadu*, chto k zapakhu . . . pota ot *konvoia* primeshivaetsia prokliataia rozovaia struia" ("It seemed to the Procurator that the . . . palms in the garden gave off the smell of roses, that the accursed smell of roses was mingled with the . . . convoy's sweat") (27/16); "I seichas zhe s ploshchadki *sada* pod kolonny na bal*kon* dvoe legionerov vveli . . . cheloveka let dvadtsati semi" ("Two legionaries immediately led in a man of about twenty-seven from the garden onto the balcony under the columns . . .") (28/18); "Prostuchali tiazhelye sapogi Marka . . . i slyshno bylo, kak vorkovali golubi na ploshchadke *sada* u bal*kona*" ("Mark's heavy boots clattered . . . and the cooing of pigeons in the garden near the balcony could be heard") (29/19); "Pilatu pokazalos', chto ischezli . . . kolonny bal*kona* i krovli . . . vdali, vnizu za *sad*om, i vse utonulo . . . v . . . zeleni kapreiskikh *sadov*" ("It seemed to Pilate that everything—the . . . columns of the balcony and the roofs in the distance below, beyond the garden—had disappeared, had drowned in the . . . greenery of Capreaen gardens") (39/28–29). And at one point Pilate's anguish at being trapped, his sense, as it were, that horse and rider are con-

---

issues. My assumption is that a detailed discussion of the role of sound play is valid only if (1) the roots and sound clusters singled out are indeed *marked* vis-à-vis other possibilities, and (2) they are thematically significant. Furthermore, it could be argued that Bulgakov's use of *un-palatalized* roots in such words as "balkon" and "konvoi" makes the connection with the palatalized *kon'* root somewhat strained. Nevertheless, just as the palatalization is lost in some words having definite equine connotations (e.g., "konnye statui"—equine statues), so too does Bulgakov presumably play not with precise etymologies, but with phonetic echoes—sounds that are close but not necessarily exact. Thus "balkon" and "konvoi" are potentially significant aspects of the setting not because they are etymologically related to the equine motif, but because they are its proximate echoes or surrogates.

[63] Bulgakov was probably familiar with the following Russian riddle: "Na bal *koni* khodiat?" (Do/can horses go to balls?) "Da, na *balkone* khodiat" (Yes, people can walk/it is possible to walk on a balcony).

spiring against him to bring about Yeshua's execution, surfaces in an especially heavy volley of "*konvoi*"—"bal*kon*"—*sad*:

> Prokurator s nenavist'iu pochemu-to gliadel na sekretaria i *kon*-
> voi. . . . Tut Pilat vskrichal: —Vyvesti *konvoi* s bal*kona*! . . . *Konvoi*
> podnial kop'ia i, merno stucha podkovannymi kaligami, vyshel s bal-
> *kona* v *sad*, a za *konvoem* vyshel i sekretar'.

> (The Procurator for some reason looked at his secretary and the con-
> voy with hatred. . . . "Let the convoy leave the balcony!" he cried
> suddenly. . . . The convoy raised their spears and, clanking rhythmi-
> cally with their metal-shod sandals, walked out into the garden. The
> secretary followed [41/30]).[64]

But perhaps the most significant sound association, for this chapter and
those that follow, involves the noun "*konets*" ("ending") and verb "*kon-
chit'sia*" ("to end"), each of which unites the phonetic image of the horse
with the semantic link to tragic finality and death. At first it seems that the
kind Yeshua has cured Pilate's *physical* discomfort (" 'No mucheniia tvoi
seichas *kon*chatsia, golova proidet. . . . Nu vot, vse i *kon*chilos' " [" 'But
your sufferings will soon be over, your headache will pass. . . . Well, see,
now it's all over' "] [34/24]); however, when the procurator yields to his
cowardice and allows Yeshua to be executed, he suddenly realizes that with
this ending his *metaphysical* anguish has only begun ("Vse bylo *kon*cheno
. . . Ga-Notsri ukhodil navsegda" ["Everything was finished. . . . Ha-
Nozri was departing forever"] [47/35]).

Bulgakov's use of paronomasia remains in evidence throughout the Yershalaim chapters, and it would prove tedious to give full treatment to those
sound patterns here. Suffice it to say that the descriptions of the Palace of
Herod the Great, Pilate's praetorium and the seat of his retributive justice,
are particularly marked by the constant repetition of the "bal*kon*" + *sad*
combination.[65] What should also be noted, however, is the presence of the
paronomasia in those scenes, such as the execution of Yeshua and the murder of Iuda, that take place away from Pilate, but which, through Bulgakov's
"acoustic programming," attest to his (Pilate's) participation. Pilate's name
(from *pilatus*—"armed with a *pilum*," a Roman javelin) suggests the Latin
version of the Russian *kop'e*, which, along with the horse, is the procurator's most dreaded attribute ("Rider of the Golden Spear") and which (apoc-

---

[64] The "bal*kon*" + *sad* and "*konvoi*" + *sad* combinations appear numerous other times in
Chapter 2. See, for instance, 42/31, 45/33–34, 50/39, 55/43.

[65] In the three chapters that contain descriptions of Pilate's praetorium, *sad* appears forty-
four times and "bal*kon*" twenty-nine times.

ryphally, by the way)[66] serves as the instrument of death at the execution. Thus Pilate presides at the execution in absentia, through his factotum Afranius, who wears a *cowl*, traditional costume of the executioner;[67] through the idea of death as ending (*"konets"*); through (metonymically) his spear, which has replaced the reed and hyssop of the Gospels (see Mark 15:36 and John 19:29) and on *the end* of which is placed the sponge; and perhaps even through the verb of death itself (*"kol'nut'"*—to prick, stab).[68] Finally, the murder of Iuda—who curses the mounted (*"konnyi"*) patrol en route to his rendezvous with death, and who meets not Niza, but the henchmen of Afranius, himself soon to be transformed into a cavalry officer—is equally resonant with auto-suggestion. Iuda's passion for Niza and, ironically, his life are reaching an *end* (*"No vse konchaetsia"* ["But everything ends"] [398/330]) as he *finally* (*"nakonets"*) reaches the *Garden*[69] of Gethsemane, where he is cornered by Afranius' men, one of whom *plunges* (*vsadit'!*) a knife into the victim's heart, after which Afranius himself, the man in the cowl, emerges from the shadows.

The equine and equestrian imagery is not nearly so explicit as we proceed from the Yershalaim chapters to the outer text, and, on first reading, it could be easily overlooked against the background of farce and whimsy. Hence it should not seem curious that, of the many commentators who have traced parallels between Yershalaim and Moscow,[70] no one has sensed a link between Pilate the unwilling rider and a city of people *driven* by their satanic impulses. But as Gasparov points out, Moscow is a splintered, reduced version of Yershalaim. In effect the tragic Pilate becomes a mass of vulgarians (*poshliaki*), the ubiquitous horse a modern system of public conveyance, and the hippodrome of history, literally and figuratively, a circular, slapstick race around the streets of Moscow.

Leitmotifs provide the first clue to Bulgakov's shift in design from tragic to comic, from hippodrome as apocalyptic metaphor to horserace as pure entertainment. Koroviev wears a jockey's cap, which he raises while show-

---

[66] There is just one reference to a canonic spear (John 19:34), and it is not an instrument of death, since the soldier pierces Jesus' side only after he has died.

[67] Earlier Bulgakov unites in one sentence Pilate the horseman, the costume of the executioner, the image of an enclosed bald skull (Golgotha), and the *kon-'* echo: "Pilate threw a hood (*kapiushon*) over his balding head" (45/34).

[68] In the few pages (227–30/192–94) describing the death of Yeshua, "konets" ("end") occurs five times, "kop'e" ("spear") five times, and "kapiushon" ("cowl") four times.

[69] *Sad* is repeated four times in the scene of Iuda's murder (399–400/330–32).

[70] For the parallels between Yershalaim and Moscow, see, e.g., Beatie and Powell, "Story and Symbol" 220–23; Ericson, "The Satanic Incarnation" 25; Gasparov, "Iz nabliudenii" 215–21; Leatherbarrow, "The Devil" 31–33; Mahlow, *Text as Cipher*; Proffer, "On *The Master and Margarita*" 548–59; and Wright, "Satan in Moscow" 1170–71.

ing Berlioz the way to the tram (and to death);[71] Behemoth sports the whiskers of a cavalryman; as Woland and his helpers make their escape from Homeless, they are referred to as a "troika" (why, one might ask, has Bulgakov left out Azazello?). On the second floor of Griboedov House there hangs a poster depicting a rider, a balcony with palms (a motif borrowed from the Yershalaim chapters),[72] and an "inspired" young writer taking a seat with his pen (his *kop'e*?); on the first floor the vaulted—probably circular—roof of the restaurant seems alive with Assyrian (as opposed to Syrian) horses. Homeless is spirited off to Stravinsky's in a truck to the dismay of a coachman who, whipping the flanks of his horse, yells "You'd do better on a racehorse!" (85/72). The circus act of bicycle riders (also a "troika") that opens the performance at the Variety Theater is colored by equine imagery ("na dyby" [on hind legs], "s sedlom naverkhu" [with the seat/saddle above] [150/133]) and by fast motion in circles (here the metaphor of the circus and the horserace coalesce). The petrified Rimsky becomes in retreat from his haunted office a rider (*sedok* can be both a horseman and a passenger) who is jostled on his seat as he is borne by a speeding taxi along the "*Sadovoe kol'tso*" (ring road).[73] It is the mounted police, together with those on foot, that are sent to break up the line of ticket buyers gathered, on Sadovoe, outside the theater (recall the combination of cavalry and foot soldiers that forms the ring around the site of Yeshua's execution [Gasparov, "Iz nabliudenii" 219]). And the unfortunate boss of the branch office of the Commission on Spectacles obsessively organizes clubs, including an equestrian circle ("kruzhok verkhovoi ezdy"). Moreover, and most-convincing, Bulgakov has placed his centers of madcap activity (here of course Margarita's and the Master's apartments are important—and logical—exceptions) along the Sadovoe Ring Road: Berlioz' ill-starred apartment, the Variety Theater, and Griboedov House are all given precise locations on this street, and, indeed, Sadovoe is the most alluded to landmark in Moscow.[74] What emerges, as various Muscovites chase Woland or are chased by him, is an atmosphere of sheer "raciness."

---

[71] Other references to the jockey's cap appear on 12/4, 121/106.

[72] The balcony and the palms resurface in other Moscow chapters: "Schizophrenia, as Said Before" (90/77) and "Ivan Splits in Two" (148–49/132).

[73] In this same chapter a mustachioed (i.e., like Behemoth) coachman drives up on Sadovoe to one of the victims of the magic show, reins in his nag, and grins diabolically (192/170).

[74] Gasparov ("Iz nabliudenii" 222) places Griboedov House on Tverskoy Boulevard. Yet the opening description of the house sets it convincingly on a ring road (my assumption is this ring road is Sadovoe): "The old, two-story, cream-colored mansion was situated on a boulevard circle (na bul'varnom *kol'tse*) [and was set] deep within a run-down garden (*sada*), divided from the sidewalk of the circle (*kol'tsa*) by a wrought-iron fence" (71/59). Whether this boulevard is Sadovoe or not really makes no difference, however, since Bulgakov deliberately links the image of the circle and the garden (thus *Sadovoe kol'tso*) from the start. Both Berlioz's

The race, one might say, begins with Berlioz's death at Patriarchs' Ponds. Intriguingly, there is a Patriarchs' Pond (*Patriarshii prud*) on the map of contemporary Jerusalem—right below that of the ancient city—in the *Encyclopedic Dictionary* of Brokgauz-Èfron that Bulgakov used while researching the novel (652–58 [insert]). It is located slightly northeast of the original site of Herod's Palace, slightly southwest of the Church of the Holy Sepulchre (near Golgotha), and right off the gabbatha, that is, the raised outdoor platform from which the historical Jesus is reputed to have begun his *via dolorosa*.[75] The unknowing Berlioz, who has been interpreted as a false or parodic Jesus (Bolen "Theme and Coherence" 428–29), begins his death march from the point, now transferred to Moscow, where Yeshua began his. But difference here is as important as similarity—in keeping with the reduced stature of the Moscow characters, Berlioz has no imagination (the correlative of religious faith in the outer text),[76] and hence has no idea of where he is going. Koroviev points the way with his jockey's cap and the editor passes through the turnstile. Before him flashes the sign "Watch out for the tram," which, if he had a better memory and more imaginative empathy, would have reminded him of Pilate's warnings to Yeshua and Caiaphas and the children alerting the spectators to the passing cavalry ala (the same verb—*berech'sia*, "beware of, watch out for"—is used in all four instances). Still standing safely behind the barrier, Berlioz sees the tram make its turn and, in what must surely be Bulgakov's deliberate use of horseracing slang, "head down the straightaway/homestretch" (*vyidia na priamuiu*) and, now animate, "let out a howl and pick up the pace" (*vzvyl i naddal* [60/49]). When Berlioz finally slips onto the rails (the modern version of the racetrack) to be mutilated by this iron horse, one of his last sights

---

apartment (97/84) and the Variety Theater (131/116) are explicitly placed by Bulgakov on Sadovoe Ring Road. As mentioned, Sadovoe is by far the most often evoked geographical landmark in Moscow: of the sixteen Moscow chapters in Book 1, eleven make precise references to Sadovoe (often several times); in Chapter 1, for example, the sun (presumably of Berlioz's life) is setting beyond Sadovoe (11/3); in Chapters 3 and 4, it is Annushka "from Sadovoe" who is responsible for Berlioz's death (62/51); in Chapter 10, Varenukha is attacked by satanic forces in the *garden* of the Variety Theater and then spirited along Sadovoe to Likhodeev's apartment (142–44/126–28); and in Chapter 14, Rimsky escapes the same forces by catching a taxi and rushing away, again along Sadovoe, from the theater (201/178).

[75] Brokgauz-Èfron XIII: 657. For maps of ancient Jerusalem during the reign of Herod the Great, see ibid. 652–58 (insert); *The Oxford Annotated Bible*, map 9 (insert); Shepherd, *Historical Atlas* 7; and Wilkinson, *Jerusalem as Jesus Knew It* 137–42, 145. There is a medieval tradition that has Jesus begin his *via dolorosa* from the Antonia at the northwest corner of the Temple area, but Bulgakov, following Brokgauz-Efron (657), has his historical Jesus begin from the gabbatha, the raised outdoor platform adjoining the Palace of Herod the Great. This means that Yeshua and the other prisoners are led out of the western gate of the city onto the Jaffa Road (see 217/182) and then in an arc northwest to Bald Mountain (Golgotha).

[76] On Berlioz's sin, see Makarovskaia and Zhuk, "O romane M. Bulgakova" 166–67.

is that of the female tram driver (the parodic horseman) furiously tugging at the brake handle (the reins) as the tram "[digs] its nose into the ground" and "[leaps] up momentarily" (61/49).

Throughout the novel's first book (Chapters 1–18) the race assumes a primarily frenetic, chaotic character. In the slapstick scenes, Woland waves the same magic wand of paronomasia that we noted in the inner text, with familiar leitmotifs, such as the balcony and garden,[77] now coming into play with new ones, such as "*konsul'tant*" ("consultant"), "*kontrakt*" ("contract"), and "*kontramarka*" ("complimentary ticket"),[78] that hide telltale signs of Satan's foreignness, his duplicity as a contractual partner, and his secret identity as chief of these festivities ("*konferans'e*"). Homeless is the first to chase the perfidious consultant, and his conversation with the doctor at Stravinsky's shows how his language constantly entangles him in Woland's snares:

—*Kon*sul'tanta ia lovliu,—otvetil Ivan Nikolaevich i trevozhno oglianulsia.

—Kakogo *kon*sul'tanta? [. . .]

—On ego [Berlioza] narochno pod tramvai pristroil! [. . .]

—A kto-nibud', krome vas, videl ètogo *kon*sul'tanta?

—To-to i beda, chto tol'ko ia i Berlioz. [. . .]

—A *ikon*ka zachem?

—Nu da, *ikon*ka . . . —Ivan pokrasnel.

—*Ikon*ka-to bol'she vsego ikh i ispugala. [. . .] No delo v tom, chto on, *kon*sul'tant, on [. . .] s nechistoi siloi znaetsia . . . i tak prosto ego ne poimaesh'. [. . .] Da-s, znaetsia! Tut fact bespovorotnyi. On lichno s Pontiem Pilatom razgovarival. [. . .] Vse videl, i bal*kon* i pal'my. [. . .] (89–90)

("I'm trying to catch the consultant," answered Ivan Nikolayevich and looked around anxiously.

"What consultant?" [. . .]

[77] The "*balkon*" + *sad* motifs show up in the following Moscow chapters of Book 1: 3 (57/45), 5 (71–72/59–60), 6 (90/77), 8 (110, 115/95, 100), 10 (131, 142, 144/116, 126, 128), 11 (149/132), 13 (168, 170, 171, 175, 180, 187, 188, 190/148, 150, 151, 155, 159, 166, 168), 14 (199/176–177), 15 (216/181), 17 (233/197).

[78] The words "*konsul'tant*," "*kontrakt*," "*kontramarka*," and "*konferans'e*" are especially marked in the early Moscow chapters and seem to be related to the chaos wrought by Woland and his band. Thus the "*konsul'tant*" might be said to be directly responsible for Homeless' schizophrenia (see 89–90/76–77), the "*kontrakt*" the undoing of Styopa Likhodeev (see 102–5/88–90), the "*kontrakt*" and "*kontramarka*" the bait for Nikanor Ivanovich (see 126, 130/110–11, 114), and the "*konferans'e*" one of the victims in Chapter 12 and the voice of conscience for Nikanor Ivanovich in Chapter 15.

"He [was the one who] deliberately got him [Berlioz] under a street-car!" [. . .]

"Did anyone else see this consultant?"

"That's the whole trouble—only Berlioz and myself." [. . .]

"And what is the little icon for?"

"Oh, yes, the icon . . ." Ivan blushed. "It was the icon that fright-ened them most of all. [. . .] But you see, the consultant, he's [. . .] in league with the Evil Spirit . . . and it's not so simple to catch him. [. . .] Oh, yes [. . .] he's in with them! This is an incontrovertible fact. He spoke personally with Pontius Pilate. [. . .] He saw everything—the balcony and the palms." [. . .] [76–77])

It would be a mistake, however, to claim that the entire outer text is governed by the atmosphere of a carnival carousel. As the fate of the Master and Margarita unfolds, and the romantic lovers—who meet as pedestrians and make every attempt to avoid the horserace whirling around them—are drawn into the disastrous present through the Master's novel about ancient history, the farce begins to take on weight and seriousness. Book I begins and ends with scenes of death, and the grotesque decapitation of Berlioz (Chapter 3) can be said to adumbrate, on a parodic level, both the figurative crucifixion of the Master's novel and his sanity by Moscow literary official-dom (Chapter 13) as well as the actual crucifixion of Yeshua in the inner text (Chapter 16: see Leatherbarrow, "The Devil" 32–33). These deaths give every appearance of being hopeless, of offering no new beginnings. As the Master, Homeless's mysterious guest from the balcony, explains, it was soon after the time when "[the novel about] Pilate was flying to its *end* ["*konets*"], and I already knew that the last words of it would be: 'The Fifth Procurator of Judea, the *horseman* [*vsadnik*] Pontius Pilate,' " (176/155), that his and Margarita's lives were shattered. Margarita had been reading the novel ceaselessly ("*bez konatsa*"); it had become her life and, in the ab-sence of children, a child born miraculously of the Master's imagination and her love. But it was "crucified" by the fearful establishment and, amid im-ages of the same apocalyptic storm that signaled the end of Yeshua's life, burned in a paroxysm of anguish by the half-mad Master.[79] "I came out into life with the novel in my hands, and that was *the end of my life* [moia zhizn' konchilas'] . . . That was my first encounter with the literary world, but now, *when everything is over* [kogda vse uzhe konchilos'] and my ruin is obvious, I recall it [the novel] with horror!" (181/160; emphasis added). The circle of history has repeated itself in the characters of the Master and Margarita; the senseless and at the same time inexorable punishment of

[79] The obvious allusion here to Gogol', Bulgakov's favorite writer, is mentioned in Gasparov ("Iz nabliudenii" 247).

Yeshua, the "good man," is repeated in the punishment of the Master, the genuine artist.

It is Maragarita, as almost everyone has remarked, with her unsponsored love and special energy (the Master's novel was read by her *bez kontsa*—"ceaselessly"), who must save the day. Book II opens onto a situation very similar to the one which earlier confronted Berlioz. Indeed, there are numerous parallels to suggest that Margarita is starting the race all over again: like Berlioz, she unwittingly summons the devil, only her Faustian gesture is distinguished by her belief ("Ia veruiu!"—"I believe!" [277/237]) in forces greater than herself; her flight to Woland's ball recalls Homeless's (another disciple's)[80] chase after the consultant; her swim in the river prior to the ball is a sort of mock baptism not unlike that experienced by Homeless in the Moscow River; and she must preside at Satan's Ball before the Master can be returned to her—just as Homeless must pass through Griboedov House, another festive hell,[81] before arriving at Stravinsky's and finally meeting the Master. This parallelism is reinforced when Margarita meets Azazello at the moment that Berlioz's funeral procession passes by. Their conversation takes place in Alexandrovsky *Garden*, across from the *Manège*, and begins with a mention of the procession, which is headed by a *mounted* policeman. Finally, the passage from the Master's novel (the one that, as a result of the fire, has "no beginning or no *end*") that Azazello uses to catch Margarita's attention is the same rich opening section, full of apocalyptic imagery and another reference to the hippodrome, of "How the Procurator tried to save Iuda of Kerioth" to which Margarita had returned, as to a holy relic, that same day.

Of all the characters that represent good faith either in a Christian or in an artistic sense (and for Bulgakov these two senses, as do the subplots in which we find them, eventually become one), Margarita alone is allowed to play havoc with the laws of time and space within her lifetime. She is the only victim who, through a satanic stroke of luck, is able to turn the tables on the victimizers. Not only does she become a witch; she becomes something more familiar:

> Margarita hung up [after speaking with Azazello], and in the next room something hobbled woodenly and began to bang on the door. Margarita flung the door open, and a broom, its bristles up, flew danc-

---

[80] See Beatie and Powell, "Story and Symbol" 227; Gasparov, "Iz nabliudenii" 209; Haber, "Mythic Structure" 400–1; and Wright, "Satan in Moscow" 1169. The most complete discussion of the character of Homeless is found in Hart, "*The Master and Margarita* as Creative Process" 169–78.

[81] See Bolen, "Theme and Coherence" 430; Gasparov, "Iz nabliudenii" 211–13; Haber, "Mythic Structure" 386–90; Krugovoi, "Gnosticheskii roman" 62; and Wright, "Satan in Moscow" 1166.

ing into the bedroom. With its end [*kontsom svoim*] it beat a tattoo on the floor, kicked and pulled toward the window. Margarita squealed for joy and jumped astride [*verkhom*] it. It was only now that the rider [*naezdnitsa*][82] remembered in a flash that in all the excitement she had forgotten to get dressed. She galloped [*galopom podskochila*] over to the bed and seized the first thing at hand—a pale-blue shift. Waving it like a banner, she flew out of the window (296/252).

Everything here bespeaks an equestrian pose, as if Bulgakov were taking pains to avoid confusing Margarita with a conventional witch. The equine broom even has a mane—its bristles are pointed upward, not downward, as we might expect. When Margarita flies out her bedroom window, then, she has suddenly taken charge, has become not only one of the judged, but one of the judges—in short, she has, on a parodic scale, become a retributive horseman. Her riding roughshod over the Judas-like Latunsky's apartment is confirmation of her new role. But since Margarita's most salient quality is forgiveness—and it is that quality which will ultimately undo what history's apocalyptic horseman has wrought—her damage is only material and her last act before leaving the Dramlit apartment house is to comfort a child frightened by her destruction.

Margarita wins her race against circular, unregenerate history. The clock is turned back, the Master is returned, and that should be enough for any happy ending. Even Bulgakov's playful signature, which seems up to now to have been signed for the most part in disappearing ink, suddenly catches the reader's eye in a flash of recognition—Woland crowns the good fortune of his winner with a horseshoe,[83] sign that the equine image has at last undergone a transformation to the good and auspicious. But that is not enough. Despite Woland's sleights-of-hand, the residue of the past cannot be entirely eliminated from the hero's reconstructed present. To achieve what they cannot have in this life, the hero and heroine must meet their own ending, their own death. And it is at this juncture in the text that Bulgakov chooses to leave the arena of history, both contemporary and ancient, and give full rein to his apocalyptic subtext. Having come full circle, he must now show how the circle is to be opened.

Chapters 30–32 contain not only one of the most "elaborate" (Ericson, "Satanic Incarnation" 36) but also one of the most *explicit* parodies of the Book of Revelation in Russian literature. This is the sort of elevating par-

[82] Natasha, Margarita's maid, is also described as a rider (*vsadnitsa*) (307–8/261). She, like her mistress, becomes a witch, mounts Nikolay Ivanovich, the neighbor turned porcine steed, and takes off for Satan's rout.

[83] Recall that in *Faust* Mephistopheles is often called the "cavalier of the horse's foot" (noted in Proffer, "On *The Master and Margarita*" 561, n.18).

ody, as Nabokov has remarked, that pays a tribute to its source and "always goes along with [the spirit of] genuine poetry" (*The Gift* 24)—not the sort, much in evidence in the Moscow chapters, that provides a "grotesque imitation" of the original (*Strong Opinions* 76). It also, of course, comes *at the end*. We know at once that we are in the presence of something serious by Bulgakov's shift to an elegiac tone, best represented in the beautiful, ghostly opening of Chapter 32:

> Gods, my gods! How sad the evening earth! How mysterious the mists over the bogs! Whoever has wandered in these mists, whoever has suffered deeply before death, whoever flew over this earth burdened beyond strength knows it. The weary one knows it. And he leaves without regret the mists of the earth, its swamps and rivers, and yields himself with an easy heart into the arms of death, knowing that it alone can soothe him.[84]

Bulgakov has cleared the stage for this race beyond history by leaving Moscow behind in mock apocalyptic ruin. Like Yershalaim before it, Moscow is the city of the devil, a getting-and-spending world of petty Judases, the fallen Whore of Babylon with her "merchants . . . grown rich with the wealth of her wantonness" (Revelation 18:3). The "temples" of satanic impulse—Berlioz's apartment,[85] Griboedov House, and *Torgsin* (a relative of the modern Beryozka store)—have all been burned to the ground:[86]

> She [the Whore of Babylon] shall be burned with fire . . . [and] when they [the kings of the earth] see the smoke of her burning, they will stand far off in fear of her torment, and say, 'Alas! Alas! thou great city, thou mighty city, Babylon! In one hour has thy judgment come' (Revelation 18:8–10).

And the cataclysmic storm that first announced the appearance of the Master to Ivan is given now, at the moment of the physical deaths of the lovers, its ultimate expression.[87] Last but not least, of all the misfortunes an angry God visits on humanity the only one conspicuously absent is the plague. Perhaps it is not too far-fetched to suggest that the elusive author has set in motion his tale about ultimate endings with the disaster-prone Annushka,

[84] This passage, argues Chudakova ("Tvorcheskaia istoriia" 252), is strongly autobiographical.

[85] The title of Chapter 27 is "The End [*Konets*] of Apartment 50."

[86] On the motif of fire, see Gasparov, "Iz nabliudenii" 222–29.

[87] Cf. Revelation 16:17–19: "The seventh angel poured his bowl into the air, and a loud voice came out of the temple, from the throne, saying, 'It is done!' And there were flashes of lightning, voices, peals of thunder, and a great earthquake such as had never been seen since men were on earth, so great was the earthquake."

alias "the plague" (*chuma*)? It is she, after all, who is the last mortal to see the Master and Margarita alive. With this apocalyptic manifold in place, the final destination of both Moscow and Yershalaim—the abyss that promises non-being and the utter insignificance of secular history—should come as no surprise.

The deaths in Chapter 30 of the Master and Margarita, arranged by Woland at the behest of (the now divine) Yeshua,[88] provide the precise moment at which the "hidden" horses in the text, both those whose presence might be too easily explained by the realistic setting of Yershalaim and those whose presence has been ingeniously masked in the swirling backdrop of contemporary Moscow, emerge to take on their genuine mythic dimensions. The seriousness of the inner text seems to have penetrated into the fantastic atmosphere of the outer text to produce a new and urgent lyricism adequate to the coming scenes of flight and freedom. The intuitive Margarita, who has been reading the same apocalyptic opening to Chapter 25, senses that a storm is on the way, but has no idea of what has caused it. Torn by the past and the knowledge of his permanent psychic debility, the Master has an attack of anxiety. Suddenly, Azazello appears with greetings from Woland and an invitation to an "outing" (*progulka*). After regaling their guest with cognac ("*koniak*"), the hosts drink Woland's gift, the poison Falernian wine that is a favorite of Pilate. (Thus Pilate the horseman, it might be said, executes not only Yeshua and Iuda, but the Master and Margarita as well.) In the pre-storm light the Master realizes immediately that his *end is approaching* ("nastaet *konets*" [464/375]). "What does this new state mean?" asks the now dead Master.

> "It means," replied Azazello, "that it is time for us to start. The storm is thundering already, do you hear? It is growing dark. The *horses* paw the earth, the little *garden* shivers. Say farewell, farewell, to your little basement flat" (466/376).

In a lovely touch, Bulgakov has made the thundering storm and the pawing horses one. Intoxicated by the lure of the open road, with the Master now in complete possession of his memory and his novel, the riders gallop off to meet Woland.[89] The chapter closes on the words of Homeless, suddenly turned prophetic as if the gift of imaginative empathy had been passed on to him by the Master after the latter's final visit: he uses the same verb ("*skonchat'sia*") to predict Margarita's end as that used by the nurse to inform him of the death of his neighbor.

[88] An earlier version has Matthu Levi visit Woland as a "violet horseman" (*fioletovyi vsadnik*) (Chudakova, "Tvorcheskaia istoriia" 238).

[89] Originally Margarita was to take off on a broom and the Master was to cling to Azazello's cloak (Chudakova, "Tvorcheskaia istoriia" 238).

As the group of riders leaves Moscow behind (in an earlier version Margarita's last gesture before departing is to save a child from the *balcony* of a burning house [Chudakova, "Tvorcheskaia istoriia" 238]), Woland, Behemoth, Koroviev, and Azazello are transformed into Bulgakov's version of the Four Horsemen of the Apocalypse.[90] Each former jester is now distinct in his somber grandeur, but it is Woland, the ultimate horseman, who is grandest of all:

> And finally, Woland himself was also flying in his true shape now. Margarita would have found it difficult to say what his horse's reins were made of. She thought they might be chains of moonlight, and the horse itself only a hulk of darkness, his mane a cloud, and the rider's spurs white blurs of stars (478/384–85).

The arrival of the horsemen at the site of Pilate's eternal torment brings us to the novel's mystifying climax. Chained Prometheus-like to the memory of his cowardice, Pilate has been reliving the immutable past for twelve thousand moons. It is time for the Master to finish his novel, to complete what he has left unresolved ("Your novel has been read . . . and the only comment on it is that, unfortunately, *it is not finished* [on . . . ne *okon*chen]" [479/385]). The Master is given the same opportunity to release Pilate that Pilate once had to release Yeshua (cf. 53/42). But the Master, urged by Margarita, is able to make the right choice, to break the chain of history, and thus to end his masterpiece ("Well, now you can finish [*kon*chit'] your novel in a single phrase!" [480/387]) with a gesture that augurs new beginnings. The forever immobile Pilate is now free to *walk* with the wandering philosopher along the lunar path toward the New Jerusalem (Revelation 21).[91] Maybe, says Woland, they will finally come to an agreement on something. The novel about Pilate finished, the Master and Margarita are rewarded with the eternal refuge and peace (*pokoi*) that neither they nor their author had in life. Interestingly, Woland suggests it is not fitting that the lovers return to historical Moscow, on the one hand, or follow after the liberated Pilate, on the other ("Why follow in the steps of that which is already finished [*kon*cheno]?" [481/387]). The reward they are to receive has somehow been specially marked for them. And so, Woland and his horsemen disappear, the couple dismount[92] and proceed—like Pilate—on foot to their idyllic resting place, and, to complete yet another circle,

---

[90] This of course makes Hella's absence logical. Beaujour ("The Use of Witches" 704, n.22) suggests, I think erroneously, that the witch's absence is carelessness on Bulgakov's part.

[91] Bulgakov considered the possibility of having Yeshua come to Pilate *on the balcony* (Chudakova, "Tvorcheskaia istoriia" 239).

[92] The couple was originally to gallop to their eternal refuge on horseback (Chudakova, "Tvorcheskaia istoriia" 247).

their story closes with the Master being released from his hero, the horseman Pontius Pilate, by his author just as he had released his hero from the burden of guilt.[93]

What is the meaning of this ending and how does it function alongside of, in dialogue with, the elaborate apocalyptic subtext? It would be a mistake, one suspects, to see this final moment as anything resembling an apocalypse of terrible judgment and retribution—that is, the Apocalypse of John. Pilate *deserves* punishment, yet the Master frees him.[94] The horses and horsemen symbolize physical death to be sure, but that death is no ending (as it is, for example, in the case of Berlioz). A great deal has been made of the fact that, in the divine hierarchy of things, the cowardly Master deserves the limbo of peace, while Yeshua and his executioner deserve the ascent into the light. Pilate, who joins the philosopher on the lunar path, has indeed suffered more than the other characters, but it does not *logically* follow that he is more worthy than the Master, his author. No, Bulgakov's unorthodox apocalyptic vision is finally benign and his horses and horsemen redemptive, at least inasmuch as death, the ultimate mystery, can be understood as a joyful opening into a state beyond history. The guiding intelligence here is not that, dominating Revelation, of the avenging Christ, but that of the merciful Lamb; for this reason Margarita's voice ("Let him go!") emerges as especially resonant. Hers is the voice of the compassionate Virgin,[95] nowhere to be found in the last book of the Bible.

There are, lest we forget, three distinct settings to suggest the rewards earned by the various characters. Homeless is left in Moscow, fated to remain a captive of history and to experience each year the return (that is, the circle) of his nightmare about Pilate. Pilate, history's relentless horseman, and Yeshua, the peripatetic "good man" whose faith in others has little or no historical justification, mount the path toward the New Jerusalem, to-

---

[93] Bulgakov here clearly links Pilate, Yeshua, the Master, and himself as ultimate author: Pilate had the chance to release Yeshua, but released Var-Ravvan (Barabas) instead ("The name of him who shall now, in your presence, be released [*otpustiat na svobodu*]" [53/42]); the Master, urged on by Margarita, is now able to release the captive Pilate (" 'Release him [*otpustite ego*]!' suddenly cried Margarita . . . The Master cupped his hands like a megaphone and shouted . . . : 'You are free! You are free! [*Svoboden! Svoboden!*]' " [480/386–87]); and finally Bulgakov releases the Master from the past and obsessive thoughts of his hero Pontius Pilate with the same phrase ("Someone released [*otpuskal na svobodu*] the Master as the Master had just released [*otpustil*] his hero" [482–83/omitted from the Ginsburg translation; emphasis added]).

[94] It must be pointed out, of course, that the essential difference between Pilate and the Master, both of whom have sinned out of cowardice, is that the former *has* expiated his crime, while the latter has not.

[95] " 'What is he [Pilate] saying?' asked Margarita, and her utterly calm face was clouded by compassion [*sostradanie*]" (479/386). For Margarita's link with the Virgin Mary, see Ericson, "Satanic Incarnation" 31–35.

ward a misty future where history is still infinite possibility, where they can at last "agree on something," where all can be well. Yeshua's concern is ethical—human perfectibility—and that is why, comforting Pilate, he continues up the path. But if Homeless is a victim of the past and Yeshua and Pilate have their sights on a vision of the distant future, where does this leave the Master and Margarita? They are left in a timeless present, a benign limbo that is both free from the pain of the past and the promise of the future, but from which, with the gift of imaginative empathy, the past can be recaptured and the future anticipated. Such a promised land for the artist cannot of course be imagined in this world, especially in the Soviet Union, but were it to exist, it would look like the little home, with its Venetian window and climbing vine, given to the Master and Margarita. Until God, the final author hovering beyond the final text, brings history and religious mystery together in this world, we must rely on Bulgakov's version of a *poeta ex machina* to make things right. With the New Jerusalem still distant, only art can free Pilate, write history from actuality back into possibility.

Yet Bulgakov, even now, is not quite finished. Like the Florensky of *Imaginaries in Geometry*, he posits a *coincidentia oppositorum*, closing, and simultaneously opening, a final circle. In the epilogue Ivan Nikolaevich (Homeless) and Nikolay Ivanovich come each spring to Margarita's *garden* to relive what has been irretrievably lost. The latter, once turned into Margarita's porcine steed, is a parodic mirror of the former (Gasparov, "Iz nabliudenii" 227), and chides himself for his faintheartedness—"What was I, an old ass [*osel*], afraid of?" (496/400) Homeless's predicament, however, is the more serious: he is haunted by a dream swarming with images of the noseless executioner, the dying Gestas, and the apocalyptic storm. Death is here in its tragic, inexorable character—Gestas is stabbed with the same spear that killed Yeshua. And, significantly, a merciful injection ("*ukol*") causes the nightmare to cease. The verb ("*kolot*/*kol*'nut' ") used to stab Gestas and Yeshua with Pilate's spear reappears in the noun whose prick releases Homeless and his lacerated ("*iskolotaia*") memory. What Bulgakov is suggesting, in this ending that *continues* what has already ended, is that Homeless, the faithful disciple, must undergo his own spiritual death each Easter season in order to be reborn, if only for an oneiric instant, into that state beyond history where the Master and Margarita now reside. Only at this point in the text, and *not* in the preceding chapter, does Yeshua swear to Pilate that the execution never happened. Suddenly we have returned to the vicious circle of history to discover how, through Homeless's experience of periodic death-in-life, the circle is to be opened. Homeless perceives that endings can be happy after all. As he asks the Master—

"So that is how it [the story of Pilate] *ended* [*konchilos'*]?"
"That's how it *ended* [*konchilos'*], my disciple . . ."

and as Margarita concludes—

"Yes, of course [*konechno*], that's how it did. Everything has *ended* [*konchilos'*], and everything *ends* [*konchaetsia*] . . . And I shall kiss you on the forehead and all will be with you as it should . . ." (498/ 402).

Little wonder, then, that Homeless wakes after his dream feeling calm and healthy. Together with the Master and Margarita, the author, the reader, and perhaps even Pilate himself, he can adjust, knowing that he is free of "the cruel fifth Procurator of Judea, the horseman Pontius Pilate," to this ending.

# FIVE

---

## *Doctor Zhivago*: The Revolution and the Red Crosse Knight

Then he mounted his faithful steed,
And began to trample the fierce serpent,
To trample it with his steed, to pierce it with his lance,
To say the following:
"Be tame, you fierce serpent!
Be quiet and calm like the beast of burden,
Like the beast of burden of the peasant."
—Russian folk poem

. . . We have a blood tie with the next world:
Who has ever been to Russia has beheld the next world
In this one.
—Marina Tsvetaeva,
*New Year's Greeting*

The example of Boris Pasternak and his famous novel provides a fitting conclusion to our study of the End in modern Russian fiction. Apocalypse, as we have said more than once, is by definition a space-time paradox: through the vivid logic of metaphor, its prophetic witness demonstrates, or tries to, that life has more than three dimensions and that what lies "beyond" can be glimpsed "within" history or brute biological time. The tension between "story" and "plot" in Pasternak's life and art, between the biographical "facts" that were often held hostage to historical necessity and the imaginative "artifacts" that served a higher dispensation, tells us that he understood the full import of this paradox. Indeed, Pasternak possessed the sort of "metapoeticizing" cast of mind that made the play with temporal and textual boundaries an indispensable element of his art. As he once wrote in *Safe Conduct* apropos of beginnings, middles, and ends, and of their relation to history and story:

[The reader] loves plots and terrors and looks at history [or story][1] as at a tale with an unending continuation. It is not known whether he

---

[1] In Russian the same word, *istoriia*, is used when describing both a "story" or anecdote and

wishes that it had a sensible ending. He is comfortable with those places beyond which his outings have not taken him. He is completely immersed in prefaces and introductions, while for me life *has been revealed* [my emphasis][2] only in those places where he is apt to sum up [*podvodit' itogi*]. It goes without saying that [despite] the internal division of history [that] is foisted on my understanding in the image of ineluctable death, I have returned to life in my own lifetime only in those instances when the tiresome hashing-over of parts [*varka chastei*] is concluded, and, having supped on the whole, a feeling, now fully fitted out, has torn itself free in all its imagined breadth (*Okhrannaia gramota* 205).

The writing of *Doctor Zhivago*, which progressed over decades and tumultuous shifts in the country's intellectual climate, encompassed periods of both hibernation and "returning to life." To an entire generation lulled into moral somnambulism[3] by the excesses of Stalinism, however, it became a cultural symbol of *life revealed*, of the feast "on the whole" after the tiresome "hashing-over of parts." As a lyrical poet of prodigious talent who felt that he was called upon, "out of respect for his epoch" ("O skromnosti i smelosti" 220), to write a work of epic prose,[4] and as an essentially private person who found himself, in the midst of the shrill civic-mindedness of the thirties, thrust into the unlikely role of Soviet poet laureate, Pasternak came to epitomize the plight of the *surviving* artist, the one severely tasked with disentangling the sprung logic of the no longer "new" Soviet state. If the "old," as of 1917, was decreed to be over, and the calendar of the "new" era had commenced, then where were the signs of genuine change? Or to pose the question in metaphorical terms familiar to readers of *Doctor Zhivago*, once the period of carnage and chaos had passed and life had been allowed to return to its accustomed "rails,"[5] when would the terminus in whose name the new tracks had been laid come into view?

---

a "history" (cf. the French *histoire* and the German *Geschichte*). The pun is obviously not lost on Pasternak here and elsewhere. See Fleishman, *Dvadtsatye gody* 204.

[2] *Otkrovenie* (Revelation), the last book of the Bible, has the same root in Russian as the verb "to open, disclose, reveal" (*otkryvat'*; "to be opened/disclosed"—*otkryvat'sia*).

[3] The connection between sleep/death and ethical compromise/fall is made often in *Doctor Zhivago*. See discussion below.

[4] See, e.g., Pasternak's letter of December 25, 1934 to his father: "Fortunately I am alive, my eyes are open, and now I am hastening to remake myself into a prose witer in the manner of Dickens, and then, if my strength holds out, into a poet in the manner of Pushkin. . . . I am naming these two to give you an idea of my internal change. I could say the same thing another way. I have become a part of my time and government [lit: 'state'—*gosudarstvo*], and its [i.e., the government's] interests have become mine" ("B. L. Pasternak. Pis'ma G. E. Sorokinu" 223–24).

[5] Using this same imagery, but at a different temporal remove, Pasternak speaks of the pre-

*Doctor Zhivago* is a logical destination for our narrative also because it recapitulates many of the issues with which we began and because it provides a compromise solution to the disjunction between history and story troubling the other post-revolutionary authors who give prominence to the apocalyptic theme (Platonov and Bulgakov). First of all, whether consciously or not, Pasternak plies the same categories of mythical thinking introduced into novel form by Dostoevsky in *The Idiot*.[6] In both novels, a feminine figure of great beauty and warmth (who is also in some sense a symbol of Russia the bride) experiences her "fall" into history, into time dominated by death, when she is seduced by an older predatory figure (Totsky, Komarovsky). This older sensualist type is associated with the bestial world, with the world *before* Christ (or the novelist's Christ-like surrogate), and with a Russia bought and sold in the capitalist marketplace. The seduction, reported elliptically as "pre-history" in *The Idiot* and as the necessary preliminary to Yury's appearance in Lara's life in *Doctor Zhivago*, serves to shatter the "before" of virginal purity and symmetry and to make the struggle for fallen humanity necessary in the first place. Thereafter, much of the remainder of the novel is given over to "the bride's" struggle to make a choice, *in time*, between the Christ-like figure (Myshkin, Yury)—who promises a spatio-temporal version of theodicy based on the possibility of real endings and beginnings—and the Antichrist-like figure (Rogozhin, Strelnikov)—who cannot forget or forgive the sins of the past (thus he is always trapped "in the middle"), and who, in response to the injustices of history, exacts punishment and retribution. Both Myshkin and Yury are noble yet socially feckless knight figures (the "knight of woeful countenance" and St. George, respectively); both Rogozhin and Strelnikov are metaphorically aligned with the cruel, inexorable, and "straightforward" movement of the train (iron horse)—that is, historical time without the guiding intelligence of God. It is telling that the fallen bride, appearing in a text written before the revolution and full of anxiety at its approach, opts for the groom as Antichrist in *The Idiot*, whereas the same figure, appearing in a text written after the revolution and keenly aware of the latter's "fibs and shallowness, . . . her unavoidable falseness" (Pasternak's letter of October 10, 1927 to Gorky in *Literaturnoe nasledstvo* 70: 297), opts for the groom as Christ and Redeemer in *Doctor Zhivago*. Against the image of

---

dicament of the artist's language in *Safe Conduct* as "shifting to the rails of epigonism" after the period of revolutionary innovation has passed.

  [6] "Probably the nearest counterpart to Yury Zhivago in the classical Russian novel is that suggested by Max Hayward ["Pasternak's 'Doctor Zhivago' " 43]—Prince Myshkin of Dostoevsky's *The Idiot*. Myshkin resembles Zhivago in not sharing the assumptions of other characters in the story; and again like Zhivago he proves incapable of taking his place in the society to which he belongs" (Gifford, *Pasternak* 182).

Nastasya Filippovna's immobile corpse in Dostoevsky (her ride is over, the terminus reached), is projected that of Lara, raised and chastened into a Mary Magdalene figure in Yury's poetry, which stands *outside* the narrative as a constant celebration of the Easter season. Dostoevsky's St. Petersburg, the city of the Antichrist, cannot separate itself from its past, and so is doomed by its inertia to reach its apocalyptic destination; Moscow, on the other hand, through its imitation of Christ's sacrifice and suffering, is shown in the last pages of *Doctor Zhivago* to be coming into its inheritance as the genuine Third Rome.[7]

Pasternak's novel, however, is more than a dialogue with Dostoevsky about Russia's role in the economy of salvation. Completed *after* the revolution, NEP, collectivization, the advent of Socialist Realism, the show trials and purges, World War II, and Stalin's death, this work betrays both a lyrical patina and a disinterested, almost "sublime" retrospectivism totally uncharacteristic of *The Idiot* and *Petersburg*.[8] Its simultaneous "lyricizing" and "ulteriorizing" of revolutionary events is precisely what generated so much initial debate over its flagrant lack of realistic motivation as *histoire politique*.[9] Isaac Deutscher's crude but not totally unfounded argument had

[7] "Thinking of this holy city and of the entire earth, of the still-living protagonists, and their children, they [Dudorov and Gordon] were filled with tenderness and peace, and they were enveloped by unheard of music of happiness that flowed all about them and into the distance. And the book [of Yury Zhivago's poetry] they held seemed to confirm and encourage their feeling" (Hayward 432/Michigan 531). For the purposes of this study the Hayward translation, modified where appropriate for clarity, will be used as the English text; page numbers will normally appear parenthetically and will be followed by the corresponding page numbers of the Michigan Russian language edition: (432/531).

Moscow, to be sure, never actually *becomes* in Pasternak's thinking the realized Third Rome, but rather is always and ever becoming it. Notice, however, the feeling of beatitude that does come *at the end* ("filled with tenderness and peace," "enveloped by unheard of music of happiness") and that is associated with the purifying power of suffering (the purges, the war) and with the message in *the Book* (which "confirm[s] and encourage[s] their feeling"). (On the Third Rome theme in *Doctor Zhivago*, see Lilly, "Moscow as City and Symbol" 249). In general, Pasternak had little interest in the future per se, but reckoned life and history from the vantage of the present: "The future is the worst of all abstractions. The future never comes in the form you expect. Or wouldn't it be truer to say that it never in fact comes at all? . . . Everything that really exists does so only within the framework of the present" (Gladkov, *Meetings* 60).

[8] As Gifford (*Pasternak* 178) suggests, Pasternak could not have written his novel *until after* World War II, when (quoting Nadezhda Mandelshtam) the people had been given back "a momentarily restored sense of community." "At the height of the purges," concludes Gifford, "that sense did not exist in Russia; but without it the novelist has no wind in his sails." See also Hampshire, "As From a Lost Culture" 3.

[9] There has been much ado over the years about the presence of heavy-handed coincidence and the absence of realistic motivation in *Doctor Zhivago*. The best English language treatment of this problem is Struve, "The Hippodrome of Life"; the best formulation of the inherent

its share of supporters in the first wave of critical response: "It is not only that he [Pasternak] lacks the gift of epic narration and has no eye for the historic scene. He runs away from history, just as all the time his chief characters flee from the scourge of revolution" ("Pasternak and the Calendar" 245). Whichever term one attaches to Pasternak's method—"symbolic realism" (Struve, "Sense and Nonsense" 233), "introspective epic" (Erlich, "A Testimony" 131), "transnaturalistic and transpsychological structure and style" (Stepun, "Boris Pasternak" 121), etc.—it is clear that *Doctor Zhivago* has little to do with Tolstoyan realism. Tolstoy insists on the essential isomorphism between history and story: there are no neat or facile dénouements in either, and there is thus a certain rightness to his alternation of family and national plots. But Pasternak insists on the radical disjunction between history, which has no meaning in itself and which people try vainly to control, and History, which *does* have meaning ever since the birth of the Christian era and whose author is God. For Tolstoy God has no existence *as distinct* from the historical process: characters and their actions appear three-dimensional (there is no other dimension to consider), utterly verisimilar, free from the hands of a crudely intrusive fate.[10] In Pasternak, on the other hand, the reader is constantly made aware of an "inscrutable providence" (Gifford, *Pasternak* 181)[11] and a lack of three-dimensionality

---

paradox in Pasternak's "lyrical" approach to the "epic" form within the Russian context is Efron, *Pis'ma iz ssylki* 21–31.

[10] Although, to be sure, there is a distinct shift toward greater symbolic patterning from *War and Peace* to *Anna Karenina*.

[11] As Pasternak once wrote on a postcard to a French correspondent:

I always had the feeling, the taste of unity of all that exists, of the totality of all that lives and moves, and that goes away, and reappears, of being, of all of life. . . . All this reality (the totality of the world) in its turn is animated by an agitation of an entirely different kind from visible, organic or material movements. . . . It is as if a painting, a painted cloth, full of tumultuousness and commotion (*The Night Watch* by Rembrandt, for example) had been torn off and carried away by the wind, by a movement other than the movements painted and known on the painting, by an unknown movement. As if that gust of wind were blowing up the cloth, made it fly, eternally fleeing and escaping being known, in some essential part.

That is my symbolism, my characterization of reality, my pendant to the determinism of the classic novel. I describe characters, situations, details, particulars, with one sole supreme aim: to shake up the ideal of iron-clad causality, of absolute necessity; to represent reality as a spectacle of a non-material [*incorporée*] and rolling inspiration; as an apparition moved by a sort of choice and freedom; as one alternative [*variante*] among others; as a willed thing.

Hence all the "defects," the not understood oddities of my new manner: the neglect of the definite, the smudging of contours just traced, the premeditated arbitrariness of "coincidences," the representation of the solid as slipping and disappearing, etc. Hence certain optimism of this manner. The translation of being not as something which deceives and enslaves, but as a mystery which astonishes, attracts, and liberates (letter of May 20, 1959

because History's plot is being worked out *through* the characters (Yury chiefly) and because every attempt by the human being (a *character* in that plot) to master fate and assume the author's role results, in metapoetic terms, in modal impasse, and, in personal terms, in tragedy.

Thus Pasternak provides the missing link between our other two post-revolutionary authors, between Platonov, with his rejection of an other-worldly intelligence guiding humanity's steps along history's road, and Bulgakov, with his belief in a mystical haven set aside for his hero and her-oine beyond death, at their story's end. In favor of the initial stages (the "morning") of the revolution,[12] Pasternak continued to maintain his inde-pendence and did not abandon himself to a dogmatic Marxism that, once vitiated in the aftermath of NEP, produced the absurdist logic of *Cheven-gur*.[13] At the same time, his personal eschatology, quite unlike Bulgakov's, never completely divorced itself from the religious nationalism, the hybrid union of Marxism and Christian millenarianism, that marked the Symbolist period.[14] Ironically, Pasternak's "*sui generis* Christian personalism" (Er-lich, "Categories" 8) and emphasis on the sacredness of the *individuum*[15] was in one important sense *populist*, that is, always invoked in the name of the *narod*[16] that had suffered revolutions, world wars, and purges. The

---

to J. de Proyart in *Pasternak* 236–37; trans. by George Gibian [see also the latter's dis-cussion in *"Doctor Zhivago"* (MS) 32–37]).

[12] For Pasternak's attitude toward 1917, see Barnes, "Boris Pasternak i Revoliutsiia 1917 goda." In a letter to Bryusov, Pasternak described a conversation he had had with Trotsky and how it had resonated with positive feelings about the *morning* of the revolution: "The stage of the revolution that is nearest to the heart and to poetry is the *morning* of the revolution, when it returns man to his *nature* as man and looks at the state [*gosudarstvo*] through the eyes of *natural* law" (cited in Barnes 319; emphasis Pasternak's). The ties between Pasternak's own initial views of the revolution and those expressed by his hero Yury Zhivago in the early sections of the novel are clear and have been discussed by a number of scholars.

[13] Commenting, for example, on Pasternak's speech of December 12, 1931 on a poetry panel organized by the All-Russian Union of Soviet Writers, Fleishman adds, "Pasternak attacked the extremist positions of the then established literary policy, speaking out against attempts—which were equally characteristic of both the 'formalist' talk given by Aseev and of the slogans of his adversaries from RAPP—to subjugate the poet to his 'time' " (*Tridtsatye gody* 51).

[14] Recall, for example, the way that religious nationalism is parodied in *White Guard*.

[15] "In general he [Trotsky] charmed and delighted me, and I also must say that from his point of view he was absolutely correct to ask me questions [as to why Pasternak refrained from civic themes in *My Sister, Life*]. My answers and explanations came to a defense of individualism, the genuine kind, which is like a new social cell of a new social organism" (letter to Bryusov cited in Barnes, "Boris Pasternak i Revoliutsiia 1917 goda" 319).

[16] The link between the revolution and the *narod* first appeared in Pasternak's work in a cycle of poems published in the journal *The Banner* (April 1936). This is an important turning point in his art because it is also the first time he enters into poetic dialogue with one of the most loaded terms of the Stalinist thirties—*narodnost'* (populism, popular quality). See Fleish-man, *Tridtsatye gody* 288.

promise held by the revolution and (later) the first socialist constitution was for a society of free personalities that would be dedicated to a life of service and inspired by a pragmatic Christianity (to be made explicit by Pasternak only in subsequent works, especially *Doctor Zhivago*).[17] If this promise remained unfulfilled and was in fact often cruelly disconfirmed, the fault was not in the revolution itself or in the letter of Stalin's constitution. Hence Pasternak's deep attachment to the kenotic role of the Russian people and to the myth of Russia's manifest destiny may have more in common with Platonov's sympathies for the *duraki* than with Bulgakov's Olympian scorn for the venal hoi polloi, the *poshliaki* (vulgarians) or "little men" in the streets. And while Platonov's novel shows what happens when an immanent (human-centered) historiosophy is taken to its logical end-point, and while Bulgakov's novel shows what happens when an imminent (god-centered) historiosophy provides a deus ex machina exit from the "hippodrome of life," *Doctor Zhivago* attempts a marriage of the two.

Before we can proceed to a detailed reading of the text, the categories of mythical thinking structuring personal and national destiny in *Doctor Zhivago* need to be examined in the broader context of Pasternak's aesthetic. By "categories of mythical thinking" I have in mind such loaded terms as "Russia," "revolution," "history," "art/poetry." These terms, which are of course not static in Pasternak's art and which, if taken in isolation, strike the average reader with the hollow thud of upper-case verities, are in context brought alive through the use of potent image clusters. Anyone familiar with the dense associative logic and the sensations of immediacy and extraordinary "thingness" (*predmetnost'*) characteristic of Pasternak's early books of verse knows that such image clusters cannot be decoded as simple, one-to-one allegory. They are part of a multifarious life *at that moment* and cannot be mechanically generalized into overarching symbols pointing to another realm distinct from that life. Still, certain repeated images achieved a privileged status, especially after the poet's famous shift to a "simpler" manner in the 1930s, and it is not accidental that they were intimately linked with the way the mature Pasternak conceptualized the passage and shape of historical time. The most prominent of all these images is the train, which over time evolved out of its supporting role as back-

---

[17] "Never have I understood freedom as a dismissal of one's debts, as a dispensation, an indulgence. . . . There is not a force on earth that can give me freedom if I do not already possess it in embryonic form and if I do not take it myself, not from God or my superior, but from the air and the future, from the earth and from myself . . . in the form of *independence*, independence from weaknesses and from the calculations of others. This is also how I imagine socialist freedom to myself" (Pasternak, "Novoe sovershennolet'e"). And "art without risk and spiritual self-sacrifice is unthinkable" ("O skromnosti i smelosti" 222).

ground and setting (an element of realia grounding the associative leaps of Pasternak's lyrical persona in the urban world of the "here" and "now") into its foregrounded role as a metaphor for the relative movement of history in a period of national crisis and heightened consciousness. With a logic first divined by Dostoevsky, this image concealed within its own metaphorical skin, as it were, the destination implied for all those who seek to control or steer it. It is at this basic *apocalyptic* level, that is, the level at which the mythical category (the End) is *prefigured* by the trope selected to give it narrative shape (the train), that the primarily pessimistic Dostoevsky and optimistic Pasternak join hands. [18]

From his earliest ventures in print it was obvious that Pasternak thought in essentially binary terms, [19] but he was always a far cry from what modern parlance would call a "structuralist." He sought meaning not in a closed system, but in life as openness, surprise, spontaneous revelation. [20] In a much cited passage of the article "The Black Goblet" (1916), he speaks of Lyric (*Lirika*) and History (*Istoriia*) as being "two opposing poles" which are "equally *a priori* and absolute" (*Stikhi 1936–59* 150–51). By this he presumably means that the oppositions between the public (political activist) and private (lyric poet), between the one's concern with the grand course of human events and the other's concern with how that course is imprinted on the present, are eternal and not subject to human intervention. The context for these thoughts is rhetorically dense and not a little mystifying, but even so a central theme of *Doctor Zhivago* can already be glimpsed: "No one can make us, even in words, set about the task *of preparing history for tomorrow*" (*Stikhi 1936–59* 150; my emphasis). Pasternak finds fault with the Symbolists (as opposed to the Futurists) because "their promises can never be kept"—"their profundity of thought [*glubokomyslie*] surpasses all boundaries of possible realization within three dimensions" (*Stikhi 1936–59* 150). In other words, what Pasternak objects to in the Symbolists is not their propensity for abstraction (after all, he is ap-

[18] On the times in the generally eupeptic Pasternak's life when he was obsessed with feelings of "the end" (e.g., death of Mayakovsky, trial of Ramzin), see Fleishman, *Tridtsatye gody* 18, 28–29, 64.

[19] "A man has equal need of both reason and unreason, of both calm and anxiety. Leave him only reason and calm, and he will become dull, colourless and lethargic. Give him only unreason and anxiety, and he will lose himself and his world. The poet is a man of extremes: he seeks reason in unreason and calm in anxiety, unreason in reason, and anxiety in calm. Everybody has this inborn need to seek for opposites in all things—just as almost everybody is born with a rudimentary gift of poetry" (Gladkov, *Meetings* 60–61).

[20] "On the earth there is death and foresight. The unknown is dear to us, and that which is known in advance is terrifying, and every passion is a blind leap away from advancing inevitability" (*Okhrannaia gramota* 266). See also "O skromnosti i smelosti" 222–23. For the revelatory theme in *Doctor Zhivago*, see Danow, "Epiphany in 'Doctor Zhivago.' "

parently comfortable with such terms as Lyric and History), but their insistence on making an a priori distinction between this and *another* world.

Thus Pasternak will always deal with the moral or philosophical equivalent of upper-case verities—which by definition imply some master design—but he will, paradoxically, conceive of their existence *within* history, on *this side* of the End. Indeed, he will invoke repeatedly the text of Revelation in *Doctor Zhivago*, but he will do so not in the Belian sense that an End to history as we know it is imminent. Quite the opposite, and with a curious disregard for the maximalist, right-angled logic of Revelation, he will make epiphany into a gradualist, ameliorative, ultimately *evolutionary* concept—one that could not be farther from the mentality of the original exile on Patmos (see Erlich, "Life By Verses" 149–51). Most striking of all, he will manage this by joining the oppositions in an unlikely and, to much of the Soviet literary establishment, highly illicit relationship. The purest expression of "poetry" will be the homely surprises of "prose" ("Poetry is prose, prose not in the sense of a combination of all possible prose works, but prose itself, the voice of prose, prose in action, and not as it is retold" ["Rech' na pervom Vsesoiuznom s"ezde" 217]); Mayakovsky's "immortal expression" can be found in his quality of "great ordinariness" ("O skromnosti i smelosti" 223); the surest feel for the genuine revolutionary content of the moment will be vouchsafed to the individual who avoids political groups and the *splochennost'* ("togetherness") of unions and who thereby, paradoxically, remains "open" to history's rhythms.[21] So the charge most often raised against the writer—his *zamknutost'* ("closedness" to history, his retreat to an aerie "outside and above time": see Fleishman, *Tridtsatye gody* 384)—is actually what allows him to remain *open* to the future. As Pasternak evolves as a writer, as he attempts to make the transition from "lyric" to "epic,"[22] and as he becomes increasingly sensitive to his role as cultural symbol, the more these oppositions interpenetrate and intermingle,[23] creating a first impression of modal confusion. Yet the confusion is intentional: in the end it makes possible a solution unthinkable to either Platonov or Bulgakov—the "Christianization" of Marxist historiosophy together with the "secularization" of a traditional afterlife. And, in effect, this

[21] On this issue Pasternak strongly disagreed with Gorky (who felt that the literary community's strength lay in unity), and during their last meeting in 1935 he told him that fellow writers "should not join ranks" (*ne ob"ediniaites'*). See Fleishman, *Tridtsatye gody* 361.

[22] "For more than a year [as of 1927] I have been working on the book *The Year 1905*, which will consist of separate epic fragments. . . . I consider that the epic is inspired by time [*vnushen vremenem*], and therefore in the book *The Year 1905* I shift from lyrical thinking to epic thinking [*èpika*], although that is very difficult" ("O sebe" 215–16).

[23] See, e.g.: "We smuggle the quotidian into prose for the sake of poetry. We draw prose into poetry for the sake of music" (*Okhrannaia gramota* 216).

also means that the revolution, despite all the failures coming after, is preserved in potentia as a bright beginning whose time is both come and continually coming.

There are a number of sources that one might consult in an attempt to
locate the genesis of this notion of "modal confusion" ("lyrical prose,"
"great ordinariness," history versus History, etc.), but here the focus will
be on three: Husserl's phenomenology, Bergson's *élan vital*, and Fyodorov's philosophy.[24] Following his return from Marburg, as he was beginning his shift from philosophy to poetry, Pasternak gave a talk on "Symbolism and Immortality" at the studio of the sculptor Konstantin Krakht
(early February 1913). In the talk he made the case for a "subjectivity" that
was in essence "objective," that is, immutable and capable of outliving its
habitation in the individual (Pasternak, "Avtobiograficheskii ocherk" 25–
26; see also Fleishman, "K kharakteristike" 81–82). Pasternak plainly did
*not* have in mind anything like a traditional afterlife in another time-space,
but an "immortality" that existed *in time, in history*. (Elsewhere he would
envision this paradoxical immortality as a kind of roving cloud of the deceased's best traits, now chastened and purged of the dross of biography,
that would continue on as part of the ambient environment of those still
living.[25]) According to Husserl's philosophy, especially as it was mediated
and championed by the young lecturer Gustav Shpet in his *Phenomenon
and Meaning: Phenomenology as a Basic Science and its Problems* (1914),
the principal method of phenomenology was that of intellectual intuition,
"the perceiving of the essence" (*Wesensschau*) (Fleishman, "K kharakteristike" 84). The Kantian barrier between subject and object, "thing in itself" and "perceived phenomenon," is removed; what remains is the unen-
cumbered flow of the consciousness into the phenomenon and of the
phenomenon into the consciousness:

> I . . . become aware that my own phenomenologically self-contained
> essence can be posited in an *absolute* sense, as I am the Ego who invests
> the being of the world which I so constantly speak about with existen-
> tial validity, as an existence (*Sein*) which wins for me from my own
> life's pure essense meaning and substantiated validity. I myself as this
> individual essence, posited absolutely, as the open infinite field of pure
> phenomenological data and their inseparable unity, am the "transcen-

[24] For the biographical context I have made heavy use of the following works: de Mallac,
*Pasternak*; Fleishman: "K kharakteristike," *Dvadtsatye gody, Tridtsatye gody*; Pasternak:
"Avtobiograficheskii ocherk," *Okhrannaia gramota*.

[25] See Gibian, *"Doctor Zhivago"* [MS] 32–35. This is very close to the "vague nebulosity"
(*nébulosité vague*) that rises above and surrounds pure intellect in Bergson (*L'Évolution* 14,
186).

dental Ego"; the absolute positing means that the world is no longer "given" to me in advance, its validity that of a simple existent, but that henceforth it is exclusively my Ego that is given (Husserl, *Ideas* 11).

Consciousness thus constituted is not a thinking *about* (or *meta*-ulteriorizing of) the relation of "thing in itself" to "phenomenon" but the actual *site*, as it were, where the phenomenon springs spontaneously into existence. (Note the necessity here of resorting to spatial metaphors.) Furthermore, this removal of cognitive barriers is spatialized into a perception of the world that is forever "open": human beings, in their isolated subjectivity, do not perceive or "think" nature, but rather nature, in its phenomenological guise as a web of immutable, transpersonal, "objective" subjectivity, thinks human beings. It is immediately clear that the "openness within history" characteristic of the novel structure of *Doctor Zhivago* as well as the great emphasis placed by the later work on the *spontaneous* communication between humankind and nature owe much to this brief period when Pasternak was turning away from the neo-Kantianism of Natorp and Cohen and turning toward the phenomenology of Husserl and Shpet.

Bergson's theories of time were much in vogue when Pasternak was studying at Moscow University. One need not belabor the obvious parallels between the philosopher's vitalism as outlined in *L'Évolution créatice* (1907), his notion that time is a great, unbounded, fluvial force ("un courant qu'on ne saurait remonter" [*L'Évolution* 55]) whose creative energies are alive and *cannot be shaped*, and the centrifugal images of rain, sea, and open windows which the author of *Doctor Zhivago* uses to describe the birth of the revolution.[26] Suffice it to say that in Pasternak one cannot (except at cost of death) separate oneself from this oceanic temporal presence and that even to try to conceptualize it one must resort to *organic* metaphors. Those who do try to channel the *élan vital* bring something moribund into their lives and the lives of others and are apt therefore to be characterized by *mechanical* metaphors. Artists, on the other hand, are uniquely equipped to overcome the mechanical fallacy by breaking down the spatial barriers that intelligence erects and by constantly placing themselves, through a leap of intuition, back into the flow of life (*L'Évolution* 185).[27] It is precisely this kind of empathizing quality, this capacity to swim in *la courant de la vie*,

[26] "La vie psychologique n'est ni unité ni multiplicité . . . elle transcende et le *mécanique* et l'*intelligent*, mecanisme et finalisme n'ayant de sens que là où il y a 'multiplicité distincte', 'spatialité', et par conséquent assemblage de parties préexistantes: 'durée réelle' signifie à la fois continuité indivisée et création" (*L'Évolution* 16). For more on this notion of Bergsonian vitalism in *Doctor Zhivago*, see de Mallac, *Pasternak* 289–91.

[27] Cf. "une metaphysique ou la totalité du réel est posée en bloc, dans l'éternité, et ou la durée apparente des choses exprime simplement l'infirmité d'un esprit qui ne peut pas connaître tout à la fois" (*L'Évolution* 55).

that Yury Zhivago possesses in the highest degree and that Strelnikov-Antipov, with his tendency to *spatialize* historical causality and teleology, lacks.[28] Having nothing to do with imitation,[29] creative intuition is finally Bergson's shorthand for "le domaine propre de la vie, qui est *compénétration réciproque*, création indéfiniment continuée" (*L'Évolution* 186; my emphasis).[30]

Nikolay Fyodorov's *idée fixe* about the literal overcoming of death within history is as present in Pasternak's *Doctor Zhivago* as it is in Platonov's *Chevengur*.[31] However, in Pasternak the fact that history's true goal and "common cause" has not been realized in Soviet times does not produce black humor or absurdist logic. Parents (Yury's mother and father, Tonya's mother Anna Ivanovna, eventually Yury himself) can still be raised from the dead and children can still act toward one another as true siblings once the process is "metapoeticized" out of the physical realm.[32] Consequently, there is in *Doctor Zhivago* none of Fyodorov's or the early Platonov's infatuation with the miracles of modern technology. On the contrary, Pasternak is apt to see blind faith in machines as dehumanizing. His application of Fyodorovian doctrine is either on a purely aesthetic plane (what conquers death is Yury's poetry) or on a moral plane that is also deeply poetical (Yury's good deeds that live on posthumously as the ambient cloud in others). Thus Pasternak is able to "succeed"—*through his art*—where Platonov, seeing no metapoetic level, no saving grace in the words themselves, "fails." And if the central optimistic message of Fyodorov was that an apocalypse of divine judgment *could be avoided* once children set about raising their parents and undoing death, Pasternak shares this optimism even as he describes the terrors suffered by his people (especially the children) as "apocalyptic" (431/530).[33] Yet such terrors, however real, are not *literally* apocalyptic,

---

[28] "L'intelligence est, avant tout, la faculté de rapporter un point de l'espace à un autre point de l'espace, un objet matériel à un objet matériel; elle s'applique a toutes choses, mais en restant en dehors d'elles, et elle n'aperçoit jamais d'une cause profonde que sa diffusion en effets juxtaposés" (*L'Évolution* 184).

[29] Recall that the young Zhivago's talent is "for life" whereas the young Antipov's talent is "for imitation."

[30] Note here the notion of opposites coming in place, *compénétration réciproque*, that would have appealed to Pasternak.

[31] See Chapter 3 of the present study. For a fine treatment of the influence of Fyodorovian thought on the central themes of *Doctor Zhivago*, see Masing-Delic, "Zhivago as Fedorovian Soldier."

[32] It is dubious whether Fyodorov himself would have approved of Pasternak's "metapoetic" treatment of his philosophy—a philosophy that was, if anything, relentlessly literalist.

[33] "Pasternak's affection for, and sense of indebtedness to the Symbolist spellbinder [i.e., Blok] may have derived additional poignancy from the fact that he had lived through the fulfillment of Blok's apocalyptic prophecies. . . . Pasternak's temperament had never been that

since history has not ended, but is continually reborn, *back into itself*, through the example of Yury Zhivago and other "gifted" individuals.

For Pasternak, history is endowed with meaning and its forward movement acquires purpose at those privileged moments when genuine change and newness are apparent. The future emerges from the camera obscura of the present as a kind of photographic negative to be later "developed." It is not in the photographer's power to change the images on the paper, only to bring them more clearly into focus. The fact that the future *already* exists in the present and at historical turning-points becomes visible in a kind of "double exposure" suggests the spatial condition of coincidence or parallax (e.g., "star-crossed lovers")—the most famous example being the candle in Lara's window on Kamerger Street which points the way to future meetings (the love affair in *Yuryatin*, Yury's poetry written at Varykino, the heroine's surprise return to the same flat to discover her lover's body and to speak with Evgraf about his legacy) even as it illumines the present (Blok as the "Christmas Star" of Yury's and Tonya's generation, Lara as a "fallen" woman who insists on speaking with Pasha in the candlelight prior to making her fateful visit to the Sventitskys). This symbolic patterning "from the end" is what allows the "story" in history, the bared device, to come to the fore. Time, as it were, wears different guises (e.g., biblical, fairy tale, poetic) to make its message known, yet each "fitting" implies its own end-determined plot. It is also, to resort again to Arthur Danto's terminology, what distinguishes the historian proper, whose function it is to narrate a closed past from the position of the present, from the artist, whose function it is to narrate a past that is curiously open to the present and the future: Yury dies in the novel and the events described therein are physically finished, but the story does not stop there. To the figure described by the historian, the consequences of one's actions cannot be known before they happen; to the character of the feckless doctor described by Pasternak, the legacy of his good works can be predicted even before he dies.

Pasternak's root metaphor for all great turning-points is the revolution (*re*-volution), which he experienced on various levels and "domesticated" through imagery. Although his early verse has almost none of the topical references we associate with 1917, it is pervaded by the same "sea of spontaneity" which is the semiautobiographical Yury's word-picture for the sensation of freedom he and the others feel when they hear the good news. As a phenomenon of temporal thinking, the revolution renders huge blocks of the past powerless and hovers in a kind of vertiginous equipoise between the old and the new, or—to put it in the antinomial terms of *Doctor Zhi-*

---

of a Utopian. By 1950 he had less use than ever for the notion of a millennium" (Erlich, "Life by Verses" 149–51).

*vago*—between the bound and the free, the national and the personal, the pre-Christian and the Christian. It is this balancing-act, this pausing before a wondrous array of freedom and choice that is celebrated in the associative leaps and striking image clusters of *My Sister, Life*; by the writing of *Doctor Zhivago* the historical choices have already been made and the clusters stabilize into something closer to conventional symbols.[34] For example, in the later novel the revolution is first described by the eponymous hero as something that "broke out willy-nilly, like a sigh suppressed too long. Everyone was revived, reborn, changed, transformed. You might say that everyone has been through two revolutions—his own personal revolution as well as the general one. It seems to me that socialism is the sea, and all these separate streams, these private, individual revolutions are flowing into it—the sea of life, the sea of spontaneity" (124/148). Everything here—"suppressed sigh," "revived," "reborn," "sea," "streams," etc.—bespeaks an organic, unrehearsed, completely natural process. Time exists fully in the present; there is no reference as yet to a "before" or "after." And subsequently, during Yury's stay in Moscow, when the revolution has developed a darker cast, the same organic metaphor is used ("the revolution is this flood"), only now the water has been replaced by a "sea of blood" (153/185). Thus throughout the novel, whenever time is stressed as a positive beginning or a "turning" toward the new, Pasternak calls on his various image clusters of "living life" (e.g., windows open to the linden trees, the unfurling of Mary Magdalene's hair) to convey this open-ended, centrifugal movement.

Conversely, the revolution as turning-point also implies an *ending* to those who simplify, take the life out of, its movement. Pasternak's word picture for this mechanizing or "logocentrifying" of the historical process is, of course, the railroad. There is no other modern Russian writer who made broader application of the railroad motif than did Pasternak, and the changes wrought in his use of this image over time tell us much about how his thinking evolved from his early lyrics and stories to his last major work. Over and over again in *Safe Conduct* and his "Autobiographical Essay" the train is the site of a turning-point in Pasternak's life, the occasion to reflect

[34] "I don't know what would have remained for me of the Revolution, and where would be her *truth* if Russian history had not had you [Gorky]. But for you—in the flesh and in your full individuality—and save for you as an immense generic personification, her fibs and shallowness became directly exposed. . . . Having—along with everyone else—breathed these ten years her unavoidable falseness, I had gradually come to think of liberation. For this it was necessary to select the revolutionary theme in a historical perspective, as a chapter among chapters, as an event among events, and raise it to the power of a tangible and live, nonsectarian pan-Russian [reality]" (letter of October 10, 1927 to Gorky in *Literaturnoe nasledstvo* 70: 297–98; cited in de Mallac, *Pasternak* 111).

on how twentieth-century history in its rapid course has brought him in contact with individuals who will change his view of the world, and hence his attitude toward the past and tradition. Such confrontations with destiny include:

(1) the chance meeting with a mysterious stranger, who later turned out to be Rilke, on a station platform ("a fabulous thought [*vymysel*] in a crowd of the unfabulizable [*nevymyshlennost'*]" [*Okhrannaia gramota* 203]);

(2) his trip on a night train with his father to witness the passing of Tolstoy (the "last *bogatyr'* "), who died at the Astapovo station ("It was somehow natural that Tolstoy grew peaceful . . . by the road [*u dorogi*], like a pilgrim [*strannik*], near the throughways of the Russia of that time, along which his heroes and heroines continued to race and describe circles and to look out the coach windows at the wretched station standing there, not knowing that the eyes which had looked at them all their lives and had embraced them with their vision and immortalized them, had closed forever" ["Avtobiograficheskii ocherk" 28]);

(3) his entrance into Marburg by train, amid thoughts of the speed and shape of history in a post-Hegelian world, to study philosophy with Cohen ("In Marburg they knew history to perfection and never tired of trundling out treasure after treasure from the archives of the Italian Renaissance, French and Scottish rationalism, and other poorly studied schools. They looked at history in Marburg through Hegelian eyes, that is, in a way that generalized brilliantly, but at the same time within the precise boundaries of common sense. . . . Like one of the particles of contemporary consciousness [within Cohen's system], I was hurtling toward the center of gravity. The train was crossing the Harz. In the hazy morning, having leapt out of the forest, the thousand-year old Goslar flashed by like a medieval coal miner. Later Göttingen rushed past. The names of the cities became louder and louder. At full speed, without bending over, the train flung the majority of them from its path" [*Okhrannaia gramota* 225]);

(4) his decision to abandon philosophy and Marburg and to enter another "faith" ("Then [that evening, after returning to Marburg] I washed up and, drying myself off, went out onto the balcony. Evening was setting in. . . . I looked into the distance at the road joining Ockershausen and Marburg. It was already impossible to recall how I had looked in that direction on the evening of my arrival. The end, the end! The end of philosophy, that is, the end of any [further] thought of it. And like a traveling companion in a train compartment, it [philosophy] would have to take account of the fact that every love is *a crossing-over into another faith*" [*Okhrannaia gramota* 241; my emphasis]);

(5) the twilight status of the tsarist regime which the returning future poet links with the train stations dressed up to celebrate the centennial of

the defeat of Napoleon ("The spectacle did not summon up recollections of the events being celebrated in those riding by. The anniversary decorations breathed the chief quality of tsarist rule—indifference to native history. And if the festivities were reflected in something, it was not in the course of one's thoughts [*na khode myslei*], but in the course of the train [*na khode poezda*], since the latter was held over longer than expected at the stations and was stopped more often than usual enroute by signals" [*Okhrannaia gramota* 267]);

(6) his initiation into the realm of poetic composition with the lyric "The Station," which was inspired by the same Brest Station where strikes—and revolution—would originate in *Doctor Zhivago* ("In the distance, at the end of the tracks and platforms, there rose, draped in clouds and smoke, the departing horizon of the railroad, which hid the trains from sight and contained an entire [hi]story of relations, [including] homecomings and leavetakings, and events before and after them" ["Avtobiograficheskii ocherk" 32]);

(7) the impression created by a young Vladimir Mayakovsky who read his famous "tragedy" amid the scent of the linden trees and the bellowing of the locomotive whistles so familiar to readers of *Doctor Zhivago* ("The poplars were growing green. The lindens were drily turning gray. . . . The locomotives on the Brest line—renamed the Alexandrovsky—were giving forth their throaty whistles. And all around people were getting haircuts, shaving, baking and cooking, bartering, moving about—and not aware of anything. It was the tragedy *Vladimir Mayakovsky*, which had only just appeared. I listened raptly, with all my heart, holding my breath. I had never before heard anything of the kind. Here was everything. The boulevard, the dogs, the poplars and butterflies. The barbers, the bakers, the tailors, the locomotives. Why quote? We all recall this stifling, mysterious, summery text, available now to everyone in the tenth edition. In the distance locomotives roared like white sturgeon. In the throaty region of his art there was the same unconditional distance that occupies the earth" [*Okhrannaia gramota* 272–73]); and

(8) the loss of his cherished letters from Tsvetaeva which were accidently left by a friend on a commuter train (*èlektrichka*).

What is striking about Pasternak's early use of a mechanical image for the revolution (train, locomotive, tracks expanding into the distance, the acceleration of time) is that it is rarely negative and in fact is usually infected by the larger semantic field of life in its organic, spontaneous forms. Mayakovsky's poetry is read in the context of life in the streets, a life characterized by the interconnectedness of the plant world (the lindens and poplars which are *turning* gray and green), the human world (whose barbers cut back the *growth* of beards and hair and whose bakers supply the *yeast*

that transforms dough into bread), and the mechanical world (with its locomotives that sound like the rush of white sturgeon). Here the train is
primarily an image for rapidly approaching change, for a time of newness.
There is little of the life-denying, pejorative coloration that will make its
way into later descriptions—the train as the absence of "free play," as a
self-contained ensemble of engine, tracks, and destination (see Schivelbusch, *Railway* 19–40). When, for example, in the title poem of *My Sister,
Life* the poet exclaims that a train schedule is grander than Holy Scripture,
or when in his famous definition of poetry in *Themes and Variations* he
likens his craft to a summer seated in a third-class coach, we are in the
presence of this initial semantic field. One is blessed to be a passenger on
this breath-taking time machine whose traits are speed, power, expansive-
ness (Mayakovsky's poetry still represents distance—*dal'*), social flux/in-
termixing (a *third-class* coach), and the unknown and unexpected. Consequently, there is as yet no inclination to look back and reconsider.

Yet, as was intimated earlier, Pasternak's selection of a mechanistic word-
picture to describe revolutionary time already contained within itself the
possibility of alternative readings *once the trip was over*. *Safe Conduct* was
written *after* Mayakovsky's suicide, at a time when Pasternak was taking
stock in his own poetic method and comparing it to that of his dead colleague. He was keenly aware of the dangers lying in wait for the loud, provocative, deliberately *engagé* artist, who more than anyone epitomized the
revolution but who, in another, later time, was doomed to live out a public
myth of perennial change and instability. As Pasternak begins to describe
the early Mayakovsky, his words are involuntarily drawn into an orbit of
nuance where even positive attributes conceal potentially fatal consequences:

> He existed as if on the next day following a vast spiritual life . . . and
> everyone came upon him in the shaft of its *irreversible consequences*.
> He sat on his chair as *on the seat of a motorcycle, leaned forward*, cut
> and quickly swallowed his Wiener Schnitzel, played cards with eyes
> squinting and *head unturned*, magisterially strolled along Kuznetsky,
> hollowly intoned through his nose, like excerpts from the liturgy,
> deep-meaning snatches of his own and others' [work], scowled, grew
> [before us], traveled and performed, and in the depths behind all this,
> as *behind the straightness of a skater racing at full speed*, there flashed
> eternally some day of his, preceding all others, when first this *running
> start* was made, *straightening* him up so boldly and effortlessly. Be-
> hind his manner of carrying himself there could be divined something
> like a decision *when it has been put into action and its consequences
> are no longer subject to repeal*. Such a decision was [apparent in] his

genius, the confrontation with which had so struck him at first that it became forever after a thematic directive, to whose embodiment he gave all of himself *without pity and hesitation.*

But he was still young, and the forms awaiting [*pred*stoiashchie] this theme were up ahead. It, however, was insatiable and would countenance no procrastination. Therefore what suited it at first was to anticipate [*predvoskhishchat'*] the future, and an anticipation [*predvoskhishchenie*] of the future, realized in the first person, is a pose. . . .

At the same time the *mainspring* [*pruzhina*] of his immodesty was a fantastic modesty, and beneath its sham freedom [*volia*] lay hidden a bondage [*bezvol'e*] that was phenomenally suspicious and given to causeless gloom. And equally deceptive was the *mechanism* of his yellow coat (my emphasis; *Okhrannaia gramota* 270–71).

I have quoted this rather well-known description of Mayakovsky at length because it indicates to what extent the gradual changes in Pasternak's temporal thinking depended on spatial imagery whose context is subtly but decidedly *post*-revolutionary. Each defining attribute of the larger portrait of the revolutionary poet tells how he is pointed—physically, spatially— toward the future. His entire past, including the very manner in which he carries himself, enters into an ensemble (the "pose of external wholeness" [271]) implying "irreversible consequences." Mayakovsky cannot simply sit still but must lean forward on his chair as though he were riding a motorcycle—a kind of mechanized, urban version of the steed.[35] There is in addition the suggestion that this poet is head-over-heels in love with the sheer velocity and danger of the ride. Even when doing something as frivolous as playing cards, he keeps his eyes fixed on his quarry and does not turn his head to consider his surroundings. Pasternak reinforces this meaning with the second metaphor of the skater (*kon'kobezhets*), whose salient traits are again precipitous speed (*razbezhavshiisia*), straightforward motion (*priamota, raspriamliavshii*), and a running start (*razgon*). Yet this picture of intense goal-directedness is not without its contradictions: the bravado is in actuality shyness, the freedom of movement a kind of bondage to a prescribed course. And so, as the essentially larger-than-life, eulogistic memoir grades into sober criticism and reservation, the images of an inorganic, mechanical nature come to the fore—the resemblance of his diction to a *piece of sheet-iron* (270), the *spring* of his immodesty, the *mechanism* of the yellow coat, the *magnet* and *horseshoe* of his art (274), etc. In the end Mayakovsky is prisoner to a motion that is rehearsed (the "playing at life" [270], the "pose"), repetitive, unfree, inevitable. Like the motorcyclist

---

[35] The phrase *sadilsia na sedlo* (Michigan 270) means both to sit on a bicycle seat and "to get into the saddle."

or skater overcome by the peculiar inertia of speed, he has no way to get off.

It has been suggested on more than one occasion that Pasternak intended his reader to divine a certain kinship between the story of Strelnikov-Antipov in *Doctor Zhivago* and the real-life fate of Vladimir Mayakovsky (see, e.g., Ivinskaya, *Captive* 187–88). Such a comparison between a commissar spreading death and destruction through the Russian countryside and a suicidal poet seems, prima facie, far-fetched, at least in the sense that the chief defining qualities of the two, the one's political acts with life-and-death consequences and the other's poetry, have nothing in common. Be this as it may, Pasternak clearly saw a similarity in their self-inflicted ends (as well as in that of his good friend the Georgian poet Paolo Yashvili [see Fleishman, *Tridtsatye gody* 418–20]). In both poets there was something too "straightforward," too forced (*nasil'stvennyi*), too committed to a historical plot superimposed from outside or above, too willing to weld their personal fates to "the locomotive of the revolution." What seems reasonable to assume in context is that the Pasternak of *Doctor Zhivago*, looking back at the great promise with which Mayakovsky and Yashvili began, saw the future revealed in these traits and gave them *spatial* form in the "iron road" lying before Pasha Antipov in the novel. In this regard, the "iron inner bearing" that Pasternak associated with Mayakovsky, the various "commandments and forms of nobility, the feeling of obligation which did not allow him to be otherwise—less handsome, less witty, less talented" ("Avtobiograficheskii ocherk" 39–40)—seem nearly identical to the terms used to describe the doomed commissar.

Thus Mayakovsky and Yashvili and (later) Strelnikov-Antipov were joined in Pasternak's mind because their views of history and their self-appointed roles within the latter could be said to *predict* their own ends.[36] They were/are faced with the same dilemma tormenting Pilate in *The Master and Margarita*—a history without God and theodicy, that is, without His position on the outside conferring meaning and direction to our actions on the inside, is finally only Realpolitik and a baffling series of plots, forever retarded, unfulfilled, and cynically manipulated. The only reality worth considering is that of death itself. It is not surprising, therefore, that one of Pasternak's metaphors for history before Christ is familiar to readers of Bulgakov's novel—the racecourse, hippodrome, coliseum. This enclosed structure creates the illusion of great speed and propulsive force on its straightaways, yet its elliptical shape always brings its competitors back to

[36] "At this point [i.e., as he was thinking of going to war], [Antipov] committed a fatal and *forever thereafter predetermining* error [*rokovaia i vse napered predreshivshaia oshibka*]" (Michigan 415).

the beginning. In this *public* arena where there is no way out, the reigning ethos is survival of the fittest. The fact that one group watches while another group vies with and destroys itself precludes the possibility of progress in human terms. Pasternak hints at this word-picture in *Safe Conduct* when he imagines Mayakovsky to be a speed skater (the rink being the implied setting).

More explicit still is his description of Kiev on the eve of the 1905 revolution in *Lieutenant Schmidt*:

> The fields and the distance were spread out in an ellipse.
> The silk of the umbrellas breathed a thirst for thunder.
> The scorching day aimed its fathomless sky
> at the stands of the hippodrome.
>
> The people, mesmerized by the melting of the distance,
> sweated like kvas on an ice-box,
> while the horses, spinning in a vortex of hooves and
> shin pads, whipped the space as though making butter.
>
> And there behind, wafting with the even beat
> of some kind of subterranean origin,
> the martial year whirled up behind the jockeys
> and the horses and the spokes of the carriages.
>
> Whatever was whispered by the crowd, whatever they drank,
> it grew up around them and crawled along the crosswalks
> and intruded itself into conversation and with a pinch
> of its ashen taste mixed with their (soft) drinks.
>
> Everything ended. Night made its approach. Through Kiev
> there rushed the darkness, flinging tight each shutter.
> And the rain poured. And then, as in the days of Batyi,
> the departed day became strangely ancient.
>
> (*Stikhi i poemy 1912–32* 139)

Here are many of the same thematic elements we recognize from Bulgakov's novel: the elliptical configuration of the hippodrome, with its ancient or pagan connotations (the Tatar Khan Batyi); the horses moving at breakneck speed around the course; the crowd oblivious to the approaching hoofbeats of doom;[37] the storm as a symbol of gathering punishment and retribution for past sins; the recognition that "everything has ended" as the circle of history closes on this era.[38] As shall be demonstrated shortly, this

[37] Cf. the sweating Romans depicted in the early pages of *Doctor Zhivago*.

[38] Cf., for example, the "second coming" of the Tatar East described by Blok in "The Field of Kulikovo" and Pasternak's phrase "the departed day became strangely ancient."

global image of deadly entrapment and meaningless re-volution will, together with that of the train, play a key role in the conception of the later
novel.

When, for example, Yury first meets Strelnikov in the coach of the latter's *armored train*, the warrior impresses the poet with his self-possession,
his ability to feel at home in any circumstances, as though he were "in the
saddle" (Michigan 254). Soon thereafter, while appraising Yury's foil, the
narrator concludes that

> Strelnikov had from his earliest years striven for what was most el-
> evated and pure. He considered life a huge *stadium* [or hippodrome—
> *ristalishche*] in which people, honorably observing the rules, competed
> in the attainment of perfection.
>
> When it happened that this was not the case, it never entered his
> head that he, simplifying the world-order, had been wrong. Having
> long since driven his hurt inward, he began to cherish the idea of be-
> coming at some point a judge [who would arbitrate] between life and
> those dark forces corrupting it, [who would] come to its defense and
> avenge on its behalf.
>
> Disenchantment embittered him. The revolution armed him (210/
> 257).

Strelnikov, whose motives are noble and pure, has built of time an arena in
which progress is made only through the dialectical to-and-fro of competi-
tion. His way of thinking does not allow the possibility that this time-place
is as cheap, lurid, and subject to excess as that of the Roman coliseum, that
it offers no escape to those who agree to compete on its terms. At the end
of his life, Yury too is confronted with the "stadium of life" (*zhiteiskoe
ristalishche*—408/502): he dies of a heart attack while trying to exit a tram
(another train) and is immediately overtaken by the same aged Mademoiselle Fleury he had once known in Melyuzeyev.[39] Life goes on and, in the
eyes of history and narrative time, "his death has no relation to the coach
[of the tram]" (409/503) or to its continued progress. Nevertheless, Yury is
protected from the implications of this senseless circular movement by his
refusal to live by its rules (even at the end he desperately tries to open a
window on the tram and then, when that fails, to get off) and by his art, his
*podvig* of celebration (as opposed to Strelnikov's "heroic feat" of revenge),
which lives on after him.

*Doctor Zhivago* presents essentially three opposing views of historical time
and the latter's relation to the fate of "Russia the bride." These views are

---

[39] Cf. Pasternak's mention of V. Inber's division of history into sketches on a tram window
in "O skromnosti i smelosti" 220.

embodied in the three principal male characters—Komarovsky, Strelnikov-Antipov, and Yury—and find clearest expression in their relationships with Lara. Moreover, each view is dominated by allegiance to a single temporal category (old, new), and each resorts to a spatial configuration in depicting the historical and biographical implications of this allegiance. It is worth noting that Pasternak is willing to take considerable liberties with actual historical chronology and its incarnation in narrative time in order to preserve the basic mythical features of this scheme. These features might be formulated as follows: (1) Time without the dimension (the new beginning) of Christ is an endless repetition of past failures, a traducing of the higher elements in human beings, and a cynical application of the carpe-diem philosophy—its geometrical figure is the closed circle;[40] (2) Time is a radical turning point, a *re*-volution that seeks to inaugurate the new by violently exterminating all those who entrap human beings in the old—its geometrical figure is the straight line into a better future;[41] and (3) Time, rather than being a destructive break with the past, is a constant celebration of that "living life" which emerges out of, and ultimately transcends, all failed beginnings, and which transforms brute history into Christian History—its geometrical figure is the seasonal cycle, the circle that opens and closes every year and is epitomized by the natural and religious connotations of Easter. One would not wish to claim that Pasternak's design here is narrowly allegorical; there are enough "lyrical" inconsistencies and idiosyncratic departures from the basic model to preserve the author's repeated emphasis on time as, first and foremost, "spontaneous life." Still, Pasternak did have a fixed number of images that could serve him in his depiction of the shape of Russian history, and our singling out of these three merely confirms this.

Let us begin our discussion with Komarovsky, who represents the old, or time "before Christ." Obviously, the well-heeled Moscow lawyer does not live in pre-Christian times, but Pasternak wishes to suggest that in his complicity in the deaths—literal *and* figurative—of those close to Yury, in his urge for lower, prurient forms of pleasure at the expense of others, and in his corrupting influence on all that is beautiful and free, he stands in relation to Russia on the eve of the Revolution as the Roman ruling class once stood in relation to the Empire's captive peoples on the eve of the Christian era. Komarovsky's close ties with the Roman ethos surface often and in marked contexts: he is first presented to the reader as a smug "thoroughbred animal" (*porodistoe zhivotnoe* [17/14]). This epithet becomes clearer

---

[40] Cf. the "closed circle" of time tormenting Pilate in *The Master and Margarita* (Chapter Four).

[41] Cf. the road taken by all the disenfranchised *duraki* in Platonov's *Chevengur* (Chapter Three).

in later evocations of the circus or coliseum; its objective correlative in the
modern Moscow setting is the lawyer's constant companion, the disgusting
bulldog Jack.[42] Lara, once seduced by Komarovsky, becomes his "slave [*ne-
vol'nitsa*] for life" (43/48); she recalls how she has been forced to sit like a
kept woman, an objet d'art, in the private rooms of an expensive restaurant:
"What was the name of that terrifying painting with the fat Roman [that
hung] in the same first room where it all began? 'Woman or Vase' " (48/
53). Finally, situated between descriptions of Lara before and after her fall
are Uncle Nikolay's (one of Pasternak's mouthpieces) explicit comments on
the "dead time" of ancient Rome:[43]

> That ancient world ended with Rome because of overpopulation. Rome
> was a flea market of borrowed gods and conquered peoples in two tiers,
> one on earth and one in the heavens, a swinishness wrapped in a triple
> knot around itself like an intestinal blockage. Dacians, Herulians,
> Scythians, Sarmatians, Hyperboreans, heavy wheels without spokes,
> eyes sunken in fat, sodomy, double chins, the feeding of fish with the
> flesh of educated slaves, illiterate emperors. There were more people
> on earth than at any time since, and they were all jammed into the
> passages of the coliseum, and they all suffered (40/43–44).

The images selected by the author to present Komarovsky's Roman ethic
(convoluted intestines, wheels without spokes, passages of the coliseum)
already anticipate the shape of time that will entrap Lara after her fall: "Oh,
what a *charmed circle*!"[44] she found herself in; "She would say to herself,

---

[42] Cf. "I [Nikolay Vedenyapin] think that if one could stop the slumbering beast in man
with threats, . . . then the highest emblem of humanity would be the circus tamer with a whip
and not a self-sacrificing preacher" (39/42).

[43] Pasternak is explicit about Lara's inner symmetry, the combined psychic and physiological
senses of well-being *before* her "fall" to Komarovsky. After the seduction, however, she no
longer experiences this *in tactus* joy (likened to the invisible string joining the salient of her
left shoulder to the big toe of her right foot as she lays in bed). Compare the change from 25/
25 to 44/49.

[44] In a letter of March 3, 1953 to V. F. Asmus, Pasternak described his condition in 1935,
when he was suicidally depressed over the falseness of his public role (poet laureate) and suffered constant insomnia, in the following terms: "Then I was eighteen years younger, Mayakovsky had still not been deified, [and so] they fussed over me, sent me abroad, and there was
no manner of inanity or muck that I wouldn't have said or wrote, and that they wouldn't have
printed; in reality I had no illness, but I was incurably unhappy and was perishing, *like he who
is charmed by an evil spirit in a fairytale*. . . . My task [i.e., to create something worthy] was
impossible—a *squared circle* [*kvadratura kruga*]" (Mossman and Aucouturier, "Perepiska
Borisa Pasternaka"). Compare the following opening to the second chapter of Blok's poem
*Retribution* as a possible subtext for Lara's (i.e., "Russia's") condition:
> In those distant and hollow years
> sleep and darkness reigned in [people's] hearts:

'And what if I were to marry him? How would that be different?' She *entered onto the path* of sophistry. But at times *a despair without issue [toska bez iskhoda]* would seize [or 'envelop'—*okhvatyvat'*] her" (43, 44/47, 48). The young heroine constantly feels the desire to fall into a physical and moral sleep—that is, she longs to forget the present by becoming a sleeping beauty who awaits the kiss of her prince. Thus the "charmed circle" keeping her in bondage to Komarovsky is both an image of religious time (Rome before her rechristening as Moscow, the third and final holy city) and folkloric time (the heroine under the spell of an evil wizard). When Yury first lays eyes on the strange girl "from another world," in the aftermath of her mother's attempted suicide (also caused by Komarovsky), he is immediately struck by all of these things:

> . . . On the other side of the dinner table, covered with a knit tablecloth, there *slept*, sitting up, a girl in an arm-chair, with her arms *wound around* its back and her cheek pressed to it. She was probably *deathly tired* if the noise and movement around her didn't bother her as she slept. . . .
>
> In the meantime a silent scene took place between the girl and the man [Komarovsky]. . . . Their understanding of one another was *frighteningly magical*, as though he were the puppetmaster and she, obedient to the movements of his hands, the marionette. . . .
>
> Yura stared transfixed at them both. From his position in the half-darkness, where he could not be seen by anyone, he looked, unable to tear himself away, into the lamp-lit *circle*. The spectacle of the *enslaved* girl had something about it unutterably mysterious and shamelessly open (54-55/61–62; my emphasis).

This scene offers an excellent example of how, according to Pasternak, History lies concealed within history, time that is meaningful and emplotted "from beyond" exists within time that is meaningless and tragic. From the viewpoint of "Fairy Tale," structurally and thematically the central

---

Pobedonostsev extended over Russia
his owlish [*sovinye*] wings,
and there was neither night nor day,
but only the shadow of his gigantic wings;
he drew around Russia an enchanted
circle [*divnyi krug*], looking into her eyes
with the glassy stare of a wizard;
to the intelligent sound of this wondrous tale
it is not difficult for a beauty to fall asleep,—
and she grew foggy-headed,
smothering hopes, thoughts, passions . . .

(*ss* III: 328).

poem in the cycle that concludes the narrative and physically stands *beyond* it, Lara is transformed into the captive maiden (also Russia), Komarovsky into the serpent (the force responsible for Russia's fallen state), and Yury into Saint George (the Dragonslayer). The context in which the poem is drafted (Varykino) is somewhat misleading, since the reader, also as it were "under a spell," is lured into believing that the process of metapoesis takes place in that narrative "here" and "now." And so it does—the wolves closing in on the old Kreuger estate become the dragon of historical necessity, and there is no actual mention of Komarovsky (although he will soon appear to take Lara away again). But this earlier scene provides the actual genesis for the poem, whose "narrative" functions as a counter-weight to the other narrative, located *inside* history, out of which it grew. Lara is caught in the circle of lamplight by the magical power of Komarovsky the wizard/puppetmaster. Her arms are entwined around the chair with the same verb of encirclement (*obvit'*) that will appear in the poem to describe the serpent's tail. She is utterly worn out by her ordeal and has fallen into a deep, death-like sleep. Yet "miraculously," Yury will make use of all these images of captivity in the later poem about liberation.

There are two representatives of a younger, "new" generation whose role it is to break the vicious circle of Lara's captivity to Komarovsky and his world. The first is Pasha Antipov, the young boy who, with his "unusual power of clear and logical reasoning," his "great moral purity," and his "talent for imitation" (208, 210/254, 256), becomes Strelnikov, the "shooter" (from *streliat'*), the "executioner" (from *rasstreliat'*), and the "straight-arrow" (from *strela*). Hidden in the commissar's *nom de guerre* is his violent reply, his volley of conscience, to the ills that caused Lara's seduction and fall. The revelation of Lara's past, which takes place on the couple's wedding night, forever transforms this swain of the revolution, this "Stepanida" or "fair maiden," into an entirely new person (the future Strelnikov): "In all Antipov's life there had not been a change more decisive and sudden than the one that night. In the morning he woke up a different person, and afterwards was surprised that people still called him by his former name" (84/98). The tragic, irreversible implications of the transformation are then made manifest on many subsequent occasions. When, for example, Lara confides to Yury how Antipov's moral purity became perverted by his commitment to remaining Strelnikov *until* the world was ready for him to return to his family, she describes his iron will as a "Roman civic virtue" (250/309)—that is, one worthy of the arena or coliseum—and his fanatic belief in an abstract ideal as the equivalent of "giving himself over to higher forces that, deadening and pitiless, would one day not spare him" (334/412). The commissar's "quarrel with history,"[45] his noble ef-

---

[45] "On stal dut'sia *na khod sobytii, na istoriiu*" (337/415; my emphasis).

forts to "pay back in full for everything that she [Lara] had suffered, to wash clean all the sad memories, so that any return to the past would be impossible" (385/473), are doomed *in advance* because he is compelled to use the same *Roman* methods, including force and Realpolitik, that corrupted the old. Finally, during the last and fatal encounter at Varykino between "Doctor Life" and his now suicidal foil, Yury conjures up Strelnikov-Antipov out of his past with precisely those images for which the whole novel has prepared us: " 'Who is this? Who is this? . . . Is it possible? A hot May morning of some year now forgotten. *The railroad station* at Razvilie. *The ill-boding coach of the commissar.* The clarity of his views, the *straightforwardness*, the severity of his principles, his rectitude, rectitude, rectitude. Strelnikov!' " (380/468)

The implicit motivation for Antipov's transformation into Strelnikov is gradually revealed through the remarkable incidence of railroad imagery in the text.[46] This transformation is quite at odds with any Christian metamorphosis, since it reduces—in the name of humanity—the human to the level of machine. The light-hearted and puckish young Pasha becomes the dour and self-destructive commissar. The complete change is also homologous, that is, conceptually equivalent, to the subtle differences wrought in, and by, the word-picture of the railroad during the course of the novel. The railroad, which both tolls out the "old" (the suicide of Yury's father on the five o'clock express) and rings in the "new" (the strikes on the Brest line that inaugurate the revolutionary movement), is where children, playing at *shooting*, grow into genuine revolutionaries. It is also where the tsar makes his final pathetic appearance to his troops; where Gints, the young officer sent to quell an angry mob, is destroyed by his stentorian allegiance to an abstract and obsolete code of honor; and where Yury, the quintessential passenger, has his vivid encounters with such revolutionary types as the deaf-mute Klintsov-Pogorevshikh and Strelnikov. Later on, after the revolutionary movement has run amok and Strelnikov the pursuer has become Strelnikov the pursued, the new atmosphere of aimlessness and destruction is captured by the same image of the railroad. Now, however, the latter has been metamorphosed into vacant stretches of tracks, with the mammoth, frozen corpses of locomotives lying alongside them, which Yury passes *on foot*, as he makes his way slowly back to Yuryatin from his forced service with the Forest Brotherhood. And later still, it is Komarovsky's special train that takes Lara from Yury, just as it is the urban version of the train (the tram) that is the site of Yury's fatal heart attack, and it is the military train that comes to rescue Yury's and Lara's orphan daughter Tanya and to exact

---

[46] The train as a leitmotif has been mentioned by several scholars (see, e.g., Danow, "Epiphany" 890–91), but little has been done to place the image within the larger context of the themes and structure of the novel and, indeed, of Pasternak's art in general.

the death penalty on the malefactor who has tortured her adoptive family. These are but a few of the instances of foregrounded railroad imagery in the text: presenting the grim trajectory—from nursery (the Brest line) to graveyard (the snowy expanse of empty tracks and abandoned locomotives)—of what began as "straightforward" revolutionary time, these descriptions also suggest that, in the hippodrome of life, there are new competitors, but no real winners.

No character is of course more closely associated with the train as emblem of revolutionary time than Strelnikov. This bond, which seems almost congenital, begins in childhood, long before his transformation into machine-like commissar. Here the young man's purity and rectitude (*pravota*) provide the motive force and direction (na*pravlenie*) for his subsequent acts of heroism and cruelty. According to Pasternak's metaphorical thinking, once the young man commits himself to *righting* the wrongs of the old through "shooting" he has also left the station, as it were, of his innocence and begun his trip down tracks that permit no reverse or lateral movement. (Yury, on the other hand, constantly insists on his status as an observer, "on the side.") Thus there is a certain logical symmetry linking: (1) Antipov's origins as the son of a railroad switchman (*strelochnik*, that is, one that regulates movement and direction on the tracks); (2) the first, seemingly innocent shots of the children "playing at war" (" 'The boys are shooting [mal'chiki *streliaiut*],' thought Lara. She was thinking this not about Nika [Dudorov] and Pasha [Antipov], but about the whole city firing its shots [obo vsem *streliavshem* gorode]. 'They are good, honest boys,' she thought. 'They are good and for that reason they are shooting [ottogo i *streliaiut*]' " [46/51]; (3) the shot (*vystrel*) fired by Lara at Komarovsky during the Sventitskys' party which is thereafter forever connected in Yury's mind with the coming revolution; (4) the shots of the soldiers at the front signaling the beginning of the revolution ("Just think, Brest St., No. 28. And now again the shooting [*strel'ba*], but this time it is much more terrifying. This is not your game of 'kids shooting' [mal'chiki *streliaiut*]" [109–10/131]); (5) the shot from the midst of the angry mob that fells Gints at the station; (6) the implicit relation between Klintsov-Pogorevshikh's extremist views ("there was an air of Petenka Verkhovensky [from Dostoevsky's *The Devils*] about him" [137/165]) and his reputation as a "crack shot [*strelok*]"; (7) the shot of the Forest Brotherhood that awakens Yury from his reverie as he rides back to Varykino and tries to make his choice between Tonya and Lara; (8) the repeated shots ("*vystrel za vystrelom*" [279/343]) that the doctor discharges into the strange tree during a skirmish between the partisans and a group of White cadets; and (9) the shot that Strelnikov administers to himself ("lezhal za*strelivshiisia Pavel Pavlovich*,"—"there lay Pavel Pavlovich who had shot himself" [386–87/476]) at the end of his road.

As in the word-picture of the railroad, of which this is part, the scenes of shooting add up to a narrative. There is in them a straightforward reasoning which might be summed up as "he who lives by the sword (or bullet) shall die by the sword." Lara and Yury are spared this kind of death because their shots do not kill and because, ultimately, in the love that brings them together, they stand for life. Again, once Lara is caught in the dizzying circles of the Sventitskys' waltzes (see 71–73/82–84), she enters a "will-less, dream-like" state, feels the chain begin to tighten around her, and fires at the wizard (and indeed at the entire world he inhabits) who has cast the spell. But she hits Boris Kornakov, the friend of the implacable prosecutor trying the case of the *striking railroad workers.* No one is seriously injured, and the wizard's circle of time remains intact until Yury is finally able to pierce it with his art. Likewise, when on the battlefield Yury fires into the gnarled *arbor crucis,* he is acting out his role as "Fyodorovian soldier," that is, trying to bring down the symbol of moribund adherence to form (the cadets' "honor"), which prevents these otherwise good young people from "living life." In this particular episode, the shot which Yury believes has killed the White recruit Seryozha has in fact been miraculously stopped by an amulet containing the ninetieth psalm; the doctor, far from causing the death of a boy, is allowed, like Christ ministering to Lazarus, to raise the latter from the dead (see Masing-Delic, "Fedorovian Soldier" 301–10).

Within the mythic structure of the novel, where comparisons are not literal but literary, metapoetic, Strelnikov-Antipov plays Laertes to Yury's Hamlet, Tybalt to his Romeo, and, *mutatis mutandis,* Antichrist to his Christ. Nowhere is this final comparison made clearer than at the moment when each character finds his "path" in life, the spatial projection onto the future of his reason for living. What is more, these paths are joined to one another as mirror opposites. In both cases their goal involves the status of Lara and the Russia she symbolizes: that is to say, both "paladins" are called at roughly the same time to do battle in the service of their maiden. Yury first realizes his mission while musing on the Christmas message of Alexander Blok's poetry; he glances up from the street to see a *candle* shining in a window on Kamerger Street (see Masing-Delic, "Zhivago's 'Christmas Star' "). It is not fortuitous that Yury looks *up* from his position as a passerby to focus on this very domestic Christmas star, since it is the same one by whose guttering light Lara is now trying, unsuccessfully, to explain to Pasha the reason for her perturbation as she sets off for the Sventitskys. In other words, even as Lara is reliving the horrifying chain of her fall and captivity, Yury—without "knowing" it, of course—is thinking *ahead* to the various ways his poet's alchemy might turn that fall and its traditional attribute in novelistic time (candlelight) into a symbol of resurrection and the *risen* soul.[47] This symbol will find its most eloquent expression in the upward movement of "Winter Night" (445–46/550–51), a central lyric in the poetic cycle that exists *beyond* the prose section, *beyond* the death of the hero and the disappearance of the heroine.

Conversely, the moment at which Pasha becomes the future Strelnikov is also the moment at which he learns the details of Lara's past. In this regard, Yury's advice to the dying Anna Ivanovna (Tonya's mother) is especially apropos: "Consciousness is a *light shining outward*; consciousness *illumines the way before us* so that we don't stumble. Consciousness is *the headlight of a forward moving locomotive. Turn the light inward* and the result will be *a crash*" (60/68; my emphasis). Once Strelnikov has translated the revolution into the settling of personal scores and "has driven his hurt inward" (Michigan 257), he becomes just such a runaway train. Indeed, when Yury later tells Lara his impressions of the commissar, this image resurfaces: "How did he strike me? As someone doomed. I think that he will end badly. He will have to atone for the evil he has wrought. These self-appointed rulers [*samoupravtsy*] of the revolution are horrifying not as villains, but as *mechanisms out of control*, as *trains that have lept the tracks*" (247/306).[48] It is not unexpected then that Pasha Antipov's Christmas star—which he finds when he decides to abandon his family, enter the army, and set in motion the play-within-the-play which casts him as Strelnikov—no longer has any connection to the domestic or natural world. The celestial bodies whose configuration in the heavens has long guided humanity in its search for divine intentionality are suddenly (as in a revelation!) *eclipsed* by manmade illumination; this blinding *cognitio* is, tragically, the only "opening" (*vykhod*) into another time that this modern Hector, with his "one-track" mind, can imagine:

> Antipov sat on the overturned boat [in his yard in Yuryatin] and looked at the stars. The thoughts to which he had grown accustomed over the last years seized him with alarming force. It seemed to him that sooner or later he would have *to think them through to the end* [my emphasis], and it would be better to do so today. . . . He looked at the stars as though he were asking them advice. They shone, in clusters and in isolation, large and small, blue and iridescent. Suddenly, blotting out

---

[47] The *topos* of the fallen woman (*padshaia zhenshchina* [see 41/45]) whose features are outlined against the artificial light of the candle—as opposed to the natural light of day—occurs in the works of a number of nineteenth-century writers, including Dostoevsky (*Notes from Underground*) and Chekhov ("An Attack of Nerves").

[48] It is ironic that R. Eideman once defined Pasternak as a "perfected locomotive" carrying an empty cargo. See A. Selivanovskii, "V zashchitu sovetskoi kul'tury" 4–5; cited in Fleishman, *Tridtsatye gody* 365).

their radiance, the yard together with the house, boat, and Antipov himself were illumined by a harsh, rapidly moving light, as though someone were running from the field to the gate and swinging a lighted torch. Hurling clouds of yellow smoke shot with flame into the sky, it was a military train moving west by the crossing, as had countless others, day and night, beginning the year before. Pavel Pavlovich smiled, got up off the boat, and went to bed. The longed-for solution [*vykhod*] had been found (92–93/110).

As Lara's other knight, Zhivago is never associated with the relentless movement of the train. He is often a passenger, to be sure, but this only underscores his willingness to be borne along by the powerful forces of history without ever trying, like the son of the *strelochnik*, to guide or re-route them. Saint George (Yegory Khrabry, Georgy Pobedonosets),[49] is, after all, a horseman (*konnyi*), and, as his novelistic incarnation, Yury expresses himself most fully when the hoofbeats of historical time are rendered in spirited trimeter (see 362–67/450–53).[50] The image of the horse is not nearly so prominent in *Doctor Zhivago*, especially in the early sections, where it is overshadowed by the train, but it is still marked. There are in fact several episodes in which its meaning is juxtaposed to that of the train (that is, "new," "revolutionary" time), and two in particular are pivotal to our understanding of Yury as modern a Saint George. At first the equine

---

[49] Of the various commentators who have glossed the Saint George theme in *Doctor Zhivago*, Bodin (*Nine Poems* 47–66) is most illuminating. Her analysis is based on the poem "Fairy Tale" ("Skazka"), with numerous cross-references to the narrative section and with helpful explications of the sources that Pasternak/Zhivago may have had in mind as he wrote the work (folk poetry, *dukhovnye stikhi* [folk verse with religious message], hymns, academic and icon painting, modern adaptations in Rilke, Chukovsky, Shvarts, and Tsvetaeva, etc.). Bodin is particularly persuasive in her conclusion about Yury's potentially confusing incarnation as Saint George: "It is important to point out . . . that Jurij only becomes St. George in his imagination, never in reality; to regard the hero of the prose portion of the novel as a St. George figure possessing the same qualities as the protagonist of 'Skazka' is consequently incorrect. The most important criterion for this—strength of will—is lacking. If we would like to understand the hero of the novel and of 'Skazka' . . . as being a single person . . . we have to see the energetic hero of the poem as a development, rather than a reflection of the passive hero of the prose portion of the novel. . . . [Hence] the novel consists of two parts, the prose portion describing a passive and the verse portion an active principle. . . . In the same way that St. George arises from death to lead a new and active life, the hero of the novel comes to life again in its verse section" (65–66). The Russian folk tradition of Saint George is also described in considerable depth in Senderovich, "Chudo Georgiia o zmie."

[50] See as well the Pushkinian image of "raising the horse [of the revolution] on its haunches" and of laying mounted siege to the citadel-like epoch in the 1936 lyric "He rises up. The centuries . . ." (*Stikhi 1936–1959* 6–7). Fleishman argues (*Tridtsatye gody* 288) that this poem was an important turning point in Pasternak's work, signaling the appearance of a civic or *engagé* element that had been almost totally absent in his earlier lyric verse.

image acquires connotations of fatality and valediction: horses, the traditional funerary symbol, bear the remains of Yury's mother to the cemetery on the novel's opening page (their movement is accompanied by the singing of "Eternal Memory"), and Anna Ivanovna's pulmonary ailment begins after a fall from a wardrobe, which is then likened to "the horse of Prince Oleg, a thing bringing death to its owner" (57/64). Elsewhere horses are described as appearing to stand in place when compared to the precipitous movement of the express train (the same one from which Yury's father will hurl himself to his death [15/12]); they are associated with the rich life of tsarist dragoons and with a show of circular prancing in Lara's dreams (25/25); they draw the handsome carriage of Fuflygin, the divisional manager of the Brest Line, and are skittish and "frightened of the railroad" (27/28); they carry armed dragoons into a defenseless crowd of demonstrators that includes Pasha Antipov (34–35/37–38); and they form a cordon of Cossack support for the threatened Gints—only the support disintegrates in the wake of the latter's bombast, and his dying pose is that, ironically, of "one mounted [*sidiashchii verkhom*] on the edge of the [water] butt" (131/157).[51] Here horses appear to be emblematic of a *pre-revolutionary* way of life and are endowed with an implicit, "animal" awareness of their *transitional* status; whether as mode of conveyance or as mounted reply to the threat of revolution, they seem almost to sense that the superiority that was once theirs belongs now to an iron counterpart.

But Yury's role as Saint George is realized through his art, not his martial exploits. Rather than the sword (or rifle) of his foil, his weapon is the pen. And as modern artist, as lone Johannine voice in the wilderness of revolutionary Russia, he "constantly contemplates death and by this act constantly creates life" (78/91). Hence the horse, for Yury and Lara, becomes something more than a conveyance in the hippodrome of life. It carries them *out* of brute history as such and *into* the magic world of mythic, folkloric, poetic time. Pasternak hints at this early in the novel when Lara, on the eve of her departure to *Yury*atin, hears a strange noise *through an open window* of her apartment:

[51] See also the description of the military types that Yury meets earlier at the commandant's: "The doctor was the only person in the room who sat normally [lit: 'like a human'—*pochelovecheski*]. . . . The commandant almost lay across his desk, his cheek on his fist, in the manner of Pechorin [i.e., the Byronic hero of Lermontov's *A Hero of Our Time*]. His aide, a massive, stout man, perched on the arm of the sofa as if *he were riding side saddle [kak v damskom sedle]*. Galiullin *sat astride a chair [sidel verkhom na stule]*, his arms folded on its back and his head resting on his arms, and the commissar kept hoisting himself by his wrists onto the window sill [i.e., as though during riding practice?] and jumping off and . . . running up and down the room with small quick steps" (116/139).

At this time a completely different and unique sound coming from the courtyard through the open window attracted her attention. Lara drew back the curtain and leaned outside.

In the courtyard a hobbled horse was shifting about [*peredvigalas'*] with lame little jumps. No one knew whose it was and it had probably wandered into the courtyard by mistake. It was already almost completely light, but still a long time before sunrise. The sleeping and, as it were, completely desolate (lit. "died out"—*vymershii*) city was drowned in the violet-gray coolness of the early [morning] hour. Lara closed her eyes. God knows into what quiet, charming country place [*derevenskaia glush'*] this distinctive and incomparable shifting about of the shod horse [*konskoe kovanoe perestupanie*] was taking [*perenosilo*] her (85/100).

This is the only instance in the text *before* Yury's and Lara's love affair in which the horse is endowed with an unmistakably positive, purely folkloric valence. Lara does not know it, but this unprepossessing steed is pointing her in the direction of Yuryatin, the town named after her Saint George. Like the heroine in earlier passages, the city has fallen into a sleep bordering on death in anticipation of the liberating horseman. The repeated emphasis on movement from one spot to another (the prefix *pere-*, with its central meaning of transit) points up the fact that the heroine (and the Russia she symbolizes) will eventually be borne from the historical "here and now" to a poetically transfigured "then and there." That Pasternak selects a *lame* horse to be the vehicle of this transformation only reinforces the incongruity, the bright irony, separating history from poetry. There is, certainly, nothing accidental ("no one knew whose it was," "it had probably wandered in by mistake," etc.) about the appearance of this animal. Indeed, as Lazar Fleishman has ingeniously demonstrated, it was a throw from a horse— after which the future poet rather than his steed came up lame—that played a crucial, even "predestined" role in Pasternak's decision to give up music and become a poet (*Stat'i o Pasternake* 103–07).[52] To the poetic imagination, a deflating spill from a horse can be precisely what gives Pegasus his wings. And that which is expressed on the plane of biography as a reconsideration of artistic calling (music → poetry) and on the plane of the novel as

[52] In a narrative fragment ("The Arrogant Beggar," wr. 1930s) that served as one of the preliminary sketches to *Doctor Zhivago*, the child (a proto-Yura) is described as having a "horse's mug" (*morda loshadinaia*: *Proza 1915–58* 301–2). This in turn recalls Akhmatova's line (of 1936) in which Pasternak "likened himself to a horse's eye" (*Sochineniia* 1: 234) and Tsvetaeva's remark that there is "something in his face at once of the Arab and his horse" (*Proza* 354). See Fleishman, "Problems in the Poetics" 55; and Gifford, *Pasternak* 178, 258.

an equine-driven restructuring of time (Lara "before" → Lara "after" Yury's poetry) is none other than the very "trimetered, syncopated rhythms of the gallop and the fall" once heard by the lame Pasternak and later given rein to in the rhythmic pace of the steed of "Fairy Tale" (E. Pasternak, "Pis'mo [1913] A. L. Shtikhu" 145).

Yury's dual role as poet-paladin is first made manifest in the text during the initial stage of his affair with Lara. Riding back to Varykino from Yuryatin, and filled with remorse over his betrayal of Tonya, the horseman is overtaken by poetic thoughts at the same time that the poet muses on the significance of his literal and literary "paths." Pasternak, it seems, intends for the two roles to merge and for the physical and emotional spaces to become coextensive. Zhivago, for example, asks himself, " 'What will be further?' . . . And finding no answer, he hoped for something impossible, for the intervention of some kind of unforeseen circumstances that would bring a resolution" (253/312). This "something impossible" will soon take the form of the Forest Brotherhood—eventually Zhivago will lose his wife and family, his "domestic circle" [rodnoi krug], but he will also gain the chance to see Lara again and to create the poetry that will save them both. But for the nonce he is, like the Hamlet to which he often compares himself,[53] unable to decide between the two women, and this indecision is made physically concrete through his desire now to "turn and gallop back to the city" (that is, to Lara), now to "overcome himself and continue his course [to Varykino]" (253/313) (that is, to Tonya).

Suddenly, in one of those moments when Yury becomes preternaturally attuned to the sights and smells of nature (the foliage of the forest, the whining of the mosquitos) and the rhythmic movement of his horse (the squeaking of the leather, the "music" of the animal's hoofbeats and farts), he hears the song of the nightingale summoning him to "Awake! Awake!", a call which his poetic imagination immediately associates with Easter and resurrection: "My soul, my soul! Why do you sleep, arise!" (254/314). The "answer" given by intuition is, within history, a *non-solution*: that is, he decides to *postpone* the "explanation" with Tonya and thereby win for himself one more trip back to Yuryatin to visit Lara. But within art, in which two different plots and two different dénouements can occupy the same space at the same time, such an outcome is possible. The mere thought that he will again see Lara soon and "receive as a gift from the hands of the Creator this God-given white loveliness" (254/314) sends Yury into a lyric swoon. It is doubly appropriate, therefore, that Pasternak's image for this

---

[53] Not necessarily the Hamlet we are accustomed to see discussed in Western scholarship, but the peculiarly "Russian" Hamlet—mediated first by Coleridge and then, more importantly, by Turgenev—who in his role as brooding observer has much in common with the "superfluous man" (lishnii chelovek) of nineteenth-century Russian literature.

state of rapture is one of *giving up the reins* and *embracing the horse*, the very movement of life itself, which responds with a spontaneous burst of speed: "Yury Andreevich threw down the reins, leaned forward in the saddle, embraced the horse around its neck, and buried his face in its mane.[54] Taking this expression of tenderness as an appeal to all its strength, the horse took off at a gallop" (254/314).[55] Time seems to become an attribute of space as the horse's hooves, endowed with a fairy-tale quality, barely touch the earth and huge stretches of the road fly into the background ("[zemlia] . . . otryvalas' ot ego kopyt i otletela nazad": *nazad*, "behind, backward," is a temporal designation as well). The experience of life "at a gallop" is short-lived, however, and Yury is quickly brought back to reality by the sound of a partisan's *shot*. Significantly, he does not force the issue of choice, presented spatio-temporally by the *crossroads* up ahead; instead, that choice is made for him by the "three armed horsemen" (*tri vooruzhennykh vsadnika*), to whom he gives over the reins of his horse.

During the second stay at Varykino, this time with Lara and her daughter Katya, Yury is completely cut off from the outside world, and the lovers' "days are numbered" (354/437). The only way in and out of this fairy-tale kingdom, where a weak-willed doctor with a bad heart becomes Saint George the Dragonslayer and a former nurse his maiden, is with the help of Savraska, a plain, workaday nag. This is no place for trains and the iron logic of revolution. Here, for the only time in the text, we get a careful look at Yury in the process of writing poetry. Here too the hero gives us his most pointed excursion yet into the meaning, and shape, of history:

He again thought that history, or that which is called the course of history [*khod istorii*], is conceivable not at all as is accepted; [instead] it depicted itself to him in its likeness to the life of the plant kingdom. In the winter the bare twigs of the leaf-bearing forest, like the hairs on an old person's mole, are sickly and pitiful underneath the snow. In the spring the forest is transfigured [les *preobrazhaetsia*] in the space of a few days; it reaches to the clouds, and in its leaf-covered thickets one can lose oneself, hide [cf. earlier image of hair/horse's mane]. This transformation [*prevrashchenie*] is achieved by a movement which surpasses the movement of animals in its forward thrust because the animal does not grow as fast as the plant. . . . The forest does not move about [les ne *peredvigaetsia*]; we cannot catch it [in the act], lie

---

[54] This connection between the horse's mane and freedom of movement is taken up later in Sima's description of Mary Magdalene as she unbinds her hair and "unbinds" herself from sin (344–45/424–25).

[55] In this passage Pasternak does not use the neutral word for "horse" (fem: *loshad'*), but the word, much more common in folklore, for "steed" (masc: *kon'*).

in wait for it to change [podsterech' za peremenoiu mesta]. We always
come upon it in a state of immobility. And it is in just such a state of
immobility that we catch unawares the life of society, history, which
is eternally growing, eternally changing, yet imperceptible in its metamorphoses [v svoikh prevrashcheniiakh] (377–78/465).[56]

The narrator represents Yury's point of view as a constant hovering between the ideas of physical transformation and spiritual transfiguration. We
cannot see nature physically move about (the Russian prefix pere-, with its
concrete orientation), but we are aware that every year it is somehow transfigured, made new (the Old Church Slavic prefix pre-, with its metaphysical
orientation). Thus the Christian linear trajectory which joins together a series of unique, one-time occurrences—the birth, death, and resurrection of
Christ—is repeated, made cyclical, "paganized."[57] At the same time, it dis-
cards its characteristic "right-angled" logic, including mention of a final
fiery judgment and condemnation of the unrighteous, and assumes a more
"evolutionary" pattern. But because the "eternally growing, eternally
changing" shape of history is meaningful, that is, entails progress, the analogy with the pagan world is only partial—each spring we do not return to
the same, ahistorical beginning, but to a new start that has moved us closer
to the ideal of Christian brotherhood and to a society of free personalities.
It need hardly be said that the only visual image for this cyclical progression
is the romantic spiral (see Abrams, Natural Supernaturalism 183–87).

The final stage in the metamorphosis of Yury Zhivago into the Red
Crosse Knight occurs during a two-night period of intense creativity. We
know the change is genuine because of the "fact" of the poetry, the legacy
which attests to the miracle and which is meant to continually "revive" the
reader even after the fictional author has suffered a fatal heart attack. Pasternak takes pains to create the illusion of a timeless "no-place" (the snow-
covered wilds of Varykino) where the confrontation between human being

---

[56] See as well the following paragraph: "Tolstoy thought of it [history] in just this way, but
he did not spell it out so clearly. He denied that history was set in motion by Napoleon or any
other ruler or general, but he did not develop this idea to its logical conclusion. No single man
makes history. History cannot be seen, just as one cannot see grass growing. Wars and revolutions, kings and Robespierres, are history's organic agents, its yeast. But revolutions are
made by fanatical men of action with one-track minds [odnostoronnie fanatiki], geniuses in
their ability to confine themselves to a limited field. They overturn the old order in a few hours
or days, the whole upheaval takes a few weeks or at most years, but the fanatical spirit that
inspired the upheavals is worshipped for decades thereafter, for centuries" (378/465–66).

[57] See the Introduction (23–25) and Eliade's and Panchenko's arguments about cyclical return discussed there. Panchenko's point about odrevlenie ("making old") seems especially pertinent.

and history can be appropriately mythologized.[58] The wolves encircling the old Kreuger house lie in wait in a dark, folkloric ravine; their presence is sensed by Savraska, tethered and defenseless in the stable. Yury realizes that his time with Lara is short, and, as he composes "Fairy Tale," he experiences the state which poets call inspiration. The frigid plain becomes the *skazochnyi krai* (fairy-tale realm) of the steppe; the wolves in the ravine become the mythical (*dopotopnyi*—"antidiluvian") serpent in the cave; the frightened work horse the valiant steed trampling the monster; and the sleeping Lara the ransomed princess, the "daughter of the earth" (cf. 365–67/450–53 and 442–44/545–48).

It is at this point, that is, as the specific becomes the general and the real the ideal, that Yury, the creator of this vision, is also himself *transfigured*:

At such moments Yury Andreevich felt that the main work was being accomplished not by him but by something *higher*, something which was located *above* him and governing him, and this was the condition of *universal* thought and poetry, whatever it was destined to do in the future, the next step to be taken in its historical development. And Yury felt himself to be only the occasion, the fulcrum, allowing it to be set in motion.

He rid himself of [the need for] self-reproach, and for a time his feelings of personal wretchedness, his dissatisfaction with himself, left him. He looked about, he took in all that surrounded him (364/448; my emphasis).

This is perhaps the best example in all of *Doctor Zhivago* of those privileged moments, those *revelations*, when *higher* forces break into the narrative and leave their divine watermark. Once again, spatiality stands in for temporality as that which is "higher" becomes *the future in the present* that moves the poet's hand. Yury qua modern prophet does not know why this is so; he knows simply that another voice speaks through him, that he is the instrument of another's will. And so it is that the ash of "personal wretchedness" and failure is burned away in an instant of triumphant illumination and ultimate "disclosure" (*apokalypsis*).

Finally, it should come as no surprise that Yury's search for the right pace for his mythical horse and rider is a search for the right meter, the right lyrical pace, as well. In the kind of "reverse perspective" celebrated by Pavel Florensky in his study of Russian icons, the shortening of the poetic meter translates into a lengthening of the horse's stride until "Saint George the

[58] This is made even more obvious in the poem ("Fairy Tale") that emerges from the narrative section: there the plain outside Varykino is metamorphosed into a "marvelous/fairy-tale realm" (*skazochnyi krai*) and the post-revolutionary winter into an "olden days, once upon a time" (*vstar', vo vremia ono*) (442/545).

Dragonslayer [Georgii Pobedonosets] [is] galloping on his steed across the boundless expanse of the steppe" (367/452). The poet, *waking up* (*probudit'sia*) and *catching fire* (*zagoret'sia*), compresses into the bare spaces of his poem a passionate, full-voiced minimalism; the myth is not superimposed on the meter, but instead grows out of it. The last thing Yury sees, stationed somewhere *behind* and looking ahead through his mind's eye, is the horseman growing smaller, disappearing into the distance (i.e., the future). Thus ends the psychological climax of *Doctor Zhivago*. The hero's tryst with History is over; Lara suddenly awakens and reminds him of the wolves, that is, of the couple's present predicament within the tightening circle of history.

These three versions of historical time—Komarovsky's charmed circle, Strelnikov's revolutionary straight line, and Zhivago's "open circle" or seasonal cycle—all interact and engage in heated dialogue within the text. Although in the last pages Dudorov and Gordon seem chastened and wiser, committed to preserving Yury's memory through his verse (hence the echo-like return to the singing of "Eternal Memory" with which the novel opened), there is no clear resolution. Instead there is the hope that Moscow will *come into* its rightful inheritance as the Holy City. "After the era of the locomotive," Pasternak once said, "will come the era of love" (de Mallac, *Pasternak* 336). This sense of muted hopefulness, preserved despite much evidence to the contrary, is, as we remarked at the outset, quite typical of Pasternak. It is also at odds with the temper of Socialist Realism, which tends to corset all sanguine predictions within the confines of the present tense, to make of them a *fait accompli* or at least an iron-clad inevitability. Yet Pasternak, who cannot conceive of history other than as a progressive cycle, is honest enough to admit that his characters, even at the end, are still unwitting participants in the hippodrome of life. The conversation of his friends still seems predictably imitative and ungifted to Yury; it is described as a "runaway cart which carried them where they didn't want to go. They couldn't turn it and so in the end they were forced to run into and crash against something" (400/493). Their thoughts are again conceived in images of inorganic springs and mechanisms and their entire circle of friends is "hopelessly ordinary" (Michigan 493). Dudorov's stories about exile in the camps is likened to "a horse that tells how it broke itself at the riding rink [manège]" (402/495). And finally, Yury's own death in the same hippodrome (*ristalishche*) goes unnoticed by the aged Mademoiselle Fleury, who continues on her way with her private concerns, as if she too were wearing blinders.

Perhaps the most curious and, for Pasternak, telling element in his use of the apocalyptic subtext is the role of Evgraf, the strange boy with Kirghiz eyes who turns out to be Yury's half-brother and who appears just in time to "cure the doctor" of typhus—raising him, like Lazarus, from the dead. His vague and distant origins and his miraculous comings and goings make him, as Edmund Wilson once remarked, a being that seems "to descend upon Yury from a higher realm" ("Legend and Symbol" 8). Although his role might be reduced to that of the helpful hen of the folktale, most commentators have acknowledged that there is something else afoot in his activities. In the midst of famine he provides the ailing Yury with white bread, butter, sugar, and coffee, and, though still a boy, he instructs the Zhivago family in how to survive. He is, in a word, a novelistic equivalent of the angel of Revelation, the messenger from another space-time come to the prophet in the wilderness. In fact, Yury recognizes him as "the spirit of his death" (174/211) who helps him write poetry, that is, create life, and as we learned earlier in Yury's musings at Anna Ivanovna's funeral, it is art's central concern to continue the Revelation of John, to meditate on death and thus create life (78/91). Hence Evgraf's function in the story of Yury's life is meant to be seen as *apocalyptic, revelatory*: he sends Yury to Yuryatin, to the rendezvous with the heroine, just as surely as the lame horse sends Lara. Moreover, the poem he inspires contains much verbal play,[59] a clear Easter message ("Time to arise, time for the resurrection" [174/211]), and the image of Mary Magdalene (Lara's poetic incarnation). Stalin, strangely enough, whose phone calls, letters, and "wonder-working intervention" (see Fleishman, *Tridtsatye gody* 283) had a great/fatal impact on the lives of poets dear to Zhivago's creator, seems to have served at some level as a prototype for Evgraf. Yet elsewhere he is called by Pasternak "a giant of the *pre-Christian* era of human history" (Gladkov, *Meetings* 78; my emphasis). How, asks the reader, can these competing mythical categories (pre-Christian/Christian) be reconciled, how can the "plowman" be transformed into a guardian angel, except in art and the skewing of historical chronology that the latter allows?

In closing, brief mention should be made of the poems, which were intended to be read together with the narrative and to resolve what is left flawed and fallen in the life of Yury Zhivago.[60] A good deal has been written about the structure and themes of the cycle as well as about its connections

[59] There is ironically no poem called "Turmoil" ("Smiatenie")—the name given the poem in the text—in the poetic cycle written by Yury Zhivago. The rhyming and vocalic instrumentation spill over into the prose paragraph following the mention of the poetic lines which Yury's thoughts of death inspire: "*Rady* kosnut'sia i *ad*, i *raspad*, i razlozhenie, i smert', i odnako, vmeste s nimi *rada* kosnut'sia i vesna, i Magdalina, i zhizn' "—"Glad to be touching him [were] hell, destruction, corruption, and death, but together with them and also glad to touch him [were] spring, Mary Magdalene, and life" (Michigan 211).

[60] Analyses of the "Poems of Yury Zhivago" are found, e.g., in the following: Bodin, *Nine Poems*; Davie, *The Poems of Dr. Zhivago*; Gifford, *Pasternak* 198–213; Masing-Delic, "Some Alternating Opposites"; and Obolensky, "The Poems of Doctor Zhivago."

to the narrative at large. The essential movement of the poems, for example, is from spring ("March," "Passion Week") to spring ("Magdalene," "The Garden of Gethsemane") (that is, from life to life), whereas the essential movement of the narrative is from autumn to late August (that is, from the death of Maria Nikolaevna to the death of Yury Andreevich).[61] Here, however, despite Pasternak's version of history and his insistence that the "lyrical" and the "historical," the mythic and the real, coexist *simultaneously*, the poems remain *outside* the narrative. The reason for this separation may be one of convenience—Pasternak may have wanted to see the poems into print without getting entangled in the question of the publishability of the novel—but that it exists at all is one of the vexed issues facing any reader trying to make sense of the entire work's generic identity. Because the poems hover, as it were, beyond the threshold of the prose portion, they serve as the optical (and aural) illusion of Yury's immortality, of the "cloud" of his creative *élan* that continues to move others after he himself is gone. They are all part of the ulterior design and patterning that constitutes the work's implicit apocalyptic structure. Yet, had Pasternak wanted to show the existence of History *within* history, and of God's *siuzhet* as it shapes time's otherwise mechanical *fabula*, would he not have placed the poems strategically throughout the text? Such a coexistence would have alerted the reader to the actual tension within history between these antinomial terms. As it is, Pasternak, while not believing in a Christian afterlife,[62] nonetheless creates the aesthetic equivalent of one. Presumably, he wants the reader to see (to apprehend spatially) that the time in which Yury becomes Saint George is *of a different order* than the one in which he gives Lara back to Komarovsky. Be this as it may, such a desire does not accord with Pasternak's basic conception of time as a polysemous unity. Pasternak used the concept of a poetic cycle as an aesthetic substitute for the Christian myth in which the Son is resurrected out of death to the right hand of the Father. There is finally a fundamental and irreconcilable difference between the Fyodorovian model (the overcoming of death within history) that governs the worldview of Pasternak and the Florenskian model (the passing through death to another realm beyond) that governs the worldview of Bulgakov.

[61] For the structural parallels between the prose narrative and the poetic cycle, see, e.g., Rowland and Rowland, *Pasternak's 'Doctor Zhivago'* 58–59, and Gifford, *Pasternak* 182.

[62] And in this limited sense he remains a son of Judaism. On the issue of Pasternak's Jewishness, see Gibian, "*Doctor Zhivago*, Russia, and *Rembrandt*"; de Mallac, *Pasternak* 326–37; and Stora, "Pasternak et le judaisme."

# Afterword:
# The End and Beyond

Along the cliff, above the abyss, by its very edge
I whip my horses on, drive them.
I can't get enough air, but I endure, swallowing the mist,
And sense with fatal rapture how I am perishing, perishing.
　　　　—Vladimir Vysotsky, "Slow Down, You Steeds"

How does one "put in perspective" this study of five novels and their relation to one Biblical subtext, the Book of Revelation, and to one historical context, the revolutionary turning-point known as 1917? The process of stock-taking would, ideally, be stereoscopic, since it would take into account the status of the reigning myth ("the End") both at the time these writers wrote about it *and* at our time coming "after." In other words, the reader of these Russian "apocalyptic fictions" is constantly asked to answer a question that vexed not only the early Christians but, indeed, all of Western civilization waiting now some two millennia "on tiptoes" for the second shoe in God's plot to drop—how can history "mean" when the *Parousia* is forever indefinitely postponed?[1] Do we, from our position "in the desert" of a middle, simply ventriloquize the voice from beyond, project a spatial boundary that will stand in for a temporal end in the latter's absence? Each of our Russian novelists was painfully aware of the potential existential homelessness implied by such questioning and each, as I have tried to demonstrate, filled the desert of his printed page with structures that undermined the temporal logic of discourse. No Russian writing in the Stalinist thirties needed to be reminded of the reality of historical context, of the fact that every utterance entered willy-nilly into a larger and often literally "end-determined" discourse—and yet Bulgakov parried *in advance* the thrusts coming from the ubiquitous "other" by building into his novel a transcendental/mystical logic whose "center" (in the language of poststructuralism) was located elsewhere. What was finally "under erasure" in Bulgakov's text was not the Derridean "trace" of a "transcendental signified,"

---

[1] "History has meaning," wrote Berdyaev well before Frank Kermode, "only because it ends" (*Russkaia ideia* 181).

but the very logic of a post-Kantian world. This, like the "open circle" which is its image, is only an optical illusion, since history cannot be un-written (or at least has not been thus far), and the mistake of cowardice committed by Pilate twelve thousand moons ago cannot be undone. There is reason to believe, on the other hand, that Bulgakov himself felt more than a conjurer's aesthetic pleasure in the dénouement of his "sunset novel." We can say this because Bulgakov has his *dead* hero and heroine speak at the end, from beyond the end, to Ivan Homeless, who is still very much trapped in the hippodrome of life. That this cannot be, that Bulgakov cannot thus step outside the "untranscendable horizon" of discourse, is beside the point, since he believed it could, and he could.

What, in the final analysis, do these novels tell us about the Russians' view of the End as it has evolved from the time of Dostoevsky to the time of Pasternak? First of all, the constituent elements of the myth, what Lévi-Strauss has called "mythemes," remain essentially intact. These are not so much the individual motifs found in the apocalyptic subtext (prophet figure, threshold space "betwixt-and-between," Christ and Antichrist foils, etc.), but their interrelations, their combinatory possibilities. And it is precisely such enduring combinatory possibilities that give mythological time its dual nature as "reversible and non-reversible, synchronic and diachronic" ("The Structural Study of Myth" 211). Conversely, the novels we have been dis-cussing do not deal simply in mythological time; the fact that they are about Russian history, with numerous allusions to real events and people, means that the mythological time implicated by the apocalyptic subtext is con-stantly forced to engage in dialogue with the "openness" of contemporary reality. To borrow again from Lévi-Strauss's terminology, the Russian so-ciety here interpreted by myth is not "cold" but "hot," and in this sense the myth means different things to different generations—it not only re-flects but, as it were, "creates" the historical moment which it is employed to "explain." And it is this historicity of myth that I had in mind when I spoke of the changing role of the horseman in the chronotope of these nov-els: Pushkin's equipoise became Gogol's precipitous forward movement be-came Dostoevsky's exhaustion (his *zagnannyi*—"overdriven"—steed) be-came Bely's simultaneous return to all three and his "leap over history," etc. Readers, so to speak, do not look through the window of the text at a stationary scene. Rather, they too are on "history's ride," and their optic, as well as their optical illusion, moves.

If national myths never completely die, it is safe to say that they lose the terms of their original potency. When Alexander Herzen was first exiled to Vyatka (present-day Kirov) in 1835 for his anti-government student activ-ities, he had very negative feelings about Siberia. At one station en route, anticipating the allusion to Dante made by Solzhenitsyn a century later

(*The First Circle*), he remarked that the lines "Through me you enter the woeful city, / Through me you enter eternal grief" could be applied just as easily to "the road to Siberia as to the gates of Hell" (*ss* viii: 219). And yet, by 1838 he was positing for Siberia those very characteristics which he felt were lacking in "European" (i.e., old, worn-out, fallen, corrupt) Russia:

> What is Siberia—this land you do not know at all. I breathed in the icy air of the Ural mountains; its breath is cold, *but fresh and healthy*. Do you realize that Siberia is an entirely new country, an America *sui generis*, precisely for the reason that it is a land without aristocracy, a land . . . which doesn't remember its ancestry, [one] in which people are renewed, shutting their eyes on their entire past existence [. . .]? There [in Siberia] life is enjoyable, and there is enlightenment, but the more important points are: freshness and newness (letter of July 18, 1835 to N. I. Sazonov and N. Kh. Ketcher in Herzen, *ss* xxi: 45–46).

Here was that sense of openness and newness, of a life free from the demoralizing residue of the past, that the Russian intelligentsia was looking for. And here was the fresh starting point that Herzen hoped would give his country's *put'*, the spatialization of its historical mission, a new lease on life. The hidden irony, of course, is that Herzen never in actuality went further East than Vyatka—that is, he never made it to Siberia, never in fact "breathed in the icy air of the Ural mountains." What is so telling is that Herzen, who combined the highest ideals of the liberal intelligentsia with a generally skeptical view of history per se, was satisfied, for the moment at least, with a New Jerusalem *of words*.

But myths cannot be secularized indefinitely, disemboweled of their essentially religious motivation, without running the risk of becoming parodies of their former selves. The limitless steppe of Gogol or the freshness and newness of Herzen's Siberia cannot exist in a vacuum, especially when one considers some of the experiments in "human engineering" that have been made in the name of the first socialist state with dizzying frequency since 1917. It is this degeneration of the "Russian idea," and of the myths and spatial metaphors that feed it, that concerns Georges Nivat in his recent study *Vers la fin du mythe russe* (1981). Edward J. Brown, in a review essay devoted to the latter, sums up the "vers" in Nivat's title in the following way:

> But what of the Russian myth, "moving toward its finale"? Like Russian culture of the nineteenth century itself, the myth has long been in a process of decomposition and decline, and I conclude that no element of it any longer exists as a national image capable of rallying the collective mind. The myth of the steppe degenerated into the Gu-

lag, the myth of the Christian peasant into atheism and alcohol, and, though indeed spared the evils of capitalism, Russia suffers the far greater evil of Zinoviev's "ratorium" (*krysarii*). Except for Solzhenitsyn, whose final religious vision of the national destiny is still in the process of creation, Russian literature of our time is symptomatic of sickness ("Some Reflections" 293–94).

All of the writers we have been discussing belonged to generations (pre-Symbolist, Symbolist, post-Symbolist) that at some level took the Russian myth seriously. If Bulgakov rejected those aspects of the Symbolist ethos that promoted apocalypticism in exclusively national or chauvinistic terms, he did not reject that ethos *in toto*. Mystic and mystifier, apocalypticist and social satirist, he remained a child of his age to the extent that the myth of the End continued to inform his work, but only in its guise as *personal* eschatology. The year 1917 had shown him the impossibility of universal ends and beginnings; he retained only that part of the apocalyptic—the individual end coming "from beyond" as opposed to "from within"—which made his work meaningful in the face of recalcitrant reality. Similar statements could be made, *mutatis mutandis*, about Platonov and Pasternak, although the former, as I have said on several occasions, was unable in the "secular" atmosphere of NEP to find an appropriate transcendent model to replace the naive faith in the proletarian experiment of his youth. Nevertheless, to repeat, all these writers were both young and old enough to come to consciousness under the impact of 1917 as epochal turning-point, to approach the Russian myth within its own, essentially religious terms. They questioned this myth, to be sure, but they still saw it as a worthy adversary.

I would suggest further that the Russian myth of the End continues quietly to assert its existence, even if, in Brown's words, it is no longer "capable of rallying the collective mind." The July 26, 1986 issue of *The New York Times* contains an article describing the psychological effects on Soviet citizens of the disaster at the Chernobyl nuclear plant three months earlier (see also July 27, 1986 issue of *New Russian Word* [*Novoe russkoe slovo*]). A well-known (but unnamed) Soviet writer is mentioned there as citing the following passage—familiar to readers of *The Idiot*—from the Book of Revelation: "The third angel blew his trumpet, and a great star fell from heaven, blazing like a torch, and it fell on a third of the rivers and on the fountains of water. The name of the star is Wormwood. A third of the waters became wormwood, and many men died of the water, because it was made bitter" (8:10–11). The writer then startled his audience by reaching for a Russian-Ukrainian dictionary and pointing out to them that "wormwood" (*polyn'*) in Ukrainian is *chernobyl*'! The atheistic public had to acknowledge, on the strength of this mesmerizing coincidence, that history's plot may not be authored by humanity "from within," but by God "from without." Perhaps the potential contamination of Kiev's water supply (the "fountains of water": lit. "sources of water"—*istochniki vod*) was not simply a human error but a sign of divine judgment? It goes without saying that had Dostoevsky been writing today he would certainly have made some reference to this event through a *porte parole* and mock exegete like Lebedev.

The article about Chernobyl confirms what readers of Soviet-Russian literature have never completely forgotten—that even in the most secular society the Book, or its equivalent, is a sine qua non. Contemporary writers, most of whom were born after the revolution and thus have no direct recollection of it as a sacred or "Great Time," still need some informing myth and the spatial metaphors that underlie it. We recall that for the Solzhenitsyn of "Matryona's Homestead" (1963) this myth finds its repository in an ailing, superstitious old woman, the one "good person" on whose frail shoulders rests the possibility of a spiritually rejuvenated Russia. If the *Rus'* in Russia still exists at all, it does so in the village, and if the spirit of the village and the *narod* still exists, it does so within the boundaries of Matryona's yard and within the walls of her tumble-down house. Echoing the fears of Dostoevsky and Tolstoy a century earlier, Solzhenitsyn has his heroine die in a railroad accident. As a representative of an ideal mythical past, with a language rich in its archaic twists and turns and resistant to modern usage, Matryona dies as she lived—helping others (the very ones who have come to dismantle her home, her roots in the past) and enduring their insults. And it is, significantly, the train, Solzhenitsyn's image for the pitiless force of the "new" (read "Soviet," "atheistic," "non-Russian," etc.) that makes its way deeper and deeper into *kondovaia* (true-timbered) Rus', that destroys Matryona.

Joseph Brodsky, in describing the haunting blackness of the horse in his early "The black firmament was brighter than those legs" (1961), is also describing the blackness in all of us ("I think: it's black inside of us too" [*Stikhotvoreniia* 94]), the willingness to judge, denounce, ignore distinction. This wild stallion, which "knows no saddle" and cannot get any blacker, is, as Anna Akhmatova attested, a kind of photographic negative of the Pale Horse of Apocalypse—the Soviet Pegasus (Simchenko, "Tema pamiati" 506ff.). The entire poem is built on the Tsvetaevan device of beginning "at the end," at the far right of the poetic keyboard, and then *going further, making blackness blacker* (cf. Brodsky, "Footnote to a Poem" 205–8). The final verse, which has split off from the preceding stanzas to assume a position of formal (spatial) as well as thematic prominence (the "punch line"), tells why at last the horse has come to pay his terrible visit:

It was as if he were someone's negative.
Why did he, having stopped his flight,
Tarry among us until the morning?
Why didn't he move away from the campfire?
Why did he breathe the black air,
Rustle about in the trampled brush?
Why did he pour forth black light from his eyes?

He was looking for a rider among us.

(Stikh 95)

In his allegorical works of the sixties and seventies, Vasily Aksyonov returns repeatedly to the question of the pseudo-apocalyptic end of Soviet
history. *The Steel Bird* (1965), for example, tells how the Stalinist traits of
fear and denunciation make their "nest" in a typical Soviet apartment
house; the bird-like title character (Popyonkov), who comes out of nowhere, uses pity and insinuation to gradually occupy more and more of the
building until the inhabitants finally revolt against his despotic presence.
The tyrant and his henchmen relatives are routed—for the time being; the
building, its foundation weakened by the bird's nesting ways, comes top-
pling down; and the formerly feckless apartment manager (Nikolay Nikolaevich), *mounted on a white charger*, leads his comrades off to the paradise
of a new housing project. In *Surplussed Barrelware* (1968), the various
characters are engaged in a kind of Soviet *Canterbury Tales*: they all board
a truck that is traveling to the city of Koryazhsk, where its cargo of empty
barrels is to be redeemed. They cease being sociological types (Volodya the
worker, Irina the teacher, Gleb the sailor, Stepanida the peasant woman-
cum-lab technician, etc.) and succeed in becoming *reborn* individuals only
through the shared experience of dreams and through their longing to find
Good Person (*khoroshii chelovek*). Thus, once in Koryazhsk, they decide
against boarding the train whose departure time is 19:17 (i.e., the train of
Soviet history which has made them into insensate types and over whose
movement they have no control) and to embark instead on mythical barrel
rides (a kind of return to the preconscious world of the womb together with
the "note in the bottle" motif) over the ocean of ahistorical time in search
of the island of Good Person (see Wilkinson and Yastremski, *Surplussed
Barrelware* 8–15).

One of the most important post-Thaw novels is Venedikt Erofeev's tragicomic *From Moscow to the End of the Line* (Moskva-Petushki, 1976). This
work revives many of the same themes and structural principles found in
the earlier "apocalyptic fictions," only the element of parody is now much
stronger. The hero (Venya), a hopeless drunkard and at the same time a

poetic soul, boards the train in Moscow to pay a visit to his girlfriend in Petushki (the "end of the line" he is looking for). But, in this world where everything is dour and drab without a drink, Venya is a contemporary Soviet Christ-figure whose gospel is alcoholic liberation and whose destination is a mock version of the Symbolist Bride. In other words, Erofeev has taken the plague of Soviet society (alcohol) and made it into a vehicle—the only one left—of salvation. Under its influence, the ride becomes, as Tsvetaeva would say, a series of "transfers from the local to the interplanetary [lit. "interspatial"—*mezhprostranstvennyi*]" train (*Stikhotvoreniia* IV: 285). And yet, in the end, the ride and the boisterous rhetoric and vodka-induced oblivion turn on themselves: Venya never makes it to his Beautiful Lady; the line becomes a vicious circle leading back to Moscow; and the angels, who had been his messengers "from beyond," end by cruelly laughing at him (as they would at a body severed in two by a train). After being betrayed by his Peter and forsaken by his God, Venichka winds up on the Sadovaya *Ring Road*, where he realizes he has made a terrible mistake. The mistake materializes in the form of four thugs (a parodic allusion to the Four Horsemen of Apocalypse?), who then pursue, beat, and "crucify" him, this wandering truth seeker and voice in the Soviet desert, by plunging an awl into his neck.

My last example comes from Yury Trifonov's novel *The Old Man* (1978). Generally speaking, Trifonov is closer to the conventions of classical realism—his works are densely populated with the quotidian concerns of educated urban dwellers—and thus is less likely to experiment with the form of parodic allegory than, say, Aksyonov or Erofeev. Still, in *The Old Man*, probably his most ambitious work, the element of myth/allegory does play a significant role. This is because, first of all, the novel is about revolutionary justice and *judgment*: the title character (Pavel Letunov) is the old man who is trying to reconstruct the events surrounding the trial and prosecution of the Cossack lieutenant-colonel Sergey Migulin (whose real-life prototype was Filipp Mironov: see Ermolaev, "Past and Present" 131). Migulin had welcomed the revolution and fought bravely for its principles (although he was categorically against the death penalty), but was disturbed by what was happening to his fellow countrymen in the Don region, who were being victimized by the Communists' policy of terror. The descriptions of violence, whether "White" or "Red," and the logic underlying it are placed in the larger context of the "court of history."[2] There is as well a constant ironic interplay between the "then" of the inner text (the story of Migulin)

---

[2] To be sure, it is not Trifonov's intention to absolve the Whites: one of his most haunting early scenes describes nineteen bodies, massacred by the Whites, that lie barefoot, stacked like firewood in the snow (*Starik* 17–18).

and the "now" of the outer text (the story of Letunov). Migulin is eventually tried for treason (he defies orders and proceeds on his own against the forces of Denikin), sentenced to death, saved at the last minute (the sentence is commuted), re-arrested a year and a half later, and presumably murdered in prison *without a trial* (the actual fate of Filipp Mironov). At the precise moment in the novel when Sergey Kirillovich decides to break ranks with the Revolutionary Military Council (the Red Army forces) and to question the justice of the cause for which he has been fighting (and for which the "old man" has continued to live ever since), the resultant chaos is described in familiarly apocalyptic terms:

> A vivid nocturnal terror in the steppe, where the burning smell of grass and the odor of wormwood [dominate]. . . . By order of the Southern Front Migulin is declared a traitor and said to be outside the law. There is some kind of young priest staying overnight with us. No, not a priest but a seminarian. He is crazy, all the time quietly laughing and crying, mumbling something. . . . Suddenly he comes up to me, squats down—he is lanky and gaunt—and says with weighty sadness, pointing his finger at me:
>
> "Understand, this star's name is Wormwood . . . And the water has become as wormwood, and the people die from its bitter taste [or: 'from bitterness'—*ot gorechi*]" (*Starik* 134).

The half-crazed seminarian dies a senseless death immediately after his prophecy, but Letunov, now on the outside of that time looking in, continues on his search for the *zachem*, the "why," of Migulin's actions, as if the meaning of his own story as well as that of Soviet history depended on it.

These various examples are, to be sure, not conclusive, but they do tell us that the theme of history and its end, and the figures that grant that theme a life as narration, have not disappeared even in times of the most corrosive doubt and irony. Russian literature in general, and the Russian novel especially, have always absorbed the roads and rails of historicist logic by turning them into hollow barrels adrift on a sea of the (im)possible; if these linguistic echo chambers and generic wombs produce, as in the case of Aksyonov's novella, sprigs of yellow blossoms, it is not because that is how things are, but how they *should* be. And as long as Russian writers, to quote Tsvetaeva again, look for the transfer "from the local to the interplanetary train," they will look past their country's long and tragic history of derailings.

# Works Cited

Abrams, M. H. "Apocalypse: Theme and Variations." In *Apocalypse in English Renaissance Thought and Literature*. Edited by C. A. Patrides and Joseph Wittreich. Ithaca: Cornell University Press, 1984. 342–68.

———. *Natural Supernaturalism*. New York: Norton, 1971.

Akhmatova, Anna. *Sochineniia*. Edited by B. A. Filippov and G. P. Struve. 3 vols. Munich: Inter-Language Literary Associates, 1965–83.

Aksyonov, Vassily. *Surplussed Barrelware*. Edited and translated by Joel Wilkinson and Slava Yastremski. Ann Arbor: Ardis, 1985.

Alexander, Paul J. *Byzantine Apocalyptic Tradition*. Edited by Dorothy deF. Abrahamse. Berkeley: University of California Press, 1985.

Alexandrov, Vladimir E. *Andrei Bely: the Major Symbolist Fiction*. Cambridge, Mass.: Harvard University Press, 1985.

———. "Unicorn Impaling a Knight: The Transcendent and Man in Andrei Belyi's *Petersburg*." *Canadian-American Slavic Studies* 16 (Spring 1982): 1–44.

Al'tman, M. S. *Chitaia Tolstogo*. Tula: Priokskoe knizhnoe izd., 1966.

———. "Zheleznaia doroga v tvorchestve L. N. Tolstogo." *Slavia* 34 (1965): 251–59.

Annenskii, Innokentii. *Stikhotvoreniia i tragedii*. Edited by A. V. Fedorov. Leningrad: Sovetskii pisatel', 1959.

Anscheutz, Carol. "Belyi's *Petersburg* and the End of the Russian Novel." In *The Russian Novel from Pushkin to Pasternak*. Edited by John Garrard. New Haven: Yale University Press, 1983. 125–53.

Antsyferov, N. *Dusha Peterburga*. Petersburg: Brokgauz-Èfron, 1922.

Anuchin, D. N. "Sani, lad'ia i koni, kak prinadlezhnosti pokhoronnago obriada." *Trudy Imperatorskogo Moskovskogo Arkheologicheskogo Obshchestva* 14 (1890): 83–226.

Arban, D. " 'Porog' u Dostoevskogo (Tema, motiv i poniatie)." In *Dostoevskii: Materialy issledovaniia*. Edited by G. M. Fridlender. Leningrad: Nauka, 1976. II: 19–29.

Arendt, Hannah. *Between Past and Future: Eight Exercises in Political Thought*. New York: Viking, 1961.

Baehr, Stephen L. "From History to National Myth: *Translatio imperii* in Eighteenth Century Russia." *Russian Review* 37 (January 1978): 1–13.

———. "In the Re-beginning: Rebirth, Renewal and *Renovatio* in Eighteenth-Century Russia." In *Russia and the West in the Eighteenth Century*. Edited by A. G. Cross. Newtonville: Oriental Research Partners, 1983. 152–66.

———. "In the Name of the Father: the Patriarchal Myth in the Russian Utopia and Orwell's *1984*." Article MS.

———. "Regaining Paradise: The 'Political Icon' in Seventeenth- and Eighteenth-Century Russia." *Russian History* 11 (Summer-Fall 1984): 148–67.

———. "The Troika and the Train: Dialogues between Tradition and Technology in Nineteenth-Century Russian Literature." In *Issues in Russian Literature Before 1917: Proceedings from the III International Congress on Soviet and East European Studies*. Edited by Douglas Clayton. Columbus: Slavica, forthcoming.

Bakhtin, M. M. "Forms of Time and of the Chronotope in the Novel: Notes Toward a Historical Poetics." In *The Dialogic Imagination*. Edited by Michael Holquist. Translated by Caryl Emerson and Michael Holquist. Austin: University of Texas Press, 1981. 84–258.

———. *Problemy poètiki Dostoevskogo*. Moscow: Sovetskaia Rossiia, 1979.

Barnes, Christopher. "Boris Pasternak i Revoliutsiia 1917 goda." In *Boris Pasternak: 1890–1960*. Paris: Institut d'études slaves, 1979. 315–27.

Barratt, A. "Apocalypse or Revelation?" Article MS.

Barskov, Ia. L. *Pamiatniki pervykh let russkogo staroobriadchestva*. St. Petersburg: Tip. Aleksandrova, 1912.

Barthes, Roland. "Historical Discourse." In *Structuralism: A Reader*. Edited and with an Introduction by Michael Lane. London: Jonathan Cape, 1970. 145–55.

Bashutskii, A. "Parovye mashiny, zheleznye dorogi i oborotnye banki." *Otechestvennye zapiski* 1 (1839): 1–17.

Bazanov, Vasilii. *Sergei Esenin i krest'ianskaia Rossiia*. Leningrad: Sovetskii pisatel', 1982.

Beatie, Bruce A., and Phyllis W. Powell. "Bulgakov, Dante, and Relativity." *Canadian-American Slavic Studies* 15 (1981): 250–70.

———. "Story and Symbol: Notes Toward a Structural Analysis of Bulgakov's *The Master and Margarita*." *Russian Literature Triquarterly* 15 (1978): 219–51.

Belinskii, V. G. *Polnoe sobranie sochinenii*. 13 vols. Moscow: Akademiia Nauk, 1953–59.

Belozerskaia, L. E. *O, med vospominanii*. Ann Arbor: Ardis, 1979.

Belyi, Andrei. "Apokalipsis v russkoi poezii." In *Lug zelenyi: Kniga statei*. Moscow: Al'tsiona, 1910; rpt. New York: Johnson Reprint, 1967. 222–47.

———. *Arabeski*. Moscow: Musaget, 1911; rpt. Munich, Wilhelm Fink Verlag, 1969.

———. *First Encounter*. Translated by Gerald Janecek. Princeton, NJ: Princeton University Press, 1979.

———. "Krugovoe dvizhenie." *Trudy i dni* 4–5 (1912): 51–73.

―――. *Kubok metelei* (Chetvertaia simfoniia). Moscow: Skorpion, 1908; rpt. Munich: Wilhelm Fink Verlag, 1971.

―――. "Liniia, krug, spiral'—simvolizma." *Trudy i dni* 4–5 (1912): 13–22.

―――. "The Magic of Words." In *Symbolism: An Anthology*. Edited and translated by T. G. West. London: Methuen, 1980. 120–43.

―――. *Masterstvo Gogolia*. Moscow-Leningrad: OGIS, 1934; rpt. Ann Arbor: Ardis, 1982.

―――. *Na rubezhe dvukh stoletii*. Moscow-Leningrad, 1930; rpt. Letchworth: Bradda, 1966.

―――. "Otkrovenie v groze i bure: Istoriia vozniknoveniia Apokalipsisa." *Pereval* 6 (1907): 56–57.

―――. *Peterburg*. Edited L. K. Dolgopolov. Moscow: Nauka, 1981.

―――. *Petersburg*. Translated and with an introduction by Robert A. Maguire and John E. Malmstad. Bloomington: Indiana University Press, 1978.

―――. *Selected Essays*. Edited and translated by Steven Cassedy. Berkeley: University of California Press, 1985.

―――. *Serebrianyi golub'*. Berlin, 1922; rpt. Munich: Wilhelm Fink Verlag, 1967.

―――. *Severnaia simfoniia* (1-aia geroicheskaia). Moscow: V. V. Pashukanis, 1917: rpt. Munich: Wilhelm Fink, 1971.

―――. *Simfoniia* (2-aia dramaticheskaia). Moscow: V. V. Pashukanis, 1917: rpt. Munich: Wilhelm Fink, 1971.

―――. *Simvolizm*. Moscow: Russkoe tovarishchestvo, 1930; rpt. Munich: Wilhelm Fink, 1969.

―――. *Stikhotvoreniia i poèmy*. Edited by T. Iu. Khmel'nitskaia, N. V. Bank, and N. G. Zakharenko. Moscow-Leningrad: Sovetskii pisatel', 1966.

―――. *Vozvrat* (III simfoniia). Moscow: Grif, 1905; rpt. Munich: Wilhelm Fink Verlag, 1971.

Benjamin, Walter. *Illuminations*. Edited by Hannah Arendt. Translated by Harry Zohn. New York: Schocken, 1969.

Bennett, Virginia. "Echoes of Friedrich Nietzsche's *The Birth of Tragedy* in Andrej Belyj's *Petersburg*." *Germano-Slavica* 3 (Fall 1980): 243–59.

Berberova, Nina. "A Memoir and a Comment: The 'Circle' of *Petersburg*." In *Andrey Bely: A Critical Anthology*. Edited by Gerald Janecek. Lexington: University of Kentucky Press, 1977. 115–20.

Berdiaev, Nikolai. *Russkaia ideia*. Paris: YMCA, 1946.

―――. *Smysl istorii*. Berlin: Obelisk, 1923.

Bergson, Henri. *L'Évolution Créatice*. 24 ed. Paris: F. Alcan, 1921.

Bethea, David M. "Aspects of the Biblical Plot in the Age of Symbolism: Blok, Bely, and the Poetics of Revelation." Article MS (forthcoming).

―――. "The Role of the *eques* in Puškin's *Mednyj vsadnik*." Article MS (forthcoming).

*Bibliia ili knigi sviashchennago pisaniia vetkhago i novago zaveta*. Valley Forge: Judson, 1964.

Billington, James H. *The Icon and the Axe: An Interpretive History of Russian Culture*. New York, Random House, 1970.

Blackmur, R. P. "*Anna Karenina*: The Dialectic of Incarnation." In *Anna Karenina*. Edited by George Gibian. Translated by Aylmer and Louise Maude. New York: Norton, 1970. 899–917.

Blok, Aleksandr. "Bezvremen'e." In *Sobranie sochinenii v vos'mi tomakh*. V: 66–82.

———. "Intelligentsiia i revoliutsiia." In *Sobranie sochinenii v vos'mi tomakh*. V: 9–20.

———. "Narod i intelligentsiia." In *Sobranie sochinenii v vos'mi tomakh*. V: 318–28.

———. *Sobranie sochinenii v vos'mi tomakh*. Edited by V. N. Orlov, A. A. Surkov and K. I. Chukovskii. Moscow: Khud. lit., 1960–63.

———. *Stikhotvoreniia*. Edited by Vl. Orlov. Leningrad: Sovetskii pisatel', 1955.

———. *Zapisnye knizhki, 1901–1920*. Edited by V. N. Orlov. Moscow: IKhL, 1965.

Bodin, Per Arne. *Nine Poems from 'Doktor Živago.'* Stockholm: Almquist and Wiksell, 1976.

Bogdanov, Alexander. *Red Star*. Edited by Loren R. Graham and Richard Stites. Translated by Charles Rougle. Bloomington: Indiana University Press, 1984.

Bolen, Val. "Theme and Coherence in Bulgakov's *The Master and Margarita*." *Slavic and East European Journal* 16 (Winter 1972): 427–37.

Borges, Jorge Luis. "Stories of Horsemen." *New Republic* (19 May 1982).

Boyde, Patrick. *Dante Philomythes and Philosopher: Man in the Cosmos*. Cambridge: Cambridge University Press, 1981.

Braudy, Leo. *Narrative Form in History and Fiction*. Princeton: Princeton University Press, 1970.

Briusov, Valerii. *Stikhotvoreniia i poèmy*. Edited by D. E. Maksimov and M. I. Dikman. Leningrad: Sovetskii pisatel', 1961.

Brodsky, Joseph. "Catastrophes in the Air." In *Less Than One*. 268–303.

———. "Footnote to a Poem." In *Less Than One*. 195–267.

———. "Less Than One." In *Less Than One*. 3–33.

———. *Less Than One: Selected Essays*. New York: Farrar, Straus and Giroux, 1986.

———. *Stikhotvoreniia i poèmy*. Washington, D.C.: Inter-Language Literary Associates, 1965.

Brokgauz-Èfron. *Èntsiklopedicheskii slovar'*. St. Petersburg: I. A. Èfron, 1894.

Brooks, Jeffrey. "*Vexi* and the *Vexi* Dispute." *Survey* 19 (Winter 1973): 21–50.

Brown, Edward J. "Some Reflections on the Russian Idea Suggested by the Reading of Nivat's *Vers la fin du mythe russe*." *Russian Review* 44 (1985): 289–94.

Brown, Marshall. " 'Errours Endlesse Traine': On Turning Points and the Dialectical Imagination." *PMLA* 99 (January 1984): 9–25.

Browning Gary L. "The Death of Anna Karenina: Anna's Share of the Blame." *Slavic and East European Journal* 30 (Fall 1986): 327–39.

Bulgakov, Mikhail. *Belaia gvardiia*. In *Romany*. Moscow: Khud lit., 1973.

———. *Master i Margarita*. 2nd ed. Frankfurt/ Main: Possev, 1971.

———. *The Master and Margarita*. Translated by Mirra Ginsburg. New York: Grove, 1967.

———. "Pis'ma protesty M. Bulgakova, A. Solzhenitsyna i A. Voznesenskogo." *Grani* 66 (1967): 151–67.

———. *Sobranie sochinenii*. Edited by Ellendea Proffer. Ann Arbor: Ardis, 1985.

———. *The White Guard*. Translated by Michael Glenny. New York: McGraw-Hill, 1971.

Bulgakov, prot. Sergii. "Pravoslavnaia èskhatologiia." In *Pravoslavie: Ocherki ucheniia pravoslavnoi tserkvi*. Paris: YMCA, 1985. 380–90.

———. "Pravoslavie i apokaliptika." In *Pravoslavie: Ocherki ucheniia pravoslavnoi tserkvi*. Paris: YMCA, 1985. 370–79.

Burkhart, Dagmar. "Leitmotivik und Symbolik in Andrej Belyjs Roman 'Peterburg'." *Die Welt der Slaven* 9 (1964): 277–323.

Carlson, Maria. "The Ableukhov Coat of Arms." In *Andrej Bely Centenary Papers*. Edited by Boris Christa. Amsterdam: Adolf M. Hakkert, 1980. 157–170.

Cassedy, Steven. "Bely the Thinker." In *Andrey Bely: the Spirit of Symbolism*. Edited by John E. Malmstad. Ithaca, NY: Cornell University Press, 1987. 313–335.

Cervantes. *Don Quixote*. Translated by J. M. Cohen. Harmondsworth: Penguin, 1950.

Chaadaev, Peter. *Philosophical Letters, and Apology of a Madman*. Translated by and with an introduction by Mary-Barbara Zeldin. Knoxville: University of Tennessee Press, 1969.

Chatman, Seymour. *Story and Discourse: Narrative Structure in Fiction and Film*. Ithaca, NY: Cornell University Press, 1978.

Cherniavsky, Michael. "Khan or Basileus: An Aspect of Russian Mediaeval Political Theory." In *The Structure of Russian History*. Edited by Michael Cherniavsky. New York: Random House, 1970. 65–79.

———. "The Old Believers and the New Religion." In *The Structure of Russian History*. Edited by Michael Cherniavsky. New York: Random House, 1970. 140–88.

———. *Tsar and People: Studies in Russian Myths*. New Haven: Yale University Press, 1961.

Chistov, K. V. *Russkie narodnye sotsial'no-utopicheskie legendy*. Moscow: Nauka, 1967.

Christian, R. F. *Tolstoy: A Critical Introduction*. Cambridge: Cambridge University Press, 1969.

Chudakova, M. "Arkhiv M. A. Bulgakova." *Zapiski Otdela Rukopisei* 37 (1976): 25–151.

———. "Tvorcheskaia istoriia romana M. Bulgakova *Master i Margarita*." *Voprosy literatury* 1 (1976): 218–53.

———. "Uslovie sushchestvovaniia." *V mire knig* 12 (1974): 79–81.

———. "A Vital Necessity (About Mikhail Bulgakov's Personal Library)." *Soviet Literature* 2 (1977): 142–47.

Cioran, Samuel D. *The Apocalyptic Symbolism of Andrej Belyj*. The Hague: Mouton, 1973.

———. *Vladimir Soloviev and the Knighthood of the Divine Sophia*. Waterloo, Ontario: Wilfrid Laurier University Press, 1977.

Clark, Katerina. "Little Heroes and Big Deeds: Literature Responds to the First Five-Year Plan." In *Cultural Revolution in Russia, 1928–1931*. Edited by Sheila Fitzpatrick. Bloomington: Indiana University Press, 1978. 189–206.

———. *The Soviet Novel: History as Ritual*. Chicago: University of Chicago Press, 1981.

Clark, Katerina, and Michael Holquist. *Mikhail Bakhtin*. Cambridge, Mass.: Harvard University Press, 1984.

Clayton, Jay. *Romantic Vision and the Novel*. Cambridge: Cambridge University Press, 1987.

Cohn, Norman. *The Pursuit of the Millenium*. 2nd ed. New York: Oxford University Press, 1970.

Collins, John J. "Introduction: Towards the Morphology of a Genre." *Semeia* 14 (1979): 1–19.

Cox, Roger L. *Between Earth and Heaven: Shakespeare, Dostoevsky, and the Meaning of Christian Tragedy*. New York: Holt, Rinehart and Winston, 1969. 164–91.

Cullmann, Oscar. *Christ and Time*. Translated by Floyd Wilson. Philadelphia: Westminster Press, 1950.

Cumont, Franz. "La fin du monde selon les mages occidentaux." *Revue de l'Histoire des Religions* (Paris) (January–June 1931): 29–96.

Dalton, Elizabeth. *Unconscious Structure in 'The Idiot'*. Princeton: Princeton University Press, 1979.

Danto, Arthur C. *Narration and Knowledge*. New York: Columbia University Press, 1985.

Danow, D. K. "Epiphany in 'Doctor Zhivago'." *Modern Language Review* 76 (October 1981): 889–903.

Davie, Donald. *Poems of Dr. Zhivago*. Manchester: Manchester University Press, 1965.

Davydov, Sergej. *'Teksty-Matreški' Vladimira Nabokova*. Munich: Verlag Otto Sagner, 1982.

Delaney, Joan. *See* Grossman, Joan Delaney.

de Mallac, Guy. *Boris Pasternak: His Life and Art*. Norman, OK: University of Oklahoma Press, 1981.

de Proyart, Jacqueline. *Pasternak*. Paris: Gallimard, 1964.

Deutscher, Isaac. "Pasternak and the Calendar of the Revolution." *Partisan Review* 26 (Spring 1959): 248–65.

Dikman, M. I. *See* Sologub, Fedor.

Dolgopolov, L. K. "Andrei Belyi v rabote nad *Peterburgom*." *Russkaia literatura* 1 (1972): 157–167.

———. *Na rubezhe vekov*. Leningrad: Sovetskii pisatel', 1977.

————. "Obraz goroda v romane A. Belogo *Peterburg*." *Izvestiia Akademii Nauk SSSR: Seriia literatury i iazyka* (1975): 46–59.

————. "Roman A Belogo 'Peterburg' i filosofsko-istoricheskie idei Dostoevskogo." In *Dostoevskii: Materialy i issledovaniia*. Edited by G. M. Fridlender. Leningrad: Nauka, 1976. II: 217–224.

Dolinin, A. S. *See* Dostoevskii, F. M.

Dostoyevsky, Fyodor. *The Idiot*. Translated by David Magarshack. Harmondsworth: Penguin, 1972.

Dostoevskii, F. M. *Literaturnoe nasledstvo: Neizdannyi Dostoevskii*. Edited by L. M. Rozenblium and I. S. Zil'bershtein. Moscow: Nauka, 1971. Vol. 83.

————. *Pis'ma*. 4 vols. Edited by A. S. Dolinin. Moscow-Leningrad: Gos. izd., 1928–59.

————. *Polnoe sobranie sochinenii v tridtsati tomakh*. Edited by G. M. Fridlender et al. Leningrad: Nauka, 1972–.

Dowling, William. *Jameson, Althusser, Marx: An Introduction to 'The Political Unconscious'*. Ithaca, NY: Cornell University Press, 1984.

Dryzhakova-Altshuller, Elena. "Andrei Platonov." In *Handbook of Russian Literature*. Edited by Victor Terras. New Haven: Yale University Press, 1985. 341–42.

Durov, V. *Russkie i sovetskie nagradnye medali*. Moscow: Gos. Istoricheskii Muzei, 1977.

Èfron, Ariadna. *Pis'ma iz ssylki (1948–1957)*. Paris: YMCA, 1982.

Eidinova, V. "K tvorcheskoi biografii A. Platonova (Po stranitsam gazetnykh i zhurnal'nykh publikatsii pisatelia 1918–1925 rodov)." *Voprosy literatury* 3 (1978): 213–28.

Èikhenbaum, Boris. *Lev Tolstoi: Semidesiatye gody*. Leningrad: Khud. lit., 1974.

Èl'baum, G. *Analiz iudeiskikh glav 'Mastera i Margarity' M. Bulgakova*. Ann Arbor: Ardis, 1981.

Eliade, Mircea. *The Myth of the Eternal Return, or Cosmos and History*. Translated by William R. Trask. Princeton, NJ: Princeton University Press, 1954.

————. *Shamanism: Archaic Techniques of Ecstasy*. Princeton, NJ: Princeton University Press, 1964.

Elsworth, J. D. *Andrey Bely*. Letchworth: Bradda, 1972.

————. *Andrey Bely: a critical study of the novels*. Cambridge: Cambridge University Press, 1983.

Emerson, Caryl. *Boris Godunov: Transpositions of a Russian Theme*. Bloomington: Indiana University Press, 1986.

Erickson, Edward. "The Satanic Incarnation: Parody in Bulgakov's *The Master and Margarita*." *Russian Review* 33 (January 1974): 20–36.

Erlich, Victor, ed. "Introduction: Categories of Passion." In *Pasternak: A Collection of Critical Essays*. Englewood Cliffs, NJ: Prentice-Hall, 1978. 1–20.

————. " 'Life by Verses': Boris Pasternak." In *The Double Image*. Baltimore, MD: Johns Hopkins University Press, 1964. 133–54.

————. "A Testimony and a Challenge: Pasternak's *Doctor Zhivago*." In *Paster-*

*nak: A Collection of Critical Essays.* Englewood Cliffs: Prentice-Hall, 1978. 131–36.

Ermolaev, G. "Proshloe i nastoiashchee v 'Starike' Iuriia Trifonova." *Russian Language Journal* 37 (Fall 1983): 131–45.

Fanger, Donald. *Dostoevsky and Romantic Realism: A Study of Dostoevsky in Relation to Balzac, Dickens, Gogol.* Chicago, IL: University of Chicago Press, 1967.

———. "Influence and Tradition in the Russian Novel." In *The Russian Novel from Pushkin to Pasternak.* Edited by John Garrard. New Haven, CT: Yale University Press, 1983. 29–50.

Fedorov, Nikolai. *Filosofiia obshchago dela.* Edited by V. A. Kozhevnikov i N. P. Peterson. 2 vols. Verny-Moscow: 1906, 1913; rpt. Heppenheim/Bergstrasse: Gregg International Publishers, 1970.

Fitzpatrick, Sheila, ed. *Cultural Revolution in Russia, 1928–1931.* Bloomington: Indiana University Press, 1978.

Fleishman, Lazar. "Avtobiograficheskoe i 'Avgust'." In *Stat'i o Pasternake.* 102–12.

———. *Boris Pasternak v dvadtsatye gody.* Munich: Wilhelm Fink Verlag, 1981.

———. *Boris Pasternak v tridtsatye gody.* Jerusalem: The Magnes Press, 1984.

———. "K kharakteristike rannego Pasternaka." In *Stat'i o Pasternake.* 4–61.

———. "Problems in the Poetics of Pasternak." *PTL* 4 (1979): 43–61.

———. *Stat'i o Pasternake.* Bremen, K-Presse, 1977.

Fletcher, Angus. *Allegory: The Theory of the Symbolic Mode.* Ithaca: Cornell University Press, 1964.

Florenskii, sviashch. Pavel. *Mnimosti v geometrii.* Moscow: Pomor'e, 1922.

———. *Stolp i utverzhdenie istiny: Opyt pravoslavnoi feoditsei v dvenadtsati pis'makh.* Berlin: Rossica, 1929.

Florovsky, Georges. "The Problem of Old Russian Culture." In *The Structure of Russian History.* Edited by Michael Cherniavsky. New York: Random House, 1970. 126–39.

Frank, Joseph. *Dostoevsky: The Seeds of Revolt, 1821–1849.* Princeton, NJ: Princeton University Press, 1976.

———. "A Reading of *The Idiot.*" *Southern Review* 5 (1969): 303–31.

Freud, Sigmund. "The Anatomy of a Mental Personality." In *New Introductory Lectures on Psychoanalysis.* Translated by W. J. H. Sprott. New York: Norton, 1933.

Friedlander, Saul, et al., eds. *Visions of Apocalypse: End or Rebirth?* New York: Holmes and Meier, 1985.

Friedman, Alan. *The Turn of the Novel.* New York: Oxford University Press, 1966.

Funkenstein, Amos. "A Schedule for the End of the World: The Origins and Persistence of the Apocalyptic Mentality." In *Visions of Apocalypse: End or Rebirth?* Edited by Saul Friedlander, Gerald Holton, Leo Marx, and Eugene Skolnikoff. New York: Holmes and Meier, 1985. 44–60.

Gallie, W. B. *Philosophical and Historical Understanding.* New York: Schocken Books, 1968.

Garrard, John, ed. *The Russian Novel from Pushkin to Pasternak*. New Haven, CT: Yale University Press, 1983.

Gasparov, B. M. "Iz nabliudenii nad motivnoi strukturoi romana M. A. Bulgakova *Master i Margarita*." *Slavica Hierosolymitana* 3 (1978): 198–251.

Gearhart, Suzanne. *The Open Boundary of History and Fiction*. Princeton, NJ: Princeton University Press, 1984.

Geller, Mikhail. *Andrei Platonov v poiskakh schast'ia*. Paris: YMCA, 1982.

———. "Ob Andree Platonove." In Andrei Platonov. *Chevengur*. Paris: YMCA, 1972. 9–22.

Gerigk, Horst-Jürgen. "Belyjs *Petersburg* und Nietzsches *Geburt der Tragödie*." *Nietzsche-Studien* 9 (1980): 356–73.

Gesemann, Wolfgang. "Zur Rezeption der Eisenbahn durch die Russische Literatur." In *Slavistische Studien zum VI Internationalen Slavistenkongress in Prag, 1968*. Edited by Erwin Koschmieder and Maximilian Braun. Munich, 1968. 349–71.

Giamatti, A. Bartlett. "Headlong Horsemen: An Essay in the Chivalric Epics of Pulci, Boiardo, and Ariosto." In *Italian Literature: Roots and Branches*. Edited by Giose Rimanelli and Kenneth John Atchity. New Haven, CT: Yale University Press, 1976. 265–307.

Gibian, George. "*Doctor Zhivago*, Russia, and Leonid Pasternak's *Rembrandt*." In *The Russian Novel From Pushkin to Pasternak*. Edited by John Garrard. New Haven, CT: Yale University Press, 1983. 203–224.

———. "*Doctor Zhivago*, Russia, and Leonid Pasternak's *Rembrandt*." (Expanded MS to above entry.)

Gifford, Henry. *Pasternak: A Critical Introduction*. Cambridge: Cambridge University Press, 1977.

Ginzburg, L. Ia., and V. S. Kiseleva-Sergenina, eds. *Poèty 1820–1830-kh godov*. 2 vols. Leningrad: Sovetskii pisatel', 1972.

Girard, René. *Deceit, Desire, and the Novel: Self and Other in Literary Structure*. Translated by Yvonne Freccero. Baltimore, MD: John Hopkins University Press, 1965.

Gireev, D. *Mikhail Bulgakov na beregakh Tereka: Dokumental'naja povest'*. Ordzhonikidze: Izd-vo "Ir," 1980.

Gladkov, Alexander. *Meetings with Pasternak*. Translated by Max Hayward. New York: Harcourt, Brace, Jovanovich, 1977.

Gogol, N. V. *Dead Souls*. Translated by Bernard Guilbert Guerney. New York: Holt, Rinehart and Winston, 1966.

———. *Polnoe sobranie sochinenii*. Edited by N. L. Meshcheriakov et al. 14 vols. Moscow-Leningrad: Akademiia Nauk, 1937–52.

Gor'kii, M. "Pis'mo A. Platonovu." In *Literaturnoe nasledstvo: Gor'kii i sovetskie pisateli*. Moscow: Nauka, 1963. 313. Vol. 70.

Gossman, Lionel. "History and Literature." In *The Writing of History: Literary Form and Historical Understanding*. Edited by Robert H. Canary and Henry Cozicki. Madison University Press, 1978. 3–39.

Greene, Diana. "Male and Female in *The Snail on the Slope* by the Strugatsky Brothers." Article MS (forthcoming).

Grossman, Joan Delaney. "*The Master and Margarita*: The Reach Exceeds the Grasp." *Slavic Review* 31 (1972): 89–100.

Guerney, Bernard Guilbert. *See* Gogol, N. V.

Haber, Edythe C. "The Lamp with the Green Shade: Mkhail Bulgakov and His Father." *Russian Review* 44 (1985): 333–50.

———. "The Mythic Structure of Bulgakov's *The Master and Margarita*." *Russian Review* 34 (October 1975): 382–409.

Hackel, Sergei. *The Poet and the Revolution: Aleksandr Blok's 'The Twelve'*. Oxford: Oxford University Press, 1975.

Hampshire, Stuart. "*Doctor Zhivago*: as from a Lost Culture." *Encounter* 11 (Nov. 1958): 3–5.

Hart, Pierre R. "*The Master and Margarita* as Creative Process." *Modern Fiction Studies* 19 (Summer 1973): 169–78.

Hayward, Max. "Pasternak's Doctor Zhivago." *Encounter* 10 (May 1958): 38–48.

Herzen, A. I. *From the Other Shore*. New York: G. Braziller, 1956.

———. *Sobranie sochinenii v tridtsati tomakh*. Moscow: Akademiia Nauk, 1954–65.

Hollander, Robert. "The Apocalyptic Framework of Dostoevsky's *The Idiot*." *Mosaic* 7 (1974): 123–139.

Holquist, Michael. *Dostoevsky and the Novel*. Princeton, NJ: Princeton University Press, 1977.

Husserl, Edmund. *Ideas: General Introduction to Pure Phenomenology*. Translated by W. R. Boyce Gibson. New York: Collier, 1962.

Ianovskaia, Lidiia. *Tvorcheskii put' Mikhaila Bulgakova*. Moscow: Sovetskii pisatel', 1983.

Ivanov, V. V. "The Category of Time in Twentieth-Century Art and Culture." *Semiotica* 8 (1973): 1–45.

———. "Opyt istolkovaniia drevneindiiskikh ritual'nykh i mifologicheskikh terminov, obrazovannykh ot asva-'kon'." *Problemy istorii iazykov i kul'tury narodov Indii*. Moscow: Nauka, 1974.

Ivinskaya, Olga. *A Captive of Time*. Translated by Max Hayward. New York: Doubleday, 1978.

Jahn, Gary R. "The Image of the Railroad in *Anna Karenina*." *Slavic and East European Journal* 25 (Summer 1981): 1–10.

Janecek, Gerald. "The Spiral as Image and Structural Principle in Andrej Belyj's *Kotik Letaev*." *Russian Literature* 4 (January 1976): 357–64.

Janson, H. W. "The Equestrian Monument from Cangrande della Scala to Peter the Great." In *Sixteen Studies*. New York: Harry N. Abrams, 1974. 159–187.

Jobes, Gertrude. *Dictionary of Mythology, Folklore, and Symbols*. New York: Scarecrow, 1962.

Jones, Rufus. *The Eternal Gospel*. New York, Macmillan Co., 1938.

Josephus. *The Jewish Antiquities*. Cambridge: Harvard University Press, 1963.

———. *The Jewish Wars*. New York: Putnam, 1927.

Kantemir, Antiokh. *Sobranie stikhotvorennii*. Leningrad: Sovetskii pisatel', 1956.

Karlinsky, Simon. "Andrei Platonov: 1899–1951 (An Early Soviet Master)." *The New Republic* (31 March 1979).

———. *Russian Drama from its Beginnings to the Age of Pushkin*. Berkeley, CA: University of California Press, 1985.

Kejna-Sharratt, Barbara. "Narrative Techniques in *The Master and Margarita*." *Canadian Slavonic Papers* 16 (1974): 1–12.

Kermode, Frank. "Apocalypse and the Modern." In *Visions of Apocalypse: End or Rebirth?*. Edited by Saul Friedlander, Gerald Holton, Leo Marx, and Eugene Skolnikoff. New York: Holmes and Meier, 1985. 84–106.

———. *The Sense of an Ending: Studies in the Theory of Fiction*. New York: Oxford University Press, 1967.

Khlebanov, A. I. *Narodnaia sotsial'naia utopiia v Rossii*. 2 vols. Moscow: Nauka, 1977–78.

Kirpotin, V. *Dostoevskii v shestidesiatye gody*. Moscow: Khud. lit., 1963.

Klosty Beaujour, Elizabeth. "The Uses of Witches in Fedin and Bulgakov." *Slavic Review* 33 (December 1974): 695–707.

Konevskoi, Ivan. *Stikhi i proza*. Moscow: Skorpion, 1904.

Kovac, Anton. "The Problem of Good and Evil in Bulgakov's Novel *The Master and Margarita*." *New Zealand Slavonic Journal* 2 (1968): 26–34.

Kovac, Arpad. "Genezis idei 'prekrasnogo cheloveka' i dvizhenie zamysla romana 'Idiota'." *Studia Slavica* 21 (1975): 309–31.

———. "The Poetics of *The Idiot*: On the Problem of Dostoevsky's Thinking about Genre." In *Critical Essays on Dostoevsky*. Edited by Robin Feuer Miller. Boston: G. K. Hall, 1986. 116–26.

Krasnov, A. "Khristos i master." *Grani* 71–73 (1969): 162–95, 150–92, 175–94.

Krieger, Murray. "Dostoevsky's *The Idiot*: The Curse of Saintliness." In René Wellek, ed. *Dostoevsky: A Collection of Essays*. Englewood Cliffs, NJ: Prentice-Hall, 1962. 39–52.

Kristeva, Julia. *Desire and Language: A Semiotic Approach to Literature and Art*. Edited by Leon S. Roudiez. Translated by Thomas Gora, Alice Jardine, and Leon S. Roudiez. New York: Columbia University Press, 1980.

Krugovoi, G. "Gnosticheskii roman M. Bulgakova." *Novyi zhurnal* 134 (1979): 47–81.

Lakier, A. B. *Russkaia geral'dika*. St. Petersburg, 1855. 2 vols.

Lakshin, Vladimir. "Èskizy k trem portretam." *Druzhba narodov* 9 (1978): 200–20.

———. "Roman M. Bulgakova *Master i Margarita*." *Noyyi mir* 6 (1968): 284–311.

Lasky, Melvin J. *Utopia and Revolution*. Chicago, IL: University of Chicago Press, 1976.

Lavrov, A. V. "Andrei Belyi i Grigorii Skovoroda." *Studia Slavica* XXI (1975): 395–404.

———. "Mifotvorchestvo 'argonavtov'." In *Mif—fol'klor—literatura*. Edited by B. G. Bazanov, A. M. Panchenko, and I. P. Smirnov. Leningrad: Nauka, 1978. 137–170.

Lavrov, A. V., E. V. Pasternak, and E. B. Pasternak. "B. L. Pasternak. Pis'ma k G. È. Sorokinu." In *Ezhegodnik rukopisnogo otdela Pushkinskogo Doma na 1979 god.* Leningrad: Nauka, 1981. 199–227.

Lawrence, D. H. *Apocalypse.* New York: The Viking Press, 1932.

Lawrence, Peter. *Road Belong Cargo.* Manchester: University Press, 1964.

Leach, Edmund, and D. Alan Aycock. *Structuralist Interpretations of Biblical Myth.* Cambridge: Cambridge University Press, 1983.

Leatherbarrov, W. J. "Apocalyptic Imagery in 'The Idiot' and 'The Devils'." *Dostoevsky Studies* 3 (1982): 43–51.

———. "The Devil and the Creative Visionary in Bulgakov's *Master i Margarita.*" *New Zealand Slavonic Journal* 1 (1975): 29–45.

Lednicki, Wacław. *Pushkin's 'Bronze Horseman'.* Berkeley, CA: University of California Press, 1955.

Leont'ev, Konstantin. "Nad mogiloi Pazukhina." In *Sobranie sochineniia.* 9 vols. Moscow: Izd. V. M. Sablina, 1912–13.

Levinton, G. A., and I. P. Smirnov. " 'Na pole Kulikovom' Bloka i pamiatniki Kulikovskogo tsikla." *Trudy Otdela Drevnerusskoi Literatury* 34 (1979): 72–95.

Lévi-Strauss, Claude. "The Structural Study of Myth." In *Structural Anthropology.* New York: Basic Books, 1963.

———. "History and Dialectic." In *The Savage Mind.* Chicago, IL: University of Chicago Press, 1966. 245–269.

Levitine, George. "The Problem of Portraits, Late Allegory, and the Epic of the Bronze Horseman." In *The Sculpture of Falconet.* Translated by Eda M. Levitine. Greenwich: New York Graphic Society, 1972. 51–60.

Levitskii, S. *Ocherki po istorii russkoi filosofskoi i obshchestvennoi mysli.* Frankfurt/Main: Posev, 1968.

Lilly, Ian K. "Moscow as City and Symbol in Pasternak's *Doctor Zhivago.*" *Slavic Review* 40 (1981): 241–50.

Lipets, R. *Obrazy batyra i ego konia v tiurko-mongol'skom èpose.* Moscow: Nauka, 1984.

Ljunggren, Magnus. *The Dream of Rebirth.* Stockholm: Almqvist and Wiksell, 1982.

Lord, Robert. *Dostoevsky: Essays and Perspectives.* Berkeley, CA: University of California Press, 1970.

Lotman, Iu. M. "Ideinaia struktura 'Kapitanskoi dochki'." *Pushkinskii sbornik.* Pskov: Pskovski Gos. Ped. Institut, 1962. 3–20.

———. "Poèziia 1790–1810-kh godov." In *Poèty 1790–1810-kh godov.* Edited by Iu. M. Lotman and M. G. Al'tshuller. Leningrad: Sovetskii pisatel', 1971. 5–62.

———. "Problema khudozhestvennogo prostranstva v proze Gogolia." *Uchenye zapiski Tartuskogo gosudarstvennogo universiteta* 209 (1968): 5–50.

Lotman, Iu. M., and B. A. Uspenskii. "Binary Models in the Dynamics of Russian Culture (to the End of the Eighteenth Century)." *The Semiotics of Russian Cultural History.* Edited by Alexander D. Nakhimovsky and Alice Stone Nakhimovsky. Ithaca: Cornell University Press, 1985. 30–66.

————. "Spory o iazyke v nachale XIX v. kak fakt russkoi kul'tury." *Trudy po russkoi i slavianskoi filologii* 24 (1975): 168–254.

Löwith, Karl. *Meaning in History: the Theological Implications of the Philosophy of History.* Chicago, IL: University of Chicago Press, 1949.

McGinn, Bernard. *Visions of the End: Apocalyptic Traditions in the Middle Ages.* New York: Columbia University Press, 1979.

————. "Early Apocalypticism: the ongoing debate." In *The Apocalypse in English Renaissance Thought and Literature.* Edited by C. A. Patrides and Joseph Wittreich. Ithaca, NY: Cornell University Press, 1984. 2–39.

McLean, Hugh. *Nikolai Leskov: The Man and His Art.* Cambridge: Harvard University Press, 1977.

Maguire, Robert A., and John E. Malmstad. "*Petersburg.*" In *Andrey Bely: Spirit of Symbolism.* Edited by John Malmstad. Ithaca, NY: Cornell University Press, 1987. 96–144.

Mahlow, Elena. *Bulgakov's 'The Master and Margarita': The Text as Cipher.* New York: Vantage, 1975.

Maimin, E. A. "Vladimir Odoevskii i ego roman *Russkie nochi.*" In V. F. Odoevskii. *Russkie nochi.* Edited by B. F. Egorov. Leningrad: Nauka, 1975. 247–76.

Makarovskaia, G., and A. Zhuk. "O romane M. Bulgakova *Master i Margarita.*" *Volga* 6 (1968): 161–81.

Maksimov, D. E. "Ideia puti v poèticheskom soznanii Al. Bloka." In *Blokovskii sbornik II.* Edited by Z. G. Mints, et al. Tartu: Tartuskii Gos. Univ., 1972. 25–121.

————. "O spiraleobraznykh formakh razvitiia literatury." In *Kul'turnoe nasledie drevnei Rusi.* Edited by D. Likhachev. Moscow: Nauka, 1976. 326–54.

Malinowski, Branislaw. *Magic, Science and Religion.* New York: Doubleday, 1954.

Malmstad, John E., ed. *Andrey Bely: Spirit of Symbolism.* Ithaca, NY: Cornell University Press, 1987.

Mann, Robert. "Path of the Bronze Horseman in *The Master and Margarita.*" Article MS.

Manuel, Frank E., and Fritzie P. *Utopian Thought in the Western World.* Cambridge: Harvard University Press, 1979.

Markus, R. A. *Saeculum: History and Society in the Theology of St. Augustine.* Cambridge: Cambridge University Press, 1970.

Marx, Karl, and Frederich Engels. *Capital and Other Works.* New York: Modern Library, 1932.

————. *Selected Works.* 2 vols. London, 1962.

Marx, Leo. *The Machine in the Garden: Technology and the Pastoral Ideal in America.* New York: Oxford University Press, 1964.

Masing-Delic, Irene. *Death and Immortality in Russian Twentieth Century Literature.* Book MS.

————. "Some Alternating Opposites in the Zhivago Poems." *Russian Review* 36 (1977): 438–72.

————. "Zhivago as Fedorovian Soldier." *Russian Review* 40 (July 1981): 300–16.

————. "Zhivago's 'Christmas Star' as Homage to Blok." In *Aleksandr Blok Cen-

*tennial Conference.* Edited by Walter N. Vickery. Columbus, OH: Slavica, 1984. 207–223.

Massie, Suzanne. *Land of the Firebird.* New York: Simon and Schuster, 1980.

Maude, Aylmer and Louise. *See* Tolstoy, Leo.

May, Herbert G., and Bruce M. Metzger. *The New Oxford Annotated Bible with the Apocrypha.* New York: Oxford University Press, 1977.

Medvedev, Pavel N. *The Formal Method in Literary Scholarship.* Translated by Albert J. Wehrle. Baltimore, MD: Johns Hopkins University Press, 1978.

Merezhkovskii, D. S. *L. Tolstoi i Dostoevskii.* St. Petersburg: Mir iskusstva, 1901–02.

———. "O prichinakh upadka i o novykh techeniiakh sovremennoi russkoi literatury." In *Izbrannye stati.* Munich: Wilhelm Fink Verlag, 1972. 209–305.

Miller, D. A. *Narrative and Its Discontents: Problems of Closure in the Traditional Novel.* Princeton, NJ: Princeton University Press, 1981.

Miller, J. Hillis. "Narrative and History." *ELH* 41 (1974): 455–73.

Miller, Robin Feuer. *Dostoevsky and 'The Idiot': Author, Narrator, Reader.* Cambridge: Harvard University Press, 1981.

Milne, Lesley. "K biografii M. A. Bulgakova." *Novyi zhurnal* 111 (June 1973): 151–74.

———. *'The Master and Margarita'—A Comedy of Victory.* Birmingham, AL: Birmingham Slavonic Monographs, 1977.

Mints, Z. G. "Blok i Dostoevskii." In *Dostoevskii i ego vremia.* Edited by V. G. Bazanov and G. M. Fridlender. Leningrad: Nauka, 1971. 217–47.

———. "Blok i Gogol'." In Z. G. Mints et al., ed. *Blokovskii sbornik II.* Tartu: Tartuskii Gos. Univ., 1972. 122–205.

———. "Poniatie teksta i simvolistskaia èstetika." In *Materialy vsesoiuznogo simpoziuma po vtorichnym modeliruiushchim sistemam.* Tartu: Tartuskii Gos. Univ., 1974. 134–41.

Mitsishvili, N. ed. *Poèty Gruzii v perevodakh B. L. Pasternaka i N. S. Tikhonova.* Tiflis: Zakgiz, 1935.

Mochulsky, Konstantin. *Dostoevsky: His Life and Work.* Translated by Michael A. Minihan. Princeton, NJ: Princeton University Press, 1967.

Morson, Gary Saul. *The Boundaries of Genre: Dostoevsky's 'Diary of a Writer' and the Traditions of Literary Utopia.* Austin, TX: University of Texas Press, 1981.

Mossman, Elliott, and Michel Aucouturier. "Perepiska Borisa Pasternaka." *Revue des études slaves* 53 (1981): 267–91.

Muchnic, Helen. *Russian Writers: Notes and Essays.* New York: Random House, 1971.

Muecke, D. C. *Irony.* London: Methuen, 1970.

Nabokov, Vladimir. *The Gift.* Translated by Michael Scammell. New York: Putnam, 1963.

———. *Strong Opinions.* New York: McGraw-Hill, 1973.

Nakhimovsky, Alexander D. and Alice Stone, eds. *The Semiotics of Russian Cultural History.* Ithaca, NY: Cornell University Press, 1985.

Nekrasov, Nikolai. *Polnoe sobranie stikhotvorenii v trekh tomakh*. Ed. K. I. Chukovskii. 3 vols. Leningrad: Sovetskii pisatel', 1967.

Nietzsche, Friedrich. *Thus Spake Zarathustra*. In *The Portable Nietzsche*. Edited and translated by Walter Kaufmann. New York: Viking, 1968.

Nigg, Walter. *Der christliche Narr*. Zurich: Artemis, 1956.

Nivat, Georges. *Vers la fin du mythe russe*. Lausanne: Editions L'Age d'Homme, 1982.

Obolensky, Dimitri. "The Poems of Doctor Zhivago." *Slavonic and East European Review* 40 (December 1961): 123–35.

———. "Russia's Byzantine Heritage." In *The Structure of Russian History*. Edited by Michael Cherniavsky. New York: Random House, 1970. 3–28.

Odoevskii, V. F. *Russkie nochi*. Edited by B. F. Egorov. Leningrad: Nauka, 1975.

Olcott, Anthony. *See* Platonov, Andrei.

Orlov, V. N., ed. *Aleksandr Blok i Andrei Belyi: Perepiska*. Moscow: Letopisi Gosudarstvennogo literaturnogo muzeia, 1940.

Ospovat, A. L., and R. D. Timenchik. *'Pechal'nu povest' sokhranit': ob avtore i chitateliakh 'Mednogo vsadnika'*. Moscow: Kniga, 1985.

Panchenko, A. M. "Istoriia i vechnost' v sisteme kul'turnykh tsennostei russkogo barokko." *Trudy otdela drevnerusskoi literatury* 34 (1979): 189–99.

Pasternak, Boris. "Avtobiograficheskii ocherk." In *Proza 1915–1958*. 1–52.

———. "Bezliub'e." In *Proza 1915–1958*. 321–27.

———. *Doctor Zhivago*. Translated by Max Hayward and Manya Harari. New York: Signet, 1958.

———. *Doktor Zhivago*. Ann Arbor: University of Michigan, 1958.

———. "Novoe sovershennolet'e." *Izvestiia* (15 June 1936).

———. *Okhrannaia gramota*. In *Proza 1915–1958*. 203–93.

———. *Perepiska s Ol'goi Freidenberg*. Edited by Elliott Mossman. New York: Harcourt, Brace, Jovanovich, 1981.

———. "Pis'ma k G. È. Sorokinu." In *Ezhegodnik rukopisnogo otdela Pushkinskogo Doma na 1979 god*. Leningrad: Nauka, 1981. 199–227.

———. *Prose and Poems*. Edited by Stefan Schimanski. London: Ernest Benn, 1959.

———. *Proza 1915–1958*. Edited by B. A. Filippov and G. P. Struve. Ann Arbor: University of Michigan Press, 1961.

———. "Rech' na pervom Vsesoiuznom s"ezde sovetskikh pisatelei, 29 avgusta 1934 goda." In *Stikhi 1936–59*. 216–18.

———. *Safe Conduct*. New York: New Directions, 1958.

———. "O sebe." In *Stikhi 1936–59*. 215–16.

———. "O skromnosti i smelosti." In *Stikhi 1936–59*. 218–24.

———. *Stikhi 1936–1959*. Edited by B. A. Filippov and G. P. Struve. Ann Arbor: University of Michigan Press, 1961.

———. *Stikhi i poèmy 1912–1932*. Ed. B. A. Filippov and G. P. Struve. Ann Arbor: University of Michigan Press, 1961.

Pasternak, E. V. "Pis'mo A. L. Shtikhu." In *Voprosy literatury* 9 (1972): 144–45.

Paszkiewicz, Henryk. *The Origin of Russia*. New York: Philosophical Library, 1954.

Pavlovich, N. A. "Vospominaniia ob Aleksandre Bloke." In *Blokovskii Sbornik I*. Edited by Iu. M. Lotman et al. Tartu: Tartuskii Gos. Univ., 1964. 446–506.

Peace, Richard. *Dostoyevsky: An Examination of the Major Novels*. Cambridge: Cambridge University Press, 1971.

Pelikan, Jaroslav. *Jesus Through the Centuries*. New Haven, CT: Yale University Press, 1985.

Piper, D.G.B. "An Approach to Bulgakov's *The Master and Margarita*." *Forum for Modern Language Studies* 7 (1971): 134–57.

Platonov, Andrei. *Chevengur*. Paris: YMCA, 1972.

———. *Chevengur*. Translated by Anthony Olcott. Ann Arbor: Ardis, 1978.

———. "Poslednii den'." *Plamia* 69 (1919): 16.

———. "Vospitanie kommunistov." *Krasnaia derevnia* (30 July 1920).

Pope, Richard W. F. "Ambiguity and Meaning in *The Master and Margarita*: The Role of Afranius." *Slavic Review* 36 (March 1977): 1–24.

Potapov, L. P. "Kon' v verovaniiakh i èpose narodov Saiano-Altaia." In *Fol'klor i ètnografiia*. Leningrad: Nauka, 1977. III: 164–178.

Prizel, Yuri. "M. Bulgakov's *Master i Margarita*: The True Absolute." *Russian Language Journal* 30 (Fall 1976): 109–18.

Proffer, Ellendea. *Bulgakov*. Ann Arbor: Ardis, 1984.

———. "Bulgakov's *The Master and Margarita*: Genre and Motif." *Canadian Slavic Studies* 3 (1969): 615–28.

———. "On *The Master and Margarita*." *Russian Literature Triquarterly* 6 (1973): 533–64.

Pushkin, A. S. *Polnoe sobranie sochinenii*. 17 vols. Moscow-Leningrad: Akademiia Nauk, 1937–59.

Raeff, Marc. "Home, School, and Service in the Life of the Eighteenth-Century Russian Nobleman." In *The Structure of Russian History*. Edited by Michael Cherniavsky. New York: Random House, 1970. 212–23.

———. "Russia's Perception of Her Relationship with the West." In *The Structure of Russian History*. Edited by Michael Cherniavsky. New York: Random House, 1970. 261–68.

Reeves, Marjorie. "The development of apocalyptic thought: medieval attitudes." In *The Apocalypse in English Renaissance Thought and Literature*. Edited by C. A. Patrides and Joseph Wittreich. Ithaca, NY: Cornell University Press, 1984. 40–72.

———. *The Influence of Prophecy in the Later Middle Ages*. Oxford: Oxford University Press, 1969.

Reiche, Harald A. T. "The Archaic Heritage: Myths of Decline and End in Antiquity." In *Visions of Apocalypse: End or Rebirth?* Edited by Saul Friedlander, Gerald Holton, Leo Marx, and Eugene Skolnikoff. New York: Holmes and Meier, 1985. 21–43.

Richter, David. *Fable's End*. Chicago, IL: University of Chicago Press, 1974.

Roberts, Henry L. "Russia and the West: A Comparison and Contrast." In *The Structure of Russian History*. Edited by Michael Cherniavsky. New York: Random House, 1970. 251–60.

Ronen, Omry. *An Approach to Mandel'štam*. Jerusalem: The Magnes Press, 1983.

Rosenthal, Bernice Glatzer. "Eschatology and the Appeal of Revolution: Merezhkovsky, Bely, Blok." *California Slavic Studies* 11 (1980): 105–39.

Rovinskii, P. A. "Zemlia i volia." In *Chernogoriia v ee proshlom i nastoiashchem*. St. Petersburg: Tip. Imp. Akademii Nauk, 1897.

Rowland, Beryl. "The Horse and Rider Figure in Chaucer's Works." *University of Toronto Quarterly* 35 (1965–66): 249–59.

Rowland, Mary F., and Paul Rowland. *Pasternak's 'Doctor Zhivago'*. Carbondale. IL: Southern Illinois Univiversity Press, 1967.

Rozenblium, L. M. "Tvorcheskie dnevniki Dostoevskogo." In *Literaturnoe nasledstvo: Neizdannyi Dostoevskii*. Edited by L. M. Rozenblium and I. S. Zil'bershtein. Vol. 83. Moscow: Nauka, 1971. 9–92.

Rzhevskii, L. "Pilatov grekh." *Novyi zhurnal* 90 (1968): 60–80.

Sackur, Ernst. *Sibyllinische Texte und Forschungen*. Halle a.d.S., 1898; reprint Torino: Bottega d'Erasmo, 1963.

Schivelbusch, Wolfgang. *The Railway Journey: Trains and Travel in the 19th Century*. Translated by Anselm Hollo. New York: Urizen Books, 1980.

Senderovich, Savely. "Chudo Georgiia o zmie: Istoriia oderzhimosti Chekhova odnim obrazom." *Russian Language Journal* 39 (1985): 135–225.

Shane, A. M. *The Life and Works of Evgenij Zamjatin*. Berkeley, CA: University of California Press, 1968.

Shepherd, William. *Shepherd's Historical Atlas*. New York: Barnes and Noble, 1976.

Simchenko, O. V. "Tema pamiati v tvorchestve Anny Akhmatovoi." In *Izvestiia AN SSSR: Seriia iazyka i literatury* 44 (1985): 506–17.

Sirotina, I. D. "Obraz konia v russkom, altaiskom i iakutskom geroicheskom èpose." In *Sibirskii fol'klor*. Novosibirsk, Novosibirskii gos. ped. institut, 1980. 41–61.

Skaftymov, A. P. "Tematicheskaia kompozitsiia romana 'Idiota'." In *Tvorcheskii put' Dostoevskogo*. Edited by Nikolai I. Brodskii. Leningrad: Seiatel', 1924. 131–86.

Slobin, Greta. *Remizov's Fictions, 1900–1921*. Book MS (forthcoming).

Smirnov, P. S. *Vnutrennie voprosy v raskole v XVII veke*. St. Petersburg, 1898.

Sologub, Fedor. *The Kiss of the Unborn*. Translated by Murl G. Barker. Knoxville: University of Tennessee Press, 1977.

———. *Stikhotvoreniia*. Edited by M. I. Dikman. Leningrad: Sovetskii pisatel', 1975.

Solov'ev, Vladimir. *Tri razgovora*. New York: Chekhov, 1954.

Speransov, N. N. *Zemel'nye gerby Rossii*. Moscow: Sovetskaia Rossiia, 1974.

Starr, Chester G. *History and the Concept of Time*. Middleton: Wesleyan University Press, 1961.

Steinberg, Ada. *Word and music in the novels of Andrey Bely*. Cambridge: Cambridge University Press, 1982.

Stenbock-Fermor, Elisabeth. "Bulgakov's *The Master and Margarita* and Goethe's *Faust*." *Slavic and East European Journal* 8 (Fall 1969): 309–25.

Stepun, Fedor. "Boris Pasternak." In *Pasternak: A Collection of Critical Essays.* Edited by Victor Erlich. Englewood Cliffs, NJ: Prentice-Hall, 1978. 110–25.

Stites, Richard. "Fantasy and Revolution: Alexander Bogdanov and the Origins of Soviet Science Fiction." In Alexander Bogdanov, *Red Star: The First Bolshevik Utopia.* Bloomington, IN: Indiana University Press, 1984. 1–16.

———. "Red Visions: Revolutionary Utopianism in Soviet Russia, 1917–30." Article MS (forthcoming).

Stora, Judith. "Pasternak et le judaïsme." *Cahiers du monde russe et soviétique* 9 (1968): 353–64.

Stremooukhoff, Dimitri. "Moscow the Third Rome: Sources of the Doctrine." In *The Structure of Russian History.* Edited by Michael Cherniavsky. New York: Random House, 1970. 108–25.

Striedter, Ju. "Three Postrevolutionary Utopian Novels." In *The Russian Novel from Pushkin to Pasternak.* Edited by John Garrard. New Haven, CT: Yale University Press, 1983. 177–201.

Struve, Gleb. "The Hippodrome of Life: The Problem of Coincidences in *Doctor Zhivago.*" *Books Abroad* 44 (Spring 1970): 231–26.

———. "Sense and Nonsense about *Doctor Zhivago.*" In *Studies in Russian and Polish Literatures in Honor of Wacław Lednicki.* Edited by Z. Foleiewski et al. The Hague: Mouton, 1962. 229–50.

Sviatlovskii, V. *Russkii utopicheskii roman.* Petersburg: Gos. izd., 1922.

Tate, Allen. "The Hovering Fly." In *The Hovering Fly and Other Essays.* New York: Books for Libraries Press, 1968. 17–23.

Terras, Victor. "Dissonans v romane F. M. Dostoevskogo 'Idiot'." *Transactions of the Association of Russian-American Scholars in the U.S.A.* 4 (1981): 60–68.

Teskey, Ayleen. *Platonov and Fyodorov: The influence of Christian philosophy on a Soviet writer.* Trowbridge-Wiltshire: Avebury, 1982.

Timofeeva (Pochinkovskaia), V. V. "God raboty s znamenitym pisatelem." In *F. M. Dostoevskii v vospominaniiakh sovremenikov.* Edited by V. V. Grigorenko et al. Moscow: Khud. lit., 1964. II: 122–185.

Tolstaia-Segal, Elena. "Ideologicheskie konteksty Platonova." *Russian Literature* 9 (1981): 231–280.

———. " 'Stikhiinye sily': Platonov i Pil'niak (1928–1929)." *Slavica Hierosolymitana* 3 (1978): 89–109.

Tolstoi, L. N. *Perepiska s russkimi pisateliami.* Moscow: GIkhL, 1962.

Tolstoy, Leo. *Anna Karenina.* Edited by George Gibian. Translated by Aylmer and Louise Maude. New York: Norton, 1970.

Torgovnik, Marianna. *Closure in the Novel.* Princeton, NJ: Princeton University Press, 1981.

Trifonov, Iu. *Starik i Drugaia zhizn'.* Moskva: Sovestskij pisatel', 1980.

Tsvetaeva, Marina. *Proza.* New York: Chekhov, 1953.

———. *Stikhotvoreniia i poèmy v piati tomakh.* New York: Russica, 1980.

Tucker, Robert C. *Philosophy and Myth in Karl Marx.* Cambridge: Cambridge, University Press, 1972.

Ulam, Adam. *The Unfinished Revolution.* New York: Random House, 1960.

Uspenskii, B. A. "Kul't Nikoly na Rusi v istoriko-kul'turnom osveshchenii." *Trudy po znakovym sistemam [Uchenye zapiski Tartuskogo Gos. Univ.]* 463 (1978): 86–140.

Uspenskii, Gleb. *Polnoe sobranie sochinenii.* 14 vols. Moscow: Akademiia Nauk SSSR, 1940–54.

Valency, Maurice. *The End of the World: An Introduction to Contemporary Drama.* New York: Schocken, 1983.

Valentinov, N. *Two Years with the Symbolists.* Edited by G. P. Struve. Stanford: Hoover Institution, 1969.

Varshavskii, V. "*Chevengur* i *Novyi Grad.*" *Novyi zhurnal* 122 (1976): 193–213.

Vasil'ev, Vladimir. *Andrei Platonov: Ocherk zhizni i tvorchestva.* Moscow: Sovremennik, 1982.

Viazemskii, P. A. *Polnoe sobranie sochinenii.* 12 vols. St. Petersburg: Izd. grafa S. D. Sheremeteva, 1878–96.

Virginskii, V. S. *Vozniknovenie zheleznykh dorog v Rossii.* Moscow: Gos. transportnoe zheleznodorozhnoe izdatel'stvo, 1949.

Walicki, Andrzej. *A History of Russian Thought from the Enlightenment to Marxism.* Translated by Hilda Andrews-Rusiecka. Stanford: Stanford University Press, 1979.

Wasiolek, Edward, ed. *Dostoevsky: The Notebooks for The Idiot.* Translated by Katherine Strelsky. Chicago, IL: University of Chicago Press, 1967.

———. *Tolstoy's Major Fiction.* Chicago, IL: University of Chicago Press, 1978.

Watson, Robert N. "Horsemanship in Shakespeare's Second Tetralogy." *English Literary Renaissance* 13 (1983): 274–300.

Weeks, Laura D. "Hebraic Antecedents in *The Master and Margarita*: Woland and Company Visited." *Slavic Review* 43 (Summer 1984): 224–41.

Weidlé, Wladimir. *Zadacha Rossii.* New York: Chekhov, 1956.

West, James. *Russian symbolism: a study of Viacheslav Ivanov and the Russian symbolist aesthetics.* London: Methuen, 1970.

Westwood, J. N. *A History of Russian Railways.* London: G. Allen and Unwin, 1964.

White, Hayden. *Metahistory: The Historical Imagination in Nineteenth-Century Europe.* Baltimore, MD: The John Hopkins Press, 1973.

Wilkinson, John. *Jerusalem as Jesus Knew It: Atchaeology as Evidence.* London: Thames and Hudson, 1978.

Williams, Raymond. *Marxism and Literature.* Oxford: Oxford University Press, 1977.

Wilson, Edmund. "Doctor Life and His Guardian Angel." *New Yorker* (15 November 1958): 213–38.

———. "Legend and Symbol in *Doctor Zhivago.*" *Encounter* 12 (June 1959): 5–16.

Worsley, Peter. *The Trumpet Shall Sound: A Study of 'Cargo' Cults in Melanasia.* London: MacGibbon & Kee, 1957.

Wright, A. Colin. *Mikhail Bulgakov: Life and Interpretations.* Toronto: University of Toronto Press, 1978.

Wright, A. Colin. "Satan In Moscow: An Approach to Bulgakov's *The Master and Margarita*." *PMLA* 88 (October 1973): 1162–72.

Yakushev, Henryka. "Andrei Platonov's Artistic Model of the World." *Russian Literature Triquarterly* 16 (1979): 171–88.

Yakushev, Henryka, and Aleksei Yakushev. "Struktura khudozhestvennogo obraza u Andreia Platonova." In *American Contributions to the VIII International Congress of Slavists*. Edited by Victor Terras. Columbus, OH: Slavica, 1978. II: 746–778.

Zenkovsky, Sergei A., ed. *Medieval Russia's Epics, Chronicles, and Tales*. New York: Dutton, 1974.

Zenkovsky, V. V. *A History of Russian Philosophy*. Translated by George L. Kline. 2 vols. New York: Columbia University Press, 1953.

Zerkalov, A. *Evangelie Mikhaila Bulgakova: Opyt issledovaniia 4-kh glav roman 'Master i Margarita'*. Ann Arbor: Ardis, 1984.

Zholkovsky, Alexander. *Themes and Texts: Toward a Poetics of Expressiveness*. Ithaca, NY: Cornell University Press, 1984.

Ziolkowski, Theodore. *Fictional Transfigurations of Jesus*. Princeton, NJ: Princeton University Press, 1972.

# Index

Abrams, M. H., 37–38, 40n.37, 108, 112, 120, 162–63, 264

Afanasyev, L. B., *Journey to Mars*, 157

Akhmatova, A. A., 60, 261n.52, 273

Aksakov, K. S., 29

Aksyonov, V. P., 275, 276; *The Steel Bird*, 274; *Surplussed Barrelware*, 274

Alaric I, 16

Albert of Cologne, Saint, 141n.64

Aldebert, 146

Alexander, Paul J., 16

Alexander I (tsar), 197

Alexander II (tsar), 74, 75n.30

Alexander III (tsar), 50

Alexander the Great, 47

Alexandrov, Vladimir E., 111n.9, 126, 129, 131, 134

Alexis (tsar), 19, 20, 23, 24, 26

Althusser, Louis, 32n.29

Altman, M. S., 57n.61, 73n.28, 77n.38

Annensky, I. F., 128n.35

Anscheutz, Carol, 108, 110n.7, 129n.36

Antsyferov, N., 52n.53, 69n.14, 124, 144

Anuchin, D. C., 47n.44, 53

apocalypse: genre of, 6–9; Judaeo-Christian tradition of, 4–12, 14; as myth, 3–12; in Russian history, 12–31

apocalyptic fiction, 46, 105–7, 136, 138, 140, 149–52, 161–63, 180–81, 269, 274; typology of, 31–44

apocalypticism, versus eschatology, 6, 14

apocalyptic plot, elements of, 39–44

apocalyptic steed, 44–61, 83–84, 123–25,
130, 132, 134, 178–80, 193–200, 206–29, 249–50, 259–66, 273

Apuleius, 138n.57

Arban, D., 66n.9

Arendt, Hannah, 120n.22

Ariosto, 51

Aristotle, 120, 141n.64, 204; *Metaphysics*, 214; *Poetics*, 214

Aseev, N. N., 235n.13

Asmus, V. F., 252n.44

Astakhov, G. A., 189

Augustine, Saint, 5, 10–11, 17, 25, 51, 111n.9, 139, 147, 195; *The City of God*, 5, 10, 120

Avicenna, 141n.64

Avraamy (monk), 20

Avvakum (archpriest), 18–20, 23, 24, 31


Baader, Franz von, 111

Babel, I. E., 59

Baehr, Stephen L., 57n.61, 73nn.28–29, 76n.33, 145n.1, 155n.15, 156

Bakhtin, M. M., 32n.30, 34, 42, 44, 66n.9, 67, 75, 80, 103, 111n.9, 138–41, 151, 169, 202, 204, 206

Bakunin, M. A., 30, 71, 72n.24, 109n.5

Balmont, K. D., 155n.13

*Banner, The (Znamia)*, 235n.16

Barnes, Christopher, 235nn.12, 15

Barratt, A., 194, 195, 197, 198

Barskov, Ya. L., 19, 20

Barthes, Roland, 32n.29, 34

Bashutsky, A., 74

*Basileus*, 16–21

Batyi, Khan, 249

Batyushkov, K. N., 56n.59

Bazanov, V. G., 53, 71

Beatie, Bruce A., 202n.32, 203n.37, 205n.39, 206, 217n.70, 222n.80

Beaujour, Elizabeth Klosty, 213n.57, 226n.90

Beckett, Samuel, 60n.69

Belinsky, V. G., 30, 71, 75–76, 172

Belobotsky, Andrey, 25

Belozerskaya, L. E. (second wife of M. A. Bulgakov), 187n.2

Bely, Andrey (B. N. Bugaev), 21n.20, 36, 37, 44, 45, 59, 150, 181, 191, 238, 270; "Circular Movement (Forty-Two Arabesques)," 121–23, 137; "The Emblematics of Meaning," 140n.62; "The Eternal Call," 136n.52; The First Encounter, 111n.9, 135; The Fourth Symphony, 125, 140n.62; Glossolalia, 131n.38; Gogol's Mastery, 131, 132n.41; Kotik Letaev, 121n.24; "The Line, the Circle, the Spiral—of Symbolism," 121; The Magic of Words," 130, 135; On the Border of Two Centuries, 109n.5, 135n.47, 136; "On the Divide," 140n.62; Petersburg, 19, 34–46, 69n.14, 70, 73, 105–44 (commentary), 151, 162, 187, 199, 214n.62, 233; The Second Symphony, 123–24n.29, 135, 136n.52, 137n.54; The Silver Dove, 117, 134n.45, 142n.66, The Third Symphony, 121n.24, 122n.27, 136n.52

Benjamin, Walter, 143

Bennett, Virginia, 110n.7, 127n.33

Bentham, Jeremy, 75n.32

Berberova, N. N., 121n.24

Berdyaev, N. A., 12, 18, 23, 27–28, 54, 60, 117, 159, 161n.23, 171–72, 269

Bergson, Henri, 110n6, 239; L'Évolution créatice, 240–41

Bernini, Giovanni, 47, 48

Bestuzhev-Marlinsky, A. A., 56n.59

Billington, James, 74, 75n.31, 77

binary oppositions, in Russian history, 12–14, 15, 18, 23, 26, 28, 60

Blackmur, R. P., 79

Blake, William, 37, 119, 160

Bloch, Ernst, 4n.2

Blok, A. A., 21n.20, 36, 48n.46, 52, 54, 59, 109, 113, 116–17, 119, 120n.21, 123–25,

135n.47, 140n.62, 186, 241n.33, 257; "The Intelligentsia and the Revolution," 116; "The New America," 175n.40; "On the Kulikovo Field," 112n.10, 249n.38; "On the Railroad," 173n.36; "The People and the Intelligentsia," 125; "A Petersburg Poem," 117n.18; Retribution, 120n.21, 252–53n.44; The Snow Mask, 119; "Stagnation," 124; The Twelve, 107–8, 110n.5, 113n.10

Bobrov, S. S., 28, 69n.15

Bodin, Per Arne, 259n.49, 267n.60

Boehme, Jakob, 111

Böethius, 112n.9, 141n.64

Bogdanov, A. A., 15n.10, 154n.12, 155n.13, 157–58; Red Star, 153, 157–58n.19

Bolen, Val, 219, 222n.81

Bologna, Giovanni, 47

Bolonikov, Ivan, 159

Book of Cyril, 19

Book of Ephrem the Syrian, 24

Borges, Jorge Luis, 54

Boyde, Patrick, 141n.64

Braudy, Leo, 32n.29

Brodsky, Joseph, 3, 60, 144n.67, 145, 155n.14, 163, 164n.28, 165; "The black firmament was brighter than those legs," 273–74

Brooks, Jeffrey, 118

Brown, Edward J., 271–72

Brown, Marshall, 130

Browning, Gary L., 77–78n.38

Bryusov, V. Ya., 36, 64n.14, 155n.13, 235nn.12 and 15; "The Coming Huns," 116n.16; "The Pale Horse," 109n.5; "Republic of the Southern Cross," 157; "The Revolt of the Machines," 157; "To the Bronze Horseman," 133n.43; "Tsushima," 116n.16

Bulavin, Kondraty, 21, 159

Bulgakov, A. I. (father of M. A.), 201, 207n.44

Bulgakov, Mikhail Afanasyevich, 36–38, 59, 106, 151, 152, 163, 232, 235, 236, 238, 268, 269–70, 272; "The Adventures of Chichikov," 192; The Cabal of Hypocrites, 189; "The Crimson Island" (story), 192; The Days of the Turbins, 186; "Diaboliad" (story), 192; The Fatal Eggs, 192; The Heart of a Dog, 192; "Kiev Town,"

188n.3; *The Last Days*, 189–90, 192; *The Life of Molière*, 200n.27; *The Master and Margarita*, 19, 32, 34–46, 139, 162, 185n.47, 186–229 (commentary), 248, 251n.40; "The Red Crown," 194; *A Theatrical Novel*, 200n.27; *The White Guard*, 186–87, 191, 193–200 (commentary), 201n.30, 208n.50, 214n.62, 235n.14
Bulgakov, N. A. (brother of M. A.), 193–94
Bulgakov, S. N., 14, 117
Bulgarin, F. V., 29
Bunin, I. A., 195n.16
Bunyan, John, 51
Burkhart, Dagmar, 127n.33, 134
Burton, Robert, 51

Calvin, John, 20n.19
Campanella, Tommaso, 11; *Civitas Solis*, 166n.33
Carlson, Maria, 127n.33, 134, 135
Cassedy, Steven, 110n.6, 138n.55
"catastrophists," 28–29, 68
Catherine II, 21, 48, 51
Cerularius, Michael, 16
Cervantes, Miguel de, *Don Quixote*, 58n.62, 168, 172, 176–79
Chaadaev, P. Ya., 30, 68; *Apologie d'un fou*, 111; *Philosophical Letters*, 29, 156
Chatman, Seymour, 31
Chaucer, Geoffrey, 51; *Canterbury Tales*, 274
Chekhov, Anton, 259n.49; "An Attack of Nerves," 258n.47; "The Peasants," 57
Cherniavsky, Michael, 16n.12, 18–22, 31, 176
Chernyshevsky, N. G., 36n.32, 75; *What Is to Be Done?*, 28, 156
Chistov, K. V., 145n.1, 155n.14, 159n.21
Christ, versus Antichrist: as characters in apocalyptic plot, 43–44
Christian, R. F., 78n.38
chronotope, 45, 59, 67–68, 138–39
Chrysippus, 120
Chudakova, M., 187n.2, 189, 199, 201n.31, 202n.32, 205, 207nn.45 and 47, 224n.84, 225nn.88 and 89, 226
Chukovsky, K. I. (N. K. Korneychuckov), 259n.49
Chulkov, M. D., 155–56n.15; *The Mocker*, 156n.15

Cioran, Samuel D., 109n.5, 110n.6, 121n.24, 122n.26, 127n.33
Clark, Katerina, 29n.28, 38, 59, 60, 118n.19, 138, 139, 165n.31, 175n.39, 202
Clayton, Jay, 92n.59
Cohen, Hermann, 240, 244
Cohn, Norman, 13n.8, 18, 118n.20, 146n.3, 159n.21
Coleridge, Samuel Taylor, 37, 262n.53
Collins, John J., 8, 40, 41
Columbus, Christopher, 11
Comte, Auguste, 11, 110n.6
Condorcet, M.J.A.N.C., 15n.10, 149n.6
Constantine I ("the Great"), 16, 47–48
*Contemporary, The (Sovremennik)*, 75n.30
Cox, Roger L., 62n.1, 64n.5, 92n.59
Cullman, Oscar, 120n.22, 146
Cumont, Franz, 6

Dalton, Elizabeth, 63n.4
Danilevsky, N. Ya., 111
Danow, D. K., 237n.20, 254n.46
Dante Alighieri, 5, 51, 111–12n.9, 139–41, 143, 181, 270; *The Divine Comedy*, 141n.63, 203–5
Danto, Arthur, 31–33, 242
Darwin, Charles, 160
Davie, Donald, 267n.60
Davydov, Sergej, 203n.38
*Dawn, The (Utrenniaia zaria)*, 73n.28
de Bonald, Louis, 29
Delvig, A. A., 77n.37
de Maistre, Joseph, 29
de Mallac, Guy, 239n.24, 240n.26, 243n.34, 266, 268n.62
de Man, Paul, 32n.29
Denikin, A. I., 276
Derrida, Jacques, 32n.29, 269
Derzhavin, G. R., 52n.53, 56n.59
Deutscher, Isaac, 233
Dickens, Charles, 231n.4
Diderot, Denis, 48n.46
Dikman, M. I., 120
Dmitriev, M. A., 29, 68
Dmitriev-Mamonov, M. A., 28, 69n.15
Dobrolyubov, A. M., 117
Dobrolyubov, N. A., 36n.32, 75
Dolgopolov, L. K., 73, 119–20, 121n.24, 124n.29, 127n.33

Dolgoruky, Yury, 49n.48
Donatello, 47
Dorosh, Efim (E. Ya. Goldberg), 60
Dostoevskaya, M. D. (first wife of F. M.), 65–66
Dostoevsky, Fyodor Mikhaylovich, 12, 15, 23, 28, 30, 36, 37, 44, 109, 110n.5, 111, 140, 149n.8, 154, 155, 158, 159, 164, 172, 181, 205, 237, 270, 273; *The Adolescent*, 72–73, 82n.43, 124, 155n.14; *The Brothers Karamazov*, 113–14, 156, 159; *Crime and Punishment*, 56–57, 64–65, 70–71, 97n.67, 139n.58, 165n.29; *The Devils*, 70–72, 75, 84n.48, 96, 106, 113n.11, 155n.14, 171, 195n.16, 256; *Diary of a Writer*, 30, 69, 70, 98n.68, 147n.4; "The Dream of the Ridiculous Man," 155n.14; *The Idiot*, 19, 34–46, 50, 57–58, 59n.67, 62–104 (commentary), 105–6, 113n.11, 139, 177, 207n.44, 232–33, 272; "The Meek One," 66n.8; *Notes from Underground*, 64, 258n.47; "On the Road," 76; *Winter Notes on Summer Impressions*, 69, 70, 73n.28
Dowling, William, 44n.42, 119
Dryzhakova, E., 164n.28
Durov, V., 49n.47

Eco, Umberto, 11
Efron, A., 234n.9
Eideman, R. P., 258n.48
Eikhenbaum, B. M., 79n.39
Elbaum, G., 208
Eliade, Mircea, 4, 6, 24, 45, 53, 120n.22, 122n.26, 139, 181, 264n.57
Elizabeth I (queen of England), 49n.47
Elsworth, J. D., 110n.6, 121
Emerson, Caryl, 45, 138n.57
Engels, Friedrich, 4n.2, 118
Eon, the Breton Christ, 146
Ericson, Edward, 207, 217n.70, 223, 227n.94
Erlich, Victor, 234, 235, 238, 241n.33
Ermolaev, Herman, 275
Erofeev, V., *Moscow to the End of the Line*, 59, 274–75
eschatology, versus apocalypticism, 6, 14
Escher, M. C., 33, 143
Esenin, S. A., 53; "Sorokoust," 59
Euripides, 50

Falconet, E. M., 48–51, 55
Fanger, Donald, 89n.56, 165n.29
Favorsky, V. A., 123n.28
Fénelon, F., 156
fiction, versus history, 31–33
Fitzpatrick, Shelia, 154n.11
Fleishman, L., 231n.1, 235nn.13 and 16, 237n.18, 238, 239, 248, 258n.48, 259n.50, 261, 267
Fletcher, Angus, 139, 181
Fletcher, Giles, 49n.47
Florensky, P. A., 36, 123n.28, 150n.8, 162, 265, 268; *Imaginaries in Geometry*, 201–5, 228; *Pillar and Foundation of Truth*, 203
Florovsky, G., 26
Fonivizina, N. D., 67n.11
Ford, Henry, 153
Foucault, Michel, 32n.29, 164
Fourier, F. M. Charles, 28
Frank, Joseph, 70n.18, 75n.32
Frank, S. L., 117
Freud, Sigmund, 51n.50, 63n.4, 136n.51
Friedman, Alan, 39n.35, 63n.2
Funkenstein, Amos, 4, 5, 7
Fyodor Ivanovich (tsar), 49
Fyodorov, G. A., 89n.55
Fyodorov, N. F., 23, 30, 36, 39, 113, 154, 162, 165, 166, 169, 177, 182, 184, 241, 257, 268; *Philosophy of the Common Cause*, 30, 160–61
Fyodorov, P. S., 73n.28

Gallie, W. B., 32n.29
Gapon, G., 116n.16
Gasparov, B. M., 50n.49, 205n.40, 206n.41, 207n.44, 214n.61, 217, 218, 221n.79, 222nn.80 and 81, 224n.86, 228
Gastev, A. K., 15n.10, 153, 154n.12, 155n.13, 157, 159
Gdeshinsky, P., 189
Gearhart, Suzanne, 32n.29
Geller, M., 152, 159n.21, 164nn.27 and 28
Genet, Jean, 60n.69
George, Saint, 48, 49, 52, 232, 254, 259–63, 268
Gerasimov, M. P., 153
Gerigk, Horst-Jürgen, 110n.7
Gesemann, Wolfgang, 57n.61
Giamatti, A. Bartlett, 47n.44, 51

Gibian, George, 239n.25, 268n.62
Gide, André, 205; *Les Faux-Monnayeurs*, 206
Gifford, Henry, 232n.6, 233n.8, 234, 261n.52, 267n.60, 268n.61
Ginzburg, L. Ya., 72n.23
Girandoux, Jean, 60n.69
Girard, René, 63, 89
Gireev, D., 189, 194
Gladkov, A., 233n.7, 237n.19, 267
Gladkov, F. V., *Cement*, 37
Glinka, F. N., 62
Goethe, Johann Wolfgang von, *Faust*, 205, 223n.83
Gogol, Nikolay Vasilyevich, 28, 35, 52–56, 70, 72, 138n.57, 149, 192–93, 221n.79, 270, 271; "The Carriage," 55n.59; *Dead Souls*, 68, 107n.3, 175, 192; "Diary of a Madman," 55n.59; *The Inspector General*, 192; *Marriage*, 55n.59; "Nevsky Prospect," 55n.59; "Rome," 55n.59; "A Terrible Vengeance," 124
Goncharov, I. A., 156
Gorky, Maxim (A. M. Peshkov), 164, 238n.21, 243n.34; *Mother*, 38, 118–19
Gossman, Lionel, 32n.29
Granovsky, T. N., 71
Great Schism, 13, 16, 18–21, 23
Great Time, 4, 5, 139, 273
Greene, Diane, 149n.7
Grossman, Joan Delaney, 213n.57
Gruzinov, I. V., 59
Gudov, I., 60

Haber, Edythe C., 188nn.2 and 3, 205n.39, 206n.41, 207n.44, 222nn.80 and 81
Hackel, Sergei, 48n.46, 108n.4, 110n.5, 117
Halévy, Ludivic, 79n.39
Hampshire, Stuart, 233n.8
Hart, Pierre R., 222n.80
Hawthorne, Nathaniel, 58n.63
Hayward, Max, 232n.6
Hegel, G.W.F., 29, 30, 37, 44, 110n.6, 111, 118, 120, 162, 244
Heine, Heinrich, 33n.31, 128n.34, 149n.8
Herbert, George, 51
Herzen, A. I., 30, 36n.32, 64, 68, 72n.22, 96, 111, 149n.8, 172, 270–71; *From the Other Shore*, 147n.4
Hilarion (metropolitan), 14

history, versus fiction, 31–33
Hilter, Adolf, 11
Hoffmann, E.T.A., 33n.31, 149n.8
Holbein, Hans, 98–99
Hölderlin, Friedrich, 37
Hollander, Robert, 62n.1, 64n.5, 81, 85, 97, 98
Holquist, Michael, 29n.28, 32n.30, 64n.5, 83n.47, 102–3, 118n.19, 138, 202
"Holy Russia," 21–23
horse. *See* apocalyptic steed
Howe, Irving, 206n.43
Husserl, Edmund, 239–40

Ilenkov, V. P., 59; *The Driving Axle*, 175n.39
Inber, V. M., 250n.39
Ionesco, Eugène, 60n.69
Itin, V., *The Country of Gonguri*, 153
Ivan III ("the Great"), 17n.14
Ivan IV ("the Terrible"), 16, 18, 19n.18, 22, 49
Ivanov, Vsevolod Vyacheslavovich, 60
Ivanov, Vyacheslav (V. I.), 36n.32, 102, 108
Ivanov, Vyacheslav Vsevolodovich, 47n.44, 123n.28
Ivanova, S. A., 63
Ivanov-Razumnik (R. V. Ivanov), 119
Ivinskaya, Olga, 248

Jahn, Gary R., 78n.38
James, Henry, 32n.30
Jameson, Fredric, 118
Janecek, Gerald, 121n.24
Janson, H. W., 47n.44, 48
Joachim of Fiore, 10–11, 109n.5, 111n.9
Jobes, Gertrude, 47n.44
Jones, Rufus, 43, 161
Jonson, Benjamin, 51
Josephus, Flavius, 200; *The Jewish Wars*, 213n.59

Kachenovsky, M. T., 29
Kant, Immanuel, 110n.6, 126, 137, 138n.55, 141n.64, 204, 239–40, 270
Kantemir, A. D., 26, 52n.53
Kapiton (monk), 19
Karamzin, N. M., 16, 29
Karlinsky, Simon, 25, 26, 164n.28
Keats, John, 191

Kejna-Sharratt, Barbara, 206n.42
Kermode, Frank, 7, 34, 37, 63n.2, 66, 148, 269
Kerzhentsev, P., 153
Ketcher, N. Kh., 271
Kheraskov, M. M., *Cadmus and Harmonia*, 156n.15; *Numa, or Flourishing Rome*, 155n.15; *Polidorus, the Son of Cadmus and Harmonia*, 155
Khlebanov, A. I., 145n.1
Khlebnikov, V. V., 37n.33, 155n.13
Khmelnitsky, Bogdan, 191, 197n.21, 198–99
Khomyakov, A. S., 23, 29, 77n.36, 111, 188n.3
Kibalchich, N., 75n.31
Kireevsky, I. V., 29, 77n.36, 111
Kirillov, V. T., 153
Kirpotin, V., 77n.36
Klyuev, N. A., 53, 59, 117
Kobylinsky-Ellis, L. L., 132n.43
Konevskoy, I., 117n.18
Korolenko, V. G., 154; *Makar's Dream*, 155
Korvin-Piotrovsky, V., 60
Kovac, Anton, 206n.41
Kovac, Arpad, 81n.42, 83n.46
Kozlov, I. I., 56n.59
Krakht, K. F., 239
Krasnov, A., 205n.39
Krieger, Murray, 63n.4
Kristeva, Julia, 35
Krugovoy, G., 206n.41, 207nn.44 and 45, 214, 222n.81
Krutikov, M., 73n.29
Krylov, I. A., 56n.59
Kurbsky, A. M., 21n.21, 22
Kutuzov, A. M., 28, 69n.15
Kuzmin, M. A., 117
Kyukhelbeker (Kuechelbeker), V. K., 56n.59

Lakier, A. B., 49n.47
Lakshin, V., 193, 205n.40, 206n.41
*Landmarks (Vekhi)*, 117
Lasky, Melvin J., 145n.1
Lavrov, A. V., 109n.5, 110n.7, 129n.37, 133n.43, 136
Lawrence, D. H., 36; *The Apocalypse*, 60–61; *The Rainbow*, 60n.70
Lawrence, Peter, 3n.1
Lazhechnikov, I. I., 29
Leach, Edmund, 45–46, 139

Leatherbarrow, W. J., 62n.1, 64n.5, 207n.44, 217n.70, 221
Lednicki, Wacław, 48n.46, 51, 52
Lenin, V. I., 28, 31, 38, 50, 153, 154, 158, 166n.33, 202
Leonardo da Vinci, 47
Leontiev, K. N., 30, 58, 68, 77n.37, 110, 113n.32, 117
Lermontov, M. Yu., 57, 68; *Hero of Our Time*, 56, 260n.51
Leskov, N. S., "Enchanted Pilgrim," 57
Lessing, G. E., 11
Levinton, G. A., 125
Lévi-Strauss, Claude, 32n.29, 270
Levitine, George, 47n.44
Levitsky, S., 77n.37, 110n.6, 112
Lilly, Ian K., 233n.7
liminality, 45–46
Lipets, R., 47n.44, 53, 179
Lisitsky, L., 123n.28
Littré, Emile, 75n.32
Ljunggren, Magnus, 136n.51
Lomonosov, M. V., 52n.53
Lord, Robert, 63n.4
Lorrain, Claude, 155n.14
Lotman, Yu. M., 12–13, 23, 26, 55n.58, 60, 69n.15, 73n.27
Louis XIV (king of France), 48
Löwith, Karl, 5
Luther, Martin, 20n.19, 51
Lvov, P. Yu., *The Russian Pamela*, 155
Lyashko, N. (N. N. Lyashchenko), 155n.13

McGinn, Bernard, 6, 8, 9, 16, 17n.13, 106
McLean, Hugh, 57
Maguire, Robert A., 121n.23, 127n.33
Mahlow, Elena, 206n.41, 217n.70
Makarovskaya, G., 219n.76
Makhno, Nestor, 159
Maksimov, D. E., 129n.35
Malinowski, Bronislaw, 3
Malmstad, John E., 121n.23, 127n.33
Mandelshtam, N. Ya., 233n.8
Mandelshtam, O. E., 145; "Concert at the Station," 59, 73n.29
Mann, Robert, 194, 199n.24, 200n.26
Mann, Thomas, *The Magic Mountain*, 43
Manuel, Frank E. and Fritzie P., 7, 9n.6, 10n.7, 11, 15n.10, 145n.1, 148nn.4 and 5, 149n.6, 157

Marcus Aurelius, 47, 48, 52
Marcus Curtius, 48
Mariengof, A. B., 59
Markus, R. A., 10
Marx, Karl, 11, 15n.10, 38, 39, 43, 44, 117–19, 147, 153, 178, 200, 235, 238
Marx, Leo, 58n.63
*Mashina* ("machine," "train"), 58, 74, 75n.30, 88, 91, 99–101, 152
Masing-Delic, Irene, 37n.33, 241n.31, 257, 267n.60
Massie, Suzanne, 76n.33
Master of Hungary, 146
Mayakovsky, V. V., 189, 237n.18, 238, 245–49, 252n.44; *About That*, 159; *Vladimir Mayakovsky, A Tragedy*, 245
Maykov, A. N., 66nn.9 and 10, 67n.12, 71, 77nn.35 and 36, 102n.73
Medvedev, P. N., 45, 138n.57
Medvedev, Silvester, 23
Meilhac, Henri, 79n.39
Melnikov-Pechersky, P. I., *In the Forests*, 117
Mendeleeva, L. D., 116
Mercier, Sébastien, 15n.10, 149n.6
Merezhkovsky, D. S., 12, 36, 107n.3, 108, 109, 130
"messenger from beyond," 41–42, 82, 85, 105, 267, 275
messianism, versus apocalypticism, 17, 20
Mickiewicz, Adam, 51–52
Miller, D. A., 39n.35, 63n.2
Miller, J. Hillis, 32n.29
Miller, Robin Feuer, 79n.40, 82n.43, 97, 98
Milne, Lesley, 193, 206n.41, 207n.45
Milton, John, 181; *Paradise Lost*, 139
Mints, Z. G., 124nn.29 and 30, 129n.37
Mitsishvili, N., 26
Mochi, Francesco, 47
Mochulsky, K., 62n.1
Molière (Jean Baptiste Poquelin), 190
Montesquieu, Charles Louis de, 156
More, Sir Thomas, 15n.10, 147n.4, 148, 156
Morson, Gary Saul, 62n.1, 70n.17, 145n.1, 147n.4, 149n.8
*Moscow* (*Moskva*), 206
"Moscow the Third Rome," 15, 17, 19, 20, 22, 45, 140, 155n.15, 233, 253
Muchnic, Helen, 78n.38
Muecke, D. C., 33n.31, 149n.8

Müntzer, Thomas, 11
Muravyov, N. N., 73n.29
Musil, Robert, 36
myth, of Apocalypse, 3–12; definition of, 3–4

Nabokov, Vladimir, 40n.36, 162n.26, 201, 206, 224; *The Gift*, 188, 230n.38
Napoleon I (emperor of France), 244, 264n.56
Natorp, Paul, 240
Nekrasov, N. A., 57, 110n.5; *About the Weather*, 56, 70; "Troika," 125n.31
Neverov, Alexander (A. S. Skobelev), 155n.13
New Enlighteners, 23–26
*New Russian Word* (*Novoe russkoe slovo*), 272
Nicholas I (tsar), 29, 57n.61, 73n.29, 190
Nicholas II (tsar), 29n.28, 108, 116n.16
Niebuhr, B. G., 29
Nietzsche, Friedrich, 109n.5, 110, 120, 123, 126, 128n.34, 129, 141n.64; *Thus Spake Zarathustra*, 122
Nigg, Walter, 102
Nikon, Patriarch, 14, 19–20, 23
Nivat, Georges, 271
*Notes of the Fatherland* (*Otechestvennye zapiski*), 74

Obolensky, Dimitri, 13, 16n.12, 267n.60
Odoevsky, V. F., 29, 68; *Russian Nights*, 156; *The Year 4338*, 156nn.16 and 17
Ognyov, N. (M. G. Rozanov), 37n.33
Okunev, Ya., *The Coming World*, 153
Olcott, Anthony, 164
Old Believers, 13, 14, 18–21, 23–25, 82, 116–17, 172
Origen, 5
Orlov, V. N., 124n.29, 125
Orwell, George (Eric Blair), *1984*, 149
Ospovat, A. L., 124
Ostrovsky, A. N., *The Storm*, 58n.64

Paley, A., *Gulfstream*, 158n.19
Panchenko, A. M., 23–25, 264n.56
Pasternak, Boris Leonidovich, 36, 37, 38, 59, 60n.69, 106, 152, 163, 181, 270, 272; "The Arrogant Beggar," 261n.52; "Auto-biographical Essay," 239, 243, 244, 245,

Pasternak, Boris Leonidovich (*cont.*)
  248; "The Black Goblet," 237; *Doctor Zhivago*, 19, 34–36, 151, 160, 162, 165n.29, 185n.47, 187, 196n.17, 230–68 (commentary); "Fairy Tale," 253, 259n.49, 262, 264n.58, 265; "He rises up. The centuries . . . ," 259n.50; *Lieutenant Schmidt*, 249–50; *My Sister, Life*, 235n.15, 243, 246; "The New Coming-of-Age," 236n.17; "On Modesty and Boldness," 231, 236n.17, 237n.20, 238, 250n.39; "On Myself," 238n.22; *Safe Conduct*, 230–31, 232n.5, 237n.20, 238n.23, 239n.24, 243–47, 249; "Speech at the First All-Union Congress," 238; "The Station," 245; *Themes and Variations*, 246, "Winter Night," 258; *The Year 1905*, 238n.22
Paszkiewicz, Henryk, 21n.21
Pavlovich, N. A., 119
Peace, Richard, 62n.1, 82n.44, 84n.48
Pecherin, V. S., 29, 68, 69n.15, 72, 96
Pelikan, Jaroslav, 5, 7
Peter I ("the Great") 13, 16, 18, 21, 23, 25–26, 27, 48–52, 58, 67n.12, 70, 73, 82, 90, 117, 124, 125, 126, 128n.34, 130, 132, 140, 199, 200
Peter III (tsar), 159n.21
Peter the Hermit, 146
Petlyura, S., 191–99
Petrashevsky Circle, 71
Petronius, 138n.57
Philo Judaeus, 51, 200
Philotheus (monk), 15–18; "Against the Astrologers and Latins, " 17
Pilnyak, Boris (B. A. Vogau), 21n.20, 155n.13; *Mahogany*, 154n.13, 171
Piper, D.G.B., 206n.41, 207n.46
Pisarev, D. I., 75
Plato, 50–51, 107, 122n.26, 156n.16, 157
Platonov (orig. "Klimentov"), Andrey, 21n.20, 36, 37, 59, 60n.69, 106, 138n.57, 232, 236, 238, 272; *Chevengur*, 34–46, 58n.62, 145–85 (commentary), 235, 241, 251n.41; *The Foundation Pit*, 155n.14, 183n.46; "The Hidden Man," 158; "Ivan Zhokh," 159; *The Origin of a Master*, 164; "The Last Day," 153; "The Rearing of Communists," 153
Plehve, V. K. von, 125

Plotinus, 120
Plutarch, 51
Pobedonostsev, K. P., 253n.44
Pogodin, M. P., 29, 50n.49
Polevoy, N. A., 29
Pope, Richard W. F., 209n.53, 210n.54
Popov, A. S., 201n.30
Popov, P. S., 192, 193
Posidonius, 120
Potapov, L. P., 47n.44
Powell, Phyllis W., 202n.32, 203n.37, 205n.39, 206, 217n.70, 222n.80
Prizel, Yuri, 206n.41
Proclus, 120
Proffer, Ellendea, 187n.2, 189, 190, 191nn.8 and 9, 192, 193, 194, 196n.18, 200, 201, 205n.40, 206n.41, 217n.70, 223n.83
Prokopovich, Feofan, 26
Propp, F. Ya., 36
Pugachyov, Emelyan, 21, 117, 159
Pushkin, Aleksandr Sergeyevich, 29, 35, 48–49n.46, 50, 55, 73, 76, 111, 154, 159, 187n.92, 231n.4, 259n.50, 270; *Boris Godunov*, 191; *The Bronze Horseman*, 49–52, 57n.61, 68, 107n.3, 115, 132, 191, 197, 198–99, 200n.26; *The Captain's Daughter*, 191, 195; "The Devils," 55n.59, 191n.7; "Earthly Power," 190; *Eugene Onegin*, 165n.29; *History of Pugachyov*, 191; *Poltava*, 191; "There lived on the earth a poor knight," 177
Put' ("path"), idea of, 26–27, 39, 54, 170–72, 184–85, 257, 262, 271
Pynchon, Thomas, 60n.69

Rabelais, François, 111n.9, 140–41n.63
Racine, Jean, 95n.65
Radishchev, A. N., 36n.32; *Journey from St. Petersburg to Moscow*, 156
Raeff, Marc, 27
Ramzin, L. K., 237n.18
Ranke, Leopold von, 29
Razin, Stenka, 21, 117, 159
Reeves, Marjorie, 5, 11
Reiche, Harald A. T., 4
Rembrandt van Ryn, 234n.11
Remizov, A. M., 36, 69n.14, 155n.13; *Sisters of the Cross*, 109n.5
Revelation of John, history of, 7–12. See *also* apocalypse

Revelations of the Pseudo-Methodius, 16–17
Richter, David, 39n.35, 63n.2
Rilke, Rainer Maria, 244, 259n.49
Roberts, Henry L., 27
Ronen, Omry, 59, 73n.29
Rosenthal, Bernice Glatzer, 108n.4, 118n.19
Rousseau, Jean-Jacques, 81n.42
Rovinsky, P. A., 53
Rowland, Beryl, 51
Rowland, Mary F., and Paul, 268n.61
Rozanov, V. V., 36, 109n.5; *The Apocalypse of Our Time*, 110n.5
Rozenblyum, L. M., 62
Russian apocalypticism, 12–31
Rzhevsky, L., 206n41

Sackur, Ernst, 17n.13
Saint-Martin, Louis Claude, 111
Saltykov-Shchedrin, M. E., 154
Savonarola, Girolamo, 11
Sazonov, N. I., 271
Schelling, F.W.J., 29, 37, 111
Schivelbusch, Wolfgang, 58–59n.66, 246
Schlegel, Friedrich, 33n.31, 149n.8
Schopenhauer, Arthur, 110n.6, 120
Selivanovsky, A. P., 258n.48
Senderovich, Savely, 259n.49
Seraphim, Saint, 29, 202
Shakespeare, William, 51, 89; *Hamlet*, 205
Shane, A. M., 54n.57
Shelley, Percy Bysshe, 92n.59, 161
Shepherd, William, 219n.75
Shershenevich, V. G., 59
Shirinsky-Shikhmatov, S. A., 28, 69n.15
Sholokhov, M. A., 59–60
Shpet, Gustav, 240; *Phenomenon and Meaning*, 239
Shvarts, E. L., 259n.49
Sidney, Sir Philip, 51
Simchenko, O. V., 60, 273
Simeon of Polotsk, 23–26; *Of the King Nebuchadnezzar*, 24–25
Sirotina, I. D., 47n.44
Skoropadsky, P. P., Hetman, 195
Skorovoda, G. S., 110n.6, 126, 141n.64
Slobin, Greta, 109n.5
Smirnov, I. P., 125
Smirnov, P. S., 19
Socialist Realism, versus apocalyptic fiction, 38–39

Solger, Karl, 33n.31, 149n.8
Sollogub, V. A., 73n.28
Sologub (Teternikov), F. K., 120, 128–29n.35, 186; "The Young Linus," 199n.24
Solovyov, A., 21
Solovyov, S. M. (father of Vladimir), 25, 90
Solovyov, Sergey (nephew of Vladimir), 109n.5
Solovyov, Vladimir, 12, 28, 30, 36, 68, 110–21, 123, 135, 140, 141n.64; *The Meaning of Love*, 111n.8; "On the Decline of the Medieval Worldview," 111n.9; *Philosophical Principles of Integral Knowledge*, 112n.10; *Three Conversations*, 112–16 (commentary), 127n.33, 159, 161n.23
Solzhenitsyn, Aleksandr, 270, 272; *First Circle*, 271; "Matryona's Homestead," 59, 273
Southey, Robert, 37
Spenser, Edmund, 51, 58, 172, 181; *The Faerie Queene*, 139
Speransov, N. N., 49n.47
Speshnev, N., 72
Stalin, I. V., 154, 157, 190, 196n.18, 201, 205, 206, 236, 269, 274
Starr, Chester G., 120n.22
Steinberg, Ada, 127n.33, 131n.38
Steiner, Rudolf, 110n.6, 120–21, 123, 141n.64; *Occult Science: An Outline*, 121
Stenbock-Fermor, Elisabeth, 205n.39
Stepun, F. A., 234
Stirner, Max, 29, 75n.32
Stites, Richard, 145n.1, 158n.19, 159nn.21 and 22
Stora, Judith, 268n.62
Strakhov, N. N., 92n.60
Stremooukhoff, Dimitri, 16n.12, 17n.16
Striedter, Jurij, 145n.1, 147n.4, 164n.28, 169n.34, 181, 183n.45, 184–85n.47
Strugatskys, the brothers (A. N. and B. N.), *The Snail on the Slope*, 149n.7
Struve, G. P., 233n.9, 234
Sumarokov, A. P., 52n.53
Svyatlovsky, V., 145n.1, 156
Swedenborg, Emanuel, 111
Swift, Jonathan, 183

Tacitus, 200
Taneev, V., *The Communist State of the Future*, 156n.17

Tate, Allen, 102
Tatlin, V., 153
Taylor, Frederick Winslow, 153
Teilhard de Chardin, Pierre, 11
Terras, Victor, 64n.5
Teskey, Ayleen, 155n.13, 161n.23
Thomas Aquinas, Saint, 141n.64
Thoreau, Henry David, 62
Tieck, Ludwig, 32n.31, 149n.8
Timenchik, R. D., 124
Timofeeva (Pochinkovskaya), V. V., 30, 69
Todorov, Tzvetan, 34
Tolstaya-Segal, E., 153n.10, 154–55nn.12
    and 13, 164n.28, 166n.32
Tolstoy, A. N., *Aelita*, 157–58n.19
Tolstoy, Lev Nikolayevich, 28, 57, 109, 113,
    164, 172, 174n.37, 205, 234, 244,
    264n.56, 273; "Alyoshka the Pot,"
    116n.17; *Anna Karenina*, 56, 77–79
    (commentary), 234n.10; *War and Peace*,
    58n.64, 165n.29, 234n.10
Tomashevsky, B. V., 34, 168
Torgovnik, Marianna, 39n.35, 63n.2
train, 57–59, 73–102, 152, 166–67, 172–75,
    236–37, 243–46, 250, 255–59, 273–75
Tretiakovsky, V. K., 52n.53
Trifonov, Yu. V., *The Old Man*, 275–76
Trotsky, L. D., 118n.20, 198, 235nn.12 and
    25
Trubetskoy, P., 50
Tsiolkovsky, K. E., 159
Tsvetaeva, M. I., 59, 230, 245, 259n.49,
    261n.52, 273, 275, 276
Tucker, Robert C., 118n.19
Turgenev, I. S., 30, 36n.32, 57, 78, 262n.53;
    "First Love," 56; "Living Relics,"
    116n.17; *Smoke*, 73n.28
Tyutchev, F. I., 23

Ulam, Adam, 118n.19
Uspensky, B. A., 12–14, 26, 69n.15, 73n.27
Uspensky, G. I., 76n.34
utopia, versus apocalypse, 8–9n.6, 15, 145–
    52, 161–63

Valency, Maurice, 60n.69
Valentinov (Volsky), N., 118
Varshavsky, V. S., 164n.28
Vasilyev, V., 159
Vasily III (grand prince), 17

Veresaev, V. V., 192
Verrochio, Andrea del, 47
Vesyoly, Artem (N. I. Kochkurov), *Russia
    Drenched in Blood*, 59
Virgil, 203
Vladimir, Saint, 26
Voloshin, M. A., 36, 54, 59, 109–10n.5
Voltaire, 50n.49
Vyazemsky, P. A., 23, 55–56n.59, 57n.61,
    76
Vysotsky, V. S., 269

Wagner, Richard, 128n.34, 131n.38,
    135n.47
Walicki, Andrzej, 110n.6, 111, 112n.10
Wasiolek, Edward, 63, 64, 78n.38, 83
Watson, Robert N., 47n.44, 50, 51
Weeks, Laura D., 195
Weidlé, V. V., 69n.14, 73n.26
West, James, 110n.6
Westwood, J. N., 77n.37
White, Hayden, 32n.29
Wilkinson, Joel, 274
Wilkinson, John, 219n.75
Williams, Raymond, 4n.2
Wilson, Edmund, 267
Wordsworth, William, 37, 112, 162
*Works and Days* (*Trudy i dni*), 121
Worsley, Peter, 31n.1
Wright, A. Colin, 187n.2, 193, 207n.44,
    217n.70, 222nn.80 and 81

Yakushev, Henryka, 164n.28, 177n.42
Yanovskaya, L., 187n.2
Yashvili, P., 248
Yastremski, Slava, 274
Yavorsky, Stephan, 23
Yeats, W. B., 105, 107, 119

Zabolotsky, N. A., 37n.33; *The Triumph of
    Agriculture*, 159–60
Zagoskin, M. N., 29
Zamyatin, E. I., 54, 154, 158; *We*, 149, 157,
    161
Zenkovsky, S. A., 16n.11
Zenkovsky, V. V., 110n.6
Zerkalov, A., 200, 205n.39, 207n.46, 208,
    209n.51
Zhirmunsky, V., M., 124n.30
Zholkovsky, A., 49n.46

Zhuk, A., 219n.76
Zhukovsky, V. A., 23, 56n.59
Zinovyev, A. A., 272

Ziolkowski, Theodore, 43
Zosimius (metropolitan), 17
Zwingli, Huldreich, 20n.19